ENVISIONING WOMEN IN WORLD HISTORY

ENVISIONING WOMEN IN WORLD HISTORY
1500–PRESENT, VOLUME 2

PAMELA McVAY
Ursuline College

 **Higher Education**

Boston   Burr Ridge, IL   Dubuque, IA   New York   San Francisco   St. Louis
Bangkok   Bogotá   Caracas   Kuala Lumpur   Lisbon   London   Madrid   Mexico City
Milan   Montreal   New Delhi   Santiago   Seoul   Singapore   Sydney   Taipei   Toronto

Mc Graw Hill **Higher Education**

Envisioning Women in World History: 1500–Present, Volume 2

Published by McGraw-Hill, an imprint of The McGraw-Hill Companies, Inc., 1221 Avenue of the Americas, New York, NY 10020. Copyright © 2009. All rights reserved. No part of this publication may be reproduced or distributed in any form or by any means, or stored in a database or retrieval system, without the prior written consent of The McGraw-Hill Companies, Inc., including, but not limited to, in any network or other electronic storage or transmission, or broadcast for distance learning.

This book is printed on acid-free paper.

1 2 3 4 5 6 7 8 9 0 DOC/DOC 1 0 9 8

Volume 2 ISBN: 978-0-07-353465-7
Volume 2 MHID: 0-07-353465-X

Editor in Chief: *Michael Ryan*
Publisher: *Lisa Moore*
Senior Sponsoring Editor: *Jon-David Hague*
Editorial Coordinator: *Sora Kim*
Executive Marketing Manager: *Pamela Cooper*
Production Editor: *Karol Jurado*
Production Service: *Anne Draus, Scratchgravel Publishing Services*
Manuscript Editor: *Carol Lombardi*
Design Manager: *Ashley Bedell*
Senior Production Supervisor: *Tandra Jorgensen*
Composition: *10/13 Palatino by Laserwords*
Printing: *45# New Era Matte Plus, R.R. Donnelley & Sons*

Library of Congress Cataloging-in-Publication

Clay, Catherine.
    Envisioning women in world history / Catherine Clay, Chandrika Paul, Christine Senecal.
        —1st ed. p. cm.
    Includes index.
    ISBN-13: 978-0-07-351322-5 (alk. paper)
    ISBN-10: 0-07-351322-9 (alk. paper)
    1. Women—History. I. Paul, Chandrika. II. Senecal, Christine. III. Title.
HQ1121.C623 2009
908.2—dc22   2007032970

The Internet addresses listed in the text were accurate at the time of publication. The inclusion of a Web site does not indicate an endorsement by the authors or McGraw-Hill, and McGraw-Hill does not guarantee the accuracy of the information presented at these sites.

Photo Credits
Figure 1.1: Det Kongelige Bibliotek, Copenhagen. Figure 2.2: © The New York Public Library, Rare Books Division, Astor, Lenox and Tilden Foundations/Art Resource, NY. Figure 3.3: Library of Congress. Figure 3.4: From *Description de l'Afrique* by Olfert Dapper, 1686. Figure 4.1: © Carousel/Laurie Platt Winfrey, Inc. Figure 4.2: Library of Congress, Prints and Photographs Division (LC-USZ62-95344). Figure 5.2: Library of Congress. Figure 6.1: National Archives and Records Administration. Figure 7.2: © Christopher Kerrigan. Figure C.1: Library of Congress, Prints and Photographs Division (LC-DIG-ppmsca-05085).

www.mhhe.com

TABLE OF CONTENTS

◀ Note from the ▶ Series Editors

World History has come of age. No longer regarded as a task simply for amateurs or philosophers, it has become an integral part of the historical profession and one of its most exciting and innovative fields of study. At the level of scholarship, a growing tide of books, articles, and conferences continues to enlarge our understanding of the many and intersecting journeys of humankind framed in global terms. At the level of teaching, more and more secondary schools as well as colleges and universities now offer, and sometimes require, World History. One of the prominent features of the World History movement has been the unusually close association of its scholarly and its teaching wings. Teachers at all levels have participated with university-based scholars in the development of this new field.

The McGraw-Hill series Explorations in World History operates at this intersection of scholarship and teaching. It seeks to convey the results of recent research in World History in a form wholly accessible to beginning students. It also provides a pedagogical alternative to or supplement for the large and inclusive core textbooks that are features of so many World History courses. Each volume in the series focuses briefly on a particular theme, set in a global and comparative context. And each of them is "open-ended," raising questions and drawing students into the larger issues that animate World History.

Women's History may be the only field of historical study more vigorous than World History over the past 40 years. Nevertheless, the sheer volume of research and writing, after millennia of neglect, has made it difficult for most scholars in Women's History to reach beyond the established conceptual traditions of national histories. World History has taught us to ask and try to answer larger questions about women than those posed by national histories. What patterns can be discerned from the separate histories of women over the globe? What historical conditions or institutions repress or liberate women? Although most women have lived in patriarchies during the past 500 years, how have their experiences differed? How have they been able to shape their own destinies?

Pamela McVay, a specialist in both World and Women's History, is ideally suited to help us answer these questions. Her approach is enriched by a deep immersion in the issues and literature of Women's Studies, but she keeps a steady eye on chronology and the processes of historical change. The result is a vibrant tapestry that is as engaging as it is profound.

Robert Strayer
Kevin Reilly

◀ PREFACE ▶

Volumes 1 and 2 of *Envisioning Women in World History* are the first text-book world histories of women. As such, they break new ground in every chapter. My goals for this volume are to make the stories of women's lives and the vast recent scholarship of Women's History accessible to every adult reader, useful in classes on World History and Women's Studies, and so tightly woven into World History that world historians could start making substantive changes in the way we teach and write. Working toward those goals meant writing a book not quite like other history or Women's Studies texts and asking general readers to think about the world a little differently. Volume 2 of *Envisioning Women in World History* focuses on seven world historical themes across cultures:

- The creation of the Atlantic World in the wake of Columbus' historic voyage in 1492
- The impact of increasing state centralization in the seventeenth and eighteenth centuries
- The emergence of social and political movements in response to industrialization and the cross-cultural exchange it fostered in the nineteenth and early twentieth centuries
- The roles of Nationalism and Imperialism during the nineteenth and early twentieth centuries
- The emergence of highly centralized, especially totalitarian, governments in the first half of the twentieth century
- The emergence of Second-Wave Feminism in the context of decolonization, the Cold War between the United States and the Soviet Union, and increasing globalization
- The political and social implications of women's intellectual and artistic achievements in the last half of the twentieth century

Each chapter compares and contrasts at least three world cultures in terms of one of these subjects, considering not only women's roles and the impact of world historical developments on women, but also the interaction of gender ideology with these events. Cross-cultural exchange—whether of ideas, goods, or people—is frequently important to women's history, as it is in world history generally, and therefore receives at least some attention in most chapters.

ix

To the General Reader

If you choose to read *Envisioning Women in World History: 1500–Present* for your own pleasure and edification, you should find that it stands alone. You will not need to read a World History or a Women's Studies textbook alongside it to understand what's happening, and in fact I recommend against doing so. Instead, I suggest you either study smaller chunks of Women's History or read the literature, view the art, and watch the performances created by some of the women described here. Each chapter's bibliography has suggestions for further reading and audio-visual material to tempt you into deeper exploration. As a rule, I have left men's experiences out unless they touch directly on women's. Thus, a few men, such as Muhammad Ali of Egypt (a major patron of women's education), receive individual attention, but the majority of individuals described in the volume are women. The references listed in the chapter bibliographies are a good starting point for learning more about both men's and women's history.

This textbook focuses on the lives of ordinary women, defined broadly to include nearly all the people one would meet in the course of daily interactions—peasants, slaves, servants, shopkeepers, housewives, laborers, sex workers, professionals—the people whose lives most interest my own students. Every chapter does name several "great" women whose actions, words, and decisions had a profound impact on many other women. No legitimate history of women could ignore Elizabeth Cady Stanton and Lucretia Mott's decision to start the world's first women's rights movement, for example. But this text focuses on the ways typical women have shaped and been shaped by the world around them—indeed, many of the women who have shaped the world in the most profound ways started their lives in ordinary obscurity.

I have borrowed women's own words to illustrate women's experiences as much as possible, but readers should be aware that this choice carries an inherent and inescapable bias. Almost by definition, any woman prior to the mid-nineteenth century (and later in many parts of the world) who managed to leave behind a record of her thoughts, feelings, or deeds was extraordinary. The vast majority of women writers had enough wealth to afford them some leisure at the time they wrote—and most of them were unmarried too. It is much harder to find the voices of laborers, servants, slaves, and other marginalized women. Among sex workers, we might have the words of a courtesan, but probably not those of a streetwalker. Among slaves and serfs, only an extremely small number of women ever achieved the freedom and leisure to write down or narrate their experiences to others, and they were all women who had been able to take advantage of unusual opportunities.

To the History Student: Reading and Researching Women's History

If you are reading *Envisioning Women in World History: 1500–Present* for a history class, your instructor will already have explained to you that researching and writing history are a kind of detective work, with the historian looking through the various bits and pieces of the past (the "primary sources") for clues as to what happened and why. The whole truth about the past is irrecoverable; just as you probably left no record of what you ate for breakfast yesterday or of how the sky looked from your window this morning, so also most of the things that have ever happened have left no trace. Historians work with the small percentage of life that has been left behind, either because it was hard to dispose of (for instance, trash) or because people took pains to preserve it (for instance, monuments, prized ceremonial objects, the stories they most wanted to tell). Both kinds of information tell us more about the wealthy and powerful than about the poor and ordinary. Poor people have less to leave behind and use up more of what they do have—most of the clothes poor people have ever worn have been patched, handed down, or finally converted to diapers, menstrual rags, pillow stuffing, and so on. Conversely, the wealthiest people have the resources to commission public monuments and works of art, build homes from durable materials and maintain them, and have the history and stories they think are most important written down—sometimes in stone. Therefore the more powerful or wealthy a person or social group was, the more likely we are to have materials surviving from their lives. This does not mean we know everything about the ruling class and nothing about ordinary people, but it does mean we know more about elites. Since most societies of the past 500 years have been male-dominated—that is, men have controlled most of the wealth, positions of prestige, definitions of kinship and lineage, and opportunities to have their voices heard—fewer records of women's history have survived. Moreover, the records that do exist have been underreported, not least because until the latter quarter of the twentieth century, professional history writing was an almost exclusively male enterprise.

   At that time women academics in the United States, Europe, and Latin America began insisting on the importance and value of women's history and began writing it. Those who wrote about women's history often did so at risk to their careers, because most departments of history considered women's history trivial and believed it could never generate more than a sort of pitiful "me too" list of women's accomplishments that would echo, but never really be as important as, "real" history. The history taught then (and mostly now) was not thought of as men's history but simply as "history." It took time for feminist academics to discover that many important female accomplishments had been written out of our history for no apparent reason—other than that they were achieved by women. As women's historians asked how that had happened, they discovered a critical problem with the discipline in general. The outline of the past, as told in supposedly neutral textbooks that they (and this author) had learned from, fit women's history poorly. Women's historians found, for instance, that just because men were gaining freedoms did not mean that women were—in fact, women's freedoms are often restricted at exactly the moment their husbands, brothers, and sons gain freedoms. Feminists found that the questions historians normally asked about people's lives left out many of the most important aspects of women's experiences, and so women's historians would have to ask new and different questions about women. Further, as we began questioning what women's lives were like and what it meant to be a woman in *this* time and place versus *that* time and place or what a woman's life was like compared with her brother's, we realized that hardly anyone had ever asked those kinds of questions about either gender.

The questions feminist academics have asked about women's lives have had some impact on the teaching of traditional history classes, but in general World History textbooks ignore most of the kinds of questions feminists ask of history. In part this is because World History is itself a newcomer to academic settings. It has been taught on college campuses only since the mid- to late 1980s—where it may supplant but more typically complements the Western Civilization survey—and the Advanced Placement exam for high school students has only been in existence for seven years. World History scholars frequently feel some anxiety about the degree to which their work will be accepted as legitimate. Much of the debate within World History has focused on the degree to which it is possible to create a truly global historical narrative, on whether comparative or global histories are more suitable, and on whether particular topics are, in and of themselves, of historical or global significance. Women's History typically gets ignored in such conversations. The major individual works and collections of comparative Women's History are unknown to most world historians. Most World History textbooks give the impression that the vast majority of changes in women's lives or activities have not affected the world as a whole and relegate Women's History to a sidebar or a few disconnected paragraphs dutifully appended to the end of each chapter.

This textbook, in contrast, was written out of a long-term familiarity with Women's History writing and a long-term commitment to feminist goals. It cannot be, therefore, simply a story of "what the women were doing" during the eras and in the places your World History textbook discusses. Nor can it be a history of individual "great women," what women's historians have come to call "women worthies"—those women who have succeeded in making a name for themselves, following the standards set by the men around them. This textbook is instead a history of how major world historical processes changed women's lives, how women influenced those processes, and how gender ideology (ideas about the proper behavior, attitudes, and predispositions of male and female people) was manipulated and changed by people participating in those processes. World historical processes often affected women very differently from men, and the shifts in gender ideology accompanying events such as the Industrial Revolution or Imperialism happened in the long term.

TO THE WOMEN'S STUDIES STUDENT

You may be reading *Envisioning Women in World History: 1500–Present* in a course that is explicitly about Women's History or Women's Studies—for instance, a course on Cross-Cultural Anthropology of Women or Women's History. If so, you will probably notice, just like students in World History classes, that this text is divided into different categories than many studies in Women's History. Life-Cycle, Sexuality, Education, Class, Race, Work, and the other topical (as opposed to chronological) categories more typically taught in Women's History courses appear as parts of chapters, but not as chapter titles. Instead, the chapters are arranged in roughly chronological order so that readers unfamiliar with Women's Studies will understand that (1) particular topics were not unchanging throughout the period or throughout the world and (2) these topics are not isolated from traditional history—therefore, any comprehensive history course must incorporate the history of women. When a reader sees chapters arranged topically, they often suppose that because "Marriage" (for example) can be described in one chapter, it was the same throughout the entire period of the textbook and very similar in every country. When readers unfamiliar with Women's Studies and Women's History look at books divided topically rather than chronologically, they often presume that the histories of those topics, while perhaps interesting, were isolated from and unimportant to other trends in history and can be left out without detracting from the real story. I intend this textbook to show how the real story of World History needs to incorporate the history of women.

In particular, this volume spends less time than most Women's History texts elucidating fine distinctions among women. The brevity of the text and the breadth of the subject matter make this almost a necessity, but it would have been appropriate even in a much longer work. Treating women as a group with common interests is in keeping with mainstream ideas about women during the past five centuries, as well as with the internationalist tradition of both First-Wave feminist movements and anti-feminist agitators. Although contemporary women activists may see themselves as divided into widely different camps—liberal or equality feminists, socialist feminists, womanists, cultural feminists, and "I'm not a feminist, but" activists—the opponents of women's interests have never had difficulty spotting such groups' similarities and labeling them the enemies of the family, the state, or whatever ideology is currently dominant. On a practical level, as seen in this text, women around the world struggle with similar political, economic, cultural, and ideological issues. In a World History context, it is more instructive to learn from the successes and failures of Chinese, Indian, French, and Argentine women's movements than to elaborate the many ways in which they differ from one another.

Although *Envisioning Women in World History: 1500–Present* is primarily a history of women, gender history plays a strong role in the text. Gender ideology is the constellation of ideas and assumptions a society has made about male and female people and how they map that ideology onto the world around them (for example, giving a baby boy a blue blanket or a little girl a pink one). Most people's mental maps tend to assign gender to the country of women, so to speak. But, of course, gender ideology is as much about men and boys as it is about women and girls, and ideas about women are often used as inverse mirrors for ideas about men. If women were supposed to be one thing, then men were supposed to be the opposite. Because masculinity and femininity are intertwined in this way, Volume 2 of *Envisioning Women in World History* explores the development of gender ideology as it applied to both sexes.

As is the custom in Women's Studies writing, I could share with readers that I have a particular position in the world and a perspective shaped and limited by the privileges I enjoy because of my race (white), family background (middle class), and citizenship (United States). Such rhetorical gestures of self-identification and hesitation are common in World History writing too, because world historians are aware of the very great degree to which their backgrounds shape the questions they choose and the questions they think are most important. But I prefer to emphasize what extraordinary good fortune it is that I have been able to write this text at all. I owe a deep debt of gratitude to the Cleveland Congregation of the Ursuline Sisters and to Ursuline College. The Ursuline

Sisters founded a Catholic women's college 136 years ago. Because of that institution's commitment to the education of and research about women, my colleagues and the administration granted me a year's paid sabbatical to write this textbook and create a new course associated with it. I have learned in the process of researching and writing it (which started long before the sabbatical) how very rare it is for any woman to have such an opportunity. The Ursuline Sisters trace their lineage as educators back through five centuries of service to girls and women of every background. It is my hope that this text reflects in some way the values, voice, and vision of Angela Merici, their foundress, and that it proves a credit to the college's and the order's history.

Although I incurred numerous other intellectual debts during the process of writing this book, I am particularly grateful to several of my friends and colleagues for providing technical expertise and emotional support: Dr. Mary Bivins (African history, editing, and textiles), Dr. Jasmin Cyril (pre-Columbian Central America, editing, and art history), Sr. Christine DeVinne (editing), Dr. Beth Johnson (editing), Dr. Nancy Kane (dance history), and Mr. Robert Kane (women's reproductive freedom).

BIBLIOGRAPHY

PRIMARY SOURCES (SOURCES CREATED IN THE TIME AND PLACE BEING STUDIED)

Aghai, Cameron Scott, and Susan Douglass, ed. and trans. *Muslim Women through the Centuries.* Los Angeles: Council on Islamic Education, 1998.

Andrea, Alfred, and Craig Overfield. *The Human Record: Sources of Global History.* Vol. II, *Since 1500.* 5th ed. Boston: Houghton Mifflin, 2005.

Collins, Robert O. *African History: Text and Readings.* 3 vols. New York: M. Wiener, 1990.

DiCaprio, Lisa, and Merry Wiesner. *Lives and Voices: Sources on European Women.* Boston: Houghton Mifflin, 2000.

Douglass, Susan L., ed. *Beyond a Thousand and One Nights: A Sampler of Literature from Muslim Civilization.* Los Angeles: Council on Islamic Education, 1999.

Ebrey, Patricia. *Chinese Civilization: A Sourcebook.* 2nd ed. New York: Free Press, 1993.

Halsall, Paul, ed. *Internet History Sourcebook Project.* www.fordham.edu/halsall/index.html. Accessed 1/11/08.

Mann, Susan, and Yu-yin Cheng. *Under Confucian Eyes: Writings on Gender in Chinese History.* Berkeley: University of California Press, 2001.

Tharu, Susie, and K. Lalita. *Women Writing in India: 600 B.C. to the Present.* 2 vols. New York: Feminist Press, 1991.

SECONDARY SOURCES

Anderson, Bonnie, and Judith Zinsser. *A History of Their Own: Women in Europe from Pre-History to the Present.* Vol. 2. Rev. ed. Oxford: Oxford University Press, 1999.

Baron, Beth, and Nikki Keddie. *Women in Middle Eastern History: Shifting Boundaries of Sex and Gender.* New Haven, CT: Yale University Press, 1991.

Bingham, Marjorie Wall, and Susan Hill Gross. *Women in World Culture.* Series published in the early 1980s with titles on Islam, Israel, India, the USSR, China, Africa, Japan, and Latin America, among others. Some volumes were released by Gary E. McCuen in Hudson, Wisconsin, and some by Glenhurst Publications in St. Louis Park, Minnesota. Each volume includes study questions and class activities.

Carrasco, David, ed. *The Oxford Encyclopedia of Mesoamerican Cultures: The Civilizations of Mexico and Central America.* New York: Oxford University Press, 2001.

Ebrey, Patricia Buckley. *The Cambridge Illustrated History of China.* London: Cambridge University Press, 1996.

Hughes, Sarah Shaver, and Brady Hughes. *Women in World History.* Vol. 2, *Readings from 1500 to the Present.* Armonk, NY: M. E. Sharpe, 1997.

Kelly, Joan. *Women, History, and Theory: The Essays of Joan Kelly.* Chicago: University of Chicago Press, 1983.

Lerner, Gerda. *The Creation of Patriarchy.* New York: Oxford University Press, 1986.

———. *The Creation of Feminist Consciousness: From the Middle Ages to Eighteen Seventy.* New York: Oxford University Press, 1993.

McNamara, Jo Ann. *Sisters in Arms: Catholic Nuns through Two Millennia.* Cambridge, MA: Harvard University Press, 1996.

Organization of American Historians. *Restoring Women to World History: Teaching Packets for Integrating Women's History into Courses on Africa, Asia, Latin America, the Caribbean, and the Middle East.* Bloomington, IN: OAH, 1988.

Scott, Joan, ed. *Feminism and History.* London: Oxford University Press, 1996.

Steer, Diana. *Native American Women.* New York: Barnes & Noble, 1996.

Tsomo, Karma Lekshe, ed. *Buddhist Women Across Cultures: Realizations.* Albany, NY: SUNY Press, 1999.

UNESCO Scientific Committee for the Drafting of a General History of Africa. *General History of Africa.* 17 volumes. Oxford: Heinemann International Literature and Textbooks, 1992–1993.

Widmer, Ellen, and Kang-i Sun Chang, eds. *Writing Women in Late Imperial China.* Stanford, CA: Stanford University Press, 1997.

AUDIO-VISUAL RESOURCES

Davidson, Basil. *Africa.* VHS. Chicago: Home Vision, 1984.

Ebrey, Patricia, ed. *Visual Sourcebook of Chinese Civilization.* http://depts.washington.edu/chinaciv/. Accessed 1/11/08.

Hall, Stuart. *Portrait of the Caribbean.* VHS. New York: Ambrose Video, 1992.

KEY QUESTIONS IN WOMEN'S HISTORY

Throughout this text, you will find that questions about family status, property rights, access to education, health care, and sexual freedom are often much more important than they might be in other history textbooks. Women's historians learned early on that studying women's lives required them to pose questions historians were unused to asking. They had to ask questions about matters considered private, trivial, and unrelated to trends and events traditionally considered worthy of research. They had to develop a new vocabulary and new research methods to compare women with each other, to find change and continuity over time, and to set women's choices and activities in the context of the opportunities and the limits different eras and cultures offer. This introduction illustrates some of the strategies historians use to investigate women's lives. Of course, the emphasis of *Envisioning Women in World History, 1500–Present,* Volume 2 is on standard world history subjects such as worldwide political movements, the emergence of global economic patterns, and comparisons across culture—not on the mainstream questions of women's studies. Nevertheless, the questions normally asked by women's historians make up the foundation of our study of women's lives. Not every women's history strategy appears in every chapter, but at least one or two of them does. Therefore, we need to begin by introducing the reader to some typical questions scholars of women's history ask of the past.

Gerda Lerner,[1] the first person ever to hold an academic chair in women's history, has suggested that we compare a woman's opportunities with her brother's. How do her education and inheritance compare with his? Does she have as wide a choice of livelihoods and marriage partners, as much opportunity for recreation, as much freedom of movement as he does? Do she and her brother have the same responsibilities toward the family? If we presume that the logical division of family resources is to parcel them out to all children equally, how many of her resources are spent

1

on her brother or brothers, especially on their education? An important advantage of this question is that we are comparing similar social categories—the children of the rich with each other, for instance, instead of with the children of the middle class.

None of the societies examined in this text attempted to provide equal resources and education to brothers and sisters during the sixteenth century. The system of simultaneous, formal co-education found in many contemporary societies—in which girls and boys study the same things at the same age in the same classroom—is a recent innovation (made in part by seventeenth-century Roman Catholic nuns). In 1500 CE, nearly all the cultures of the world divided childcare responsibilities and education according to the sex of the children by the time they could walk and talk intelligibly. Boys went to be with the men during the day, and girls went to be with the women. The men and women would gradually teach the children all the things they needed to know to function as adults—not, in most societies, by sitting them down in a classroom, but by engaging them in the activities they needed to learn. The degree to which girls felt this as discrimination depended on the degree to which adult women had authority equivalent to adult men. Early on, then, girls learned women's responsibilities and boys learned men's.

LINEAGE

Lineage and family structure have great power to shape women's experiences. One reason families may allocate more resources to boys may have to do with the way their culture understands descent within a lineage (the family including ancestors and descendants). Woman's history must therefore ask, "Who inherits?"

Patrilineal societies reckon descent only through the father's family (the patriline), whereas matrilineal societies reckon descent through the mother's family (the matriline). In a strictly patrilineal society, a married woman's children will be considered the heirs of their father's family, not their mother's. When her children describe their family heritage, they will describe only the line of fathers and their father's brothers that preceded them. The Chinese, for instance, have historically recognized almost purely patrilineal kinship structures, with family names taken from the father, authority and titles handed from father to the oldest son, and married daughters considered lost to the family. Strictly matrilineal families will do the opposite—children will describe themselves as descended from their mothers and their mother's sisters that preceded them. The Cherokee Indians, like many other Native American groups, have historically practiced matrilineal kinship. This has meant not just that children were their mothers' heirs, but that tribal membership limited to those who had, by birth or by adoption, Cherokee mothers. Some cultures reckon descent bilaterally, from both parents and their siblings. For example, although most Americans take the names of their fathers' families, families recognize relatives as coming from both their parents' lineages.

Lineage systems matter to women and men because they are usually the basis on which families give each other resources during life and at their deaths. If the family holds aristocratic titles or ceremonial offices that can pass from one generation to another, these will be handed on in accordance with the rules of the family lineage. Important resources—real estate, movable goods, and debts owed the lineage by other lineages—will be inherited either by women or by their children. So, in a matrilineal society, a woman's first natural heir would be her daughter, and then her sister if she had no daughters, and then her nieces if her sister were dead. A man's natural heirs would not be the children of his wife, but those of his sister—possibly her sons. About 15 percent of West African societies hand down property and titles in this way. The women will be critical to the process, and their alliances with each other and with males in their own matriline will carry great weight. In a patrilineal society, resources will be handed off through the male lines, usually from male to male. Family power and prestige will be linked to the men, and women will frequently invest more energy in their husbands and sons than in their brothers.

Lineage will also influence choices of marriage partners and decisions about the guardianship of children. Although almost all people leave children in the care of their mothers until the children are old enough to walk and talk, rules for child care, guardianship, and matchmaking for older children vary widely. Societies that reckon kinship along the father's or mother's line may prefer cousin marriage. For instance, in a matriline, a woman's son may be encouraged to marry one of the daughters of his mother's sister, so that his children will stay part of his mother's lineage. Children may belong to their lineage first and to their parents second. For example, in many patrilineal societies the father and the father's family are responsible for children. If a marriage ends in divorce or the death of the husband, the father's family may take custody of the children, regardless of the mother's wishes. Societies that practice bilateral kinship (children belong to the lineages of both parents) are more likely to leave children in the care of the surviving parent, whatever their sex.

MARRIAGE AND SEXUAL FREEDOM

Marriage is another key variable in a woman's life. Can she initiate a divorce? Can her husband? If there is a divorce or separation, who gets custody of any children, and how will the property of the partners be divided? If widowed, can she remarry? Is she able to marry more than one man at a time? Can her husband take other wives, and if so, what is her status relative to them? Does marriage mean becoming part of the same economic unit as the husband? What kind of relationship is she expected to have with her husband?

Sexuality is a major issue in women's history and women's studies, as it is in the emerging field of men's studies. Does a woman's culture consider sexual pleasure important for women, and does marriage change that in any way? Is there a penalty for her having sexual partners outside marriage? Does her culture even admit the existence of same-sex eroticism, and if so, does it punish women who choose other women as sexual partners? Does her culture permit birth control of any kind, and if so, does it permit any method a woman can control independent of her partner? Do women even have an opportunity to learn about birth control? Although contemporary contraceptive methods are much more effective than traditional ones, barrier methods of contraception have been used in some cultures for thousands of years. In addition, whereas some cultures make knowledge of non-reproductive sexual practices and birth control widely available, others not only restrict knowledge of birth control methods but also penalize at least some forms of non-reproductive sex. Whether a woman has 3 pregnancies or 15 makes a huge difference in her overall health and in her ability to care for children.

These questions lead us naturally to wonder about women's sexual freedom. Who decides whether, when, and whom a woman or man should marry, and when she should first have sexual contact? Early in the time period under study, most women in the world lived in cultures where someone besides the bride decided the answers to these questions, at least with respect to her first marriage. Usually, parents chose their children's spouses, often (especially for girls) early in life. For girls the decision could often be made before the onset of menarche, and in many societies (China, India, Western Europe, Africa, and the entire Muslim world), the decision could be made without the girl's consent and without consulting her.

In studying the history of women, it is crucial to remember how common it has been and still is for women to have other people decide who their first sexual partners will be and at what age they are to begin having sexual relationships. Whether a woman starts having children at age 12 or age 25, or never, has an enormous impact on her quality of life, as does her ability to accept, refuse, or initiate sexual activity with partners of her own choice. In most societies, for most of recorded history, women (even very young women and pre-pubescent girls) have lacked the power to refuse sexual relations, at least not with the men chosen for them by their families—and so they have often not had the power to consent in meaningful ways to these sexual relationships, either. That is, women have lived (and continue to live) in cultures that practice extreme forms of what feminist theorist Adrienne Rich has called "compulsory heterosexuality":[2] women have not just been expected to marry and (at least try) to have children but were compelled to. Even where women have been able to choose their own sexual partners, the framework within which a culture produces and distributes goods may make it extremely difficult for a woman to support herself (let alone children or elderly relatives) without a man in her household. Either women will be paid much less than men, or most of the work in the culture will be divided by sex, or both.

Compulsory heterosexuality has also been a feature of the lives of many men, but it is and always was less restrictive. Many cultures tolerated some homosexuality, and almost all have tolerated a much greater degree of promiscuity among men than among women. Usually a man could choose additional partners freely outside marriage, whereas societies that chose women's husbands did so specifically to prevent the women from having freedom of choice—to be certain the women's children were fathered by a particular man. Most cultures have made it relatively easy for men to support themselves alone, although it would be unusual for men to be able to do so and raise children without female help. Men's work is rarely structured in a way that makes childcare possible.

DIVORCE, WIDOWHOOD, CELIBACY

How much freedom do widows and divorced women have to determine their choice of sexual and marriage partners? It was common for widowed women to be able to choose their own second husband or to choose not to remarry at all—although most societies favored one or the other and applied pressure accordingly. Whether a widow or divorcée remarried depended on multiple factors besides just her own desire for a husband or perhaps a father for her children: whether her society and family encouraged widows to remarry; whether widows had independent access to income; and whether widows could remarry and still retain custody of their children.

Could a woman refuse to marry? Surprisingly, the decision to refuse marriage was tolerated, even encouraged, in some places, for women who wanted to dedicate themselves to the spiritual realm. Most cultures, even today, consider celibacy deviant for women. Unmarried adult women and men may be seen as a threat to stability. Single adult women may be considered a danger to a family's sexual honor; this is a reason to marry girls off before they are old enough to choose sexual partners on their own. Nevertheless, many peoples seem to associate female sexual abstention with a connection to the divine.

In Europe, Lebanon, and Egypt, Catholic, Orthodox, and Coptic women lived in all-female monastic communities throughout the whole of our period. In pre-colonial Africa some single women occupied important religious positions as mediums, priestesses, or oracles. In other parts of the world, some women could become Buddhist or Daoist nuns or even recluses and—although the choice was most common for widows—a few women were able to force their families to accept this choice before marriage. Chinese Girls whose betrothals had been cut short by the unexpected deaths of their fiancés could also force their families to accept celibacy. Of course, we must not take too rosy a view of the women's autonomy in monasticism; not every nun chose the celibate life. Christians often dedicated very young children to the church the same way they might dedicate a child to a particular apprenticeship. Buddhist and Daoist widows might become nuns because they had no way to support themselves. But many—probably most—nuns chose to renounce the world and family life. We see this most clearly by the fact that affluent, independent widows in both Europe and China frequently visited, became lay members of, and joined convents in large numbers.

IMPLICATIONS FOR WOMEN'S HISTORY

The following chapters treat these topical questions as touchstones within world historical movements, considering the aspects of women's history that were most important within particular eras and across cultures. For instance, the development of Atlantic slavery had profound implications for women's status within the family, sexual freedom of choice, and legal rights in West Africa and the Americas. Since its origin in the late eighteenth century, industrialization has relied heavily on family structures that guarantee large pools of cheap female labor moving in and out of the paid workforce. In Nazi Germany, Stalinist Russia, and Maoist China, widely differing gender ideologies nevertheless led countries to similarly restrict reproductive freedom. In short, each chapter explores one or two world historical themes in terms of women's lives and decision making, and women's history topics form the inevitable backdrop to these comparisons.

MAKING HISTORY

The history of any oppressed group, whether it be peasants, colonized peoples, slaves, or women in general, can be disheartening. The reader may feel anger or despair over repeated evidence of injustice that they feel helpless to change. There are many examples of ways women have been able to act on their own behalf, to resist oppression, and express themselves throughout this book. Yet my experience has been that students first confronting women's history may struggle to recognize women's agency (that is, their ability to act and make decisions for themselves) because it is so painful to discover the inequities of the past—inequities that are often still part of the present. To help alleviate this normal reaction to the text's subject matter, the Conclusion of this text focuses on women's activism and accomplishments in the latter half of the twentieth century. In no way do I intend to suggest that the late twentieth century is the first era in which women have made major contributions to world culture. However, the enormous increase in world population in the twentieth century coupled with the widespread availability of public education has meant that far more women are alive and making history than ever before. It would be even more impossible to list all the accomplishments of women in this era than it would be for previous ones, but the text restricts itself to highlights and reminds the reader that women can and do act on their own behalf.

STUDY QUESTIONS

These are particularly good for discussion across generations.

1. What kinds of history have you studied in the past, and to what extent did it include women's history?

2. What would you most want people to remember about your era? Make a list of five things and explain why each is important to you.

3. When you were growing up, to what extent did brothers and sisters have the same educational opportunities? Inheritances? Freedom to choose romantic partners and access to family planning?

4. What physical spaces in your society are single-sex or are used primarily only by one sex? Can you find any common themes among these spaces?

BIBLIOGRAPHY

Lerner, Gerda. *The Creation of Patriarchy.* New York: Oxford University Press, 1986.

McNamara, Jo Ann. *Sisters in Arms: Catholic Nuns Through Two Millennia.* Cambridge: Harvard University Press, 1996.

Rich, Adrienne. "Compulsory Heterosexuality and Lesbian Existence," *Signs* 5, no. 4 (Summer 1980): 631–660.

Scott, Joan. "Gender as a Useful Category of Analysis," in *Gender and the Politics of History.* Rev. ed. New York: Columbia University Press, 1999.

Scott, Joan, ed. *Feminism and History: A Reader.* A volume of the series *Oxford Readings in Feminism.* New York: Oxford University Press, 1996.

❧ PART ONE ❧

THE EARLY MODERN WORLD, 1500–1750

The era from 1500 to 1750 was dominated by the political and economic joining of the Americas and coastal Africa with Europe and by the increasing size and centralization of states throughout the agricultural world. Women participated in and reacted against political and economic change. They were often targets of state control, their behavior deemed a symbolic measure of social harmony or disorder.

Chapter One, "Setting the Stage: Directions in and Resources for Women's History before 1500," examines the status quo for women at the start of our era, in and around the year 1500. Even though the year of Christopher Columbus' voyage is traditionally considered a watershed in world history, women in many world cultures had already been experiencing changes in the kinds of freedoms and challenges they faced. The Columbian moment accelerated and in some cases altered the direction of those changes. Chapter One therefore briefly reviews shifts that had occurred in much of the world prior to 1492. Chapter Two, "Ideological Transformations in Eurasia, 1500–1750," uses case studies of four expansionist states to consider the ways women responded to and felt the impact of governments' quest for power. The chapter pays particular attention to the kinds of sources available to historians to study women in these regions, showing how politics, gender expectations, and assumptions about what constitutes historical evidence influence our ability to construct women's history. Chapter Three, "The Atlantic World, 1492–1750: Speaking for Cortés," addresses one of the most important arenas of world history, women's contribution to it, and the ways the creation of the Atlantic World depended on and created expectations of gender roles. Over the course of these three chapters we will see that women's paid and unpaid work, legal status, and relations with their families were critical components of political and economic expansion.

The early modern era was in many ways a bleak one for women. In governments' quest for greater control of free male and slave subjects of both sexes, they typically demanded more work, more conformity, and more self-sacrifice from women and girls and rarely provided much compensation for these losses. Not all women acquiesced to these plans, of course, and many engaged in passive or active resistance; others created or seized opportunities from ideological and legal loopholes.

CHAPTER ONE

SETTING THE STAGE: DIRECTIONS IN AND RESOURCES FOR WOMEN'S HISTORY BEFORE 1500

The voyage of Christopher Columbus to the Americas in 1492 marks one of the most important watersheds in world history. Major civilizations that had never before come in contact merged within a few generations, trade routes expanded to cover the entire globe, and wars quickly followed those trade routes. In addition, the time period from around 1400 to 1600 saw major political, economic, and social change in the Middle East, China, Japan, Russia, Western Europe, West Africa, the Andes, Central America, and (we suspect) in the Great Lakes region of North America. Thus, world history course sequences typically break at 1500 CE, with the first segment devoted to the ancient and medieval worlds and the second to the world after Columbus. The events of this era were just as vital for women as for men, although the impact was rarely the same for both sexes. *Envisioning Women in World History* therefore follows the custom of other world history texts by beginning at the traditional break. Before embarking on an analysis of those profound changes, however, we will consider the state of women's affairs before Columbus' voyage.

History never stops to take a breath. We should not imagine that before 1500 women's histories were standing still and that the Columbian moment jolted them into action. Rather, changes already in motion accelerated or altered direction after the impact. For instance, the process of state centralization and militarization sped up in West Africa. There were also important continuities with the past and with the direction of past change. In the year 1500 nearly all societies practiced division of labor by gender and tasked girls and women with the care of small children, and this would not change. The rise of stronger centralized states that had begun in many parts of the world in the previous two to three centuries not only continued but also speeded up. As Chapters Two and

Six show in more detail, growth in state power often goes hand-in-hand with diminished freedom for women, making that particular continuity troubling.

INFLUENCES AND LIMITS ON EVIDENCE

For many parts of the world, we have limited evidence remaining about the era before 1500. Instead of treating this limitation as a weakness, this chapter takes the opportunity to examine the ways ideology and social practice influence what kinds of materials about women get produced and saved. We first consider the lives of the groups of women who are least well documented: foraging (that is, hunting and gathering) women and women from agricultural societies in North America, Africa, and Australia. We then examine three cultures for which we have considerable surviving evidence and research available—Ming China, Renaissance Europe, and Aztec Meso-America—and discuss both what is known of women's lives and what kinds of resources have been available to scholars to reconstruct those lives. We will see that gender ideology and political history both play roles in determining what we know about women.

AGRARIAN AND FORAGING CIVILIZATIONS IN NORTH AMERICA, SUB-SAHARAN AFRICA, AND AUSTRALIA, CA. 1500

Foragers had been under pressure from agriculturalists for thousands of years, gradually being forced into less desirable (for farming) regions as farming societies expanded. This process accelerated during the late medieval period as new, more powerful, and more aggressive agricultural states and urban empires surfaced in the Andes, Central America, the Great Lakes, Southeast Asia, and sub-Saharan Africa. The current state of research gives us only a cloudy vision of how all this touched women's lives, however. The next few pages can give us only a rough approximation of the state of their world, but should suffice to give the reader a sense of the range of different experiences, opportunities, and responsibilities they encountered.

For several reasons, American, sub-Saharan African, and Australian women are the least well documented for the sixteenth century. First, outside Ethiopia, West African urban centers, and the Swahili-speaking parts of the East Africa, these regions produced few written documents or inscriptions, and little of what was written had to do with women's lives. Until recently, historians restricted themselves to evidence from written materials. They were limited to writings by travelers—quite a few of them visited Africa in the fifteenth and sixteenth centuries. Unfortunately, these people were observers and outsiders and almost all men, and they naturally saw and heard and wrote about things from their perspective. They wrote haphazard, fragmented accounts of women's lives and they rarely understood the nuances of social interaction. Muslim and Christian merchants, missionaries, soldiers, sailors, and diplomats—their main concerns when writing about women were to describe how they were more or less chaste than women from the writers' own countries and how the women were more or less properly respectful of the men in their societies. The men often did not know what women did all day, and they rarely conversed with local women in depth—or at least, they rarely reported such conversations. Therefore written accounts of women in the period are of only limited use.

Archaeological evidence is of some help in telling us about the lives of women, but not as much as we would hope. Little work has been done on the urban centers of sub-Saharan Africa outside Ethiopia, Great Zimbabwe, and West Africa. Some urban centers left no monumental or even stone architecture, so we do not have the huge sites (even refuse collections) that could inform us about daily life. In North America, the only semi-urban center, that of the cave dwellers of Chaco Canyon and Mesa Verde, had been abandoned prior to our period. The mound-building cultures of the Mississippian regions left numerous earthwork monuments, but these are burial sites, and restrictions on digging up the cemeteries of Native Americans limit the archaeological studies that can be performed.

One source that remained unused until recently is oral history—the history people have not written down, but that can tell us about their past and the past of their families and societies. Western European and American historians—members of the historical tradition that produces the kind of textbook you are reading right now—once thought oral history was much less reliable than written history, and they ignored it for a long time. In truth, among Westerners oral tradition *is* often unreliable, because our tradition of writing down everything we think important means that we remember relatively little of what we hear. But we have learned in the last 50 years that in oral cultures, the case is quite different. First, peoples who do not or rarely read remember the things they hear much longer and more accurately than people in literate societies. They are accustomed to keeping their most important records in their heads rather than in a filing cabinet. Non-literate peoples often have specialists trained for much of their lives to remember and pass on history, genealogy, legends, and mythology. In comparing these kinds of histories with archaeological records, we have found that oral histories are much more likely to be accurate than previously thought. Although none of these records is perfect, we nevertheless can put together some accurate data and make some educated guesses. Part of the process involves making some assumptions about past people's lives by talking with people who still live as hunter/gatherers or in village farming cultures.

FORAGING PEOPLES

Nearly all the peoples of Australia, half the inhabitants of North America, and some Africans lived as foragers during the fifteenth and sixteenth centuries. Foragers leave behind remains, but not in the concentrations that city or even village dwellers do. And, because they move so frequently, they have fewer possessions to begin with than sedentary peoples. Foragers therefore leave behind a very limited portion of their lives in the archaeological record. Metal, stone, pottery, and beads survive (and hence often jewelry and tools for piercing, cutting, and scraping), as do some foundations of dwellings. But the perishable tools and conveniences of daily life—clothes, nets, blankets, foodstuffs—rot quickly. Even when by some fluke they survive, their mere existence is not enough to tell us how they were used. We can make some guesses, however, based on the earliest historical and anthropological accounts of travelers. We also can make some guesses based on the lives of contemporary foraging peoples. This last source of evidence is the trickiest, because foragers' customs change over time, just like everyone else's. However, it seems that foraging societies all share some characteristics, and scholars cautiously assume those characteristics were also shared by earlier foragers. Scholars also cautiously assume that the current diversity among foraging groups reflects historical diversity: Foraging cultures today differ quite a lot from each other, so scholars assume that foraging cultures of the past were equally diverse.[1]

Two stereotypes of hunter-gatherer peoples are very common. One is that they are savage brutes—wild, violent, and untouched by any of the finer feelings of civilized peoples. Another is that they are all "noble savages," living in peace and harmony with nature, untouched by history and by the money-grubbing, power-hungry sins of civilization—a natural democracy of equals.

In fact, foraging peoples were and are neither particularly violent and authoritarian nor particularly peaceful. Although hunter-gatherer groups today and in the past seem more egalitarian than sedentary cultures, none are or were entirely so. Some foraging peoples rarely come into conflict with other people, fight little among themselves, and have highly egalitarian practices. Some, like the Yanomami of Brazil, have strong traditions of collective violence. A certain amount of male dominance is also common—for example, among the Caribou Inuit of the Hudson Bay region, only men could be family heads—but not universal. Scholars assume this much variety was the case among premodern foragers, and travel accounts from the 1400s and 1500s also suggest that this was so.

Commonalities include the fact that leadership among foraging peoples is rarely hereditary, long term, or accompanied with coercive authority. Leaders are chosen on merit for specific situations and have to work with others through persuasion. Also, foraging societies almost all accord men and women much more equal status than is typical of sedentary peoples. This is not the same as saying that they are not sexist; most divide the responsibilities necessary to keep their societies going between men and women. It is common to have part of a task done by one sex and another part by the other, even if both sexes know how to do the task. Whale and seal hunting might be done by men in boats manufactured by women, for instance, as among the aforementioned Caribou Inuit. Many foraging societies deliberately prevent big-game hunters from using their skills to build up a power base by insisting that all game (or even all foodstuffs) be put into a pool and divided up by someone other than the hunter. Thus among the Witsuwit'en and Gitxsan of southeast Alaska, men hunted, but women (who also gathered and produced food) stored all the food and thereafter shared it out. Scholars believe these kinds of checks and balances to power were common among earlier foragers, but the truth is that archaeological and written evidence neither supports nor contradicts this assumption. Archaeology can give only the roughest guide to hierarchy, and travelers rarely understand the cultures they are describing well enough to catch this level of detail in their descriptions.[2]

Although short descriptions of foragers usually describe men as hunters and women as gatherers, few contemporary foraging societies divide labor exactly this way, and there seems no reason to suppose pre-modern foragers were less diverse. Big-game hunting done in the context of following animals for days at a time *is* almost entirely limited to men, although there are a number of foraging societies in which some women hunt big game. What seems to be most universally true is that small children stay with their mothers or other female relatives, and this makes it impossible and undesirable for most adult women to travel long distances to hunt. It is also true that in practically all foraging societies, men do some kinds of gathering and women fish and hunt some kinds of animals. Fishing with lines, nets, and spears is a very common female activity, and the hunting and killing of small game is a typical part of the daily activities of most contemporary women foragers. Women typically provide most of the calories necessary for daily life through their daily activities, whereas men provide some of the most difficult nutrition to get through their own hunting. We cannot assume this tells us anything about the relative status of men and women, however. Contemporary hunter-gatherer societies, as we have seen, don't use hunting or food production as bases for according respect and authority.

Outside Australia, probably every group of foragers had ties with groups of agriculturalists or pastoralists—and even in Australia, we know that some coastal peoples sent young men across the seas with traders to Indonesia. The picture many of us have in our heads of hunter/gatherers living in isolation in the forest, unknown and unseen by any outsiders, is mostly wrong. There *are* foragers who never actually see outsiders—but they are well known to the agriculturalists near them, with whom they trade. This group of foragers is, moreover, extraordinarily reticent because their territories and way of life have been encroached on so steadily that they have legitimate fear of being captured or attacked by outsiders. At the time of Columbus, the vast majority of foraging peoples were living near agriculturalists, pastoralists, and other foragers with whom they were much more equal in power. They fought with their neighbors as much as any other groups of humans, but they traded just as often. Thus, foraging peoples in the Americas, sub-Saharan Africa, and Australia were embedded in short- and long-distance networks of trade, typically exchanging products of hunting and gathering either for foods they had difficulty gathering (starches), ceremonial items (tobacco in the Americas, cowrie shells in Africa), or items for adornment (beads, jewelry, and textiles). People often express surprise when they see photographic images of contemporary foragers wearing modern clothes or jewelry, but foraging peoples are and have always been engaged in exchange networks, and since they retain only possessions they can easily carry, most of the non-food items they trade for are things they can wear. Such exchange networks could have different implications for men than for women, depending on whether the items the foragers brought to the exchanges were primarily caught, gathered, and produced by one sex, by the other, or by both.

It used to be common for historians and anthropologists to wonder why peoples remained foragers or to ask what prevented them from undergoing the kind of development into urbanization we have seen across most of the world. Why would people remain in what we think of as the Stone Age, even when they had access (as all now do) to metal tools and modern agriculture? But perhaps we have been asking the wrong question. For the vast majority of history, humans lived as hunter/gatherers. It turns out that foragers can live long lives, have few diseases, and spend only about half of every day doing work, while the rest of their time is devoted to what we would think of as leisure activities. Foragers strongly prefer their lifestyles to those of settled peoples and hold on to them tenaciously. For instance, three-quarters of contemporary Cree in Quebec live in settled villages, but nearly all of them still manage to spend a few months of every year hunting, and family members choose jobs that permit this kind of absence.[3]

VILLAGE-BASED AGRICULTURALISTS

Even though foraging was for many millennia the dominant lifestyle of humans, settled farming gradually spread to the majority of human populations by 1500. Foraging was by then almost unknown in Eurasia outside pockets of India and Southeast Asia, and agricultural societies had been spreading out and pushing foragers away from the most fertile lands of sub-Saharan Africa and the Americas for thousands of years. Most people in most of the world were farmers, even in empires built around great cities. Methods of farming, crops grown, and traditions of land tenure (ownership, rights to use, and inheritance) varied widely from region to region, as did women's roles in farming. In some cultures (for instance, Native Americans in the eastern woodlands of the Americas), women grew and tended nearly all the crops, and men helped out with some labor-intensive tasks. In other areas, men grew some crops while women grew others (for example, the Ibo of West Africa); in some areas men grew grains while women grew vegetables (most of Europe and the Mediterranean Middle East). Most agricultural peoples also practiced some hunting and gathering, although foraging opportunities could be severely limited if local aristocrats controlled rights of access to uncultivated land. At a minimum nearly all peasant women and girls engaged in gathering firewood. Women frequently gathered wild plants (edible and medicinal), berries, mushrooms, nuts, and edible invertebrates.

Most Africans and many North Americans lived in farming cultures. Throughout both areas, women were the primary agricultural workers, owning or having primary rights in the lands villages farmed and farming them either collectively or individually. It was very common for women to do almost all the subsistence farming and/or local gathering while men hunted big game and engaged in warfare, defense, and/or herding. Among the many farming peoples of North America (unlike among their distant Aztec and Maya neighbors), women were almost universally responsible for growing grain, beans, and squash, the staples of North American diets.

Where agriculture and cattle herding were combined—as in much of Eastern, Central, and Southern Africa—usually women farmed and men raised cattle. Sometimes cattle-raising people, similar to the contemporary Masai of Kenya, lived on the edges of settled areas and both traded with the locals and raided them.

One notable exception to the rule of female farming seems to have been in the Torres Straits Islands off the northern coast of Australia, where people lived on a combination of gathering; horticulture (fruit trees, mangroves, yam, taro); and fishing with net, hook, and line. Among Torres Straits islanders, the men did most of the agriculture and hunting of large aquatic game, while the women gathered and fished from shore.[4]

Settled agricultural and pastoral societies tend to be more hierarchical than foraging societies—if only because they have to organize larger numbers of people to work together, and the ways they choose to organize vary depending on family arrangements. Sub-Saharan societies practiced nearly universal marriage. Every woman's and every man's life was profoundly shaped by marriage customs and the expectations of kinship and inheritance embedded in them. If a society were patrilineal, patrilocal (married people living with the husband's family), and polygynous (men permitted or even expected to have more than one wife at a time), a woman in it was usually very disadvantaged compared with men. Her children would be considered to belong to her husband's lineage and family; her husband and his family would decide what resources she had access to; her co-wives (and in particular her senior co-wife) would be both her primary competition and her primary source of assistance. Some societies, such as the Hausa of the Western Sudan, added enclosure and veiling to these practices, expecting adult women and older girls to stay within the family compound at all times, greatly restricting their freedom of movement.

However, it would be a mistake to assume that women in very patriarchal societies have no authority, power, or access to resources. African men traditionally had to rely on their wives to feed and house them, and even today many do not know how to cook, keep house, or care for children themselves. When African women farmed, they usually decided which farmer would plant where, and the senior women decided how the fruits of their labor should be divided up. Moreover, some of the most patriarchal societies were partially matrilineal in practice. Thus women's closest ties were not to their husbands but to their brothers and sons, with whom they forged alliances. Some West African societies consider a man's natural heirs to be his sister's sons, not his own, and a number of African traditions of kingship have traditionally split leadership responsibilities among men and women in a family. Traditions in the Great Lakes Region called for a king, a queen mother, and a queen sister to divide responsibilities; the Ashanti of West Africa had separate offices for kings and queens.[5]

In almost every region of Africa, women formed social allegiances with other women. Women in African societies go through rites of passage (as do men) in groups with other women, and these age-association groups form alliances and friendships. Some African societies formalize friendships between women, and they form officially recognized friendships through a series of exchanges of gifts and messages sent through intermediaries, for example. The two women are expected to support each other financially, to leave gifts for each other and each other's children upon death, and in short become kin to one another. Influential women might even take wives of their own. The "husbands" in such marriages would take any children of the wives as their own, and the wives would do all the kinds of work on their husbands' behalf that they would have been expected to do for a male husband. Whatever the nature of the personal relationships between these women, these marriages tell us that these cultures could not conceive of a prestigious person without a wife.

About 15 percent of West African and many North American societies were matrilineal and/or matrilocal, and a few were both.[6] The Iroquois Confederacy actually advantaged women over men. Not only were they matrilineal and matrilocal, but they also passed down titles of prestige to women (not men) in their lineages. Iroquois women could depose heads of men's councils and had a right to representation in men's meetings (the men had no such representation in the women's councils). Iroquois men's first wives were usually chosen by their mothers and sisters. Husbands lived with their wives' families. Any game the men had caught or any products they had gathered were brought home and shared out either by their wives or the female heads of their wives' families, and all their possessions other than hunting tools were made by and given to them by their female relatives. In short, the Iroquois were (and according to contemporary Iroquois, still are) matriarchal. The Iroquois were not typical of farming women, but they were not anomalies in the Americas. The typical division of labor among the farming peoples of North America was that men cleared fields but women then planted, tended, and harvested crops. Typically women—sometimes as individuals but more often collectively—controlled agricultural products, and often the women decided among themselves which woman would farm what land. They also gathered resources from the areas around their settlements. Men hunted, fished, and practiced some environmental management in addition to diplomacy and war. In short, North Americans combined agriculture with foraging, with the women doing most of the farming and the men doing most of the foraging.

Agrarian peoples were expanding their territorial range, often moving into foraging territories. Farming peoples throughout the Americas built stockades around their villages with walls substantially higher than would be needed just to keep out wild animals, for example. Agriculturalists could muster more armed men to conflicts than foragers, and they occupied land much more densely than hunters. In the Americas, the arrival of the horse with the Spanish would temporarily shift the balance of power to the foragers, but as of the start of our text, agriculturalists were pushing foragers into more and more marginal lands everywhere but Australia.

EMERGING STATE SYSTEMS IN WEST AFRICA:
TRANSITIONAL EXAMPLES

For West African women, in particular, the centuries prior to the start of our period had been ones of rapid political and cultural change, and their effects on women are not yet well known. City-states conquered and otherwise absorbed their neighbors to become empires and then fell in their turn to successor states and conquerors. The expansion of the power base of states like Mali and Benin led to an increased militarization and increased centralization, trends that did not bode well for women's participation in public life any more than they did for women under Aztec rule. Nevertheless, these hierarchical societies sometimes placed women in positions of great public responsibility, although their positions derived from their relationships with men. Queen mothers (the mothers of reigning kings) held great power in Benin and Ashanti, and in Bornu the king's senior female relatives—his mother, wife, or sister—held important government positions and ran fiefs, a responsibility that required them to act as appellate judges, tax collectors, and military recruiters. On a level more consonant with the lives of ordinary women, West African legal decisions and laws of all kinds were made in open courts, with all adults able to participate in the conversation, if not to make the final decision.[7]

Finally, these states' expansion accompanied the spread of Islam throughout the African Middle Ages. Rulers of emerging states adopted Islam and/or promoted greater ties with other Muslim nations and scholars, which in turn integrated West Africans more fully into international trade and the international Arabic language culture. The spread of Islam encouraged greater literacy and different forms of religious participation for women, thus giving more women a religious education and access to literacy (for instance, in Timbuktu, the greatest center of Arabic language learning in Africa, nearly all adults were literate), but Islamic law must also have conflicted with local laws in terms of women's legal rights. The famed fourteenth-century traveler Ibn Battuta[8] remarked in surprise at how much more freedom of movement West African Muslim women had than the Muslim women he knew from the Mediterranean. One imagines that, as the works of Arab and Persian scholars and traditional forms of Muslim education became more widespread, Muslim women must have conformed more to the ideals of their co-religionists to the north.

URBAN CIVILIZATIONS, CA. 1500: THREE EXAMPLES

If most women lived as farmers, the majority of farmers lived in urban civilizations where 90 to 95 percent of the population worked the land, but surplus wealth and population were concentrated in cities that dominated the countryside around them. Although most cultures had substantial numbers of free peasants, in most places a large percentage of farmers worked land they did not own and lived in some form of bondage to the person, family, or institution that *did* own the land.

The states and empires that controlled urban centers and their farming hinterlands had all been undergoing rapid change during the fifteenth century. Some regions seemed to be deteriorating badly. Japan was suffering through what would be a century and a half of civil war, while Persia and Northern India were deteriorating into a series of small warring states. The major powers of Western Europe fought a seemingly endless series of wars through France and Italy before attempting to conquer the Americas and the world's ocean trade routes. Other states flourished during the fifteenth and early sixteenth centuries. The Ming dynasty in China, the Aztec empire in Meso-America, the Inca empire in the Andes of South America, the Malay and Javanese states in Southeast Asia, the Muscovite (soon to be Russian) empire, and the Ottoman empire in the Middle East all made successful bids for regional dominance in the fifteenth century. In Central and Western Europe, the Habsburgs built an empire with possessions spanning the globe. Rather than attempt to detail the histories of every major urban culture, this chapter considers three widely scattered ones in detail and then touches briefly on Africa. We will examine Ming China, Renaissance Europe, and the Aztec empire, as well as the role of ideology in the creation and survival of evidence and the degree to which women's lives differed from place to place.

CHINA: THE MING DYNASTY, 1368–1644

The year 1500 falls at the height of the Ming Dynasty. After the terrible losses caused by the Black Death, China's population had rebounded and urban life flourished. The Great Ming, as its inhabitants called it, had restored native rule after two centuries of foreign domination under the Mongols. At its height in the fifteenth and sixteenth centuries the Ming was the wonder of the world, with dozens of cities flourishing on a scale without equal among its contemporaries. Cities like Beijing, Suzhou, and Hangzhou had populations numbering in the millions. Trade overland and overseas expanded, and luxury goods flowed through the shops and marketplaces. Fine and applied arts, poetry, literature, scholarship, and science all throve. Roads and canals were in good repair and increasing in number and length. Merchants interacted with foreigners from all over the world, trading ideas and ways of thinking about the world along with their goods and services. China's population and its cities grew rapidly. More wealth—and more beggars—flowed through China than had been seen since the golden age of the Tang dynasty (581–907). The burgeoning business opportunities of the Great Ming affected girls and women as well as men, bringing job opportunities that hadn't existed before. The numbers of midwives and women physicians, marriage brokers, seamstresses, market women, entertainers, and small-scale entrepreneurs grew with the size of the government and the court and with the increasing numbers of wealthy gentry and merchants. Women strolled the streets of cities in search of exotic foodstuffs and entertainment just as men did. Households and families throughout China got richer; literacy spread farther into the general population; in short, the standard of living increased for everyone, including girls and women, during the central Ming.[9]

Living in an era of relative peace and considerable prosperity, Chinese writers, artists, and artisans took up new forms and subjects. The exploration of individual feelings and psychology achieved a new cultural importance. Many men chose to write about women, imagining the world from the perspective of the opposite sex, and more women than ever before took up the brush and ink on their own behalf. Much of what they wrote has survived to tell us in profuse detail about the lives of gentry women (women from families that had produced the scholar officials who ran China's central and regional government) and courtesans. Furthermore, the Chinese tradition of scholarly history writing (which is as old as and more continuous than the European tradition) has always been interested in describing the living conditions and ideas of ordinary people, as has its literary tradition, even if the descriptions are condescending or idealized. We therefore also know at least what Chinese literati and artists *thought* ordinary women's lives were like.

Despite the economic boom of the Ming, China remained a particularly difficult place for most girls and women to grow up. Chinese gender ideology placed women in perpetual servitude. The Chinese lived in extended patrilineal families, preferably made up of a father, his sons, and their sons, and all the dependents of those men living under the same roof. Daughters went to their husbands' households, worked for their parents-in-law, and provided children for their husbands' lineages, not their own. Sons were considered the greatest blessing a family could have; the birth of a daughter was cause for sadness. Sons would grow up to continue the lineage and care for their parents, but the expense of raising a girl was seen as money wasted on her husband's family. The grim reality was that when families fell on hard times, two common solutions were the infanticide of female daughters and the sale of daughters into slavery or concubinage. Parents chose husbands for girls at a young age; wealthy men had multiple wives and concubines.

The combination of these practices with a veneration for widow chastity meant that there was always a shortage of marriageable virgins and widowed women from "honorable" families for ordinary men to marry. Girls who survived childhood therefore almost invariably were married in their mid-to-late teens to men in their late 20s or early 30s. Because of the shortage of honorable women, "marrying up" was more the rule than the exception for girls. As in Africa, the possibility of co-wives was always present, even for peasant women. A wife who failed to produce sons could expect her husband to add a wife. Wives were subject to the authority of their husbands, their mothers-in-law, and any wives that might be senior to them. Concubines ranked below even the most junior wife. Divorce was common, but in most cases could only be initiated by husbands. Wives sometimes left their husbands and returned to their own parents. Except in cases of egregious abuse, a woman's parents would try to make her return. Respectable women, however well educated and virtuous they were, lived in obedience to higher authority until and unless they reached the age at which they were senior to most of the people around them.

Girls were responsible for their younger siblings as soon as they could handle any child care. If a family were poor, it might sell a daughter to pay for food, or even for a son's education. If a family aspired to marry their daughter to a wealthy man, they bound her feet. This practice, which historians guess started during the tenth century CE in the Song dynasty (907–1276 CE), spread among the gentry during the Ming dynasty. Earlier foot-binding practices had sought to narrow the foot, probably by curling the toes up or under. This produced feet that were of close to normal length but narrower than unmodified feet. Starting in the late fifteenth century, a new style developed that sought to make the foot not just narrow but short, with a high arch. To achieve this style very young girls' feet would be tightly bound into the equivalent of a fist, with the big toe curled under the little toes and the whole foot curled under itself, which results in some of the metatarsal bones staying very small and moving the heel close to the ball of the foot. Small feet were a symbol of a girl's fragility and beauty, as well as a demonstration that she never did heavy physical labor, because the deformity made it nearly impossible. Elite women had tiny (bound) feet; women who labored (farmers and workers in the city) had "big" (normal) feet. It was an unmistakable marker and one that no adult could fake; the lotus foot, as it was called, can only be deformed into shape before the bones have finished growing, in early childhood.

Wives and mothers could achieve honor and respect, but there were only a few ways to do so. A senior wife with several daughters-in-law was a force to be reckoned with; if her husband were deceased and her son the nominal head of the household, then for all practical purposes she ruled the house and everyone in it. But the highest honor a woman could achieve (and one incompatible with her responsibilities as a mother) was that of the widow suicide. Towns and villages venerated widows who refused to remarry, especially if they had committed suicide to avoid remarriage or rape. Practically every village and town had a commemorative arch and altar built to a local suicide, and people prayed to her memory for protection.

For gentry women in particular, the Ming was an era of intellectual expansion. The Chinese had always valued education, and it had always been customary to extol the virtues of a few pious and learned women. During the Ming period, gentry families began to expend significant resources to educate their daughters—not as well as their sons, but well enough for the girls to be a credit to the family. The popular image of feminine gentility now insisted on a woman of refinement, one with a classical education. A truly good woman should be not only virtuous and fiercely devoted to the honor of her lineage and her husband's family, but also a connoisseur and creator of poetry, painting, and literature. Gentry women joined circles of female friends and family to read, write, and critique poetry—often illustrated with paintings of their own devising. If they married and moved too far away to visit, they continued to write the members of their circle and join new ones. Without actually meeting men from outside their families, these women nevertheless often engaged in literary correspondence with a few men. Such gentry women created albums of their own and their friends' favorite poems, including some they themselves had written. They edited anthologies of each other's works and sometimes found themselves included in anthologies edited by famous men. Sometimes writers' own families sponsored the publication of collections of their works.

Courtesans were even more active in intellectual circles. These women, like Japanese geishas, were highly educated musicians, dancers, artists, caterers, and sex workers. Courtesans had been employed in the sex industry since the seventh century, and they sold their skills as artists and performers as well as their bodies. The Ming emperors had revived the custom of having courtesan halls where men would meet to talk about the classics, write and recite poetry, and compete in writing poetry and capping (finishing) each others' quotations from famous poets. Courtesans—who planned these banquets and invited the men who attended them—were supposed to be as proficient as the men at reciting and writing poetry. They were also dancers and opera singers, with reputations based on their talent and skill as performers and on their willingness to defy convention. Courtesans could become famous; make large sums of money; travel, write, engage in poetic and literary conversations; and debate directly with groups of men. They were treated as (mostly) intellectual equals, and the most famous of them were quoted, published, and anthologized. Some married their clients and joined the gentry class.

Even so, few women chose the life of a courtesan. Some were enslaved; many wives of Mongol men captured during the Ming restoration of Chinese rule had been forced into this form of servitude, and by our period many of their descendants had been born into it. Other women were sold into the profession by their families; some became courtesans or were forced to live by working as prostitutes (without any of the refinement courtesans provided in the form of artistic and intellectual performance) when all their male relatives died and they had no other way to support themselves. Judging from the poetry they and their clients left behind, courtesans were not especially pleased with their work. A major genre of courtesan writing depicts their distaste for the profession and their desire to leave it. An anonymous Ming courtesan described herself as "A tiny piece of worthless bone [dice] cast over and over again. Since falling into disgrace I go tumbling without end . . .". Other times courtesans wrote about their love affairs with clients, not always fondly. We find Jing Pianpian, one of the best known courtesan poets, scolding an insufficiently attentive admirer, "Why do you complain that the distance is great when it is your hesitation that keeps you away?"[10]

Peasant women and laborers made up by far the majority of all Chinese women. Their feet were not normally bound, and they rarely had much formal education. Peasant women either lived on farms their family owned or else on farms they sharecropped, renting from landlords. They worked in rice and wheat fields, cultivated fruit trees and silkworms (in mulberry trees), and processed silk from the cultivation of the worm in the tree to the final fabrication of clothing. They cooked and cleaned for their families, and they were responsible for teaching their children the basics of virtue, good manners, and filial piety. Filial piety describes a complex set of behaviors, attitudes, and rituals stemming from the Chinese belief that the family lineage extends back through all deceased ancestors to the first ancestor in Heaven and forward through all future generations. Actions of the family on earth would affect the lineage in Heaven as well as in the future, and actions of the ancestors in Heaven would affect the lineage on earth. Each family member was both an acolyte and a priest in the cult of filial piety, acting out their reverence for the ancestors and their representatives on earth (the elders) and acting the part of the ancestors' representative for younger members of the lineage.

China's population doubled during the Ming dynasty. Families had more surviving children and more members, but they also had more people to feed on the same amount of land. Whereas cities grew and the upper crust of China grew much wealthier during the Ming, in the countryside more and more peasants were left out of family farms, working as sharecroppers or becoming bondservants. Thus, the absolute number of girls killed in infancy and sold into slavery increased at a faster rate than the population grew.

Although the ideal life Chinese society imagined for its women was one of limited movement, subservience, and complete self-sacrifice, the lives of Chinese women surviving in fiction, poetry, folk songs, and history often refused to fit the models society laid out for them. The pages of Ming writing are filled with rebellious women, bossy women, promiscuous women, warrior women—and one gets the impression from nonfiction sources that these portraits, however stereotyped, resonated with the lives of real women. Despite the heavy emphasis the official culture of late imperial China placed on propriety, filial piety, and respect for authority, the fabric of Chinese culture has always been shot through with yearning for escape, rebellion, and the solitary individual's pursuit of ideals. People of the Ming era wrote longingly of solitude, of their love for quiet, contemplation, and communion with the natural world, and many women shared that longing. Female monasticism (both Daoist and Buddhist) and asceticism seems to have increased during the Ming. Gentry women and elite courtesans created study spaces for themselves, or went on retreat into the mountains to cultivate a habit of solitude like Lu Qingzi, who wrote a collection of poems about her mountain retreat. Women with less money nevertheless sometimes retreated into a life of wandering through mountains, becoming wise women whose advice was eagerly sought by those still living under the pressures of city life. Herbalists, matchmakers, shamans, midwives, and other "grannies" (a title for unattached professional women, unrelated to the practitioner's actual age) abounded, giving opinionated advice and the rough edge of the tongue to their clients. Some women refused marriage to become scholars and teachers to their family like the legendary Elder Maiden Hua, and some became warriors. China has always had a tradition of martial women, skilled not just as warriors but as generals and rebel leaders. Popular wisdom held that women warriors had magic powers in addition to their fighting skills, and although they were never very numerous, they were a mainstay of popular plays and songs.

Even if a Chinese girl lived a sedate life quietly at home, the possibility of leaving to become a recluse, a warrior, a shaman always lingered to stir the imagination. The Ming, with its explosion of novels, short stories, plays, and fine crafts—plus the leisure to make and enjoy them—was a time of romantic longing for the finer things, the highest ambitions of the human spirit. Even when their families and neighbors did everything to keep women pursuing the straight and narrow path of married life and filial devotion, in their hearts the people of the Ming knew there were other paths for women to follow, and that some women always would.

WESTERN EUROPE IN THE HIGH RENAISSANCE, CA. 1450–1600

Europe was in the middle of what contemporaries called the Renaissance, or the rebirth of classical civilization. Like China and the rest of Eurasia, Western Europe had largely recovered from the terrible onset of the Black Death in the fourteenth century. Its population had largely recovered, and its peasantry and artisan classes had capitalized on the population and labor shortages of the previous century to wrest more independence from land-owning classes. Despite—perhaps even because of—the numerous wars of the fifteenth and sixteenth centuries, European visual and performing arts, literature, science, and the humanities throve. New ideas, techniques, and inventions appeared in all areas of life. The invention of printing with movable type (which originated entirely separately from East Asian woodblock printing) made it possible to distribute these ideas to a wider population than ever before and fed an ever-increasing hunger for books. Everywhere, people were reading religious devotionals and how-to manuals, printed for an audience ranging from the erudite university graduate who could read Latin and Greek to the semiliterate peasant or town dweller who could make out a few words (if they were accompanied by explanatory illustrations). Artists like Leonardo da Vinci and Michelangelo were becoming legends in their own lifetimes, and city economies flowered despite near-constant war.

Sources for Renaissance European women's history are therefore comparable in abundance to those available for the history of women in Ming China, but they are of very different kinds. In contrast to the Ming sources, early Renaissance documents tell us a great deal about women's finances and their material life, and—despite a large number of works written by women—much less about what they thought and felt. The writing available to us in Ming women's own words comes in the form of poetry and letters—mostly letters written in the context of poetry circles. Ming gender ideology considered poetry an appropriate expression of feminine feelings and was, moreover, interested in writing about women's lives and in hearing women's voice (even if the bulk of the writers were men and even if the women's voices were invented by men). Society in general encouraged Chinese women to write poetry, think about poetry, and write about poetry.[11]

Renaissance Europeans felt very differently. First, despite its reputation as a hotbed of individualism, European culture's fascination with the faces, lives, and voices of individuals was only in its infancy. Portraiture, especially of ordinary people, was a relatively new art form. Autobiographies were scarce. Even romantic songs and poems rarely spoke about the actual experiences of real individuals. The most famous poet of late Middle Ages, Petrarch, carried on (in pen) a lifelong fantasy relationship with Laura, a girl whom had he met briefly when they were both children.[12]

Second, even if the topic were something besides their own feelings and experiences, women had virtually no legitimate public space in which to speak or write in their own voice; women who did so could be accused of being promiscuous, mannish, or otherwise unwomanly. As wealthier peasants and artisans gained corporate political power against the nobility, ordinary men began to draw stricter lines between public (male) and private (female) spaces. Men spoke for their families in the public arena, and such public kinds of recognition as licenses, diplomas, and craft guild memberships came to be seen as appropriate for men only. Renaissance women writers prefaced their published works with apologies for daring to speak and explained that only the demands of (male) friends, family members, and authorities had persuaded them to take up the pen. Though Renaissance elites began to pay tutors to educate their daughters, they expected their daughters to use that education purely in the service of their family's interests. As the sixteenth century progressed, women scholars were more likely to write translations or produce scholarly editions of some man's work than to write their own. Christine de Pisan was the last woman of the late Middle Ages to make a living as a scholar, working for the French court and producing many works over several decades. Even the diaries and commonplace books kept by some women in this era—which do sometimes record their daily activities—almost never mention the writer's own feelings or thoughts. Personal correspondence, which the Ming used for recreation, was an almost purely utilitarian form of writing in the Renaissance. Women's letters (like men's) were about family business—what price was paid that month for candles and firewood, for example, or whether a particular family was suitable for their son to marry into. For ordinary women who left behind more than the records of their birth, death, marriage, and children born, often the one or two other surviving sources are lists of their possessions at the time they ordered their wills to be written. Despite the high value European Jews set on education, even Jewish women were not encouraged to study in depth, produce scholarship, or engage in creative writing. Jewish publishing aimed specifically at women—a late sixteenth-century development— was limited to tracts describing women's appropriate behavior and to collections of prayers.[13]

The censure of women's voices and ideas extended into the performing arts. Elite women learned to dance and play musical instruments, but performances were acceptable only in the privacy of the home—alone or in the company of a few friends. Where the central Middle Ages had given rise to professional women singer/composers (*trobaritza*), by the late fifteenth and early sixteenth centuries, professional music education outside elite circles and convents was limited to men. As visual artists began to demand and receive treatment as equals to the nobility and to gain widespread fame for their art forms, important work in the visual arts also came to be seen as an exclusively masculine activity.

Thus, at the start of our period there was very little tradition of creative expression among European women, even among the elite, and even though most elite families hired private tutors to educate their daughters. We therefore have few records produced by early Renaissance women about themselves or even about other women—Christine de Pisan's fifteenth-century advice manual, *The Treasure of the City of Ladies, or, The Book of the Three Virtues*, and her feminist revision of world history, *The Book of the City of Ladies*, are almost the only such texts. We must rely heavily on the writings by men about women and on financial, church, and government documents such as marriage contracts, baptismal rolls, wills, and trial records.

Western Europe was less homogeneous than Ming China, with more mutually unintelligible languages and somewhat wider disparities in family structure. The only form of marriage permitted in Europe was monogamy, which was supposed to be for life. The average age at first marriage varied widely. In Florence girls of 17 or 18 married men in their late 20s or early 30s and went to live in the same household as their husband, his parents, and his brothers. In Northern Europe, young women married in their early 20s to men in their mid-to-late 20s and then formed a household separate from both sets of parents. Jewish families arranged early marriages for both boys and girls and brought the teenaged couples into the household of one or the other sets of parents. Except for Jews, divorce was illegal throughout Europe, but annulment (a declaration that a marriage had been invalid and therefore never really existed) was sometimes possible for Christians. Many regions had mechanisms to permit married couples to separate, but remarriage was not permissible unless one of the separated spouses died. Fathers were the presumed guardians of children, but even in patrilineal regions where the fathers' family was assumed to be responsible for maintaining his children, widows often managed their children's and their own affairs at least until they remarried. Widows and widowers usually remarried—and there was no cult of widow chastity like the one in China. Western, central, and eastern Europe also had large numbers—as much as 10 percent of the population—of people who never married. Most of these were monks, nuns, and priests, but some were just people who had not found the right mate or been able to scrounge up the resources to set up their own household.[14]

Here, as in China, most women lived as peasants. As a class, Western European peasants were becoming more autonomous in the late Middle Ages. More of them owned their land or held very long-term leases, and many others were contracting sharecroppers. In most regions, peasants could not be sold. Although they had to pay their lord a tax to marry, peasants did not need his permission, and although the physical abuse of employees was common, many regions permitted peasants to leave abusive employers. An affluent peasant would maintain a kitchen garden (for vegetables, herbs, and medicinals), chickens, pigs, in some regions perhaps a female goat or sheep, and, if she were *very* well off, cows or even a dairy. She might also keep bees and maintain a small stand of fruit trees. Her husband would farm the major grains and legumes—barley, spelt, rye, wheat, peas, beans—but it was likely she helped at planting and harvest time. It was unlikely that she and her husband would both survive until her children were adults, so ensuring her children's financial stability and moral development was even more urgent for her than for us today. The couple would try to find a respectable household to employ the children before they reached their early teens, and the parents would seek out suitable candidates for betrothal as soon as possible—with suitability defined as much by the ability of candidate's *family* to provide appropriate financial support and moral guidance as on the qualities of the candidate him- or herself.[15]

A poor peasant woman might come from a family that had no land, keep a few chickens or a goat on the common land most villages maintained, and hire herself out to work in the fields and dairies of more well-off peasants. Her family probably would only be able to provide a small dowry, if any, so she would have to earn it herself if she wanted to marry. Europeans expected a bride to bring assets into a marriage, rather than having the groom's family pay her family a bride-price for her, and in most regions parents reserved more family assets for boys than for girls. Women were thus more likely to marry down than up the social ladder, even if they came from well-to-do families. Poor peasants usually had to work for others for a living, even sometimes in places where they risked physical or sexual abuse. Unlike a Ming dynasty servant, who would probably be taken in as a concubine and have her master's child recognized as legitimate, the European peasant was likely to lose her job and be abandoned by the father if she got pregnant by a member of her employer's family.

Although the Renaissance was expanding opportunities for men, it was limiting opportunities for women: taking away guild (professional association) memberships, clapping women who worked as prostitutes into state-controlled brothels, and embarking on the first decades of large witch-hunts. The fifteenth century had been one of expanding religious opportunities, but those began to dry up. Poor and working women had been joining groups of pious lay women (Beguines and Beatas) in small houses and neighborhoods, living in prayer and worship together without taking vows. This trend had made it easier for poor women to start and join religious orders, because they did not need generous dowries to do so. Members would live at home with their families or live together as roommates, two or three to a house, and earn an income through their own labor. In the sixteenth century the activities of these single women came to be viewed with suspicion—municipalities and religious authorities tried to shut them down.[16]

Traditional monasticism was a prestigious career path for women as well as men and required entrants to either arrive with some formal education or acquire one. Women who wanted to profess as nuns had to bring a substantial dowry or, in rare cases, special skills like accounting or music composition, to support them, because nuns were not supposed to support themselves through work, but to support the community through prayer. Families usually sent their daughters to the same convent over many generations, so that most nuns would be living with an aunt or cousin in the same house rather than entirely with strangers. Late medieval European convents were pleasant spaces. Nuns' "cells" were often apartments. Mature convents almost all owned at least a large courtyard and often-extensive gardens, sometimes rooms for servants, and always if at all possible room for women in retreat. It was common for widows to take partial vows and move to convents. As a young woman, Christine de Pisan herself said she would have entered a convent if she had not had so many family responsibilities—although when she was confined to house arrest in a convent during the last years of the Hundred Years' War, she did not find it so congenial, describing herself as "I, Christine, who have wept for eleven years in a closed abbey."[17]

The ideals Renaissance women were supposed to strive for were exemplified by the Virgin Mary, the Christian saints, and the princesses and fair ladies of epic and troubadour poetry. The relatively few favorable images of women emphasized an almost militant chastity and/or submission to authority. Popular art and literature depicted ordinary women as gossips, scolds, and prostitutes—bad women who had slipped the leashes of their men. With the rise of popular printing and secular subjects, humorous depictions of fallible women became even more common. Probably the most important thing about these ideals and distortions for ordinary women was that the most admired models of womanhood—saintly nuns, princesses, and the ladies of courtly romance—were noblewomen. Artists often showed even the Virgin Mary, who in real life would have been poor, as the daughter of a wealthy household. Where an ordinary Ming woman could imagine herself becoming a recluse, a woman warrior, or respected granny, ordinary Renaissance women had few, if any, positive images of themselves.

The fifteenth and early sixteenth centuries in Western Europe was a time of increasing misogyny and decreasing female access to public spaces and opportunities for personal growth. The great scientific, literary, theological, and artistic advances of the later Renaissance did little to alter this, although the Protestant and Catholic Reformations of the sixteenth and seventeenth centuries would.

MESO-AMERICA, 1400–1525

The 200 years from 1400 to 1600 brought rapid and mostly unpleasant changes for women in Central America. While China was in the middle of a kind of golden age and Europe was at least experiencing economic prosperity—even as it limited women's access to public spaces—Central America witnessed two waves of conquest and empire building. The most familiar was the arrival of the Spanish in the sixteenth century (discussed extensively in Chapter Three). They, however, were only the second wave of conquerors. Central America—the territory that is now Mexico, Guatemala, and Honduras—was a wealthy region. Extensive farmlands supported cities, which served as ceremonial and political centers as well as loci for trade and craft production. Over the course of the fifteenth century, Central and Eastern Mexico had been conquered by the *Mexica*, also called the Aztec. The Aztec had built a loosely connected empire of cities, which sent tribute in specialty and luxury goods to their capital, Tenochtitlán (now Mexico City). They also practiced human sacrifice on an unprecedented scale. All previous Central American societies had practiced blood sacrifice and human sacrifice as a regular part of their religions, but the Aztec based men's prestige and promotions on the number of men they captured in battle and sacrificed. Warriors garnered the most prestige because they captured men directly, but even merchants would purchase slaves to sacrifice for status. On major holidays, the Aztec would apparently sacrifice hundreds, even thousands of people. In addition, they demanded women as tribute from cities they had conquered. This seems to have also been a new practice in Central America. Remaining inscriptions suggest that previous civilizations built alliances and sealed conquests by exchanging high-ranking women, but the women sent to Tenochtitlán were not captives. Rather, the women exchanged were seen as providing legitimacy to the regime they joined; their lineages would be celebrated, and the women themselves would appear as major, honored figures in the inscriptions on monumental architecture—much of which the women themselves seem to have commissioned. The Aztec, however, seized women rather than honoring them. The combination of what other Central Americans considered excessive sacrifice, humiliating taxation, and the abuse of women made the Aztec deeply unpopular throughout the region—one reason Hernán Cortés would find them easy prey in the sixteenth century.[18]

The peoples of Central America had an extensive written culture, abundantly documented in the inscriptions on their monumental architecture, and we know that some women participated in that culture as patrons of art and as authors. But we have only the tiniest sample of their other writings. The Spanish systematically destroyed all the writing they found, so that we have only three Mayan scrolls and a few hundred Aztec scrolls surviving. What little we have left tells us how enormous the loss was, especially for women's history—the remaining documents contain brief descriptions of childhood education for girls and boys, of cycles of myths, and of the poems composed and sung by educated women.

But this evidence was not enough to decode Aztec and Mayan inscriptions carved in stone on monuments and stelae, because most inscriptions used earlier, more complex, forms of writing. Ancient Central Americans used a combination alphabet and syllabary (a system in which each letter indicates a vowel/consonant combination) that employed abbreviations for prefixes, suffixes, and infixes. They also used abbreviations in their images. To take an example from contemporary pop culture, if the Maya were to depict Superman, they might have chosen to show him in his entirety. Or they could have shown the peculiar letter S from his suit, the laser beams he could shoot from his eyes, some glowing kryptonite—or a combination of these things. Imagine trying to understand the meaning of the word "Superman" if we had no comic books, movies, or television about him, and these fragments of images were all the evidence we had left. This is what decoding Mayan images is like for art historians and archaeologists. Because we lack the written accounts of the religion, history, legends, myths, and literature of Central America, we lack the context to interpret most of the images on and in the remaining architecture. Just differentiating between images of real, historical women (quite a few still exist) and those of mythological beings is challenging. Art historians are not even certain which images are of gods, and which of goddesses—or whether Central American gods are both at different times! Therefore the chief determinants of what we currently know about Aztec women's lives are the haphazard nature of surviving records and our struggle to read what remains. Rather than comparing the reasons the Aztecs produced many examples of certain kinds of materials relating to women's lives and not others (as we have done for China and Europe), we must content ourselves with considering a much more limited range of evidence.

Despite the destruction of many sources, we know quite a bit about how Maya and Aztec people thought little girls should be raised and educated and about the roles adult women should play. There was considerable similarity between the Maya and Aztec, probably because the whole of Central America was an area of continuous cultural contact for over 2,000 years. An Aztec manuscript, the *Codex Mendoza,* describes the ideal upbringing of Aztec children. The birth of both girls and boys was cause for celebration. Children were given symbols of their adult roles—girls tiny brooms to indicate their responsibility to sweep and clean the house, and boys tiny plows to indicate they were to farm. In Central America, as in Europe, the major starch crops (here, corn and beans) were grown by men. Women's work included collecting water, weaving textiles, caring for children, and preparing food. The latter was very hard: Corn had to be soaked, dried, bleached, and then slowly ground into flour using a grindstone and pestle—there were no mills in the pre-Columbian Americas. It was labor-intensive and time-consuming and required multiple women and young girls to work together.

Women wove textiles from cotton and maguey (a kind of thorn) using portable backstrap looms (shown in Figure 1.1). A properly reared woman could take the fibers from harvest through cleaning, spinning, and dying; design the pattern to be woven; weave it; do any necessary sewing; and attach any embellishments such as beadwork, embroidery, or fancy netting. She might base her patterns on inherited designs, devise them herself, or combine tradition and innovation. Just because women knew how to do all the steps in the process did not necessarily mean that every piece of Central American clothing was made by one person from local materials. Adult (married) women were expected to buy and sell in the marketplace, especially their textiles. There was a vigorous trade in fiber, dyes, and cloth throughout Central America. When we see a contemporary Central American woman weaving with modern dyes, dressing her children in clothing or fabrics purchased in a market and made thousands of miles away, or creating textiles for sale to an international market, we in fact see her acting as a traditionalist.

Central American educations were supposed to emphasize the importance of truthfulness, self-sacrifice, hard work, honor, respect for elders, and obedience to authority. The Aztecs practiced corporal punishments for persistent disobedience by pricking children with maguey thorns or, if all else failed, tying them up and leaving them overnight

FIGURE 1.1   INCA WOMAN WEAVING
Like women in Aztec Central America in the same period, Inca
women in the Andes paid tribute to their ruler in the form of
textiles. This Inca woman is weaving on a backstrap loom—the
kind also used by Aztec and Maya women of this era. The loom
was portable. How does portability make it easier for the weaver to
work, especially if she is a woman with small children? Given that
Central and South American women used the same kind of loom
to produce textiles, what kinds of similarities would you expect to
find in their cloth?

outside in the damp (one imagines the adults must have stayed hidden
nearby in case of real danger, although the texts we have left behind do
not say this). Children were introduced to the community on at least
two occasions—their naming and their official acceptance as adults
with adult responsibilities. Boys typically learned to become farmers,
although some in cities were craftsmen or members of merchant families, and aristocratic boys all had to learn to become warriors or priests.
Some children, apparently fewer girls than boys, learned to read, write,
and recite literature.

Whereas Central Americans may have used writing to keep records
of taxes and exchanges of goods and lands, the images of people reading and speaking emphasize that writing was primarily a form of *belles
lettres* (literature esteemed for its aesthetic style rather than its factual content) intended to preserve words that would then be recited as "beautiful
speech."[19] When Central American men or women are shown speaking in
vase paintings, frescoes, and inscriptions, they are accompanied by pictures
of small scrolls that emerge from their mouths to indicate the beautiful

speech being made. Ideally writing was for song, poetry, myth, legend, and religious ceremony, and beautiful speech was supposed to be within the competence of all adults. Child-rearing instructions tell the parents (of both sexes) repeatedly to admonish and instruct their children in beautiful and moving language. Since some women were literate, it should not surprise us to learn that among the small number of poems and songs to escape the bonfire, some are attributed to women and contain references to other women writers. For instance, Macuilxochitzin wrote a poem praising the military campaign planned by her aristocratic father, saying, "I raise my songs . . . with these I gladden the Giver of Life."[20]

Women were subordinate to men in Aztec society. Parents chose the husbands of their daughters, but gave sons choices in choosing their wives. Aristocrats practiced polygyny and concubinage, and the state ran brothels in the cities. Public honors and public authority went to men, even though women had important positions in the priesthood. But despite the double standard that assumed married women would be chaste and husbands would not be, the picture for women's sexual lives was not all bleak: Sexual and sensual pleasure were celebrated, and women were not considered sources of pollution as they were in Western Europe. Girls were celebrated as much as boys were, and women's activities were considered crucial to the smooth functioning of society, even if they were not as worthy of public praise.

Although the Aztec were recent arrivals, they borrowed and/or shared much of the ideology of previous regimes. This borrowing could be quite literal—for example, stone monuments from the oldest urban center of Central America, Teotihuacán, were transported to Tenochtitlán. Like other Central American peoples, they practiced polygyny among the most aristocratic families, but not among ordinary people. A handful of wives for a ruler was not uncommon, but the rule in their society was monogamy. Aside from the practice of capturing and enslaving women (male captives were usually ritually sacrificed), the Aztecs effected other changes in the lives of the women of West and Central Mexico. They insisted on receiving a large portion of their tribute in cloth and levied specific quotas on tributary cities and their surrounding territories. Clearly this was intended to be a kind of corvée labor tax on women—unpaid labor demanded by an overlord. Yet, the archaeological evidence indicates that women throughout the Aztec-dominated regions did *not* universally step up cloth production. Women in regions that had traditionally produced less cloth did not suddenly start producing more or better-quality cloth, although women in regions that were already large-scale producers seem to have stepped up production. Instead, what seems to have happened is that villages simply bought more cloth from people already producing it for trade. Thus, the Aztec stimulated more regional trade by causing women to purchase more cloth.

It is difficult to tell how much the rise of the Aztec affected ordinary women's lives in the fifteenth century. Certainly, the increasing militarization of society, the many conquests of city-states, and the large numbers of captives required for sacrifice all hurt women. Male family members were lost to warfare and sacrificial altars, and women themselves were subject to capture, enslavement, and human sacrifice. It is also possible the Aztec were responsible for starting or at least accelerating the trade in women captives that was firmly in place by the sixteenth century.

Under Aztec domination, taxes went up without commensurate increases in government services. On the other hand, trade in urban centers (a major economic activity for women) flourished, and networks of roads and canals grew. Still, the positive reaction of most Aztec allies to the arrival of potential rivals (the Spanish) suggests most people thought the Aztec empire's impact was negative.

CONCLUSION

Few women lived in cities at the start of the era this study examines. Instead, nearly all women (and nearly all men) were agriculturalists (farmers), pastoralists (herders, although there are always fewer herders than farmers), hunter/gatherers, or a combination of the three. While the specific tasks done by women as opposed to those done by men could vary immensely from society to society, one aspect remained consistent almost everywhere. No matter what tasks men and women actually did, every society practiced division of labor by gender and presumed that the roles of men and women were mutually complementary and indispensable. In East and Southeast Asia, India, Europe, the Middle East, and Meso-America it was mostly the case that men's tasks held higher prestige than women's, even where cultural rhetoric emphasized equivalence. But in Australia, the Pacific Islands, sub-Saharan Africa, and North America, things were much less predictable. Frequently men's and women's tasks really were held to be equivalent and complementary, and women's collective institutions had as much power and influence as men's. Sometimes—though not often—women's corporate authority was even greater than men's.

STUDY QUESTIONS

1. Compare and contrast women's opportunities for self-expression in the various societies described in this chapter.

2. In which society would you rather be a woman agriculturalist? A man? Why?

3. List several ways politics (that is, changes in government, shifts in power between social groups, warfare) shaped women's lives during this period. In what ways could women respond to these changes to help themselves and their families?

4. Compare and contrast the family structures of the societies in this chapter. Which ones seem most favorable to girls? Least favorable? Why?

BIBLIOGRAPHY

*indicates contains whole primary sources or secondary works containing substantial extracts.

AFRICA

Atmore, Oliver, and Anthony Atmore. *Medieval Africa: 1250–1800.* Cambridge: Cambridge University Press, 2001.

Bingham, Marjorie Wall, and Susan Hill Gross. *Women in Africa of the Sub-Sahara.* Vol. I, *Ancient Times to the 20th Century.* Hudson, WI: Gary E. McCuen Publications, 1982.

Coquerey-Vidrovitch, Catherine. *African Women: A Modern History.* Translated by Beth Gillian-Raps. Boulder, CO: Westview Press, 1997.

General History of Africa. Vols. 4–5. UNESCO International Scientific Committee for the Drafting of a General History of Africa. Oxford: Heinemann International Literature and Textbooks, 1992–1992.

*Niane, D. T. *Sundiata: An Epic of Old Mali.* Translated by G. D. Fisher. London: Longmans, 1967.

Page, Willie F., ed. *Encyclopedia of African History and Culture.* Vols. 2–3. New York: Facts on File, 2005.

FORAGING PEOPLES

Dahlberg, Frances, ed. *Woman the Gatherer.* Cambridge: Yale University Press, 1983.

Lee, Richard, and Richard Daly. *The Cambridge Encyclopedia of Hunters and Gatherers.* Cambridge: Cambridge University Press, 1999.

MESO-AMERICA

Carrasco, Davíd, and Scott Sessions. *Daily Life of the Aztecs: People of the Sun and Earth.* Westport, CT: Greenwood Press, 1998.

Clendinnen, Inge. *Aztecs: An Interpretation.* Cambridge: Cambridge University Press, 1991.

Klein, Cecilia, ed. *Gender in Pre-Hispanic America.* Washington, DC: Dumbarton Oaks Research Library and Collection, 2001. (Not suited for undergraduate reading.)

*Leon-Portilla, Miguel, trans. and ed. *Fifteen Poets of the Aztec World.* Norman: University of Oklahoma Press, 1992.

*———. *In the Language of Kings: An Anthology of Meso-American Literature, Pre-Columbian to the Present.* New York: Norton, 2001.

*Miller, Mary Ellen. *The Art of Mesoamerica from Olmec to Aztec.* London: Thames and Hudson, 1986.

Sharer, Robert. *The Ancient Maya.* 5th ed. Stanford, CA: Stanford University Press, 1994.

MING CHINA

Cass, Victoria. *Dangerous Women: Warriors, Grannies, and Geishas of the Ming.* Lanham, MD: Rowman and Littlefield, 1999.

Ko, Dorothy. *Cinderella's Sisters: A Revisionist History of Footbinding.* Berkeley: University of California Press, 2005.

Widmer, Ellen, and Kang-i Sun Chang. *Writing Women in Late Imperial China.* Stanford, CA: Stanford University Press, 1997.

WESTERN EUROPE

*Bayard, Tanya. *The Medieval Home Companion. Housekeeping in the Fourteenth Century.* New York: Harper Perennial, 1992.

Hufton, Olwen. *The Prospect Before Her: A History of Women in Western Europe.* New York: Alfred Knopf, 1996.

*Petrarch. *Canzoniere.* Translated by A. S. Kline. *Petrarch: The Canzoniere.* http://www.tonykline.co.uk/PITBR/Italian/Petrarchhome.htm.

*Pisan, Christine de. *The Treasure of the City of Ladies.* Translated by Sarah Lawson. Harmondsworth, UK: Penguin Classics, 1985.

Wiesner, Merry. *Women and Gender in Early Modern Europe.* 2nd ed. Cambridge: Cambridge University Press, 2000.

Weissler, Chava. "The Traditional Piety of Ashkenazic Women," in *Jewish Spirituality,* vol. 2. Edited by Arthur Green. New York: Crossroads, 1987.

ORAL HISTORY

Oral History Association. *Oral History Association.* http://alpha.dickinson.edu/organizations/oha/pub_ohr.html

Thompson, Paul. *The Voice of the Past: Oral History.* Oxford: Oxford University Press, 2000.

CHAPTER TWO

IDEOLOGICAL TRANSFORMATIONS IN EURASIA, 1500–1750

During the sixteenth and seventeenth centuries, women in Eurasia lived in societies that sought to regulate femininity and masculinity in new ways—some harmful and some beneficial to women. Early modern states were becoming more centralized and more powerful; rulers and regimes had a greater ability to make their presence felt (for better or worse) in the daily lives of their subjects or citizens. Thus in this era many changes in gender ideology were at least partly state-driven—often through changes in state religious institutions. State regulation of gender almost never focused solely on women; instead, the goal would be to create a particular kind of man, another particular kind of woman, and by extension a society of families who produced properly behaved male and female children. Proper behavior for women, it is important to point out, was not necessarily imagined as only docile and submissive. Furthermore, because states wanted to produce particular kinds of subjects and families, they often wanted girls to embrace and pass on to their children the ideologies the state supported. Thus, they encouraged better-off families to provide at least a limited amount of education for girls and prescribed or recommended content. Education for boys was of course a much higher priority. A woman's brothers were still much more likely to be literate and numerate than she was, but early modern Eurasian women made definite gains in access to education.

When states increase their power over their subjects, they often compensate for their subjects' loss of autonomy by giving them greater power over their households, by providing increased services, by giving one social group increased leverage over a rival or oppressive group, or by scapegoating a particular group of people. Each of the Eurasian states we will examine used at least one and sometimes all four of these techniques to shore up their authority. Often a change created opportunities for one set of women while limiting choices for another.

State centralization is often partly the product of territorial expansion, conquest, or large-scale, extended warfare. In order to raise the funds to field large armies and navies and administer new territories, states needed more efficient methods of extracting taxes, faster ways of passing laws, and quicker methods of extracting compliance from their populace—not just when handing over taxes but in responding to the government during crises. The size of governments and their militaries expanded, providing both more access to government jobs for ordinary men but also putting far more men into military and naval service. This development obviously had different implications for the women whose husbands, brothers, and sons were employed by the government than for those whose family members were serving in the military.

Just as often, centralization leads to the creation of national (as opposed to regional or customary) legal systems. Regional and class differences in laws defining family formation, inheritance, marriage, and divorce may be smoothed over or replaced by statewide codes. At the very least, appellate court systems will be put in place, providing a forum for those unhappy with a particular decision to take their complaint to a higher level. This encouraged plaintiffs and defendants to consider the possibility that the central government might be a better source of justice than their local government—if they had the resources to continue to pursue a case. Women would find their choices expanded or diminished based on their ethnic and economic background and on which local laws the state chose to modify.

Most Eurasian states of this period experienced population growth, urban and economic expansion, and a rising standard of living in urban areas that made it possible for artisanal and merchant classes to have greater cultural (and in some cases political) influence. Wives, daughters, and sisters of artisans and craftsmen often had new choices and opportunities unavailable to rural women. But since, like almost all premodern people, urban women depended on their lineage and their marital family for financial, social, and emotional connections, they allied themselves with the interests of their urban families rather than with women in general, even with other urban women. Thus, women might well support projects that hurt women in general, even women of their own social class, if those projects served their families' interests.

This chapter, like Chapter One, limits itself to a few major case studies—China, Japan, the Ottoman empire, and Western Europe. Processes analogous to those described here occurred in the Russian empire, parts of India, and Southeast Asia. Women's history in these latter regions is, however, less well understood: The secondary and primary source literature is often not readily available in publications or languages likely to be accessible to readers of this text. Recent groundbreaking work on Russia and Southeast Asia may do a great deal to address those gaps, and the outlook for study of women's history in India improves steadily as that nation's economy expands.

QING CHINA, 1644–1795

The Qing dynasty came to power through conquest of the earlier Ming dynasty. Its emperors and leadership were not Han Chinese (the dominant Chinese ethnic group), but Manchu, and their empire encompassed not just the boundaries of Ming China but also Manchuria in the north and considerable non-Han territories to the west. The first three Manchu emperors started and completed the conquest of China. They and the very long-reigning fifth emperor, Qianlong (r. 1736–1795) were vigorous reformers, expanding the role of government in civic life, creating more government offices, and recreating a paid, professional military. The Ming dynasty had diminished the size of government to the point that basic services—road building, disaster relief, policing, access to civil and criminal justice—were almost impossible to maintain. Thus, early Qing reforms in many ways brought greater stability and more government-sponsored employment, and the families of soldiers could rely on a stable income and greater respect. On the other hand, the Qing struggled with even more rapid population growth than the Ming had faced. Between 1650 and 1850, the population of China tripled, and this had already begun to put a strain on the dynasty by the middle of the eighteenth century.[1] Figure 2.1 shows the extent of territories ruled by both dynasties.

　　Some early Qing policies had immediate negative results on women. First, the state made it almost impossible for women to prosecute rape or to demand child support if a child's father abandoned them. The main purpose of this legislation was to protect the Manchu military from prosecution for rape. As one ethnic group conquering another, early Manchu soldiers sometimes saw Han women as the property and spoils of the victors and were more likely to sexually abuse Han women than their own. Second, the Manchu had a general policy of promoting traditional Confucian values. This was meant to demonstrate that even though the dynasty was founded by people whom the ethnic Han considered foreigners, they were committed to what they perceived as the Chinese way of life. Wedded far more tightly to a conservative understanding of traditional Chinese values than the Ming, the Manchu publicized the old cult of widow chastity more than any preceding dynasty. They erected hundreds of new memorials to chaste widows and published testimonials to their virtues.

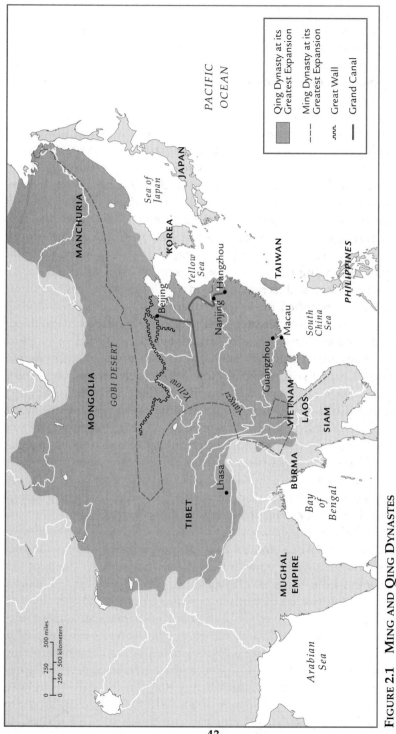

FIGURE 2.1 MING AND QING DYNASTIES

The map shows the Ming (1366–1644) and Qing (1644–ca. 1750) dynasties at their greatest expanses.

Presses released hundreds of stories about such women, and every city and village had its own small shrine or memorial to one. The most poignant and affecting stories were, of course, those of virgin suicides—women so loyal to the memory of the fiancé they had *almost* married that they gave up life itself for him. The invigorated cult of widow chastity did have some advantages for those women who married into affluent families: Widows who did not want to remarry were more able to persuade their families to permit this choice, for example, and daughters-in-law could expect more respect and financial support from their husband's family if they were widowed. The Chinese idealized a notion of extended families in which husbands and wives lived in the household of the husband's parents, but frequently a woman's husband died after his parents and without surviving brothers. It also was common for a widow to have one aging in-law or parent who, rather than being able to support her, needed her help to survive. The glorification of widow chastity therefore meant that those widows who remarried—and many did—were perceived as somehow less honorable, even if their choice had been marriage or extreme poverty. Their neighbors might condemn them for sexual impurity—even in-laws whom they were helping to support might do so. The veneration afforded some heroic role models for women.

Qing dynasty attempts to push women into a more conservative sexuality were accompanied by punitive laws forcing Chinese men to display their submission and loyalty to the new state and by repeated emphasis on the individual man's Confucian duty to obey the state and all his superiors. All men were supposed to wear the Manchu hairstyle shown in Figure 2.2—the forehead shaved and the rest of the hair braided in a single, long plait—as a symbol of their obedience to the dynasty. After 1645, not wearing it was a capital offense. The policy was part of a larger program to make Han Chinese men obedient to Manchu policies and change the kinds of education considered most desirable for men.

For most of the last 2,000 years, Chinese governments have used variations of an examination system to build up a pool of highly educated (male) civil servants and citizens. Entrance to central government offices was often limited to those who have passed certain very difficult examinations, and the subject of those examinations was, until the twentieth century, the classics of Confucius. A thorough education in Confucian ideology was thus the essential element of any boy's chance for high office, and the Chinese came to prize a Confucian education above almost any other value in raising their sons. For every student who passed the exams, there were dozens who had also studied for them and been indoctrinated in the same values and same habits of mind. The Ming had attempted to make this system more egalitarian, setting quotas for each province, so

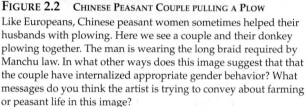

FIGURE 2.2   CHINESE PEASANT COUPLE PULLING A PLOW
Like Europeans, Chinese peasant women sometimes helped their
husbands with plowing. Here we see a couple and their donkey
plowing together. The man is wearing the long braid required by
Manchu law. In what other ways does this image suggest that that
the couple have internalized appropriate gender behavior? What
messages do you think the artist is trying to convey about farming
or peasant life in this image?

that poor regions could have their local candidates win preferment. They
also created a new category of passing candidates, the "government students," who numbered about 100,000 by the end of the dynasty.[2] These
men did not hold offices but held prizes and certificates and could usually
gain employment on that basis. Thus, the literati (the educated) class had
expanded not just in real numbers under the Ming but also in comparison to the population increase. The Qing chose not to expand the pool of
degree holders, and so competition for preferment grew ever fiercer as
the overall population of Chinese expanded. Because the government's
outlook remained conservative, more examination candidates pursued
orthodoxy in their attempts to pass the exams.

In their hunt for success, literati clung tightly to old traditions, becoming more interested in the philological sources of old texts and in correct
interpretations of classic thinkers than in devising new philosophical
insights or expressing their innermost beings. Being more classically conservative than the next fellow was a better guarantee of success than innovation, and so during the Qing dynasty scholars emphasized hierarchy,
duty, and obedience at the expense of reciprocity, honor, and individual
growth. Although creative expression and spiritual interests continued
during the Qing, the passionate fervor of Ming creativity and the celebration of individual spiritual growth diminished. The powerful championed a restrictive Confucian philosophy, called neo-Confucianism, which
encouraged orthodoxy and filial piety, with puritanical literati calling for

the censorship of novels, plays, and other literature they considered frivolous. Rather than joining heterodox religious movements and seeking hermitlike isolation, Qing literati recommended the government crush "superstition." Parents could not only beat, but also order the execution of disobedient children, and adults convicted of disrespect or disobedience in court could be exiled. Neo-Confucianism told women to be obedient and chaste, to serve their mothers-in-law and husbands, and to consider their personal desires unimportant. In short, if Han men under the Manchu had lost influence and authority, they could at least count on the government to support them in their roles as masters of their own households and lords of their wives, children, and servants.

On the other hand, for gentry women the Qing emphasis on new forms of education blossomed into a greater interest in educating women. The vast majority of Chinese women continued to receive little formal education, but among the families of the literati and families aspiring to that status it remained fashionable to educate girls. In privileged families, more and more girls were expected to read and write poetry, to display the beauty of their characters through their calligraphy, and demonstrate their refinement through their tasteful understanding of the fine arts and appreciation of nature. Elite families still spent far less on daughters' education than on their sons', but they were spending more than they had before. Popular literature continued to celebrate literate girls as delicate, refined, and exquisitely spiritual. Women's writing and women's poetry circles continued to flourish, and we find women working with and corresponding with other women, sometimes visiting each other to collaborate.

The status of the courtesan, however, seems to have declined in the early Qing. It is hard to tell for certain, because so much of the material written about courtesan life was written by men and is not always intended to be a faithful representation of women's lives. The sufferings of courtesans were a useful metaphor for the sufferings of Han literati—poems about the miserable lives of courtesans echoed the powerlessness Chinese male intellectuals felt under Qing rule. Nevertheless, far fewer women became well-known during the Qing for their work done as courtesans. Fewer still married into elite households. And compilations of women's writing in the early Qing, especially compilations made by women, began to exclude courtesans' writing or else include their work only among the writers of lesser merit. Gentry women seem to have adopted as their own the Qing emphasis on sexual purity and treated chastity and wifely (or daughterly) service as a prerequisite for any woman to produce worthwhile art or literature.

The lives of peasants and other working women grew harder in some ways. The burden of coping with China's rapid population growth fell most heavily on girls and young women, as it had during the Ming. Families continued to outgrow the land they occupied, even though the Qing colonized new regions in southern and western China. Tens of thousands of Chinese (mostly men) emigrated to Southeast Asia, even though it was illegal to leave the country, so that today they are the majority in Singapore and the largest minorities in Indonesia, Thailand, and Malaysia. Infanticide and the sale of children, most of whom were daughters, remained common and probably increased in frequency throughout the Qing period. The increasing difficulty of passing exams also meant that more family resources had to be devoted to the education of any son who was a promising examination candidate, including the small amount of family resources devoted to girls.

On the other hand, the large pool of free labor created by population growth meant that cities continued to grow. International trade expanded, and silver poured into the ports from overseas purchases of silk, porcelain, and lacquer. More and more positions for artisans and merchants appeared, and Chinese presses continued to issue new printed books in large numbers. Novels became more popular, and in addition to telling thrilling adventure stories, they explored people's interior lives and slyly pointed out the foibles and hypocrisy of official life. The most famous work of the era, *The Dream of the Red Mansions*,[3] tells the romantic story of several idealistic teenagers raised in a corrupt gentry household, their struggles to do good, and the machinations of their elders, to which the teenagers (male and female) are largely oblivious for most of the book.

In part because population growth was making it harder for ordinary men to own their own land or support themselves (let alone a family) as laborers and perhaps in part because neo-Confucianism laid such an emphasis on female subordination, footbinding (which helped make a girl an attractive daughter-in-law to wealthier families) was becoming less limited to the upper classes during the Qing. Women whose families intended daughters to be peasants or laborers were still unlikely to have their feet bound as girls, but it became increasingly the norm for women of higher social status. Mothers who wanted their daughters to marry into affluent families found it more and more necessary to bind their daughters' feet, and with the lotus foot becoming the standard form of footbinding in much of the Han world, that meant continuously forcing a daughter's feet into shape from the age of five or six until adulthood. What it cost mothers to do this to their daughters is hard to say; enduring the regular wrapping of the feet must have been an exercise in stoicism and self-denial for both parties. Mothers may also have understood footbinding as a method of teaching daughters the self-control they would need as adult women who had to obey their mothers-in-law and husbands. If it was painful to have one's feet bound, in the end they would be beautifully covered with wonderfully small shoes; if it was difficult to submit to the whims of a girls' marital family, in the end the daughter would be rewarded with children of her own and a harmonious family life.

The Qing dynasty expanded the size of government and the military, meaning that more women found their husbands employed in such occupations. At the same time, the conservative ideology of the early Qing seems to have spilled over into many areas of women's lives. Elite women and those who aspired to elite status for themselves, their sons, or their daughters had to embrace that conservative ideology to stay ahead or get ahead. In doing so they sometimes had to reject unorthodox women, acquiesce in the infanticide or sale of daughters, and ignore the tears and pain of daughters whose feet they bound. The expanding economy helped urban women but had little impact on rural women, whose families were struggling to feed larger numbers on the same amount of land.

EARLY TOKUGAWA JAPAN, 1568–1750

Japanese women's status had been in decline for some time before the start of this era. The period from 1467–1568 was filled with frequent coups, civil wars, and other disruptions caused by a series of weak governments. At the same time, neo-Confucian ideas had been brought over from China by the Buddhist monk Keian, and the Tendai and Shingon sects of Japanese Buddhism began to proclaim that women had to be reborn as men in order to achieve enlightenment.[4] As aristocratic families increasingly needed sons for war, strength and military prowess became more and more valued. These were characteristics men were supposedly more likely to possess than women. From the fourteenth century onward, families had begun to practice inheritance according to primogeniture—that is, property was passed from oldest son to oldest son. Before this, women had been the principal heirs of their parents, with the chief family estate usually going to a daughter. In short, women faced increasing misogyny and declining property rights. At the start of our period women in Japan had been losing authority, power, and access to family resources for several centuries, and the incoming Tokugawa shogunate (regency) would only accelerate that process.

The era of civil wars (Sengoku era) ended, and Tokugawa Ieyasu founded the Tokugawa shogunate in 1603. The new government, which is called by his family name, halted nearly 300 years of internal warfare and established a prosperous state where art, crafts, and learning flourished. It would be wrong to insist, therefore, that the Tokugawa shogunate did nothing for women. On the contrary, the Tokugawa state kept nearly all their husbands and sons out of war, made subsistence easier for peasants, and generated enough excess wealth to create a large middle class of merchants and craftspeople. All these things benefited women as well as men. However, despite the general improvement in material welfare, women's position within the family, legal status, access to education, and ability to possess property declined even further under Tokugawa leadership. Unlike the Qing government, which advocated family policies largely in pursuit of a reputation for traditionalism and (except for their policies on rape) only hurt women incidentally, the Tokugawa used women as hostages to enforce elite male obedience and as scapegoats for perceived cultural weaknesses.

Unlike the Manchus, who were foreign conquerors, the Tokugawa were native Japanese. They did not have to prove themselves by conforming to traditional ideology. In fact, the shoguns expended a great deal of effort to undermine and replace traditional Japanese ideology. Before the first Tokugawa shogun ended the civil wars, Japan had been divided into numerous small principalities run by individual aristocrats. All these families fought with each other using private armies of men called samurai. Having subdued the hundreds of warlords throughout Japan, Ieyasu's first concern as shogun was to prevent them from splitting the country back up into tiny fiefdoms and restarting civil wars. Part of the new shogun's approach was to make it costly for aristocratic leaders to build up a power base. He moved them from castle to castle so that they could not consolidate influence and followers in any one region. At the same time, Ieyasu insisted that the wives and children of aristocrats live at the imperial court, where they were hostages for the good behavior of their men. Obviously such policies had a major impact on the lives of aristocratic women, who were now much less likely to be individually responsible for managing or defending a castle and much more likely to pay an immediate price for any disobedience of their husbands.

At the ideological level, part of the government's method of keeping peace was to work on changing the way Japanese people, especially elites, thought about their place in the world. The old feudal system was a way of living, of navigating human relationships and the spiritual world, not to be given up easily just because the Tokugawa now forbade the formation of private armies. So, the government set out to transform the old samurai ethic into something that would be more tolerable to the state, and the guiding ethic they chose to replace it was neo-Confucianism. The egalitarian and reciprocal aspects of Confucianism were passed over in favor of its potential for authoritarianism and its emphasis on patriarchy. The Tokugawa gave their loyalty to an even less egalitarian form of neo-Confucianism than was becoming prevalent in Qing China. If the ways of samurai men were to change, the ways of samurai women also had to change. The violence and warrior ethic of the Sengoku period of civil war had tended generally to weaken the power of Japanese elite women versus that of their men—but the samurai code had also demanded much of elite women, who were expected to be able to manage and defend the household in their husbands' absence. They had to be able to take over the family finances and business. Aristocratic women almost always received some military education—a tradition that continued into the twentieth century. In short, the old system had made elite women into military auxiliaries, and to do so it had fostered an ideology of female competence alongside the ideology of female submission to parental and spousal authority. This competent-yet-submissive mythology was no longer necessary or, from the government's point of view, desirable. In its place they substituted an ideology of female unreliability and stupidity.

The Tokugawa demanded all members of society act in ways the government considered respectful, prudent, thrifty, and industrious and laid down rules of conduct for the whole day. People were divided into four ranks: soldiers, farmers, craftsmen, and merchants, with soldiers highest and merchants lowest, and women always lower than men. Each class was supposed to address the higher ranks using specific honorific forms, just as women were to address men with specific honorifics. No intermarriage between classes was acceptable, and only certain clothes and foods were permitted to particular classes. Women were to obey men.

Now the government also considered women to be inferior, silly, stupid, and troublemakers. Listening to women supposedly led honest men to rebellion, so good women should be silent, and talkative ones silenced. Government edicts and policies kept women out of many spaces. The government emphasized the importance of education of both sexes, but the education women received (and they were never more than half as likely to receive any education as their brothers) limited their ambitions and self-expression as much as it prepared them for their lives as wives and mothers. They were to read a little, do enough arithmetic to keep track of household expenditures, study homemaking, and absorb the moral lessons of neo-Confucianism. They were not to read the Japanese classics (they might have learned something from the sexual and personal freedom of medieval women), keep diaries, or engage in creative self-expression—other than perhaps flower arranging or calligraphy. Even having women perform in public speaking lines written by someone else was deemed too dangerous, and the state decreed in 1629 that no women were to perform in the theater because of the danger their presence posed for public morality.

Controlling women's behavior was very important to the Tokugawa shogunate, which took many of men's freedoms away from them at the same time as granting men previously unheard-of authority over women. Women under the Tokugawa lost almost all rights in marriage. Their husbands could divorce them unilaterally only by writing a short bill of divorce, and for almost any reason. Jealousy, disobedience, and talking too much were all sufficient reason for divorce, and none required proof. The divorced woman had no custody rights to her children and no right to the property of the married couple—she had to leave the house immediately. Japanese women of the Tokugawa period were expected to obey their husbands blindly, with an obedience unmodified by common sense, legal concerns, or any other consideration the woman thought important. If her husband wanted something of her, she was to do it, and if he broke the law—even if he were to murder her parents—it was not really expected that she should report him. Adultery became a capital crime, but only if a woman committed it. In the early medieval period the greatest writers in Japan's history, Murasaki Shikibu and Sei Shonagon,[5] had recounted the many affairs of single and married ladies of the court without any trace of embarrassment. Now, women were expected to remain sexually loyal even to philandering husbands on pain of death! Women themselves had no right to divorce even in the face of adultery, physical abuse, or abandonment. Tokugawa divorce law was even crueler to women than divorce laws in China under the Manchu, who protected wives from divorce in three important cases: if the wife had mourned her parents-in-law for the proper 3 years, if she had no family to return to, or if her husband had become rich over the course of the marriage. Just as Qing scholars were able to console themselves for their loss of influence in the government by running their households without much government interference, so formerly independent Japanese aristocrats and samurai could look to the enormous authority they had over their wives and daughters as a reward for their obedience to the shogunate. Of course, the general prosperity of the period must also have sweetened the deal.

The decline in women's status relative to men did not begin during the Tokugawa period, but the state chose to continue it. Even though the early Tokugawa led to a long period of prosperity and flourishing of the arts in Japan, it was a bad era for women, whose access to creative expression was sharply curtailed and who could share in the era's increased prosperity only with the permission of their men. It was not until the Meiji Restoration and the late nineteenth century that some of women's losses began to be reversed—this time as part of new state policies advocating somewhat higher status and much greater participation in national life for women.

THE GOLDEN AGE OF THE OTTOMAN EMPIRE, CA. 1500–1700

The Ottoman empire was one of the largest and most long-lasting empires in history, lasting from ca. 1350 to 1923 and covering, at its greatest extent, all of southeast Europe, Anatolia, the Levant, the Arabian Peninsula, the Sudan, and much of North Africa. Ottoman subjects came from many different religious and ethnic backgrounds. Sunni, Shiite, Greek Orthodox, Roman Catholic, Coptic Christian, Jewish, Zoroastrian, and other religious traditions were all represented in the Ottoman empire. Arabic, Turkish, Farsi, Greek, Croatian, Serbian, Slovakian, and numerous other languages were all native to various regions of the empire, and every major urban center (other than Mecca) had representatives from practically every religious and ethnic group. The empire's diversity—for most of its history more than half of this "Turkish Muslim" empire's subjects were non-Turks and non-Muslims—was also a source of the government's strength. The Ottoman rulers used members of conquered minorities to administer and coordinate much of the government and local society—so that these administrators would be loyal to the government and not to their local constituencies. The ruling administrative and military classes were particularly multiethnic in background. The military leadership was made up of slave soldiers, men whose only allegiance was to the government. because they were often slaves or sons of slaves taken from their Christian parents and raised as Muslims by the government. They never saw their birth parents again, and the government, which became their substitute parent, was the only authority they obeyed and the only source of their position. The use of such elite slave soldiers was established tradition in the Muslim Mediterranean long before the arrival of the Ottomans and had proven very effective. Turkish Ottoman administrators were in many instances themselves the children of wealthy men by purchased concubines or women who were descended from former slaves. Administrators were all Muslim, but they had family ties throughout the Middle East, and they rarely found themselves stationed anywhere where their own ethnic or family background matched those of the local populace.

The Ottomans were a successor state to a long history of multiethnic empires in the region dating from the second millennium BCE. The new and expansive state was an extension of past traditions on which the government consciously built. By privileging some parts of what its subjects considered traditional over others, the rulers made significant changes in the lives and ideology of ordinary people. Traditional assessments of a Sunni government's quality and legitimacy depended on its ability to protect Muslims; to uphold sharia (the legal traditions of the Muslim world);

to protect the holy cities of Mecca and Medina and make the routes to them safe for pilgrims (if the government controlled these territories); and to support charities, mosques, and intellectual life in general. The Ottomans added to this a spirit of Muslim expansionism—their state was forged in the cauldron of combat with the remains of the Christian Byzantine empire in what is now Greece. They did not just want to protect Muslim territory, but to increase the borders of the *ummah*, the community of the faithful. At the start of our era, the Ottoman empire was at its most expansionist, marching into and across southeastern Europe and eventually through Hungary to Budapest and the very gates of Vienna, taking over the holy lands of Palestine and the Arabian Peninsula, and conquering Egypt. The greatest extent of their empire in Europe is shown in Figure 2.3. Naturally, their expansionism left the Sunni Ottoman rulers in charge of tens of millions of Arabs, Greeks, and Slavs, many of whom were Christian, Jewish, or Shia.[6]

As it happens, the Ottoman empire provides a particularly good example of the way an imperial state's attempts to centralize and rationalize legal systems could affect women's lives. Unlike the Tokugawa or the Qing, the early Ottomans do not seem to have had any particular policy of promoting male control of women or of trying to appeal to conquered peoples' sensibilities by supporting the ideology of those they had conquered. They seem to have felt their evident military successes proved their claim to authority was legitimate, and successive Ottoman rulers promoted whatever legal, intellectual, military, cultural, and economic programs they thought appropriate. The Ottomans were not especially interested in supporting or undermining women's roles, but they did create a climate of peace and prosperity within the empire, and they tried to regularize administration.

Over the course of the early Ottoman era (the fifteenth, sixteenth, and seventeenth centuries), women gained increasing access to wealth, greater influence in setting the tone of cultural and civic life, greater access to education, and greater protection from the courts. The first three of these were the result of a rising standard of living and population growth; the last was a result of Ottoman attempts to provide evenhanded justice. Women also lost access to many urban spaces, to some aspects of religious participation, and (at least among the wealthier classes) to parts of their own homes. These losses were imposed by government policies, but came about partly because the government did not care to protect women's ability to participate in public life. It would be unfair to blame either the government or Ottoman men entirely, however, because it seems quite clear that Ottoman women participated in and helped generate the cultural and economic transformations that set new limits on their lives.

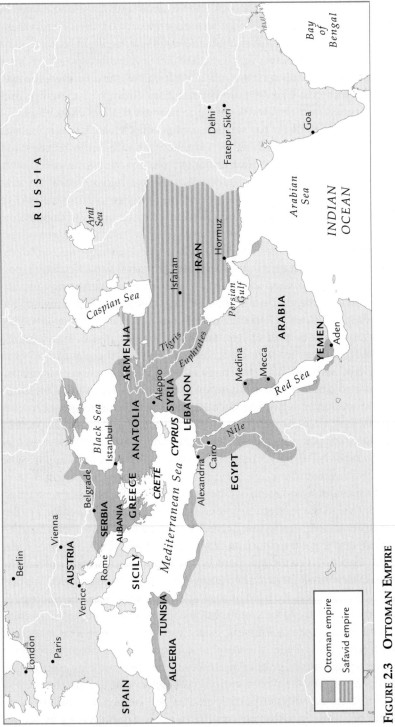

FIGURE 2.3 **OTTOMAN EMPIRE**
The map shows the Ottoman empire, ca. 1750, at its greatest expanse.

Despite the empire's diversity, there was a good deal of common expectation and common experience throughout the region. Ottoman elites could almost all speak Turkish, Arabic, and Farsi. The vocabulary in which laws, government, religion, and family disputes were discussed was similar across the whole empire, and much gender ideology seems to have been universal. The Abrahamic traditions—Islam, Christianity, and Judaism—had dominated the region since at least the fifth century ce.

All three religions (especially as practiced at the start of our period) emphasized women's inferiority to men in political and military life and the submission they owed their husbands in marriage, and all three emphasized women's roles in the family as wives and mothers. Muslim and Jewish people of this era practiced nearly universal marriage, usually expecting widows, widowers, and divorced people to remarry quickly, so a life of marital submission was the expected lot of all women in these social groups. It was also the expectation for most Christian women. The Christian sects were unique in permitting some women and men to become celibates, and this did affect Christian women in some parts of the empire. Roman Catholics in Lebanon still practiced monasticism, as did the Greek and Russian Orthodox in Ottoman southeast Europe. Coptic Christian monks and nuns still existed in scattered Egyptian monasteries, but we know little about their traditions.

On the other hand, all three religions recognized women as the spiritual equals of men, at least in theory—equally beloved of the Deity and equally capable of spiritual growth and salvation. Furthermore, among Muslims and Christians it was possible for women to become important spiritual leaders, though not as frequently and not in as many ways as it was possible for their brothers. Muslims in particular thought it was important for everyone to be able to recite (and read if possible) some of their holiest text, and it was rather common for girls to attend schools long enough to learn some or all of the Quran. Some women studied the traditions of the life of the Prophet Muhammad (the *hadith*) and became officially recognized transmitters of these traditions. Because these were the core sources for all legal decisions and for guidance in one's own life, education in the Quran and hadith provided opportunities for some women to participate in legal, political, and religious discourse, which they apparently did. Moreover, Muslims throughout the empire venerated saints of both sexes, built shrines and mosques in their honor, and made pilgrimages to honor them.

The collection of Islamic movements emphasizing mysticism, personal piety, and asceticism called *Sufism* was especially important to women. In Islam, Sufi orders served (and still serve) many of the same functions as monasticism does in Christianity and Buddhism. Sufi masters and orders taught the masses, assisted individuals in seeking spiritual growth, and provided frameworks for many kinds of charitable giving and corporate worship. Rather than attending Friday services in mosques, many women practiced their religion through individual prayer and study, supported by friends and Sufi religious orders. Sufism provided some women with opportunities for leadership and was the avenue by which most of the venerated female saints achieved their recognition. The emotional and richly descriptive language Sufis used to describe love for the divine was especially important as a model for love poetry and romances, and their examples of individual spirituality offered an important cultural and political counterweight to more official religious authorities sponsored by governments.

Nevertheless, Islamic legal traditions disempowered women in many specific ways. In all Middle Eastern societies, Islamic laws and legal commentaries pertaining to marriage, divorce, custody, guardianship, and inheritance all assumed and supported a family system that was both patrilineal and patriarchal. That is, the father and husband was in charge of and responsible for his wife and children. His children were descendants of his lineage and not of their mother's, and the ultimate decisions about who and on what basis his virgin daughters married were his, not their mother's or their own. Child marriage of girls was common, with the understanding that the marriage could not legally be consummated until the girl reached the age of menarche. At that point, Ottoman law gave a bride the right to repudiate a marriage—but only immediately at the onset of menarche. If she waited, her consent was presumed. In theory a virgin had to consent to a marriage, but in practice silence and even tears counted as consent, if she was not openly sobbing during the ceremony. A woman who had been married before was presumed to be less shy and was expected to articulate her consent rather than let it be presumed. Any child of a man's wife or concubine (or, indeed, any child he recognized as his own) was a full heir in the eyes of the law, regardless of the mother's status. The protection of the family's honor, the moral education of its members, and the provision of necessities were the father's responsibility, and the legal systems of Muslim societies all supported him in these endeavors as much as possible. Thus, for legal purposes, men counted twice as much as women. Inheritance customs gave male relatives twice as much as female relatives, and one man's testimony was as valuable as two women's of equal standing and credibility. In principle, men had an unlimited right to divorce, having only to pronounce a divorce three times to have it take effect (*talaq* divorce). Such a divorce did not even have to be registered to be effective. Talaq divorce *did* require, however, that the husband return his wife's dowry, and because of that we have numerous records of legal proceedings relating to talaq divorce still sitting in Ottoman city archives.

Women have significant property rights in Islamic jurisprudence (sharia), and in the early Ottoman period it seems clear that local, regional, and imperial courts upheld that right. Females had a right to a share of inheritances within their lineage and from their husbands equivalent to half that of the men in their family. Upon the consummation of their marriage, they were entitled to a *mahr*, a sum given to the bride by the husband in return for sexual access to her. Sharia, especially as interpreted in the Ottoman era, treats the bodies of individuals as their property and imposes penalties analogous to those for property damage to those who injure another's body or use it without permission. The only permissible context for intercourse was marriage; hence, to be legal a marriage had to include the exchange of mahr for the wife's favors, and part of the penalty for proved rape cases was the payment of mahr to the victim—if she was female. Cases of male/male rape were well known and also prosecuted, but did not involve mahr. The amount of the mahr was tied to the woman's status and could be very large for women of prominent families. It could not, however, be less than a certain value, set in Ottoman times at ten *dirhams*. A man who divorced his wife was liable to return it, and if he predeceased her, the wife had the first claim on his estate for her mahr, even before other debts or his inheritors (including herself and her children) were paid. Ottoman courts enforced these rules vigorously. They also assisted women in attaining *hul* divorce, in which the wife requests a divorce from her husband and he grants it, usually with conditions. The most common conditions husbands demanded for divorce were that the wife give up her right to mahr and agree to take over custody and possibly maintenance of the children for a certain number of years. Married, widowed, and divorced women, unlike girls, do not seem to have required a guardian to act on their behalf in legal and economic matters, and they were entitled to manage for themselves any inheritances they received, any properties they were given, and any income they might earn from them. Wives were entitled to maintenance from their husbands: In theory if not always in practice, anything wives gave to the household or to their husband could be considered a loan (although they had to stipulate this at the time of the loan). Likewise, wives could borrow from their husbands. Divorce settlements frequently include a reckoning of monies and goods owed between husband and wife, so we know that these loans were common.

Ottoman women could own all kinds of goods and real property in addition to clothes, jewels, textiles, and furnishings, and from the records of charitable endowments established by individual Ottoman citizens (*waqfs*), it seems that women could be very wealthy indeed. These endowments created mosques, schools, shrines, and libraries, or else they assigned the ownership of the property to a religious institution but gave the income from it to the endower and/or her family, usually until the family died out. In both cases, we see that women were assigning houses, warehouses, apartment complexes, and groups of shops to charity— presumably out of the much larger holdings that they were living on and passing on as inheritances. Women who set up endowments usually made themselves the administrator. Frequently the next administrator was simply the "most worthy," in the next generation. Men usually used the same system to choose future waqf administrators. When there were disputes over who was the most worthy in the generation to administer an endowment, women were as likely as men to be the courts' choice. "Worthiness" from the courts' perspective often meant just naming the oldest person, male or female, in the generation closest to the previous administrator. So even though men were far more frequently administrators of waqfs and founders of waqfs than women, it was also the case that whether a waqf was founded by a man or a woman, at some point it would probably be administered by a woman. Creation of waqf endowments became more and more popular from the sixteenth century onward and seems to have been a major feature of Muslim women's public lives. Even though the creation of a waqf may have provided a woman and her descendants with an income and a publicly recognized legacy, the institutions supported by waqfs—the mosques and schools and shrines—were run by men. Frequently, only men attended them. Therefore, when they created or supported a waqf, Ottoman women were often supporting or helping expand the physical and cultural spaces that were open only to men.

In theory men were responsible for the upkeep of their children; in divorce, small children were to be cared for by the mother at the father's expense, then given into the custody of the father later. If a woman was widowed, her husband's family was to pay the maintenance of her children until they were of age to join their husband's families. In practice, all sorts of arrangements were common, with children quite often staying indefinitely with their mothers or their mothers' relatives, children staying only with their father or his relatives, and children moving back and forth among relatives. When children were orphaned (in sharia, any child whose father is deceased is considered an orphan), their mothers were the most likely to be chosen as guardians, and they frequently remained guardians even after remarrying. This was because Ottoman gender ideology assumed that women were better nurturers than men and were naturally better at giving children the loving care they required. Thus, although there was never any question that children were members of the father's lineage and that life-altering decisions—like arranging marriages, choosing occupations, or deciding educational institutions—were fundamentally up to the father (or his family, if he were deceased), mothers were nevertheless considered critically important, even past the time of nursing and early childhood.

Women themselves went to court to demand justice, and although they were not in theory considered as strong a witness as a man, in reality the courts seem to have evaluated individual women's cases on the plaintiff's personal credibility, her witnesses, and any evidence she had to support her claim. In cases that were purely about property and its management, women seem to have done as well as men in persuading courts to uphold their rights (always keeping in mind, of course, that women had fewer property rights than men). They and their families also went to court to report crimes of assault and rape, which is rather more surprising, especially as rape was reported frequently. As mentioned above, rape was not just a form of assault but a form of theft—the rapist took something from the victim that was only to be had at a price and on prior agreement. It was, however, very difficult to prove, as the victim needed to bring four witnesses to the event and could be prosecuted for lying if she did not prove her case. Under such circumstances it is surprising that women and families brought rape cases to court. Yet Ottoman women and families seem to have sued rapists pretty often, demanding that at the very least they pay the victim a mahr equivalent to what a woman of her social status could expect to receive from a legitimate husband. If the victim agreed to marry the man, she had to withdraw the rape charge, and the marriage contract would be separately negotiated. That Ottoman women felt able to bring such charges in their own names in public forums suggests that they had an attachment to their own sexual honor. Moreover, it suggests that they and their families believed that a woman's value and personal integrity could survive sexual violation.

As *dhimmi*, non-Muslims living in an empire that was officially Muslim, women who belonged to minority religions lived under the jurisdiction of their own religious courts. There has been less research on the lives of minority women in the early Ottoman empire, but one thing we do know is that they were quite likely to appeal cases to sharia law or to higher state courts, especially with regard to marriage and inheritance. Apparently under sharia (as practiced Ottomans), women could have greater rights to property in divorce and inheritance than they did in Jewish and Christian communities, and enough minority women knew this that they would bring their divorce and property cases forward when they knew they had received less than sharia required.

The early Ottoman period was hardly one of sexual equality, of course, no matter how well the government might have upheld laws that protected the weak. Slavery was common throughout the Ottoman empire, with women, especially, being imported from Circassia (the northwest Caucasus Mountains) and the Sudan. Official censuses did not count women and girls, so that they did not exist in the eyes of the law unless a case came before the courts concerning them. They were therefore much more at the mercy of the men who ran their households than their brothers were. Although the state systematically chose, adopted, and educated boys to become senior administrators (and formally slaves of the state), no such programs existed for girls. City elites also increasingly felt that religious practices needed to be purified, clarified, and made orthodox. As usual with these sorts of movements, restricting women's freedoms more than men's became part of the purification. The veneration of female saints fell off, as did the prominence of Sufi organizations and, consequently, women's opportunities for collective worship, individual spiritual growth, and communal authority. The new orthodoxy also led to the persecution of unorthodox religious gatherings in the home, which were among the most important ways women had worshipped and studied together in medieval Islam. Because women are not required to attend mosque on Friday (as men are), in many areas women do not. Indeed, in many areas Muslim men even today will argue that because women are permitted to miss services, they should not be allowed to attend at all—or at least should only attend if they stay behind screens and silent. Ottoman Muslim women (and women in other times and places) often achieved corporate worship by holding single-sex prayer and study groups. These were organized by the women, but they sometimes invited men to teach. In the new atmosphere of the seventeenth century, some authorities decided that it was not only improper but illegal for a man to teach a group of women. Women organizers and male teachers now faced the possibility of arrest and prosecution for holding mixed-gender study groups.

Two other factors changing women's status were urbanization and a strengthening international economy. Larger cities and greater cash flow had mixed results. On the one hand, wealthy women invested in new businesses and participated actively in the growing economy. On the other, the landscapes of the cities themselves were changing in ways that separated male and female cultures. The city of Mosul became quite wealthy in this period, and leaders spent huge sums of money building public monuments and new commercial buildings. Like urban European neighborhoods, which centered around churches, urban Ottoman neighborhoods centered around houses of worship—usually mosques but also synagogues and churches in Jewish and Christian neighborhoods. Wealthy men and women founded and/or expanded mosques throughout the city, creating new neighborhoods and making some old neighborhoods more desirable than they had been. Older, unfashionable shrines were ignored, and new shrines built at the edges of town. Since one of the ways women used public space was in processions and pilgrimages to shrines, and since women went to shrines on different days than men, this changed the areas women traveled to—and expanded the numbers of places they frequently visited in the city. On the other hand, the new sites were no longer in the heart of the city, but on its outskirts, giving women fewer reasons to come into the city centers. Commercial buildings and districts went up, and although the evidence from waqf records is that many women owned shops and warehouses, these were spaces that were, in general, *used* by men most of the time. Beginning in 1475, coffee houses spread throughout the empire, becoming ubiquitous by the seventeenth century, and among the Ottomans (and, indeed, in much of Turkey and the Arab world today) they were places where men, and not women, gathered to socialize. With the movement of men's work and business spaces into separate commercial districts, women's daily lives became more separate from men's, while women themselves probably had greater scope for neighborhood solidarity.

Women, regardless of their class, tended to stay within the quarter, or neighborhood, where their house was located, except for travel to shrines and mosques and public processions (of which there were many). The quarters of Mosul, like those of many other neighborhoods in urban centers throughout the world, were close-knit. A quarter made up of five or six streets might be actually closed off except for one entrance; the alleys and streets through the houses could be privately owned; and the lane granting entrance to an apartment might or might not be a public thoroughfare. Early in this period most of life's necessities were to be found in the quarter—a religious building (a run-down temple or a church in minority areas—creating new buildings for minority worship was forbidden), shops for food and daily needs, and door-to-door salesmen for anything a woman did not need on a daily basis. Within the quarter women moved freely, less heavily veiled than they would be outside, more or less free to visit other women who lived in the quarter, and frequently doing so. Even if a woman did not go out on a particular day, throughout the Islamic world the windows and doors of houses that looked out on the street were built with screens to let the women look out without being seen, and they were *expected* to watch the street. The Ottoman government expected individual neighborhoods to keep watch for wrong-doers and suspicious activities, and given that men were gone for much of the day, it was obviously women who were supposed to do the watching. But, as the commercial districts expanded and the city created a central marketplace (where women were less likely to go than men), the quarters became less self-sufficient.

By the eighteenth century, political and commercial elites had become much wealthier than they were before, and they began to demonstrate their wealth by building impressive houses—fortified mansions that allowed the wealthiest families to house not just female domestic servants, eunuchs, and members of the family but also some of the men employed by the family for work outside the home. Before, women could move freely through the whole house (except through a co-wife's territory, for which other wives needed permission), whereas men could enter the women's space only with the women's permission. Now, there were semipublic spaces within the household that women could not enter, and there had to be extra protection around the women's area, the *haram*, to protect them from the men who were not members of the family. Less-elite merchants and scholars copied this system as much as possible, creating houses built with two courtyards—one for the men and one for the women—and with separate quarters for each individual woman and her children. Thus among the more privileged classes, the home itself became compartmentalized in a way that only royal households had been prior to this. We do not know yet how these changes in elite households affected ordinary women. It seems likely that over time even poor families must have aspired to creating this kind of sex segregation within the household.

In brief, even though Ottoman policy sought to uphold women's existing legal rights, women's privileges nevertheless diminished. New wealth provided urban women with a better standard of living and access to new types of goods, but the desire to show off family wealth by building elaborate women's quarters in wealthy homes ended up closing parts of their own homes to the women who lived in them. The development of new types of businesses provided new investment opportunities for wealthy women, but the new town planning put those investments in neighborhoods restricted to men. A conservative turn in religion tended to isolate women from the intellectual life of men, and even though women helped sponsor new religious buildings, this did not necessarily increase women's presence in public spaces or in the development of civic culture. Perhaps the state could have prevented the increased segregation, but it did not try.

REFORMATION AND COUNTER-REFORMATION EUROPE, 1517–1700

The sixteenth and seventeenth centuries were tumultuous times throughout Western Europe. Prior to the sixteenth century, European rulers fought over rival claims to territory and kingships. During the sixteenth and seventeenth centuries, many conflicts were fought over religion. Unlike the other cultural regions discussed here, all of which were dominated by one political system, Western Europe was made up of a collection of small states. Although the population and economy were expanding, just as in the other regions, European states spent much of this period engaged in wars. The presence of military and political rivals on all sides spurred monarchies and republics to spend lavishly on armies and navies and on any research that might improve their military effectiveness. Navigation techniques improved. Ships became more seaworthy and larger, and they began to carry artillery—an innovation that allowed the Portuguese, Spanish, Dutch, and English to demand protection money from merchant ships sailing in the Indian Ocean and South China Sea. Artillery became more powerful, firearms and crossbows more reliable, armor more useful, fortifications thicker and heavier, and armies larger and larger as they came to rely on masses of infantry instead of mounted knights. As terrible as the many wars of this era were, the enormous expansion in the size and expense of armies had one very positive result: By the middle of the seventeenth century, Europe's nobility could no longer settle their quarrels by marching privately hired troops a to neighbor's household and firing cannon at the doors. Only a central government could afford to field an army.

Much of the tumult was the direct result of the Protestant Reformation, finally triggered (after at least a century of hiccups) when a German monk named Martin Luther began openly opposing church fundraising policies in 1517. The Protestant Reformation began as an attempt to reform certain practices of the church, but it became a series of movements creating independent church institutions and new theologies. In an era when kings styled themselves as "Defender of the Faith," rulers demanded orthodox practice at the very least from their subjects, and most wanted orthodox belief as well. Civil wars, alliances built on the basis of religious affiliation, and rivalries exacerbated by religious hatred followed. The uneasy alliance between church and state that had characterized the Middle Ages became a union as rulers and governing bodies chose the sect or the beliefs that they thought were right for their country, turned religion into a branch of the government, and began to force their subjects to practice the state religion. The titanic struggle over religious truth affected all Europeans for good and ill. The persecution of heretics (people not subscribing to local, officially sanctioned doctrine) flowed naturally from the desire to enforce orthodoxy, and where one prince persecuted one group of believers, another would champion a group holding those same beliefs. Persecutions could spur civil war (as in France, 1662–1629) and rebellions (as in the 80-year Dutch revolt and war of independence against Spain), or they could crush rebellion (Mary of England, r. 1553–1558).

Women were as likely as men to experience war firsthand. Pitched battles were fought all over Europe, and towns were besieged for months or even years at a time. Women felt the force of recruitment and war, even when they were not part of the actual battlefield. When an army camped—even a friendly army—it needed supplies from local people. Food, clothes, firewood, and water all came from local sources. The price of foods and medicine were driven up by the increased demand the army produced. On the one hand the rise in prices was good for the people selling goods; on the other, it produced local scarcity at a time when the local need for food and medicine increased. The dangers of camp life—the infections, fevers, and dysentery that plagued encampments of soldiers—spread to the local population. Furthermore, friendly armies often recruited or simply forced young men into service, taking them away from families who often needed their sons' labor to be self-supporting. Even friendly armies could turn violent. Though very few women were ever on the front lines of battle (there were always a few who dressed as men and enlisted), they fulfilled many of the support functions that in the twentieth century would be done by regular soldiers. All the armies that marched across Europe in ever-larger sizes (by the middle of the seventeenth century, troops on the march could have 100,000 soldiers under arms) needed women to work for them as laundresses, cooks, and prostitutes. Every army had numerous women with it, most of them the wives of soldiers or hired laundresses or both. Some were on the payroll, but most were surviving on their husbands' pay.

Catholic and Protestant rulers persecuted members of the unauthorized minority religion as heretics, and women were caught in that net just as men were. In the upheaval of the Reformation and the wars that wracked Europe because of it, women were as likely to become religious martyrs as men. Religious martyrdom, although horrible, did however provide a new, heroic image of women—often of ordinary women—supporting their husbands in prison, defending their own beliefs to the death, and (in some Protestant sects), preaching their husbands' ideas when those men were imprisoned.

The Spanish Inquisition, despite its unjustified fame for witch burning, persecuted what the government considered heretics. These heretics were nominal Catholic Christians, persecuted for being crypto (that is, hidden) Jews or Muslims. These were people whose families had in 1492 been forced to convert from Judaism or Islam to Christianity. In that year the crown ordered all Jews and Muslims to leave with only the goods they could carry or be baptized. Subsequently the Spanish church and the government began to suspect some converts of being crypto, or secret, Jews. (Muslims were also targeted, although the bulk of the persecutions were against formerly Jewish families.) In fact, many families *did* secretly continue to practice Judaism, and in these families it was primarily the responsibility of the women to do so. Synagogues, which had been run by men, were closed, and it was almost impossible to maintain schools for sons to study in. But women were responsible for many less-prestigious rituals of Jewish life, especially lighting the Sabbath candles, maintaining the day of rest, and preparing special meals. Spanish Judaism survived underground by being passed from mothers to their children. Jewish men in Spain acted assimilated while their wives maintained their heritage as much as possible. Because Spanish women lived a more enclosed life— going into the street as little as possible and socializing only with women friends and with their own families—they needed to spend far less time concealing their religion and pretending to be Christian.

The sixteenth and seventeenth centuries were also the heyday of the infamous witch hunts, which were another kind of persecution of heresy, across most of Western Europe. Although many people believed they could do various kinds of magic for healing or for ill-wishing, and many Europeans believed witches could help or harm them, witches were rare targets for prosecution before the sixteenth century. Part of the impetus for the furor was a book, *The Hammer of Witches (Malleus Maleficarum)*, published in 1487 by two extraordinarily misogynist authors named Jacob Sprenger and Heinrich Krämer. They believed that witches were really heretics and insisted that, in addition to practicing harmful magic (*malificium*), witches pledged their loyalty to Satan in exchange for their powers and had sex with him to seal the deal. Later writers developed the concept of the Black Mass, in which participants supposedly gathered in the countryside to dance naked, drink babies' blood, have orgies, and so on. These practices were supposedly an inversion of the proper Mass; hence the name. Such writers thought witches were usually women because women were more susceptible to the lures of the devil, being both too stupid to turn him down and too easily lured into sin by their own near-uncontrollable lusts. Thus, witches were not merely superstitious and ignorant, as most intellectuals and jurists had believed prior to this (and as the Spanish Inquisition continued to believe), but in fact were heretics worshipping the devil. This new viewpoint changed the way judges, magistrates, lawyers, and the law in general thought about magic and became the official framework through which most states dealt with accusations of witchcraft. Unlike other kinds of trials for heresy, which targeted both sexes, witchcraft trials usually focused on women. Although some men faced prosecution in witchcraft trials, two-thirds of defendants were women, and most of the men tried for witchcraft were the relatives of prosecuted female witches.[7]

Four popular misconceptions about the era of the witch hunts need to be addressed here. First, they were not, as is often claimed, a Roman Catholic phenomenon. Witch hunts and witch trials were carried out in Protestant and Catholic countries alike. Even though witchcraft was a religious crime, a form of heresy, witch hunts and prosecutors always acted with the assistance of secular governments, who were the only institutions authorized to issue death sentences and carry out any executions. In some areas, in fact, witch hunters worked for the state rather than for the church.

Second, as mentioned above, the Spanish Inquisition did not prosecute people for witchcraft, although the offices of the Inquisition in Italy, France, and the various German states did.

Third, early feminist historians of the Middle Ages and Renaissance speculated that the witch hunts may have targeted women who worked as midwives and folk healers. Some suggested further that such women were holdovers from pre-Christian times, practicing traditional pre-Christian religion. Both these hypotheses are now frequently asserted as truths in popular media. However, numerous subsequent investigations in the 1980s and 1990s have found little support for these two hypotheses, and they are no longer to be found in contemporary research on women's history and witchcraft. Midwives were not specially targeted, although folk healers could come to the attention of witch hunts and of the Inquisition. Records of their trials show that the "cunning" men and women who made magic to ward away illness, bad luck, and so on thought of themselves as Christians. They used Christian elements (holy water, communion wafers, Latin prayers) in making charms and spells, and they thought what they were doing was normal and approved practice. There is no evidence of pre-Christian religious beliefs (as opposed to pre-Christian practices and festivals, which were often picked up, renamed, given patron saints, and celebrated by the established church) surviving into the Renaissance. Witch hunts instead focused on the weak and the unprotected. They hounded mostly impoverished older women (and some old men) who had no family alive or nearby to protect them. Their neighbors accused them of drying up cow's milk and killing babies with the evil eye, and then the courts prosecuted them for having joined a satanic cult. Hunts were sporadic, springing up with little warning rather like epidemic diseases, and procedures for dealing with accusations and trials varied from one jurisdiction to another.

Fourth, the total number of people caught up in witch hunts has often been wildly exaggerated. A death toll of 6 to 9 million killed by burning is a frequent assertion. That number is simply unsupportable. Absolute numbers are hard to come by for this subject. However, historians' best guess is that over the course of the sixteenth and seventeenth centuries between 100,000 and 200,000 people, 90 percent of them women, faced prosecution for witchcraft.[8] Of these, roughly half received death sentences, and most of the rest spent some time in prison and had to do some form of public and humiliating penance. Given the very large number of crimes for which early modern people could be imprisoned, executed, whipped, beaten, and sent on humiliating penances, witchcraft prosecution was far from the most frequently punished crime of the era. But the trials were spectacular, infrequent, and unpredictable, often involving dozens of witnesses and accused, casting a wide net throughout the populace and taking people into custody—where they would be held for months at a time before their actual trial. The trials stuck in memory and local legend for generations—for example, the witch trials that started in Salem, the only large-scale witch hunt in North America, which has lived on in national memory for over 300 years.

Women living in western and central Europe during this time knew about witch hunts, and older women living alone probably knew they were vulnerable to accusations of witchcraft, especially if they insisted on getting their own way too emphatically or got into too many disagreements. In this sense the witch hunts must have operated to help keep women "in their place." On the other hand, some women were willing to exploit people's fears of older women. Many women prosecuted for witchcraft seem to have been cultivating local fears of the evil eye for many years to protect themselves or to get their way in disputes before their neighbors finally denounced them to officials.

Warfare, religious persecution, and witch hunting may have been the most spectacular results of the Reformation for women, but institutional and ideological changes also made a big difference in women's lives. Some institutions disappeared, some new ones were invented, and societies paid new attention to developing women's spiritual lives and preparing girls for successful adult lives. Just as the Tokugawa wanted to produce a particular kind of Japanese subject, early modern Europeans wanted to produce particular kinds of Christians and created institutions to help them do it.

Protestants had originally argued for church reform. They had wanted educated priests; they had wanted priests who worked with their congregations instead of farming out their jobs to less-qualified men while skimming the income from the parish and taking on multiple jobs; they had wanted a church where the leadership lived respectably and served their congregations. In the wake of the Reformation, Protestant churches and the Roman Catholic Church alike instituted numerous reforms of religious institutions and religious life. During this era it therefore became the norm, rather than the exception, for priests and pastors to be well educated in theology, prepared to write and deliver appropriate sermons (or at least read them from a book), and able to educate their parishioners about Christianity. This meant that when women attended services, they were likely to hear at least a short sermon dealing with a serious subject— a mini-public lecture, as it were, that gave them some access to the intellectual life of the era. In Protestant areas, church leaders insisted that Christians should know the doctrines of their church and be able to read the Bible for themselves. They created a teaching tool called the catechism, which was a series of theological questions about the Christian faith—for example, it might ask for a definition of the Trinity, which was followed by their institutional church's sanctioned answers. Protestants were supposed to memorize their catechism, and children in Protestant areas all over Europe labored over the task.

Not to be outdone, Roman Catholics developed their own catechism for Catholic children to memorize. To judge by the complaints of parish priests and congregational pastors over the next couple of centuries, adults remembered their catechism as poorly as most modern adults remember studying algebra—but they did get some kind of religious education. For many women, this religious education was the only formal schooling they would ever receive. Female literacy gradually climbed, faster in Protestant than in Catholic areas, but nevertheless steadily until the creation of public schools in the nineteenth century. In some urban Protestant areas, we have evidence that up to 40 percent of women were literate by the mid-seventeenth century.[9]

Because of this, the early modern era saw a sharp increase in the number of women writers in Western Europe—similar to that in Ming China—and for the first time, most of the learned women would not be nuns but married women, living in the world. In addition, most of them were not from elite families but wives and daughters of merchants, craftsmen, and small farmers. Just taking pen in hand was a risky act; early modern women authors routinely began any work they wrote for public consumption with a lengthy apology for even daring to metaphorically speak in public, for thinking that anyone would care what a woman's opinion on the matter was, or for believing that they had anything of value to contribute to intellectual debate. Having taken the risk of public speech, women did not necessarily write the kinds of works that would get them approval from their teachers. They wrote treatises and sermons, poems and plays, and polemical pamphlets denouncing their intellectual opponents as dangerous fools, as the Quaker Margaret Fell (1614–1702) did in "Women's Speaking Justified."[10] Late in the seventeenth century, women began writing novels, a genre that became a staple of Western

European literature, and in short order women became the most widely read producers of fiction.

In terms of gender ideology, Protestant and Catholic areas alike continued and magnified a trend toward glorifying the roles of fathers and husbands that had emerged in the late fifteenth century. Protestant and Catholic authorities all also celebrated motherhood, and the medieval emphasis on celibacy as the lifestyle most pleasing to God eased somewhat, even in Catholic areas, where wives and widows were given more respect in law and in custom than they had received before. Yes, wives were expected to obey their husbands, but the ideal marriage was now a partnership, where the wife might be the junior partner but also the husband's undisputed representative whenever he was away from home or she was engaged in family business on his behalf. Parents throughout Europe gained greater authority over their children, as states made clandestine marriages harder for minors and raised the age of majority to 25 for men and 21 or 25 for women. The emphasis on women's roles as wives and mothers was seen as more natural than previous ideologies, a return to more authentic early Christian values.

Some aspects of Protestant theology actually promoted positive views of women. Protestants emphasized what Martin Luther had called the "priesthood of all believers," by which he meant that it was not just priests, nuns, and monks who were called to a particular life of service to God but that all lay people, too, were called to service through the tasks they did. Sermons described marriage and motherhood as women's special calling. Preaching against women's bodies and their sexuality grew less frequent. For centuries the established church had put more and more restrictions on when and how and why married couples could have sex, strongly suggesting that marriage was less pleasing to the Lord than celibacy and that women's bodies and sex drive were little more than dangerous temptations. Protestants turned the tables on such assertions, insisting sexual relations within marriage were good, but that celibacy was unnatural and led to unacceptable ideas and behavior.

The downside of the new Protestant emphasis on the important roles of wives and mothers was its loathing for celibacy and monasticism. If the most natural way of life was marriage, then, Protestant theologians reasoned, everyone should marry. Protestant governments did not actually force men and women to marry, and in fact the average age of first marriage in Protestant regions was high throughout the early modern period, with most women remaining single until their 20s and many marrying in their late 20s or even their early 30s in times of economic hardship. But the option of living a celibate religious life was taken away from women in Protestant countries. Convents were closed, even in the face of strong opposition from nuns. Even just staying single, doing charitable work, and attending prayers in the company of other women was problematic—most of the many small communities that did this, called Beguines, closed. The women were pressured to move in with their parents or marry. "Spinster," which originally meant a woman who spun thread for income, came to mean a woman who was unmarried. Meanwhile, in Protestant eyes, the nuns and monks who lived in Catholic countries were peculiar, repressed people who probably engaged in all sorts of sexual nastiness behind their closed walls.

Closing monasteries and convents affected women more than men. Although both men and women were now denied the option of monastic life, men experienced far less social pressure to marry and were not considered failures if they did not marry. None of the various words in European languages for an unmarried adult man ("bachelor") were pejorative. Moreover, men could and typically did pursue scholarship and the arts whether they were married, single, or cloistered. Women, however, had fewer opportunities for advanced education or the advanced pursuit of the arts without convents to support them in daily study. Protestant women also missed the revolution in the lives of nuns and sisters that took place in the sixteenth and seventeenth centuries, as Catholic women carved out new roles for themselves in the church.

Even as the Protestant church celebrated motherhood and marriage for the first time, the Catholic church hierarchy and many religious women and men themselves sought to reform monastic life. New orders and new branches of orders sprang up and flourished. Just as the areas that became Protestant had produced reformers, so too did the areas that remained in the established Catholic church. Teresa of Avila (1515–1582) is the only woman recognized as a Doctor of the Church by the Roman Catholic hierarchy. At about age 40, she experienced a series of religious visions, which she described in a book, *The Interior Castle*. She reformed her own convent and most of the Carmelite order in Spain, persuading her sisters to return to a more thorough observance of the primitive rule. The renewed piety of the many religious houses she reformed and helped establish attracted thousands of women into the religious life. Angela Merici (1474–1540) an Italian peasant woman, founded a company of women to live separately, worship together, and bring the teachings of Christ to their families and neighbors while doing good works and teaching children. Her company of sisters, the Company of St. Ursula, became the first order of women ever permitted to teach church doctrine. They specialized in teaching the daughters of the poor. To pay for the day schools (which they offered for free or at the lowest cost they possibly could), they took on the daughters of the wealthy as boarding students. These girls' parents were extremely uncomfortable with having their daughters taught by sisters who went out into the world, and so, frankly, was the church hierarchy. The Ursulines therefore went into claustration (enclosure), but continued to teach. The revised order was hugely popular—thousands of Frenchwomen joined in the seventeenth century, forming hundreds of new houses. The Ursuline Sisters and their contemporaries, the Sisters of Notre Dame, went on to become the backbone of Catholic education for women throughout the French-speaking world until the mid-nineteenth century.

Even though Catholic women's monastic and service traditions flour-ished in the sixteenth and seventeenth centuries, they did so in the teeth of the hierarchy's opposition. At the Council of Trent (1545–1563), Catho-lic bishops and theologians determined their church's official response to Protestantism, and in addition to numerous statements distinguishing Catholic theology from the various Protestant theologies (these would be enshrined in the Catholic catechism), the church decided that fifteenth- and early sixteenth-century nuns and sisters had far too much freedom. Convents were much too lax, they thought, permitting many women to stay in convents who had little calling for the celibate life, and many convents permitted too many visitors and frivolous activities. The cure for this was a combination of genuine reform—for instance, refusing to accept novices under the age of 17 and instituting long waiting periods, often five to seven years, before taking final vows—with harsh restric-tions. The Beguine tradition of communal living among lay women was cut off in Catholic countries as well as in Protestant, and all nuns and sis-ters were required (at least at first) to live in enclosure, behind walls and screens where people could not visit. In part this helped defend sisters and nuns, who were taking on new public activities, from being harassed by people who thought they should not partake of them. When sisters had first started walking together in the streets to reach out to the laity, some of them were followed by groups of men and boys who called them offen-sive names and threw stones and debris at them.[11] But it also restricted them a great deal. In one Italian convent in Bologna, for instance, succes-sive archbishops forced the nuns to perform music for the Mass while hid-den from view, to use more "appropriate" and ladylike instruments, and to give up bringing in teachers from outside the convent.[12]

In this context, the seventeenth-century emergence of Catholic female associations dedicated to public service and mission seem even more rad-ical. In 1633, St. Vincent de Paul (1581–1660), Marguerite Naseu (a peasant from the French suburbs, baptized 1594), and the aristocrat who would become St. Louise de Marillac (1591–1660) brought together a group of young women from poor families to visit the sick with food, compan-ionship, and religious instruction in urban areas. The women traveled in pairs, worked in pairs, and at first were neither nuns nor sisters but simply pious laywomen providing charity. Wealthy urban women provided the supplies; poor women joined the order and performed the services. They wore the attire of Parisian area peasants: a gray dress and a white turban. The Sisters of Charity, as they came to be called, saw their primary mission as home visitation and home nursing of the sick, but they were quickly pulled into hospitals. Always working as volunteers—not at the discretion of the local bishop or the hospital administration—they were able to keep their independence by being willing to leave whenever a local authority tried to make them work against their mission. Because they were from ordinary families and dressed as ordinary peasants instead of as nuns, they did not suffer the harassment the Ursulines had faced. They became an officially recognized order of sisters and a model for other orders that sprang up in their wake to follow similar callings.

The final piece of ideological change that swept over early modern Europe resulted from Columbus' voyage to the Americas and European travels and conquests throughout the Americas and the Indian Ocean. Experience with new peoples and continents had a profound effect on European ideas of human nature, and with those changes in ideas came new concepts about the natures of men and women. One of the more popular genres of the new printing press was travel literature: stories about strange lands and the peoples, customs, and artifacts found there. Europeans gaped at the sight of peoples who practiced completely different religions, held different ideas of morality, applied different divisions of labor among men and women, and even possessed different ideas about sexuality and parenting. Many cultures granted women more sexual freedom than Europeans did, and European men noticed this immediately! The response to this sort of difference was not, however, to decide that Europeans were too restrictive in their ideas about female sexuality and women's activities, but to decide that the peoples of the Americas, India, and Southeast Asia granted their women too much license, and that non-Western women were just naturally more sexual than Europeans.

Before this period, all women were considered to be more sexual than men—with women of the lower classes more sexually available than those of the upper classes—and now a new stereotype arose. All non-European women were believed to be more erotic and sexually available than European women. Travel literature emphasized foreign women's dress as evidence of their loose lifestyle. European women covered themselves pretty thoroughly in this period, with Spanish and Italian women frequently veiling themselves in public and all adult women covering their heads, their bodies, and their legs down to at least their ankles and usually down to their toes. Women elsewhere who wore less were, in European minds, obviously freer with their sexual favors. In many cases, they were considered to be more beautiful than their European sisters and were often described as more humble and submissive. Frequently their menfolk would be described as lazy, overly sexed, or not caring properly for their women—who would, by implication, be better off under the protection of European men. The "age of discovery" had many other consequences for women across the world (which will be discussed in more detail in Chapter Three). But for European women in particular, some important consequences were the ideas (based more on fantasy than reality) that they were better treated than women elsewhere in the world, that European women were both more naturally chaste and more independent than all other women. These peculiar ideas—completely unsubstantiated by the evidence historians have accumulated over the last 35 years about the lives of women across the early modern world—were very influential in the expansion of European empires and in the creation of the first modern feminist movements.

Conclusion

If the dominant themes of Qing, Tokugawa, and Ottoman history during this era were political stability and growing economies, the dominant theme of Western European history was warfare and growing economies in which much of the new wealth was spent on military hardware and fielding armies and navies. The result in all regions, however, was that the state became much more powerful and able to monopolize large-scale violence. In three cases—Tokugawa Japan, Reformation Europe, and Qing China—government policies sought to create a particular kind of citizen. They encouraged not just female obedience to household authorities but also female education. They also tried to celebrate particular kinds of heroic (but conventionally virtuous) women. Women themselves took advantage of new opportunities for education and new economic niches. Women scholars sought a voice in creating popular notions of women and gender ideology—indeed, they sought a voice in most areas of human endeavor.

Economic growth was important for women's freedom in all these societies, which reacted to the increasing influx of new wealth, new ideas, new goods, and potentially burgeoning movements for social change by championing a reputed return to traditional notions of masculinity and femininity. The new versions (which included neo-Confucianism, aspects of Reformation Christianity, and emerging Ottoman limits on women's access to male educators) of these traditional ideas were often more restrictive to women than their previous incarnations had been. In general, women's status, freedom of movement, and opportunities for individual choice declined in early modern Eurasia.

STUDY QUESTIONS

1. What models of womanhood did early modern Eurasian states want to promote? Have you ever found that your own government promotes a particular model of womanhood?

2. Why do you think the Ottomans were less interested in promoting models of femininity than the other states? (Hint: Consider the role of ethnic diversity in Eurasian states and the expectations Sunni Muslims had of legitimate governments.)

3. Early modern governments did not promote education in order to empower women. Why did they promote it? Why does your own government promote education?

4. Compare and contrast the differences in female educational content and in the institutions and/or methods of delivering education. How might Eurasian women have used these educations to benefit themselves? Their families?

5. Discuss the roles of institutional religion in women's lives during this period. For each of these societies, consider whether new trends of the period were more beneficial or more limiting/destructive for women. Consider changes in at least one institutional religion present in your society during your lifetime. How have these changes affected its female members?

BIBLIOGRAPHY

*indicates contains whole primary sources or secondary works containing substantial extracts.

CHINA

*Cao Xueqin. *Dream of the Red Mansions.* Translated by Yang Xianyi and Gladys Yang. Peking: Foreign Language Press, 2001.
Ebrey, Patrica. *The Cambridge Illustrated History of China.* Cambridge: Cambridge University Press, 1996.
———, ed. *Chinese Civilization: A Sourcebook.* New York: The Free Press, 1993.
Ko, Dorothy. *Teachers of the Inner Chambers: Women and Culture in Seventeenth-century China.* Stanford, CA: Stanford University Press, 1994.
Spence, Jonathon. *The Death of Woman Wang.* New York: Penguin Books, 1979.

THE OTTOMAN EMPIRE

Goodwin, Geoffrey. *A History of Ottoman Architecture.* New York: Thames and Hudson, 1987.
Greene, Molly, ed. *Minorities in the Ottoman Empire.* Princeton, NJ: Markus Wiener, 2005.
Imber, Colin. *The Ottoman Empire 1300–1650: The Structure of Power.* New York: Palgrave, 2002.
Levy, Avigdar. *The Jews of the Ottoman Empire.* Princeton, NJ: Darwin Press, 1994.

*Peirce, Leslie P. *The Imperial Harem: Women and Sovereignty in the Ottoman Empire.* New York: Oxford University Press, 1993.

Zilfi, Madeline C., ed. *Women in the Ottoman Empire: Middle Eastern Women in the Early Modern Era.* Leiden, Netherlands: Brill, 1997.

RUSSIA

Engel, Barbara Alpern. *Women in Russia, 1700–1900.* Cambridge: Cambridge University Press, 2002.

Levin, Eve. *Sex and Society in the World of Orthodox Slavs, 900–1700.* Ithaca, NY: Cornell University Press, 1989.

TOKUGAWA JAPAN

Bernstein, Gail Lee, ed. *Recreating Japanese Women, 1600–1945.* Berkeley: University of California Press, 1991.

Bingham, Marjorie Wall, and Susan Hill Gross. *Women in Japan from Ancient Times to the Present.* St. Louis Park, MN: Glenhurst Publications, 1987.

WESTERN EUROPE

*Dixon, Annette, ed. *Women Who Ruled: Goddesses, Queens, Amazons in Renaissance and Baroque Art.* Ann Arbor: University of Michigan Museum of Art, 2002.

*Levack, Brian P. *The Witchcraft Sourcebook.* New York: Rutledge, 2004.

———. *The Witch-Hunt in Early Modern Europe.* 3rd ed. New York: Pearson Longman, 2006.

*Otten, Charlotte F. *English Women's Voices 1540–1700.* Miami: Florida International University, 1992.

Wiesner, Merry. *Women and Gender in Early Modern Europe.* 2nd ed. Cambridge: Cambridge University Press, 2000.

RELIGIOUS LIFE

Atiya, Aziz Suryal. *History of Eastern Christianity.* Notre Dame, IN: University of Notre Dame Press, 1968.

Doorn-Harder, Pieternella van. *Contemporary Coptic Nuns.* Columbia: University of South Carolina Press, 1995.

Falk, Nancy, and Rita Gross, eds. *Unspoken Worlds: Women's Religious Lives in Non-Western Cultures.* San Francisco: Harper, 1980.

Findley, Ellison Banks, ed. *Women's Buddhism, Buddhism's Women: Tradition, Revision, Renewal.* Somerville, MA: Wisdom, 2000.

Melammed, Renée Levine. *Heretics or Daughters of Israel? The Crypto-Jewish Women of Castile.* New York: Oxford University Press, 2002.

Monson, Craig. *Disembodied Voices: Music and Culture in an Early Modern Italian Convent.* Berkeley: University of California Press, 1995.

Rapley, Elizabeth. *The Dévotes: Women and Church in Seventeenth-Century France.* Montreal, Canada: McGill-Queen's University Press, 1990.

Ruch, Barbara, ed. *Engendering Faith: Women and Buddhism in Pre-modern Japan.* Ann Arbor: Center for Japanese Studies, The University of Michigan Press, 2002.

CHAPTER THREE

THE ATLANTIC WORLD, 1492–1750:
SPEAKING FOR CORTÉS

In 1492, Christopher Columbus persuaded Queen Isabella of Castile to finance an expedition west across the Atlantic Ocean in search of China and India. She was able to do so because Castile had just finished conquering Granada, the last Muslim-held area in Spain—thus ending 800 years of recurring religious war. In celebration, the Spanish rulers ordered all Jews and Muslims in the kingdom to convert to Catholicism or leave. They also dropped from the monarchy's title the designation "of the three faiths" in favor of "Catholic." Centuries of religious war and conquest had created a culture that combined a passion for Christian mission with an expectation that conquest was the normal venue through which to convert unbelievers. When Columbus actually found land and inhabitants he claimed were friendly, the crown's response was to export the mission of conquest and conversion to the Americas. In doing so they created a political, economic, and cultural network that historians call the Atlantic World.

This chapter summarizes the consequences of that decision over the next several hundred years for Native American Indian, European, and enslaved African women as well as white European women in America. Obviously women's lives changed in many direct, material ways because of the conquest and resulting trans-Atlantic interaction. But women's intellectual and spiritual lives also changed because their ideas about the world and their own roles in it changed. Partly because of the European tendency to equate political and economic subordination with sexual availability, and partly because of the imposition and adoption of Christianity, new gender expectations arose for women in the Americas. Stereotypes of women were divided by economic status, skin color, and ethnicity, and women's access to positions of prestige and authority diminished.

Rather than try to detail the histories of every Native American group, this chapter will study three of the best-known: the Aztec of Mexico; the

Iroquois of New York and Ohio; and the Ojibwa, or Chippewa, of Ontario and the Northern Great Lakes. We will then explore the history of the slave trade and the roles it played in the lives of women of all races. The presence of first, thousands, and later, millions, of enslaved laborers doing the same jobs as similar numbers of wage workers contributed to a transformation in notions of work, productivity, and child rearing. The sheer numbers of people sold over the Atlantic had a broad impact on West and Central African societies, quite different from the effects of the large-scale Arab slave trade in East Africa. The third part of the chapter discusses the lives of Euro-American women in the New World.

MESO-AMERICA, 1519–1700

CONQUEST

Columbus' voyage to the Americas changed the world, joining the trans-Atlantic hemispheres in dramatic and complicated ways. For many, Native women's history conjures images of women assisting Europeans or even collaborating in their own people's conquest: Pocahontas saving John Smith in Virginia, or Sacajawea traveling with Lewis and Clark. The reality of Native women's experience was much more ambiguous. They fought against and sometimes with the Europeans. Their social structure changed in the face of European and Euro-American political power and expectations as if in response to military conquest, and they interacted with and suffered the presence of new diseases, flora and fauna, daily use objects, and religions.[1]

To understand the role of the conquest in Aztec women's lives, we have to understand the background of their conquerors. Although Queen Isabella was married to King Ferdinand of Aragon and their kingdoms were united after their deaths, the bulk of the conquistadors came from her kingdom, Castile. Most were minor aristocrats from the poorest, most underdeveloped province there, Extremadura. They saw the Americas as their opportunity to carve out land, gold, and glory for themselves—to become powerful, landholding aristocrats in the European style. They perceived the social customs of Amerindian peoples as barbarous, their religious practices horrific, their women promiscuous, and the resources of conquered peoples legitimate spoils of war. Ruthless, often desperate, they fought ferociously and died in large numbers in early expeditions; they were merciless in battle and in victory. They came from a military tradition that fought wars in order to seize territory, not captives. Native troops found Spanish warfare terrifying and dishonorable—as terrifying and dishonorable as the Spanish found human sacrifice.

The Spanish first acted in much of the Caribbean, based in Hispaniola (modern Haiti and the Dominican Republic). They found the women attractive and raped many. They enslaved much of the population and relocated thousands of people from one island to another or to and from the mainland. These atrocities became in many ways the model for all initial European conquests in the Americas. The Spanish based their early empire on fortified towns and sent out expeditions to new lands on a regular basis. By 1519, the Spanish began sending expeditions to wrest the mainland from its native rulers. The first of these, led by Hernán Cortés (1485–1547) without any orders from his superiors, was the most spectacularly successful. Cortés, 449 other men, and 16 horses landed first on the Yucatan peninsula, where they acquired from the Maya there a translator, Jermino de Aguilar, a Spaniard who had been captured and held long enough that he spoke Maya. They traveled down the coast and conquered towns. One of these followed local practice (see Chapter One) and presented the Spanish with women as tribute, and among these women was the one who came to be known as Doña Marina (also as La Malinche and Malinache). She had been given away to the Xicalango Indians by her parents, the rulers of Paynala, a Mayan town, because her new stepfather wanted to disinherit her in favor of his new son. The Xicalango had given her to the Tobasco Indians as tribute, and the Tobasco in turn gave her to Cortés as tribute. Cortés made her his interpreter and followed her political advice. Not surprisingly, given the way her family, the Xicalango, and finally the Tobasco had handed her away, Doña Marina sided with the Spanish. As the Spanish moved on to conquer the Aztecs, she became Cortés' chief informant, translator, and advisor on Maya and Aztec culture. She assisted the Spanish by foiling the political plots of their enemies and actively promoting Spanish interests in negotiations. She became Cortés' mistress (never his legal wife), and they had a son, Martin, whom Cortés acknowledged and who went to Spain to become a knight. Doña Marina married Juan Jaramillo, another conquistador, and they had a daughter, Maria. Marina received a substantial grant of land and labor (*encomienda*) for her services, but her daughter Maria never inherited it, instead spending most of her adult life litigating against Juan Jaramillo's second wife's claim to it. Doña Marina died young, one of the millions of unfortunate victims of the epidemic diseases that came to the New World with the Spanish.

Marina's story illustrates the tension between reality and myth in Native American history. As with her North American counterparts Pocahontas and Sacajawea, we know so little about her that it has been possible to use her as a blank canvas on which to paint whatever version of the Aztec defeat we want. Modern Mexican nationalists often consider her a traitor and collaborator, the first villain of Mexican history. Colonial historians used her story to whitewash the conquest and give the impression that the conquerors were welcome liberators. She has even been used as the model of a good Native woman, the example others should live up to. When Native peoples interacted with, allied with, and traded with Europeans, women were often the ones doing the interacting. It was mostly Native women who married, lived with, or had children with Euro-Americans. It was Native women who were kidnapped and raped, because raping women was mostly not an Amerindian practice. Women have therefore often been credited or blamed for colonization and conquest, whether because they slept with the enemy or clamored to buy his wares, or because, in European eyes, Native women supposedly led such degraded lives that Europeans felt forced to liberate them. Doña Marina's story contains the seeds of all this blame, and so this chapter is named for her. Her own feelings and motives are invisible to us, however, because all the male Spanish, Aztec, and Mayan scribes recorded was what she said as an agent for the Spanish—speaking for Cortés.

THE "COLUMBIAN EXCHANGE"

The first two centuries of European contact and conquest affected all phases of life in the Americas and, ultimately, in Europe and parts of Africa as well. More than people and political power traveled back and forth across the Atlantic. People carried microbes, plants, animals, technologies, and cultural practices over the waters—some deliberately and some by accident. These transfers had enormous ecological, economic, and social consequences. Historians call this collection of trades and consequences the Columbian Exchange.[2] The extents of various nations' holdings on both sides of the Atlantic are shown in Figure 3.1. Of course, exchanges were even more widespread than this map indicates, for the European powers were also embedded in trade networks spanning Eurasia and the Philippines.

DISEASE.   In the Americas, most women's lives changed as a result of epidemic disease; political and labor structures established by the conquerors; and the importation of new plants, animals, and tools. The changes were diverse, but some patterns recurred throughout the Americas. First, epidemic disease accompanied, hastened, and in some cases even caused European conquest and was as disruptive. European colonizers brought with them a host of deadly microbes previously unknown in the Americas: measles, mumps, chicken pox, rubella, influenza, and bubonic plague among them. The population of Meso-America dropped from an estimated 25 million at the start of the sixteenth century to 1.5 million

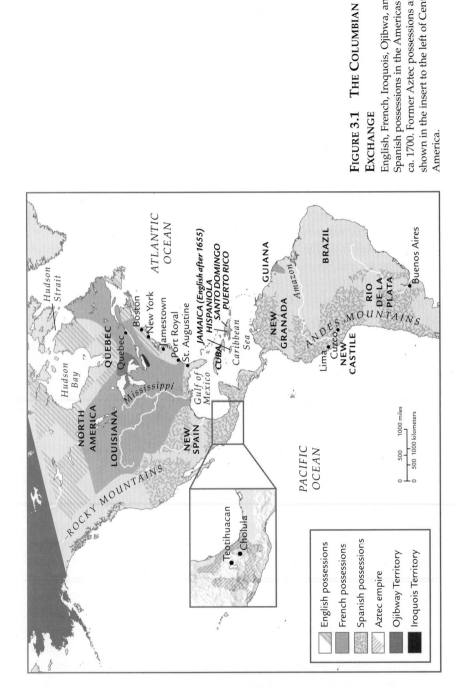

FIGURE 3.1 THE COLUMBIAN EXCHANGE

English, French, Iroquois, Ojibwa, and Spanish possessions in the Americas ca. 1700. Former Aztec possessions are shown in the insert to the left of Central America.

130 years later.[3] Outside Meso-America and the Andes, where the first Eurasian microbes arrived with the first Europeans, disease often arrived prior to colonization, spreading outward from the points of initial European landfall and advancing at a faster pace than exploration and conquest. One early consequence of disease was often to increase women's importance to their societies, which soon were desperate for children to replace their lost families. Of course, since this elevation in status typically accompanied the loss of 30 to 75 percent of an ethnic group, it was hardly cause for celebration.[4] The increase in social importance usually disappeared, however, as Native territories were conquered. For five or six generations, Maya and Nahuatl women watched most of their children, spouses, and siblings die of diseases that became all too familiar—a pattern of destruction that would be repeated throughout the Americas until the mid-nineteenth century. The psychological, spiritual, and emotional consequences must have been enormous.

For the conquistadors, these plagues were also disastrous, because disease decimated their labor supply. Cortés had established encomiendas throughout the region. These were grants of land and labor: The conquistador who owned the land was entitled to tribute and personal household service from the Indians on it, who were now legally his wards. In exchange he was to provide them with food, clothing, housing, medicine, technical advice, and a priest to care for their souls. This was the method the Spanish had used in formerly Muslim areas to reward the conquistadors (whom the government could not afford to pay), create a system of governance, and convert the local people. Although it failed entirely in the Caribbean, where people were unaccustomed to settled farming, in Central Mexico the encomienda system worked well until the onset of the first wave of epidemics. So many Natives died that many *encomienderos* (holders of encomiendas) had to sell their land back to the crown or free the few remaining wards they had. Impoverished, the sons and grandsons of conquistadors often went marching into other parts of the Americas in search of plunder, while the disasters of multiple plagues and foreign conquest made the lives of most of the population miserable.

PLANTS, ANIMALS, AND MATERIAL CULTURE.   Finally, the introduction of new flora, fauna, and tools had mixed results on women's lives. New European methods of cloth making and new sources of textiles—threads, dyes, finished cloth, and styles of looms—were popular among Native peoples throughout the Americas. So were iron and steel tools, especially cooking pots, needles, and axes, which Native peoples seem to have strongly preferred and adopted in their own craft productions. Rice, wheat, pork, beef, chicken, sugar, and all the foodstuffs and pharmacopoeia the Spanish and Europeans could make grow in the Americas made welcome additions to Native diets, even as Native foodstuffs and pharmacopoeia transformed the diets and medicines of everyone else in the world. Tomatoes, peppers, chiles, corn, potatoes, chocolate, and cassava—all Native crops—are now staples in the diets of nearly all the world's peoples. But such additions were disruptive as well as useful. The new European versions of crafts that Native women had produced in the past were manufactured by men, so that people valued crafts done by Native women less. New plants and animals displaced existing ones. Pigs overran entire islands, and whole regions of cultivated land were trampled by cattle and horses and transformed to pasture. The movement of feral horses and cattle north into the Great Plains eventually upended the social and political landscape. Plants that women had relied on for dyes, medicines, and fibers for weaving and basketry sometimes became rare or even extinct as foreign plants invaded and took over their niches, a process that continues today.

Much of the movement of flora and fauna had unintended and profound consequences for women in Europe and the Americas. In an era when no one had thought about biological conservation, the Spaniards were astonished and delighted by the new plants and animals they encountered, and they also demanded the foods, flowers, pets, and medicine from home. They shipped Native American plants and animals back home to Europe wholesale. They borrowed not just Indian staple crops, but also untold numbers of ornamental plant species and varieties that today fill the gardens and greenhouses of people all over the world. The newcomers brought with them to the Americas not just the useful plants and animals they normally consumed—like fruits, herbs, flowers, horses, donkeys, ducks, geese, cats, and chickens—but also rats, fleas, lice, and dandelions. The swarms of cattle, horses, and pigs mentioned earlier came to replace the missing human peasants, turning farmland into pasture and woodland into prairie. Plants and animal species that had filled the woods became harder to find, and Native peoples occupying the land had to change their ways of life. Animal droppings from large herds of cattle and pigs could contaminate water supplies, and those droppings also left behind not just seeds but new varieties of plant and animal disease, some of which crossbred with local diseases to create new ones. All this accelerated the spread of disease and also made it harder to find clean water sources.

CHRISTIANITY AND SPANISH LAW.   Aztec and Nahuatl cultures were based on agriculture centered on city-states. Men had done most of the farming, and the Aztec had placed a high value on sexual restraint, if not on virginity. They were hierarchical, with a hereditary aristocracy and a patriarchal family structure. Though the elites sometimes practiced polygyny and divorce, monogamy and lifetime marriage were the rule. At first, especially in Nahuatl areas, the Spanish often married daughters of local elites and worked through elite rulers. Thus there was considerable continuity of experience for Aztec women. They were still expected to do most of their work in the home, to be chaste, and to follow their husbands. They also continued to have property rights in marriage, as Castilian law gave girls inheritance rights and dowry rights and protected married women's rights to control the disposal of property and wealth in their own names.[5]

Christianity, however, caused profound cultural changes, as it would for women throughout the Americas. Many priests, shamans, and medicine people had been women, but Catholicism forbade female priests and discouraged nuns from leadership. The state persecuted practitioners of traditional religions, especially religious leaders. Gradually, female religious leadership diminished. Even today, although most Mexicans, Hondurans, Guatemalans, and El Salvadorans are all or part Indian, their religious practices are more male-dominated than they were prior to conquest.

Catholicism itself had contradictory impacts on women's status, especially after most of the population had converted to Christianity. Mary and the female saints came to occupy the sacred spaces formerly accorded gods—both female and hermaphroditic—in Meso-America. In 1531, Juan Diego reported being visited by the Virgin Mary on a hill outside Mexico City. Diego reported that she spoke of herself as being merciful, compassionate, a source of aid, and a protector for all. Her image, which appeared on his cloak during a meeting with the bishop, is very widely reproduced, and reverence for the Virgin became central to Mexican religious devotion.

Some women received religious educations, and some Aztec noblewomen were permitted to become nuns. In general, however, only Spanish women could become nuns. After the Council of Trent ended in 1563, Catholic Christianity emphasized the role of the father and of wifely submission more than in the past, exalting celibate womanhood less and praising motherly virtue more, so that women were ideologically even more connected to the household than before. Mexico was actually one of the more liberal areas in Latin America. In Brazil, a Portuguese colony, there were convents only for white women, and not for many of those. Instead, non-European women went to Portugal or the Atlantic Islands when they wanted to take up monastic life. In Peru, lay women who *were not* nuns were expected to live their lives in cloister as much as possible.

Spanish-American law, like the legal systems of subsequent Euro-American regimes, degraded Native women's status by forcing changes in agricultural production, property distribution, lineage formation, and rules of inheritance. For example, where the Aztecs had insisted on monogamy and chastity outside marriage for both sexes, the Spanish permitted males' promiscuity while penalizing women's. Thus, the Spanish recognized five kinds of illegitimacy among the children of Native and mestizo (mixed-race people, part Indian and part European) women and classified some women as virtuous and others as impure. By the early seventeenth century, even aristocratic Aztec and Maya women no longer married into the powerful Spanish families. By the early nineteenth century, the bulk of the Mexican population was Native or mestizo, with the women of both groups categorized as less than fully honorable.

In the new Spanish order, Indian women generally held lower status than the small numbers of Spanish and Spanish-American women in the colonies. Many Indian women worked as servants in the cities—often the only places they could find work. Although many Indians were captured and enslaved, the huge loss of Native population due to disease had made it impossible to maintain a slave-holding economy using Indian labor. Even the huge silver mines of Zapoteca and Potosi came to employ wage laborers, and slaves were mostly imported from Africa.

NORTH AMERICA: THE OJIBWA/CHIPPEWA AND IROQUOIS INDIANS

The changes wrought by colonization were even more pronounced in North America than in Meso-America. Although we will be focusing on women of the eastern woodlands—because they are among the most well studied, both pre- and post-conquest—most of the farming peoples experienced change similar to those of the Iroquois, and most of the hunter/gatherer peoples similar to those of the Ojibwa (Chippewa).

THE OJIBWA, SEVENTEENTH AND EIGHTEENTH CENTURIES

The Ojibwa occupied the Northern Great Lakes, their territory spreading roughly around Lake Superior and the northern shore of Lake Michigan. They were primarily a hunting and gathering people in the seventeenth century,[6] and traditionalists today still maintain that lifestyle as much as possible. Clans came together in the summer, which was the busiest season for women. At the summer camps, they gathered most of their working materials and processed most of the plant foods they needed for winter. One of the most important of these was wild rice, which the women harvested by pulling the stalks over and shaking them into a canoe while a male relative paddled under their direction. In the winter, individual families separated from the group to live alone, in winter quarters. The men hunted game, and the women processed the kills and the materials gathered over the summer to make the clothing, nets, and tools of daily life. Spiritual life was gender-segregated; men had their own spiritual tasks and celebrations, and women had theirs. In particular, each man had his own spirit guide and so was in a way the main priest and celebrant in his own religion. Women worshipped in groups more often than men did. Among both men and women, certain people could prophesy and communicate messages from the spirit world. Only a few major ceremonies involved both sexes.[7]

Among the Ojibwa, missionaries arrived at the same time as Eurasian diseases. Seventeenth-century Christianity—for the Ojibwa, Roman Catholic Christianity—forbade female leadership and insisted on the primacy of male authority, not just in religion but in all areas of life. Missionaries seemed to be immune to the diseases that were devastating the Native population, and it seems many people were tempted toward Christianity purely because they thought it might offer protection from plague. The division between male and female religious practice meant that the men could convert without losing an arena for prestige, but women could not become Christian without giving up their claim to formal spiritual leadership. Men thus converted in larger numbers than women, which proved a source of great dissension. Missionaries insisted that men direct their wives' and children's religious observances and that polygyny (one husband having multiple wives) was impermissible. Obviously, telling women how to practice religion was nontraditional and unpopular. Less obviously, although monogamy might be good for later women's status, it was a disaster in a society where sisters often married the same husband. For the Ojibwa women, sharing husbands had been a way to have adult companionship and cooperation in sharing tasks while their husbands were away hunting for the many months of the winter. For husbands to have to choose one wife over the other meant not only that the relationship between husband and wife was damaged, but also that one sister would lose her husband to the other, and both would now have to work and raise children in isolation throughout the winter.

These problems were exacerbated by changes in the economy. The fur trade was a potent engine of change. At the same time as missionaries arrived, traders arrived, too. The furs of North American mammals, especially but far from exclusively beaver fur, were highly prized in Europe. Indians throughout the Northeast recognized this quickly and began to catch animals not just for subsistence and personal use but also for sale. Throughout the eastern coast of North America, it was men who were in charge of hunting in Amerindian societies, and so the new trade and women's contribution to it were controlled by their men.

Ojibwa women's historical economic power was largely the result of their control over the process of making finished goods, although gathering was also an important part of their production. Their male relatives caught most of the animals whose hides and flesh the women processed into the staple foods, clothing, adornments, and utensils of daily living. As their men began to trap animals for sale instead of for subsistence, they brought home many finished goods that replaced materials the women had previously crafted. The women spent more and more of their time processing their men's furs for sale. They had less and less time to make the traditional crafts that increased their status. Moreover, some of their most important crafts were being replaced with purchased goods—and those purchases were made with money the men controlled. Finally, as the men focused more on hunting for sale, resources were depleted, and households had to live farther apart during the hunting seasons than they had in the past. Women lived most of their time in isolation from other women, with only their children. Thus women lost authority and prestige during the first two centuries of contact.

THE IROQUOIS, 1600–1848

Iroquois women's status, by contrast, seems to have increased during the period of early contact in the seventeenth and eighteenth centuries. Because the Iroquois lived in villages, depended on women's farming for most of their food, and practiced matrilineal descent, Iroquois women were able to retain more authority than their Ojibwa counterparts. The Six Nations'[8] first encounters with Europeans, like those of other North American Natives, were with traders and missionaries. Here, too, the desire for new goods drove economic change. Men desired axes and firearms as much as women desired iron pots and steel knives. Although quill embroidery remains a living craft (for example, the Seneca Nation Museum in Salamanca, New York, sponsors classes on quillwork and displays contemporary handicrafts), almost everyone preferred glass beads to porcupine quills in clothing and accessories. Beads are easier to use, require no processing on the user's end, come in a much wider variety of shapes and colors than the natural dyes then available, and permit designs with curving lines. For most purposes besides the ceremonial, glass beads also replaced or supplemented the shell beads called *wampum* in the Northeast.[9]

The currency of exchange by which the Iroquois acquired beads was fur—again, mostly beaver. Finding themselves positioned near the Dutch, French, and English, yet surrounded by a number of smaller and weaker nations, the Iroquois went to war to control the fur trade. The seventeenth and early eighteenth centuries saw their territory expand from what is now western New York State to include for a time nearly the entire state, parts of western Pennsylvania, northern Ohio up to the Sandusky River, and much of the region between Lakes Ontario, Erie, and Huron. War served not just to control the fur trade. It also provided captives for both sacrifice and adoption. Because Iroquois women leaders traditionally decided the fate of war captives, appointed and deposed chiefs, and decided with whom the Iroquois would ally, the activist foreign policy of the seventeenth and eighteenth centuries led to women having even more political power than before.

The Iroquois were "missionized" by Jesuits, Moravians, Methodists, and eventually Quakers, among others. None of these groups were initially very successful, particularly among Iroquois women, at least partly because the group most comfortable with female leadership (the Quakers) was the one doing the least mission work. It took a long time—until late in the eighteenth century—for Christian ideas even to begin appearing in Iroquois descriptions of religious and ceremonial matters, and even then it was men, not women, who did so. In fact, the Six Nations persecuted Christian converts, went to war with the Huron partly over the conversion of a large number of Huron Indians to Christianity, and tried to make adopted clan members give up the religion. By the end of the eighteenth century, however, attitudes had begun to shift. Few Iroquois became Christian yet, but the prophet Handsome Lake founded Longhouse, a new version of traditional religion that was more specifically monotheist than the Six Nations had ever practiced before. Longhouse taught and teaches its practitioners to eschew alcohol and witchcraft, to resist cultural assimilation, and to remain grounded in Iroquois tradition. A living religion, today Longhouse is also a powerful source for cultural revival and renewal among the Iroquois, especially the Seneca. When first instituted, Longhouse was not concerned with improving women's social status and was in fact in active conflict with the traditional matriarchs. But today Longhouse practitioners live and pass on the matrilineal and matriarchal heritage of their past. A group of Oneida converted to Methodism and in 1816 moved to Wisconsin, where many others (of widely varying religious practices) later followed. The Oneida reservation in Wisconsin now has the largest Iroquois population in the world.

SLAVERY AND THE SLAVE TRADES

ORIGINS

The slave trade in the Americas began with Columbus, who seized several Caribbean people and brought them back to Spain as trophies. The Spanish in the Caribbean used forced slave labor, relocating the indigenous peoples in many cases. In Mexico the Spanish had originally used the *encomienda* system, where conquistadors had legal standing similar to that of European feudal lords relative to the Indian peasants. In this economic system, the peasants had legal rights and the lord had some obligations. However, the encomiendas died out, replaced by slavery as the spread of Eurasian diseases gutted the Native population. Landholders tried to replace workers who had died by capturing and enslaving Indians from farther afield. Catholic missionaries protested vehemently on the grounds that many of these peoples were either Christian or the object of missionary activities. They argued that Indians were not intended by God to be servile. In the end, the newly captured and enslaved Indians were just as vulnerable to European diseases as their neighbors had been. The Spanish then turned to the slave trade from West and Central Africa, regions from which the Portuguese had been importing slaves to work on the sugar plantations of the Azores. Figure 3.2 shows Africa during the time of slavery and the slave trades. Thus began the African slave trade into the Americas, spreading from New Spain (the parts of Central and South American conquered by Spain; see Figure 3.1 on page 80) and the Caribbean to all of Latin America, the east coast of North America, and the Ohio and Mississippi River valleys. It arrived in Mexico and Peru in the sixteenth century to replace farmworkers and expanded across much of the Americas later in the seventeenth and eighteenth centuries as plantations sought large numbers of workers to grow sugar, tobacco, and eventually cotton for export.

THE MIDDLE PASSAGE

On the way across the Atlantic and into the New World (The Middle Passage), life for African women, who made up about one-third of the enslaved, was usually short and hard. An unknown number of captives lost their lives between their acquisition by African slave traders in the African interior and their sale to slave ship captains. During the voyage aboard ship to the Americas, women and men would typically be stored—chained shoulder-to-foot on the deck and on shelves 3 or 4 feet above the deck—separately, and the women were often subject to the unwanted attentions of the slave traders. In the seventeenth century, the mortality rate among the captives aboard ship could be as high as 24 percent; in the eighteenth and nineteenth centuries the mortality rate for captives was between 10 and 15 percent. These voyages were dangerous for the slavers, too—mortality rates among crew also ran between 10 and 15 percent. After the British outlawed the slave trade between Africa and British colonies, and British vessels hunted down slave traders of all nations in the

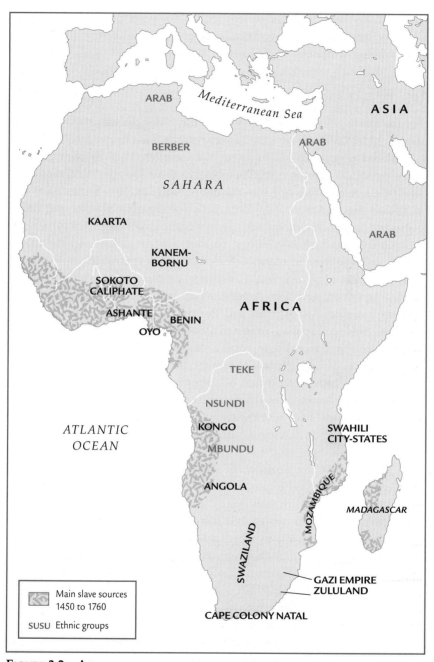

FIGURE 3.2   AFRICA IN THE NINETEENTH CENTURY

1820s, more lives were lost when panicked slavers dumped their entire cargo of human beings overboard rather than face British justice from approaching warships.[10]

LIFE IN THE AMERICAS

For the many who survived, slavery in the Americas was harsher than in Africa. Most slaves in Africa had some protections under law; they were considered people, so killing them was murder. They or their children could eventually become full members of their societies, and manumission (the freeing of slaves) was common. None of these things were true in British North America. In Latin America, Spanish Florida, the Caribbean, and Louisiana, manumission was common, though not typical, for women who had borne children to their owners. Although the majority of enslaved people were of African descent, many Indians—mostly women—were also enslaved. Thus, slave culture came to blend African, Native American, and Euro-American customs, and many people of slave descent have not just African and European, but also Native American ancestry. Enslaved women in urban areas had very different work experiences from those working in rural areas, especially plantations. In New Spain, where about 1 free white woman arrived for every 10 white men for the first century and a half of colonization, slave women and their sometimes-manumitted (freed) daughters made up the bulk of the female urban population. They worked as household servants or were hired out as day laborers and frequently found that they were also expected to provide sex to their owners.

In the Caribbean and North America, the number of free white women was higher, with about two to three white men for every white woman. This meant not only that there was a much larger number of men married to white wives, but also that there were many more single white women trying to make a living. These women lived mostly in towns and cities, and they owned almost half the slaves in urban areas. Moreover, free women of any color were much more likely to own women than men. In short, slave women in urban areas were usually the property of other women. This does not mean that there was great female solidarity between white and free colored women and their slaves; reports from witnesses and escaped slaves indicate that women were just as physically abusive as men were. In the urban areas of the Caribbean and North America, many urban slave women worked in the household cooking, doing laundry, drawing water, cleaning, and caring for any small children or livestock. This could be exhausting physical labor, especially for a woman past her first youth. Mary Prince (1788–at least 1831) in her memoirs and Ursala da Jesús (freed at about age 40) in her spiritual diary—both former slaves—complained of their declining ability to endure chores like laundry and scrubbing floors as well as of debilitating illnesses.

Free women who owned multiple slaves used them to run businesses, rather like temporary agencies whose employees had no rights. Some of their slaves would be hired out as laborers to other houses, shops, laundries, and so on. If the slave women came home pregnant, this was no problem, because there was a market for children as well. Innkeepers and brothel owners were often women, and both kinds of businesses frequently used slaves and sold their children. Women enslaved in such situations could often earn some wages from their work, however, so it was most often urban slave women who were able to save enough to purchase their freedom.

In addition to the indignities of their work and owners' attempts to control their fertility, many enslaved women suffered sexual abuse through brute force, threats, or pseudo-courtship. Planters, overseers, and affluent urban men could maintain long-standing involvements with individual women, especially in parts of the Caribbean where overseers were not permitted to marry at all or where the marriage of white and negro men and women was forbidden. It is very difficult to tell which, if any such relationships might have been consensual or loving. Enslaved women did not often have the power to refuse white men's sexual advances. There would have been a strong element of coercion in any of these relationships—just as we saw with Doña Marina—whether that coercion was overt or circumstantial. For instance, in the nineteenth century Harriet Jacobs chose to have a child by a white neighbor rather than by her owner, so she could prevent her owner from making her bear his children and because she hoped her chosen partner would purchase and free the children. Taking this lover was definitely her own choice, but it was not made freely: She regretted the necessity of it deeply for much of her life. She would have chosen differently if she had been allowed to control access to her own body.

Most enslaved women and girls in the Americas would find themselves doing the heaviest plantation labor, working as field hands. The prized, skilled workers in American slave societies were men, so they were the ones most likely to be assigned away from the fields, and nearly all field-gang bosses (many of whom were slaves) were men. Even though women were always a minority among slaves, they usually made up a little more than half the field hands at a plantation. Women spent their work hours clearing fields, planting cash crops, and harvesting. Their life expectancy on the plantation was shortened, though we do not know by how much. The worst conditions were in the Caribbean and on the sugar plantations of North America. At first, slaveholders encouraged women to have children, but by the middle of the eighteenth century, mono-cropping took over the plantation economy, and slaveholders seem to have concluded it was more profitable to work a slave to death and buy another than to lose any of her labor to pregnancy and raise her child to adulthood.

Slavery often hurt women's fertility. Terrible sanitation, frequent beatings, and constant malnourishment combined with daily hard physical labor often caused the menses to flow continuously or stop entirely. Mary Prince, the only Caribbean slave to have left a narrative of her life, described the time her owner, whom she calls "Captain I_," beat her friend Hetty hard enough to cause Hetty to miscarry:

> One of the cows had dragged the rope away from the stake to which Hetty had fastened it, and got loose. My master flew into a terrible passion, and ordered the poor creature to be stripped quite naked, not withstanding her pregnancy, and to be tied up to a tree in the yard. He then flogged her as hard as he could lick, both with the whip and cow-skin, till she was all over streaming with blood. He rested, and then beat her again and again. Her shrieks were terrible. The consequence was that poor Hetty was brought to bed before her time, and was delivered after severe labour of a dead child. She appeared to recover after her confinement, so far that she was repeatedly flogged by both master and mistress afterwards; but her former strength never returned to her. Ere long her body and limbs swelled to a great size; and she lay on a mat in the kitchen, till the water burst out of her body and she died.[11]

Women worked in the fields to the latest stage of pregnancy, which may be safe for women experiencing a normal pregnancy, but in an abnormal pregnancy can be quite dangerous to the woman and the fetus. Between a quarter and a fifth of enslaved women never had children, let alone children who lived to adulthood. Those who did have children had fewer on average than did free women. Abortion and infanticide seem to have been common, perhaps because women did not want to raise their children as slaves.

Enslaved people had their lowest fertility during the eighteenth century. At that time planters tried their best to discourage slaves from forming families—forbidding marriage, selling children away from parents, and lovers from one another. Few women were imported at all into the Spanish Caribbean, because the planters wanted there to be no time lost to pregnancy.

RESISTANCE

Among slaves, resistance came in several forms. The most obvious was open revolt. In slave rebellions—whether in successful ones like those in seventeenth-century Surinam and early nineteenth-century Haiti, or in failures like the short-lived revolts in eighteenth-century Manhattan—the nominal leaders were men. Some women participated in leadership as *obeah* practitioners, who were people with magical spiritual powers based on their experience in African traditional religions, shamanism, and medicines. Conjuring, or magic, was common among blacks in the Americas as a way to take some control over their condition—as (so many people believed) was the poisoning of owners and overseers. Women also participated as messengers and go-betweens, and they joined in the actual mass uprisings.

The most common forms of rebellion were less showy: avoiding tasks, misunderstanding instructions, leaving tasks unfinished, and covertly breaking tools. The so-called Negro Markets in every slaveholding community were the best indication of what enslaved people could do when they really wanted to. During their very small amounts of free time, enslaved people grew crops and fabricated goods to be bought and sold on their one day off at market. Slave women with a reputation for industry and skill in their own homes and in their production for the Negro Market could be the most active of the covert rebels described above, appearing hopelessly inept when it came to doing the slave owner's business instead of their own. Sometimes slaves refused tasks outright, even when it meant they would be beaten or whipped. Especially after laws went into effect forbidding Caribbean owners from actually whipping women, female slaves were famously recalcitrant, so that records of slave punishments (carefully recorded in detail at many plantations) list women as frequent recidivists, punished many times for the same kinds of incidents of insolence, disobedience, and quarreling.

Enslaved women were subjected to pressures that tended to de-feminize them; that is, their work was often the same as men's and was often in areas considered too strenuous for white women. Owners treated enslaved women as if they were men, and treated enslaved men themselves as irresponsible, foolish, brutal, or otherwise incapable. Among themselves, blacks resisted internalizing this gender ideology. Instead, to maintain their sense of dignity, they emphasized gender distinctions wherever possible. Enslaved men refused work they considered too feminine, such as washing clothes—even carrying their laundry miles to their wives' plantations rather than doing it themselves—and enslaved wives sought to keep their own houses as best they could. An example of separate slave quarters appears in Figure 3.3, where an early photograph shows all the enslaved people from one plantation posed in front of their homes.

Although today we might think that physical punishments would have been the worst aspect of slave life, autobiographies written by escaped slaves and interviews with survivors of Atlantic slavery indicate

FIGURE 3.3   PLANTATION SLAVES
A large group of slaves standing in front of Smith's Plantation,
Beaufort, South Carolina. Note that the building to the right has
two doors; it almost certainly housed two families. From their
postures and body language, how happy do you think they were
to pose for this picture? Does knowing that plantation slaves
struggled fiercely to force owners to give them housing separate
from the "Big House" give you any insight into the image?

that it was the vulnerability of the family unit that frightened them the
most. Both Mary Prince and Harriet Jacobs describe these fears—Prince
recalled her panic on the day her mother was forced to bring her and her
sisters to the market for sale: "My heart throbbed with grief and terror
so violently, that I pressed my hands quite tightly across my chest, but I
could not keep it still, and it continued to leap as though it would burst
out of my body."[12]

Participating in some kind of family life seems to have been the most
important value in slave communities. Slaves resisted all attempts to
impose communal meals and child rearing so that they could maintain a
separate home life. They lived as much as they could in patriarchal family
units and within their own households distinguished between men's and
women's roles. They conducted marriage ceremonies (as Mary Prince and
her husband, Daniel James, did), even though the law did not recognize
their marriages. Fathers were accorded the respect due the head of the
household, even if their wives held higher social status. For example, in
the United States it was common for enslaved men to marry free black
women. Because children were accorded the legal status of their mother,
an enslaved man could have free children if his wife were free, whereas

if a free man had children with an enslaved woman, his children would be born into slavery. In such situations, the enslaved man was still treated as the head of the household when dealing with his family and the black community.

THE EFFECTS OF THE SLAVE TRADE ON AFRICA

African women experienced immense consequences from the slave trade. First, from its earliest records, the Atlantic slave trade exported two to three times more men than women, and it did so out of a limited number of ports in West and Central Africa. Slave kingdoms like Benin (formerly Dahomey) and Sokoto arose, becoming wealthy and powerful by raiding their neighbors and selling war captives for firearms. Regions that had already lost considerable portions of their healthy adult men to slavery responded by focusing on warfare and on producing young warriors for the nation. The end result was that in West and Central Africa, each woman had 50 percent more children and elderly people to care for than her foremothers had. Women had a larger share of agricultural and productive responsibilities than before because there were fewer able-bodied men, and those still present were much more likely to be involved in war. Women also had less value as wives, because able-bodied men were in short supply. Contemporary accounts, Christian and Muslim, all mention the high incidence of polygyny in West and Central Africa at the time: Hardly any man had just one wife, and chiefs might have 20 or 30. These travelers said that the kings of West and Central Africa were so cavalier about their wives that they might marry a slave, have a child with her, and then sell both if the formerly enslaved wife displeased him. Although we do not have many examples of this happening, just knowing such a thing was possible must have had a chilling effect on wives.[13]

The continuing expansion of states in West and Central Africa also offered a few elite women opportunities to become major political players. Queen (or possibly Princess) Amina (1533–1610) of Zazzau (a Hausa state in modern Nigeria) led armies throughout her adulthood. Under her leadership, the state expanded substantially. She made numerous reforms of the military, including arranging for the fortifications of all the towns under Zazzau control. Queen Nzingha (1582–1683) of Matamba (modern Angola) led resistance against Portuguese encroachment and against the expansion of the slave trade into southern Africa. She pitted her enemies against each other and kept her people free from foreign control for decades. Amina's conquests provided West Africans with a model of successful female leadership and military prowess, but her rule would have affected the women of her country and its surroundings in much the same way as the expansion and centralization of other African states of era, sending large numbers of men to war, leaving women with more responsibilities at home, and making it harder for women to find marriageable men. On the other hand, Nzingha's resistance to the slave trade distinguished her; her policies would have protected women more than those of most other rulers. Her meeting with the Portuguese ambassador is depicted in Figure 3.4. The artist was a European, and Nzingha's appearance is therefore filtered through the expectations Europeans had already developed about sub-Saharan Africans.

The pressure of slave labor in the Caribbean and southern colonies of North America lowered the price of wage labor—not just in the New World, but also across the Atlantic. However, its most harmful contribution to African life would come later: the development of racism. The presence of a large class of unfree people who all shared some aspects of their appearance and heritage—brown skin and recent African descent—could only be justified by creating the myth that slavery was the natural role of some people. Spurious theories of race developed to explain the peculiar social structures of American societies. In this context, race supposedly encompassed not just physical characteristics such as skin color, hair texture, and the shape of facial features, but also moral, intellectual, and spiritual capacities. Slavery was justified on the pretext that

FIGURE 3.4   QUEEN NZINGHA

European depiction of Queen Nzingha meeting with the Portuguese ambassador. The ambassador refused to provide her a chair, so she sat on one of her male companions. Given what you have learned about early modern European attitudes toward women, what impression do you think a European audience would have of Nzingha from this image?

the enslaved were intellectually and morally inferior—like animals, children, or women—and needed to be guided with a firm hand. They were supposed to be better off in civilization than in the wilds of Africa, better off enslaved than forced to make decisions on their own in freedom. These attitudes, so harmful to enslaved peoples in the New World, would later become the ideological justification for Europeans to conquer most of Africa in the nineteenth and early twentieth centuries. The ideology of race also inflected the ideology of gender, so that stereotypes about men and women came to be partly determined by race.

WHITE WOMEN, GENDER IDEOLOGY, AND DAILY LIFE

With the Spanish, Portuguese, Dutch, French, and English eventually came many women. Until the middle of the nineteenth century, women always immigrated in much smaller numbers than men, but they came to stay. Unlike the colonial settlements Europeans were building in the Indian Ocean region at this time, the outposts in the Americas were always intended to be permanent. Women's presence symbolized this intention. From their first arrival in the Americas, therefore, Euro-American women represented the wholesale importation of European culture. They were presumed to be the standard bearers of civilization. Colonial leaders, both in the Americas and elsewhere, expected or at least wanted Euro-American women to behave in ways that would reflect well on their communities—to model to Native and enslaved women (often believed to be unfeminine) an appropriate level of piety, modesty, and wifely submission. So, just as Native women's partial cooperation with and adjustment to colonial authority came to symbolize the delusion of colonizers that they had been welcome, Euro-American women personified the fantasy of European superiority.[14]

Of course, this role of shy, retiring, and submissive wife working only within the house fit poorly with the actual roles most Euro-American women had to play—often, those of farmer or trader. Colonial administrators came, themselves, primarily from social classes in which their own female relatives performed no heavy manual labor and where most of the tasks of daily life were performed by servants. These men were often appalled to observe that real settler women performed heavy labor and so were often dirty; that they quarreled and yelled and stood up to each other and to their husbands. Transplanted to the Americas, far from manorial obligations and most of the nobility of Europe, women and men whose families had been peasants and small-scale craftspeople became landowners, citizens, and—in fact—the ruling class of much more egalitarian societies.

At least, for Euro-Americans, these societies seemed more egalitarian. What actually happened was that, because slavery was associated with darker-skinned peoples, Euro-Americans developed an idealized concept of whiteness, wherein white people were considered to be naturally free, independent, resourceful, and intelligent. The children they had with members of other races—although never presumed to be equal to children of two white parents—were supposed to be different from and better than children with no white blood. In Spanish, French, and Portuguese territories this led to extensive systems of classification by various definitions of race: dividing Euro-Americans into two groups—those born in Europe (castas) and those born in the Americas (creoles)—and then everyone else into many further tiny categories. In the north, English practice became the norm: White was white, and any African or Native ancestry at all made the children into members of another race. This is partly why so many modern members of American Indian nations are said to "look white" or "appear black" by outsiders accustomed to assigning group membership based on visual characteristics. Especially in the east, Indians treated the race of one or the other parent as irrelevant in determinations of group membership: Only the formal rules for defining a lineage and for recognizing adoption (which was common in all tribes) counted.

Because white people were patrilineal and patriarchal, their system of classification depended on white women's attachment to white men. It was common for elite men to sexually harass or abuse slaves or (on military campaigns) free Native women; but white women's sexual purity was to be guarded fiercely from any and all approaches by Native or black men. In fact, white men—who already associated sexual license with female disobedience and immorality—came to interpret all rebellion, resistance, or aggression on the part of Indian and black men as a direct threat to their control of white women's sexuality. White women were portrayed as the most desirable prize of civilization and, when slaves or freedmen or Indians were hunted down and killed for whatever reason, this was seen as a way of protecting white women from dark-skinned men, whose advances would have (whites presumed) been horrible to the women in question. Just as stereotypes arose about black women's sexuality, stereotypes of black men and Indians often focused on their sexuality, their supposedly greater sexual prowess and sex drive, their supposedly insatiable drive to possess white women. Assigning to slaves the intention to commit crimes that had already been committed a thousandfold by slave traders and slave owners presents a striking and ironic example of cultural projection apparently based upon guilt.

Most of the white women who went to the Spanish and Portuguese New World during the sixteenth and seventeenth centuries were free, but many of the British ones who went to the Caribbean and North America during the seventeenth and early eighteenth centuries arrived as indentured servants. In English territories, many of these were Irish. Indentured servants received free passage to the Americas, where a free person—often a plantation owner—would buy them for a period of up to 7 years, after which they would have earned a small sum of money and a patch of land, usually about 30 acres. Indentured servants had somewhat more privileges than slaves—murdering indentured servants was legally risky—and if they were very bold and very lucky, laborers could sometimes get some relief from mistreatment. They were subjected to physical correction, as slaves were, and often worked as field hands. After they were freed, the land they received was often quite marginal and usually lay along borders between the wealthy and various Native peoples—where they would be the first attacked in any outbreak of war. Often their land could not support them solely as farmers, so they also worked as day laborers in economies that required them to compete directly with slave labor. For women, this usually meant employment as servants, laundresses, or sex workers.[15] Descendants of poor whites who could not climb out of poverty were given insulting labels like "cracker," "red neck," or "red legs"—the latter referring to white Jamaican day laborers who often got sunburned on their legs because they could not afford trousers.

Most Euro-Americans' standard of living in the Americas was much higher than it had been in Europe. Women married younger and men much younger than they had in Europe and set up households quickly. Birth and survival rates were high—it was not uncommon for women to have 12 to 14 children and for most or all of them to survive to adulthood. The population expanded rapidly.

The economic lives of free Euro-American women were like the lives of wealthy European peasants and remained so for most of the next two centuries. Men farmed grain and cared for cattle and horses. Women raised small livestock like hens and pigs; fetched firewood and water; cooked, cleaned, gardened, and processed foodstuffs; and spun, wove, or otherwise fabricated clothes. Unlike their counterparts in Europe, Euro-American women could be confident that their husbands could someday own and farm their own land. They might not have access to a commons, but they did not need it, because the uncultivated and fallow lands around them did not belong to a local nobleman or king who forbade foraging. Euro-American women's families kept most of the fruit of their labors, and they could depend on all their adult children being able to own land or enter into a trade that paid enough to raise a family and assume that, over time, all the lowest-status jobs would come to be done by darker-skinned peoples.

MISSIONARIES

Even though most of the mission work of the seventeenth century was done by male Jesuits and Franciscans, European women tried hard to be included. It was very difficult, however. The Reformation in Germany and England was driving nuns from the cloister, and the reforms of the Council of Trent were limiting the roles of sisters and nuns, forcing them into claustration—that is, lifetime enclosure inside the convent. Nevertheless, some women yearned for the romance and excitement of mission work, and achieved it against the odds. In the eastern woodlands, women were more successful than men in their attempts at serving Native women, usually despite strong opposition from portions of their church hierarchies. Since women always made up part of the spiritual leadership in these Native matrilineal societies, they rarely converted without having examples of female leadership.[16]

When white women were allowed to work with Indian women, they had more success than male missionaries. French women were particularly active. The Duchess of Aigullon had paid the way of the Hospitalières de Dieppe—nuns who nursed patients from inside the walls of the convent—to found a hospital in Quebec, and Mare de la Petrie founded an Ursuline house there that received papal approval in 1647. The Ursulines went to Canada in 1633, but were forbidden by the bishop to witness to anyone except the settlers. It was to the hospital, then, that Marie de Saint-Josèph and her mother superior, Marie de l'Incarnation, traveled in 1650 on their own recognizance. The pair hoped to work with, heal, and convert Native girls. Marie de Saint-Josèph wrote an Algonquin-language dictionary and a book on their sacred history as well as an Iroquoisan catechism, and l'Incarnation taught her European novices Native languages. But the convent never had the funds to pay for supporting many Native pupils. The church excluded Native women from becoming professed religious, and very few of them were interested. Marie de l'Incarnation wrote in her letters that Native women had difficulty adapting to enclosure. Another group in Montreal, the Hospitalières, succeeded in founding a hospital that treated Native women but were forced by their bishop into claustration in 1669.[17]

Still, women's orders kept trying. In 1688 the Spanish Sisters of Bethlehem went to Mexico to found a hospital. In 1727, the Sisters of Saint Paul of Chartres went out to work in the hospital there, and the Ursulines of Rouen opened an Indian mission in Louisiana, where the Ursuline convent in New Orleans remains the oldest surviving building in the state. Late in the seventeenth century, the Moravians had great initial success converting Mahican women, partly because the sexes worshipped separately and

employed white and Native women as missionaries and religious leaders. The brief honeymoon ended, however, at the end of the eighteenth
century, when the Moravians decided church leadership should be exclusively male; conversions among the Mahicans declined.

Conclusion: Gender and Race Ideology Intertwine

Throughout the New World, gender ideology was deeply shaped by
developing racist assumptions. In much of the Atlantic World, where the
sexual abuse of enslaved and low-status women was common, gender ideology justified the abuse by creating an image of enslaved and low-status
women as sexually aggressive, lewd, and ignorant. Enslaved women and
their menfolk resisted attempts to treat men and women alike and maintained strict gender roles within the household.

For free white women, it became more important than ever to avoid
any hint of overt sexuality. Where European ideology had earlier considered all women weak and lustful, in the era of slavery an ideology of white
superiority began to endow middle- and upper-class white women with
the traditional European feminine virtues and assign traditional European feminine vices to enslaved women and the working poor. Among
the largely mestiza (mixed-race, Euro-American, and Indian) women of
New Spain and Peru, an ideology of Spanish-style honor and respectable
seclusion became interwoven with notions of racial superiority and inferiority, so that women's (and men's) value as marriage partners was evaluated on a combination of personal behavior, racial make-up, and financial
background.

Native women in North America also felt the force of changing gender
expectations. As these peoples entered into the wider Atlantic economic
system and were pursued by missionaries, changes in gender expectations followed. Although Iroquois women gained greater power during
the first two centuries of contact, in other societies men gained greater
power over their wives, and women's control of goods began to decline.
Polygyny gradually disappeared, but did so by breaking up many marriages. The Atlantic World was created by conquest and colonization, by
biological and cultural exchange, and by women as well as men. Though
men led expeditions of conquest and exploration, women's assistance
and support were essential to their comfort and their success. Though
Native men fought against and with Europeans, they did so with the support of and sometimes on behalf of their women. European and African
women brought as much of their home culture with them as they could,
transforming themselves, their culture, and the landscape as they did so.

Native women adapted to new peoples and resisted changes imposed by Europeans and by their own men. Everyone's material culture changed as a result of contact with new customs, technologies, and agriculture. The confluence of Native, African, and European societies led to new social hierarchies and gender ideologies.

In general, women's roles in the creation of the Atlantic World have been downplayed in our national and regional histories. Changes in women's lives appear as stand-ins for progress or emblems of a particular government's backwardness, and the women themselves are often portrayed as helpless before the decisions of the wider, male-dominated society. The hard work, hard choices, and the good and bad decisions made by hundreds of thousands of ordinary women that added up to widespread social change somehow vanish from the historical record. Metaphorically, histories of women embedded in traditional accounts of the Atlantic World often "speak for" nationalist concerns, just as Doña Marina spoke for Cortés. Yet, as this chapter shows, women in the Atlantic World did not passively accept a society and restraints imposed by men—they helped build, alter, and injure societies. They resisted some restraints and imposed others of their own. They were not just witnesses or victims, but active participants in the creation of the Atlantic World.

STUDY QUESTIONS

1. In what ways did European colonization affect the material culture (tools, housing, food, clothing, and so on) of Native American women during this era? Keeping in mind what you learned about Meso-American women in Chapter One, compare and contrast the Aztecs with the Iroquois or the Ojibwa.

2. What kinds of work did enslaved women do in the Americas? White women? Compare and contrast these kinds of work with what you know about the work done by their sisters in Europe and in West Africa at the same time. Remember what you learned about women and work in Chapters One and Two.

3. How and to what extent did the various churches and missionaries play a role in changing women's lives?

4. How did the Atlantic slave trade change gender ideology and the relationships between men and women in the Americas and in West Africa?

5. To what extent are the sexual stereotypes developed in response to racism present in your own culture today? What impact, if any, do they have on your own sense of identity?

BIBLIOGRAPHY

*indicates contains whole primary sources or secondary works containing substantial extracts.

GENERAL

Carrasco, David, ed. *Oxford Encyclopedia of Mesoamerican Cultures: The Civilizations of Mexico and Central America.* 3 vols. New York: Oxford University Press, 2001.

Crosby, Alfred. *The Columbian Exchange: Biological and Cultural Consequences of 1492.* Westport, CT: Praeger, 2003.

———. *Ecological Imperialism: The Ecological Expansion of Europe 900–1900.* Cambridge: Cambridge University Press, 2004.

———. *Germs, Seeds, and Animals: Studies in Ecological History.* Armonk, NY: M. E. Sharpe, 1994.

Keller, Rosemary Skinner, and Rosemary Radford Ruether, eds. *Encyclopedia of Women and Religion in North America.* Vols. 1–2. Bloomington: Indiana University Press, 2006.

Magner, Lois N. *A History of Medicine.* New York: Marcel Dekker, 1992.

McNeill, William H. *Plagues and People.* Garden City, NY: Anchor Press, 1976.

Sturtevant, William C., general ed. *Handbook of North American Indians.* 17 volumes. Washington, DC: Smithsonian Institution, for sale by the Government Printing Office, 1986.

Vivante, Bella, ed. *Women's Roles in Ancient Civilizations: A Reference Guide.* Westport, CT: Greenwood Press, 1999.

NATIVE AMERICANS

Anderson, Karen. *Chain Her by One Foot: The Subjugation of Native Women in New France.* New York: Routledge, 1993.

Devens, Carol. *Countering Colonization: Native American Women and the Great Lake Missions.* Berkeley: University of California Press, 1992.

Graymont, Barbara. *The Iroquois.* New York: Chelsea House, 1988.

*Landes, Ruth. *The Ojibwa Woman.* Lincoln: University of Nebraska Press, 1997.

*Lawn, Katherine E., and Claudio Salvucci, eds. *Women in New France: Extracts from the Jesuit Relations.* Bristol, PA: Evolution Publishers, 2005.

*Leon-Portilla, Miguel, ed. *The Broken Spears: The Aztec Account of the Conquest of Mexico.* Boston: Beacon Press, 1962.

Mann, Barbara Alice. *Iroquoisan Women: The Gantowisas.* New York: Peter Lang, 2000.

Pencak, William, and Daniel Richter, eds. *Friends and Enemies in Penn's Woods: Indians, Colonists, and the Racial Construction of Pennsylvania.* University Park: Pennsylvania University Press, 2004.

Perdue, Theda. *Cherokee Women: Gender and Culture Change, 1700–1835.* Lincoln: University of Nebraska Press, 1998.

Spittal, G., ed. *Iroquois Women: An Anthology.* Ontario, Canada: Iroqrafts Ltd., Iroquois Publications, 1990.

Steer, Diana. *Native American Women.* New York: Barnes and Noble Books, 1996.

SPANISH RULE

*Diaz, Bernal. *The Conquest of New Spain.* Translated by J. M. Cohen. Baltimore, MD: Penguin, 1963.

*Jesús, Ursala de. *The Souls of Purgatory: The Spiritual Diary of a Seventeenth Century Afro-Peruvian Mystic, Ursala de Jesús.* Translated by Nancy E. van Deusen. Albuquerque: University of New Mexico Press, 2004.

Lavrin, Asunción, ed. *Latin American Women: Historical Perspectives.* Westport, CT: Greenwood Press, 1978.

Meyer, Michael C., and William Breezely, eds. *The Oxford History of Mexico.* New York: Oxford University Press, 2000.

Navarro, Marisa, and Virgina Sanchez Korrol. *Women in Latin America and the Caribbean: Restoring Women to History.* Bloomington: University of Indiana Press, 1999.

Socolow, Susan. *The Women of Colonial Latin America.* New York: Cambridge University Press, 2000.

Stolcke, Verena. *Marriage, Class and Colour in Nineteenth Century Cuba: A Study of Racial Attitudes and Sexual Values in a Slave Society.* 2nd ed. Ann Arbor: University of Michigan Press, 1989. (First edition 1974; author's name was then Verena Martinez-Alier.)

Van Deusen, Nancy E. *The Sacred and the Worldly: The Institution and Cultural Practice of Recogimiento in Colonial Lima.* Stanford, CA: Stanford University Press, 2001.

Veira, Karen. *Women in the Crucible of Conquest: The Gendered Genesis of Spanish American Society.* Albuquerque: University of New Mexico Press, 2005.

IMPACT OF THE SLAVE TRADE

Bonlanle, Awe, ed. *Nigerian Women in Historical Perspective.* Lagos, Nigeria: Bookcraft, 1992.

Bush, Barbara. *Slave Women in Caribbean Society, 1650–1838.* Kingston, Jamaica: Heinemann, 1990.

Curtin, Philip D. *The Atlantic Slave Trade: A Census.* Madison: University of Wisconsin Press, 1969.

Hine, Darlene Clark, Wilma King, and Linda Reed, eds. *We Specialize in the Wholly Impossible: A Reader in Black Women's History.* Brooklyn, NY: Carlson Publications, 1995.

*Jacobs, Harriet. *Incidents in the Life of a Slave Girl.* New York: Oxford University Press, 1990.

McKissick, Patricia. *Nzingha: Warrior Queen of Angola.* New York: Scholastic Press, 2000. (Fiction)

Mvuyekure, Pierre-Damien. *West African Kingdoms 500–1590.* Detroit, MI: Gale Group, 2004.

Ogunyemi, Wale. *Queen Amina of Zazzau.* Ibada, Nigeria: University Press, 1994.

*Prince, Mary. *The History of Mary Prince, A West Indian Slave. Related by Herself. With a Supplement by the Editor. To Which Is Added, the Narrative of Asa-Asa, a Captured African.* Electronic Edition. From series, *Documenting the American South.* Chapel Hill: University of North Carolina Chapel Hill. http://docsouth.unc.edu/neh/prince/prince.html

Shepherd, Verene, ed. *Women in Caribbean History: The British-Colonized Territories.* Princeton, NJ: Markus Wiener, 1999.

Shepherd, Verene, and Hilary M. Beckles, eds. *Caribbean Slavery in the Atlantic World: A Student Reader.* Princeton, NJ: Markus Wiener, 2000.

Spruill, Julia Cherry. *Women's Life and Work in the Southern Colonies.* New York: Norton, 1972. (Reprint of 1938 edition.)

Walvin, James. *Atlas of Slavery.* Harlow, England: Pearson, 2000.

White, Deborah Gray. *Ar'n't I a Woman? Female Slaves in the Plantation South.* New York: Norton, 1985.

AUDIO-VISUAL RESOURCES:

Columbus and the Age of Discovery. 7 parts. Princeton, NJ: Films for the Humanities and Sciences, 1991.

Gates, Henry Louis, Jr. "The Slave Kingdoms," "The Road to Timbuktu." *Wonders of the African World.* VHS. Alexandria, VA: PBS Home Video, 1999.

Hall, Stuart. "Iron in the Soul." *Portrait of the Caribbean.* VHS. New York: Ambrose Video, 1992.

Shako:wi Cultural Center at the Oneida Indian Nation. http://oneida-nation.net/culture/index.html

Woods, Michael. *The Conquistadors.* VHS. Alexandria, VA: PBS Home Video, 2001.

PART TWO

NEW PATTERNS OF WORK AND POLITICAL INVOLVEMENT IN THE LONG NINETEENTH CENTURY

The nineteenth century began a long era of economic expansion and political turmoil. Starting in Europe and the Americas, a series of political revolutions resulted in the development of three powerful new ideologies that would undergird political movements throughout the nineteenth and twentieth centuries. At the same time, the Industrial Revolution turned labor relations, family organization, and world trade upside down. The Industrial Revolution also helped drive a sudden expansion of Western imperialism. Chapter Four tells the story of these developments as they occurred in Western countries, describing the Industrial Revolution, the development of new political ideologies, and the women's organizations that formed in independent countries. Chapter Five recounts their continuation in the colonial world, including their effect on the white women who traveled there. Two examples—British India and Zimbabwe—give some idea of the scope of research on women in the European empires. Chapter Five also examines the Sokoto Caliphate, a Muslim empire in what is now northern Nigeria that transformed the physical, economic, and gender landscapes of a portion of the Sudan as big as Western Europe.

Both chapters devote considerable space to a particular aspect of women's response to the economic, political, and cultural upheavals of the era: the creation of women's organizations, women's movements, and, indeed, First-Wave Feminism.

CHAPTER FOUR

INDUSTRIALIZATION, ACTIVISM, AND IDEOLOGIES OF PROGRESS, 1780–1930

Chapters Two and Three examined the ways colonization in the New World and the increasing wealth of governments affected women around the world. We saw the profound impact of the slave trade on women throughout the Atlantic and discovered that leaders of powerful, wealthy states of the seventeenth and eighteenth centuries rarely chose to use their power to increase women's opportunity. The nineteenth century would be very different because of three major developments.

The first of these, the Industrial Revolution, began in the 1750s with the first uses of hand cranks, water mills, and steam power for textile production. Industrialization spread over the world. By 1914 few parts of the world would be untouched by railroads, steamboats, telegraph, and printing presses. The Industrial Revolution forced profound changes in the division of labor inside and outside the home. New ideals of domestic life and fervent religiosity arose as people in the regions most affected adapted to the new realities.

Second, from the American Revolution (1776–1781) to the European Revolutions of 1848, European countries and their Atlantic colonies were wracked by revolutions, wars of independence, and popular uprisings demanding greater political power for the common man. (Except for a brief moment in the French Revolution, the common woman's right to political participation was ignored.) Three major political ideologies emerged from these struggles—Liberalism, Socialism, and Nationalism—and have remained at the heart of political movements ever since.

Third, technological and economic advances led to an intensified control of colonies and a new wave of imperialist expansion. As had happened in the Renaissance, the Industrial Revolution included the development of more sophisticated military and naval technologies. Faced with their capitalist economies' need for constant expansion and the loss of many Atlantic territories, the nineteenth-century industrial powers renewed their process of conquest and imperialism. Africa, Australia, the Pacific Islands, and most of India became parts of landed empires, and regions in Central and Southeast Asia that had been appropriated in earlier centuries experienced intensified control. The racist ideologies developed in the Atlantic World traveled with imperial powers. The new biological sciences of the period seemed to legitimize racism and sexism. The concept of Social Darwinism emerged from this combination of imperialism, racism, and misunderstood science. Social Darwinism argued in essence that any one person or group that was weak enough to be exploited must be biologically inferior—less fit. The strongest individuals and the strongest societies would inevitably be the ones most likely to survive, and this was considered desirable. Thus, Social Darwinism explained that differences in economic and political standing were simply products of a natural evolutionary process in which it was foolish to interfere.

Women involved themselves in and got caught up in industrialization, revolutionary ideologies, imperialism, and Social Darwinism. But they also had their own agendas. During the nineteenth century, women began to form political, social, educational, and cultural organizations on their own, to serve agendas of their own. New technologies and new access to education made it easier for women to form regional, national, and even international connections. Women found themselves increasingly able to have a voice in communal, national, and foreign affairs, and as they organized they began to have leverage to influence decisions.

INDUSTRIALIZATION AS WOMEN'S WORK

The economic changes that accompanied the Industrial Revolution transformed the lives of women and their families in the nineteenth century. Just as the presence of the fur trade in North America had turned Ojibway women's productive work upside down and given Iroquois women an opportunity to expand their authority within the family, the Industrial Revolution caused women to reorganize their families, develop new gender ideology, and imagine themselves capable of transforming the world. The industrial era conjures contrasting visions: on the one hand, glorious labor-saving devices that liberated humans from untold drudgery, and on the other the low and insecure wages, job losses among artisans, savagely long work days, and terrible pollution that accompanied the early period. The Industrial Revolution generated enormous wealth, not just in Britain but in every major industrial country that followed, and much of that wealth went into the pockets of ordinary people or into public buildings and amenities like schools, libraries, parks, roads, railroads, sewers, and running water. The blessings of industrialization did not arrive overnight and were accompanied by severe economic and social problems. They all happened within a few generations, so that nineteenth-century people lived in a world of rapid change. These changes were uncomfortable for most people, but they also led to a world where people believed change was normal, inevitable, and manageable. By the late nineteenth century, even the most conservative and traditional people in industrialized societies were interested in retaining only certain aspects of tradition and were perfectly willing to throw out others.

From the perspective of women's history, one of the most interesting aspects of the early Industrial Revolution was that it happened first in a sector of the economy—textile production—that women dominated in most cultural areas. Even in its earliest stages in any given world region, industrialization therefore had immediate consequences for women's productive labor and for their daily lives. Early industrial manufacturing employed women in greater numbers than men, particularly for low-skill and unskilled labor. It also expanded women's participation in low-wage manual labor. Textile production was and is particularly likely to employ girls and young women in temporary, seasonal, or entry-level positions for the lowest pay in the industry. This has had widely differing affects on local, regional, and national economies depending on the infrastructure and cultural expectations in place at the time of industrialization and on the goals of local governments with respect to manufacturing.

An important aspect of industrialization was that it forced peoples to redefine the accepted, traditional roles of wives and husbands. Earlier, most production could be done in the household. Factories employed people by putting out work to families: People assembled products or parts of products in their own homes, whether using materials supplied by the factory, materials the workers themselves purchased, or a combination of both. From our vantage point, the importance of this system is that it imposed relatively little change in family and household relations. It created a kind of work for pay that could be fitted in around the time devoted to other tasks in the household, and it could be done by one or all family members together, so that it did not have to disrupt work relationships within the family. As industrialization spread, more and more people got most of their income from the work they did for the factory, so that the work was not so much squeezed in around other productive activities but became the main household activity. Putting out would be an important feature of work in every country's early industrial era. However, full-time manufacturing labor (work performed inside a manufacturing plant instead of put out to workers in their own homes) eventually replaced most putting-out work.

This meant either that whole families had to work together (to make sure the children were watched), or one parent (always imagined as the mother) had to stay home with their children, or that the parents had to have some kind of day care available. The solution European labor movements strove for was to have mothers stay at home with the children while men worked full-time for wages sufficient to support the family. Work space, wages, and the public arena became associated with men (at least ideally), while the home, housework, child care, and voluntarism became associated with women and with leisure. Only paid work was considered productive. (In Chapter Five we will see that manufacturers and male laborers outside the West assumed similar ideals should apply in their own industries.) Of course, few ordinary couples could survive without the wife working. As a result, women who engaged in industrial labor almost always did so as an addition to the work responsibilities they had within the family. Since women earned much less money than men, they could not support themselves, let alone their families, by industrial work.

ENGLAND, 1750–1850

The Industrial Revolution began in rural England with the invention of devices that could replace repetitive labor normally done by women. The very first labor-saving device was meant to be operated by a child. The spinning jenny (patented in 1770) made it possible for the wielder to spin multiple threads of cotton at a time instead of only one. The worker cranked a horizontal wheel built too low for an adult to use comfortably for any length of time. Most inventors of early manufacturing devices intended women or children to work with them. When they applied for patents on new equipment, inventors often explained how the devices were particularly suited for women or children to use. Even though men worked in all sorts of fields that required fine motor skills—jewelry and watch making, for instance—manufacturers believed that women and girls were better suited to working with machines because they had smaller hands and fingers. Because the government was concerned about rising unemployment among men and the household poverty it caused, manufacturers also pointed out that the jobs they gave women and children—which did not pay enough to attract large numbers of men—would help keep families out of the poorhouse. The sexist assumptions early manufacturers brought to their hiring policies traveled with industrialization across the world. The conceptualization of male work as public and female work as private reached its first full development in Britain.[1]

Women made up the majority of British industrial workers before the mid-nineteenth century, because most of those jobs were originally intended for women and children. Manufacturing jobs attracted women because the pay was higher than for other women workers' jobs. Of course, women received much less than men for any individual manufacturing job (keeping in mind that the lowest-paying tasks were always done by women and children), but when the industries were young, women often made close to as much as a male agricultural laborer, and sometimes much more. Thus, from a woman's perspective, these were high-paying jobs, at least for a time. Even these jobs did not pay enough to support a family entirely, but they provided reliable supplemental family income. British women entered the wage labor market partly because men's real wages (as measured against inflation) were at best stable and at worst declining until 1820, while demand for consumer goods climbed in every family. Families needed the income wives and children could earn, even if their wages were lower than men's and even if they were inconsistent. For instance, in Corfe Castle, men's wages stayed the same throughout the seventeenth and eighteenth centuries. But family wealth had increased by the end of the eighteenth century, probably because of the work women and children were doing as spinners of flax and embroiderers of muslin.

Of course, women were not suddenly entering the paid labor force for the first time, nor did manufacturers necessarily increase the total number of paid jobs for women. In fact, women probably lost access to income-earning opportunities, because most labor-saving devices replaced jobs women had done. The first spinning jenny replaced 10 workers for every worker it employed. The framework loom displaced hand knitters; the power loom displaced weavers. The new textile plants hired women to do new tasks, but they employed fewer women than had been employed before.[2]

Over time industrialization made Britain wealthier, and British women's daily lives became much easier. Even poor families owned multiple sets of clothing for each member and partook of luxury goods like tea, coffee, and sugar. Standards for sanitation, health care, and diet improved, and the increasing success of Liberal and Socialist political action gave more and more families a political voice, public education, workforce protection, and pensions. To what degree the increased material comfort of individual citizens resulted from increased production (rather than from the exploitation of the labor and resources of weaker countries) is a matter of heated debate among world historians and economists. What *is* certain is that the patterns established in early industrial Britain repeated themselves in other countries in later decades as industrialization spread.

RUSSIA, 1850–1930

Russia was very nearly the last region of Europe to industrialize and therefore provides a good contrast to England. Despite many decades of government pressure and resources poured into creating an industrial infrastructure, most Russians continued to live in rural areas and work in agriculture until the 1960s. Nevertheless, industrialization had important consequences for both sexes, especially for peasants. Russia was neither industrialized nor a major center of capitalist growth in the nineteenth century. The region has a short growing season, making its farmland less productive. It was a poor country by any standard. Birth rates and child mortality were very high, and so far as we can tell most peasants (called *serfs* in Russia) were malnourished. Aleksandr Nikitenko (one of very few serfs to have published an autobiography), for instance, writes that his mother routinely chose to go hungry in order to give her children enough to eat—and his family was relatively prosperous. Although it freed them to travel, marry, and take jobs without getting permission from an owner, the emancipation of the serfs in 1861 did little for women's material welfare in the short term. In the long term, changes in military conscription helped all women. Before War Minister Dmitry Milyutin reformed the military in 1874, peasant men could be drafted for decades at a time. Soldiers' wives had been treated as if they had become widows, because they might never see their husbands again. After the reforms, all Russian men had a duty to serve at least one term in the military. Because this greatly enlarged the field of conscripts, soldiers served much shorter terms, and conscripts were likely to return home eventually.[3]

Unlike in Britain, in Russia men made up the majority of industrial workers. Because farms were often not productive enough to feed everyone in the family, and because families needed cash to pay taxes, they sent their young men out to work for wages. Russian factories, located in and around large cities, imported male workers from the countryside. Toward the end of the nineteenth century, it was clear that men could make better wages working in the city or in the factory than they could make as profits from farming, so many peasant men chose to leave the country altogether. Factory workers' wives would then live with their parents-in-law while their husbands worked far away. Daughters-in-law were vulnerable to economic and sexual exploitation by their husbands' families and, without their husbands to protect them, could find themselves expelled from their in-laws' household. They could also find that the work they did in the family counted for nothing, and that there was no place for them back in their own parents' or brothers' home. In short, for Russian women it might be almost as bad to have a husband go to the city to work in a factory as it was to have him drafted before the 1874 reform. Worse, the hardship a factory wife endured was not socially recognized, as it was for a soldier's wife.

Even if they traveled to the city to work, peasant men did not give up the family interest in farming, which was the source of their respectability and identity. Instead, we find increasing reports from observers and government officials that peasant women took on the responsibility for *all* their husbands' farming, not just for the household garden plot or for helping out at peak periods of harvest. Although it was always rare for women to plow fields without men, it was increasingly common for them to do everything else. The hard manual labor of farming—sowing, thinning, and weeding crops (much of which was done by hand as late as the early 1990s)—became more and more a woman's task.

Women were not excluded from industrialization, however. Although putting-out manufacturing declined rapidly in Britain, it continued to be an important part of the industrial economies of many other world regions, including Russia. In Russian provinces and localities where nearby factories existed, they put out work to peasant women. Like women in other regions, Russians found it difficult to leave home for an entire day, but could do wage work if it could be accomplished within their homes. Women did small-craft production and assembly from their homes, the work pieced in around the other responsibilities they had to accomplish. At first putting-out tasks required skilled workers: Women made lace, or gloves, or other finished goods requiring multiple steps. As industrialization progressed, there was less and less need for such skilled labor and more for very simple, highly repetitive tasks. One major area of women's low-skill work was making cigars. The task involved cutting, gluing, and shaping a cardboard roll and then filling it. There were machines that could do this task, but Russian peasant women (like their Ottoman contemporaries) worked so cheaply that for a long time it was cost-effective to have cigars assembled by hand. Such piecework was not only monotonous, but it also frequently led to carpal tunnel syndrome and arthritis because it required fine motor skills and repetitive motion.

The general pattern established in the late nineteenth century—with men working in factories, and women doing most of the farming and the unskilled manual labor of production—persisted until the late twentieth century. Russian farmers did almost all their work by hand, and most of it was done by women. High-paying skilled manufacturing and supervisory jobs went to men; repetitive low-skill, heavy manual labor in industries would be done by women. Neither two world wars, nor the imposition of a socialist economy, nor the introduction of mechanized farming changed this dynamic. The Russian pattern is especially interesting because it has been repeated in other agricultural economies in the twentieth century. Industrialization in Africa and India, for example, has also sent men far from home as migrant workers and left women to farm family plots still owned by the men in their families. In regions where women hold few full-time manufacturing or day labor positions, they often remain subsistence farmers—the primary producers of food for their households.

MEIJI JAPAN, 1870–1930

Japan's industrial revolution, which occurred at about the same time as Russia's, is one of the most famous in world history, and Japanese women made up the majority of industrial workers. The Tokugawa Shogunate came to an abrupt end shortly after American Matthew "Commodore" Perry brought a steamboat armed with artillery into Urage Harbor in 1853. Considerable political upheaval followed and, when Emperor Kumei died in 1867, the Tokugawa Shogunate was replaced with a monarchy headed by his successor, Tenno—who immediately embarked on a policy of rapid Westernization. Rejecting the isolationist policies of the Tokugawa, which he and much of the intelligentsia blamed for the country's inferior technology, he abolished the old feudal system and over the course of the next 20 years turned Japan into a constitutional monarchy with a representational legislature. Japan's new leadership embarked on a vigorous program of international activity, modernization, and conquest, following the models of Germany and England.[4]

Meiji Japan was successful at transforming the economy without losing any of its national identity or working against any cherished Japanese values—or so it seemed to outsiders, and so the government proclaimed. Japan inspired countries who wanted to become militarily and economically competitive with Europe, but who were afraid that copying European industry would cost them important aspects of their own culture. Japan seemed to have the best of both worlds—a modern, industrial economy; prosperity; a talent for borrowing only what it found valuable; and the creativity to transform those borrowings to make them more Japanese than foreign. The image of Meiji Japan as a sort of international version of the self-made man, pulling himself up by his bootstraps with nothing but luck and pluck contains a lot of truth. Meiji Japan became a major industrial and military power; its schools educated most of its male citizens and a large number of the girls; its colleges and universities attracted international students from all over Asia and Africa; and its artists and intellectuals were powerful influences on their contemporaries on the other side of the world.

Statistics for Japanese industry are available only from the late nineteenth century forward, but stories told by industrial workers are strikingly similar to those of workers in British industries during the first half of the nineteenth century. Mine laborers worked in constant danger and heat, under ceilings too low to allow standing upright. The women mine workers pulled heavy loads up steep slopes and maneuvered them slowly down, rising hours before dawn to bring children to day care before work and wondering from day to day if this would be the last time they lived to return to their children.

As in Britain, it was in textiles that women's work was the most important. Japan's textile industry was their first modern industry to produce a large profit and was the engine of Japan's later economic growth. The vast majority of textile workers were women—roughly 80 percent in the early part of the century (see Figure 4.1). Some of the first workers came from upper-class families, who sent their daughters to the mills because they and the government wanted to set an example for the Japanese people. Eiko Wada, one of these early volunteers, said that she joined the factory workers out of a sense of duty and a desire to learn skills that would be of service to her country. However, she earned only the tiniest sums of money—from 1.25 to 3 percent of the wages of the handful of European women who had been brought to the factories to model good industrial work habits for their Japanese colleagues. The European male supervisors earned 300 to 600 times as much as she did.[5]

Soon, however, workers were recruited from poor families. Jobbers would travel from village to village, recruiting girls by making contracts with their parents, who received a lump sum the girls would have to pay

FIGURE 4.1   TOMIOKA SILK FACTORY

The Tomioka silk factory, established in the 1870s, was one of Japan's first textile factories. The managers are all men. In what ways does the organization of space in the factory and the postures of the people in it indicate who the more powerful people are? In what ways would the floor managers' experiences be different from the workers'?

off through work before receiving any more wages (contemporary Southeast Asian prostitutes are recruited the same way). A worker therefore might not make any money at all in her first year or two of employment. The girls lived in dormitories owned by the factory, where they worked at least 12 hours a day and frequently 17 or 18 hours. The factory provided food (an important benefit during the Depression of the 1930s), a roof over their heads, and a little personal space. But the dormitories were often unheated, and the girls still had to do all their own washing in addition to personal toiletries. Because the girls had been sold to the factory, they were easily victimized. Sexual harassment and rape were common, and working conditions were dirty and dangerous.

The poorly ventilated, moist air of the plants and the close living conditions led to the rapid spread of disease. The textiles produced dust and fiber that floated in the air and nested in the lungs just like coal dust, leading to long-term health problems, and like all textile factories the buildings were prone to fire. Girls sometimes ran away, but the police would bring them back and punish them. Some committed suicide, although neither the government nor the industry kept records of names and numbers. The work was so unpopular and dangerous that the average worker stayed only two years, indicating that those who survived generally left as soon as they had recouped the price of their original contract. This high turnover meant not only that a very large number of women worked in manufacturing for part of their lives, but also that they were rarely together long enough to organize. Nevertheless, they did lead a number of strikes. As in the United States and England, the first strike in Japan was led by women workers: At the Amamiya silk mills in 1886, the women succeeded in preventing the addition of 30 more minutes to their work day.

Most of these workers came from peasant families and, on their return home, would work on small family plots and also take whatever manual day labor jobs they could get locally. This represented a firm rejection of factory labor, since farm life was very difficult. Japanese farms, especially rice farms, were among the last in the world to mechanize (the tools were not invented until the 1950s), and few farm families could support themselves on farming alone. Successive governments invested heavily in developing an infrastructure of roads, railroads, waterways, electricity, and plumbing. Rural women considered themselves fortunate to land part-time, seasonal, or long-term employment in these projects, combining outside work with their duties as farmworkers, as mothers, and as wives to support their families.

In the late twentieth century the Japanese government would subsidize farming heavily; but prior to that, rural life in industrial Japan looked similar to that in the industrial economies in much of Southeast Asia,

Central America, and North America. In all these regions, many rural families retain their sense of continuity and prestige through attachment to parcels of farmland which do not, in fact, provide enough income to support a family. Members of farm families hire themselves out to local business or industry or send members out to low-skill, seasonal manual or migrant labor. Girls and women float in and out of the lowest-skill jobs; men hold most of the scarce long-term, full-time jobs and all but a few supervisory positions. This division of labor holds roughly true even among the relatively affluent farm families of North America, where the main distinction is that jobs outside the farm are usually of a higher quality than those available in Central America, India, and Southeast Asia.[6]

POLITICS

Rapid economic change accompanied rapid political change. During the late eighteenth and early nineteenth centuries, Europe suffered cataclysmic military and political upheaval and was divided over what direction modernization should take. At the end of the eighteenth century, the United States had wrested independence from Great Britain and created a new kind of state—one without a ruler or a national religion, where all the free, adult, property-holding male citizens exercised collective sovereignty. Shortly afterward, the French Revolution created, for a short time, the first European state where every adult male could vote for representatives to a national legislature, called the National Convention. The lands of aristocrats were redistributed to the peasants who had farmed them; price controls were set on such necessities as bread; and crowds in the streets of Paris set the tone of popular opinion in the minds of legislators. As the countries surrounding France threatened invasion, the fragile new government succumbed to the temptations of tyranny, encouraging citizens to spy on one another to root out traitors and treating any political opposition as treason.

As the invading armies of Austria entered France in April of 1792, accusation and counter-accusation became a bloodbath, and in a military coup of international significance, the French army marched into Paris to install a military dictatorship. The entire healthy male population became eligible for the draft, and for the first time in European history were often eager to fight for the new France. The new military dictatorship, headed by Napoleon Bonaparte, turned the energies of the revolution outward into the conquest of all their neighboring countries. In addition to the terrible bloodshed and destruction caused by many years of war, the new government made long-lasting changes in the laws of every country the French invaded. They introduced the metric system; put peasants, nobles, and tradesmen alike on the same legal footing; created civil service exami-nations; and (at least officially) based promotions in government offices and in the military on merit. Thus, even as Napoleon had himself declared emperor and installed his relatives as the new royal families of the coun-tries his armies conquered, he habituated a generation of Europeans to thinking and acting as if, at least in government service, all men were cre-ated equal. Napoleon also rewrote the family laws of Europe, introducing one code throughout France, Belgium, the Netherlands, Spain, and Italy. He increased the power of husbands over wives, diminished the property rights of women in marriage, and decreased the authority of fathers over their adult sons. Whether this improved the lives of women depended on what the previous legal systems had been. In Italy the new laws pro-vided more protection for some women; in the Netherlands they dimin-ished almost all women's property rights, whether they were single or married.

Haiti, Brazil, and Spanish Latin America had likewise succeeded in securing independence by the end of the 1820s. In the most successful of all slave revolts, the Haitian slave population rose simultaneously in 1791, fought successfully in traditional battles and guerrilla action, overthrew the plantation owners and the government, and installed a new govern-ment of their own. The Haitian constitution, the most radical of this era, declared not only that all adult men were free citizens, but also that any-one standing on Haitian soil, no matter how they arrived there, was a free person. They dealt with the long Caribbean history of grading legal rights along a continuum of skin colors and privileging lighter skin colors by declaring that not only all Haitians but also anyone standing on Haitian soil was black. The Spanish colonies of Central America went next, secur-ing themselves independence under the leadership of Simon Bolivar.

Three political ideologies forged in these conflicts would dominate nineteenth- and twentieth-century world politics: Liberalism, Socialism, and Nationalism. All three shared similar gender ideology, which had been built in the Industrial Revolution and continued under industrial-ization and imperialism. The stereotype that middle-class, elite, white women were all more chaste, moral, intelligent, and asexually lovely than working-class or darker-skinned women traveled with Westernization— as did the stereotype that working-class and darker-skinned men were unreliable, lazy, foolish, promiscuous, prone to violence, and incapable of supporting their families. Sexual divisions of labor in manufacturing would add to this the idea that virtuous wives and mothers stayed in the private home caring for children, cooking, sewing, cleaning, and doing charitable work while their husbands fought for wages in the brutal com-mercial and political world. A good husband was one whose wife did not have to work for pay; a good wife was one who stretched her husband's income as far as possible and devoted herself wholeheartedly to his and their children's comfort and spiritual welfare.

LIBERALISM

Liberalism's origins lay in seventeenth-century England, where Thomas Hobbes and John Locke had articulated the idea that political sovereignty was based not on divine right but on the implied consent of the governed. Later the American Revolution built a society on the principle that sovereignty rested in the citizenry. Men, it was thought, should be equal before the law, independent in their own households, and free from the authority of their fathers. Liberalism disapproved of any government interference in the economy, feeling that most government regulation served only to make goods more expensive, diminish competition, and stifle innovation. Over time Liberalism's vision of citizen sovereignty expanded to include the right to vote for all free adult males, support for the abolition of slavery and serfdom, and universal public education—because only education permitted male adults to compete on an equal footing in public life. Female suffrage (the right to vote) was considered too radical by most Liberals until the twentieth century. However, nineteenth-century equal rights feminists often supported Liberal political parties anyway. Believing as they did that public education was the best vehicle for putting men on equal footing and accepting the principle that women should be the spiritual and cultural educators of young children, Liberals often supported the education of girls and women. The more widespread Liberal ideas were in any country, the more popular education for girls and women would be.

SOCIALISM

Socialism experienced its first political growth in middle phases of the French Revolution, but it began with several early nineteenth-century movements that attempted to create Utopian societies. Robert Owen instituted the most famous and successful of these. Owen envisioned a society without distinctions of class or race, where women had an equal voice in decision making. He created a small experimental society in Lanarkshire, Scotland, based on these principles, and many later British socialists borrowed from his ideas. Elsewhere, beginning in 1838, English workers banded together to form the Chartist movement, which petitioned Parliament three times for changes in the government. They sought to create working-class representation in the British Parliament by giving Parliamentary posts a salary and a secret ballot, among other things. When

Chartism and other similar labor movements in Europe were cut down, with demonstrators killed and injured in the streets by armed soldiers, there were a series of revolutions in 1848. Some achieved temporary success (notably, in France); others failed. These movements were put down just as brutally, which radicalized labor movements, turning them into political parties where it was legal for them to organize and into underground resistance organizations where political opposition was made illegal.

Socialism differed from Liberalism in that it valued the welfare of the group over the individual and wanted governments to take an active role in protecting the welfare of workers. Socialists were suspicious of distinctions based on class or wealth and generally wanted to eliminate class differences, and they gradually became more and more willing to take radical or even violent action to promote their views. Socialism was an international movement; on the ideological level, it sought to improve the lives of all workers everywhere. On the practical level, some governments forbade political organization and/or labor organization, so that frontline activists worked in constant danger of arrest and imprisonment. To exist with any continuity, Socialist parties in such countries had to become international organizations, keeping some of their leadership and communication apparatus in countries where their activities were legal and outside the most dangerous regions. The most successful Socialist Party came to be the Communists, whose supporters were followers of Karl Marx and Friedrich Engels. Increasingly organized, the Communists eventually merged and internationalized the major Socialist parties of Europe and the Americas, forming the Second International Socialist Party in 1889. Marx and Engels had a vision of how to accomplish the Socialist vision of equality, and they built a systematic intellectual framework and political program to support it. They believed industrial capitalism would inevitably lead to economic revolutions in every nation. Industrial workers would seize control of factories and machines and take over production on their own, without capitalists, individual owners, corporations, or merchants to tell them how to do things. Because they believed industrialization was the road to "Progress" (always capitalized in the nineteenth-century imagination), Socialists considered industrial workers the most economically progressive part of the economy. Socialists therefore campaigned primarily among the industrial working class and were very influential in the labor movement, even though most full-time activists came from middle-class and propertied backgrounds. The most fervent Socialists believed their goal was not only possible but also (because of the natural progress of history) inevitable, so their followers needed only to hasten the process through labor organization, political agitation, and popular revolution. They prized the collective good of workers more than profit and distrusted business leaders, who their experience told them were rarely willing to raise wages, improve safety conditions, or accept worker criticism without collective bargaining to strengthen workers' voices.

Socialists, like Liberals, shared a view of women as naturally maternal and supportive of men, bound by ties of love to the home. Although Socialist Party platforms rejected stereotypes of class, race, and sex, it was impossible for party members as individuals to overcome the prejudices they had been raised with and remained surrounded by. Socialist parties would therefore recruit chiefly men, promote men to positions of leadership, and extend political and material support for working class men's issues.

It is possible to argue women's influence in workers movements declined as Socialists became more organized. In England, the United States, and Japan, the first industrial strikes were held in textile factories, and the strikers were the young women employees. As industrial labor movements became widespread, regional in scope, and dominated by men, their activities came to be dominated by the interests of male workers. Socialists would campaign to keep women and children out of dangerous work, to limit women's work hours, and even sometimes to protect women from sexual harassment, but they had little interest in raising women's wages and none at all in making it possible for women to compete with men for paid labor.

Socialist movements within a country sometimes supported women suffrage, at least in official statements, but rarely devoted political muscle to it. They (and male labor activists in general) were more interested in preserving the dignity of the male worker and making it possible for him to earn a living wage—one large enough to support a family. Obviously, success in this area would also benefit many women: Nineteenth-century married women very often preferred not to work outside the home if they could avoid it, not least because (having no legal access to birth control, and in most cases no information about it) they typically had many children. However, widowed, divorced, never-married, and abandoned women made up a significant share of most industrial workforces. The woman who had to support herself and her children on paid wages was poorly served by nineteenth century Socialism. On the other hand, Socialism promised, and its adherents believed, that the end of economic inequality would bring the end of male domination. They welcomed women activists into positions of serious responsibility and encouraged their participation in discussions of policy. Women intellectuals with a radical bent therefore frequently worked as Socialists and were significant to the rank-and-file membership.[7]

NATIONALISM

Nationalism as an ideology was first articulated by Johann Gottfried Herder, a linguist, literature scholar, and Protestant pastor, who thought of culture not just as an invention of the human mind but also as a result of human interactions with their environment and their neighbors. He thought any one nationality or people (*Volk*) expressed its particular worldview and deepest self through its legends, poetry, and folklore. As a Christian minister, he thought all people were equal at the level of the soul—but he believed living and working in a particular climate, environment, and system of social interactions shaped the soul and the body. A volk shared language, religions, cultural assumptions—a worldview. They were nations, not just collections of people with some things in common, and nations had collective identities, memories, responsibilities, and contributions. They belonged to certain landscapes, too, and had a certain independent value and right to autonomy. Herder developed and published this notion of the volk at the turn of the eighteenth century, just as French armies were invading the rest of Europe. Nationalism seemed to provide an explanation not only of how the French could be so successful as conquerors: The entire nation was working toward one goal that all desired, rather than working for one monarch. It also explained why it was wrong for the French to continue to maintain their control over peoples with whom they had little cultural connection. Indeed, Nationalism justified the separatist longings of Central Europe, the Balkans, Italy, and Sicily, where foreign kingdoms and empires had lorded it over the local people for centuries.

Nationalism was never an exclusive political loyalty. It usually conflicted with Socialism, which saw itself by necessity as an international movement, but Nationalists could be flexible and could attach to Liberal political parties or bastions of conservatism. In some ways, Nationalism could be hard to distinguish from simple patriotism or pride in one's own country. What distinguished Nationalism from Liberalism was that the Nationalist set the collective good of the nation ahead of individual liberty or economic progress. It was more important for the people as a whole to be free of foreign influence and make their own decisions than for individuals of the nation to have a say in the government. Nationalist movements were strongest in regions where both national and individual liberties were stifled, such as the Habsburg and Ottoman empires. Czechs, Slovenians, Serbs, and Greeks could all perceive that they were oppressed both as a cultural group (they were ruled by foreigners, government officials spoke a foreign language, and their own traditions were considered barbaric) and as individuals (they were treated as second-class citizens, even if they acculturated to their foreign rulers).

Nationalists, like Liberals and Socialists, held conservative ideas about women. On the other hand, they typically glorified what they saw as traditional motherhood and traditional religious values. Nationalists saw women as mothers of the nation and believed that, as poet William Ross Wallace (1819–1881) put it, "the hand that rocks the cradle is the hand that rules the world."[8] They supported enough education for women so that they could teach traditional values. They also supported religious institutions, and this probably contributed to their appeal for women. Especially outside the English-speaking world and throughout the nineteenth century, Liberalism and Socialism became increasingly hostile toward organized religion. Many nineteenth-century women, however, were very religious. This is hardly surprising, since the mainstream ideology of the day expected women to act as the moral and spiritual center of the household. Liberal and Socialist political parties often referred to organized religion, particularly Catholicism and Christian Orthodoxy, as superstition, and to highly religious people as ignorant and foolish. Thus women, who were more likely to be highly religious than men, were also more likely to reject Liberalism and Socialism in favor of more conservative political parties that supported their religious views.

Activist Women and First-Wave Feminism

Women did not only work in industries and raise children. They thought about the world around them and sought to make it better. Increasing opportunities for education meant that more women had the intellectual tools to reflect on their own and the world's condition. The increasing size of the middle class in industrializing societies meant that more of these educated women had enough relative leisure to work for change. The entrance of women into factory labor gave many a new consciousness of their role as members of the working class and motivated them to join and start labor movements. Women's experiences under colonization taught them to see themselves as citizens of oppressed nations, and many entered into Nationalist politics on behalf of their beleaguered people. Women joined movements run by men, started their own movements, and established women's auxiliaries to existing organizations. Even where they did not organize directly on behalf of women, as participants in political and social movements they often pointed out women's particular needs and interests.

AMERICAN AND BRITISH ACTIVISM

The first formal feminist movements began in England and the United States as outgrowths of earlier political and social movements. They did not call themselves feminists—this word was invented by French activists several decades later and was re-invigorated during the early Second-Wave movements of the late 1960s and 1970s. American women entered the political arena during the Revolutionary War (1776–1781). In addition to running farms and businesses while the men and the family were away at war, a few women like Deborah Sampson and Sally St. Clair joined the Revolutionary army as soldiers. Larger numbers served as paid nurses and matrons, as scouts, as washerwomen, and in other supporting auxiliaries. Most famous of all were women like Molly Pitcher (probably Mary Ludwig Hayes; d. approx. 1822) who, like many women, carried water to soldiers on the front line. At the Battle of Monmouth in 1778, she took over cooling, loading, and reloading a cannon. Far more women supported the American Revolution by fundraising and by boycotting sugar, tea, linen, silk, paper, and glass. U.S. women remained politically engaged and active after the Revolution was over, joining wholeheartedly in the three social and political movements of the late eighteenth and early nineteenth century: the abolition of slavery in the United States, the anti-alcohol temperance movement, and the religious movement called the Second Great Awakening (ca. 1820s to ca. 1900), which was in fact the catalyst for the other two movements. Political activity by and among women gradually became normalized in the United States, so that by the 1830s several of the most important leaders in the abolition movement were women: Angelina and Sarah Grimke, Abigail Kelley Foster, and Maria Miller Stewart were all well-known activists. Abolition and temperance activists often enjoyed strong support from institutional religion (Congregationalists, Quakers, Methodists, and Unitarians all had congregations supporting either or both movements).[9]

The intellectual mother of Anglo-American feminism was an Englishwoman, Mary Wollstonecraft (1759–1797). Although British progressives knew of her and her ideas, they avoided publicly recognizing her contribution until the twentieth century. Living in France at the height of the French Revolution, she had written *A Vindication of the Rights of Man* and her most influential work, *A Vindication of the Rights of Woman,* in which she argued in favor of a high-quality education for women. Since so many women became widows or lived years of their adult lives single, she argued, they should learn to reason through problems and acquire the vocational skills to support a family. In her novel *Maria, or the Wrongs of Women* and her published correspondence from Sweden, she pointed to the difficulties poor women had earning a living even if they did marry and how terribly women could suffer if their husbands had bad tempers, poor judgment, addictions, or a debilitating illness. As a young woman, Wollstonecraft herself had been abandoned by the father (Gilbert Imlay) of her first child, Fanny. She later married William Godwin, who became the father of her second child, Mary (the author of *Frankenstein*). Because her private life was known, critics grafted her reputation as a loose woman to all her works. Yet her ideas were the backbone of the nineteenth-century equal rights movements in Britain and the United States, and the correspondence of her successors shows that later feminists were well aware of her work and of the damage her bid for limited sexual freedom allowed her enemies to do her and her ideas. Anglo-American feminists would expend considerable energy during the nineteenth century to exude an aura of impeccable middle-class respectability to defend themselves against similar charges of immorality. English and American women organizers chose to project an image of themselves as Ladies Bountiful, giving their best service to the poor, indigent, and downtrodden.

This image was the work of Hannah More (1745–1833), another Briton and an ardent opponent of Mary Wollstonecraft's ideas as well as of the idea of women's rights activism. More's writings rather demanded the active, pious obligations of honorable behavior from upper- and middle-class women. Affluent women were not to live lives of idle pleasure, but to feed the hungry, visit and nurse the sick, rescue prostitutes, preach to the lost, and establish or actively work with institutions that did these things. In short, they were to take on all the kinds of functions performed by the active orders of nuns in Catholic countries (though More, sharing the strong anti-Catholic sentiments of most of her social class, would never have acknowledged the comparison), and they were to be similarly committed to the spiritual welfare of the community around them. More's ideas gained enough popular currency that by the late 1820s, women activists on both sides of the Atlantic began starting independent societies to rescue alcoholics, prostitutes, and victims of domestic abuse. These organizations could be militant, even by twenty-first century standards. The New York Moral Reform Society, the Boston Moral Reform Society, and the Boston Society for Employing the Poor—all formed between 1834 and 1836—had at least 576 auxiliary branches by the end of the decade. All engaged in creating shelters for prostitutes and battered or abandoned women. The movement's national newspaper, the *Advocate for Moral Reform,* had a circulation of over 16,000, and it published names of men who patronized prostitutes.

Feminism in the United States split early into multiple movements, only a few of which were explicitly devoted to women's rights. U.S. feminism developed out of movements for abolition and temperance, and feminist organizations relied on organizational and fundraising strategies they had developed during the American Revolution. They had developed an ideology that historian Linda Kerber has called "Republican Motherhood,"[10] in which it was the duty of each woman to raise her children to be civic-minded, patriotic, moral, and competent citizens of the new republic. Because U.S. women were going to be raising the new sovereign citizens of the nation, they had to be prepared to do the best possible job as mothers. Late eighteenth- and early nineteenth-century women activists imagined that all women would marry and have children eventually—so they were not much worried about the concerns of single women and seem to have forgotten that many women would be widows. As in Europe, this vision of the mother as the tutor of citizens was the ground women used to make their assault for access to an ever-greater share of male-dominated public spaces such as lecture halls, schools, and any other institution that could be perceived as potentially affecting the welfare of children or a mother's ability to care for them. Even as the ideology of domesticity and separate spheres for women and men was reaching its greatest currency in popular culture, U.S. women were using that ideology to explain why women should leave the home to go into teaching, participate in selecting members of school boards, and contribute to public debate about economics and social welfare. American women came to speak of their attempts to change the world outside their homes as "social housekeeping" and to claim that education, poverty, sanitation, and public health were clearly within their natural area of responsibility. It was in this context that U.S. women first founded self-help and women's rights organizations.

Although the earliest women's groups advocated specific assistance to needy women and prostitutes, the earliest women's rights campaigners got their first organizational experience as abolitionists, working to end slavery. Free women raised money and did much of the service work for abolitionist organizations, and in the United States they had begun to expect to have a voice in decision making—if not an authoritative or public one—and an acknowledged role in public meetings. The American Anti-Slavery Society (the largest abolitionist organization in the United States) had three women on its board of directors and had sent several women delegates to the 1840 World Anti-Slavery Convention in London. When these abolitionists arrived at the convention, however, they learned that not only were the women delegates not going to be allowed to speak, they would not be permitted to remain in the regular meeting hall. Joined in protest by William Lloyd Garrison, the senior AAS delegate, they had to stay outside the convention hall during debates. Lucretia Mott (1793–1880) and Elizabeth Cady Stanton (1815–1902), who both had traveled to attend the meeting, began to think it might be necessary to agitate specifically on behalf of women.

In 1848 Mott, Stanton, and Stanton's neighbor and new ally Susan B. Anthony (1820–1906) organized the first public meeting ever to be devoted to women's rights in the Wesleyan Chapel of Seneca Falls, New York (now the site of the Women's Rights National Historical Museum). The organizers had so little experience running meetings that they asked Lucretia Mott's husband, James, to chair the meeting for them. Elizabeth Cady Stanton delivered her first speech, possibly the first political address ever made by an American woman. The attendees wrote and published a Declaration of Sentiments, stating among other things that "Men and women were CREATED EQUAL; they are both moral and accountable beings, and whatever is *right* for a man is *right* for a woman" (emphases in original). This insistence on the equality of women with men was the hallmark of the women's rights movement in the United States and characterized the decisions of all the leadership during formative years. Mott, Cady Stanton, and Anthony founded the first equal rights organization, the National Women's Suffrage Association (NWSA), but their goals were not limited to getting women the vote. Although white women did not gain suffrage throughout the United States until 1919 (see Figure 4.2), women's rights campaigners enjoyed success on many other fronts. As early as 1848, Paulina Wright Davis and Elizabeth Cady Stanton persuaded New York State to pass legislation permitting a wife to manage and retain her own property. This measure enjoyed considerable popularity, and 14 states had passed similar legislation by 1860. By 1887, married women had achieved the right to control their own wages in 37 states and

FIGURE 4.2   VOTES FOR WOMEN
The words on this 1913 postcard give the reader one kind of political message. Why do you think the cartoonist chose to draw the two figures as children? If an adult woman stood in the same posture as the girl, how would she be perceived?

the District of Columbia. Feminists persuaded colleges to admit women, founded women's colleges, and earned entry into the most prestigious professional fields.

Because these early feminists began their work as part of an international (or at least transnational) movement, organized feminism was also an international movement from its earliest inception, and it attracted followers from throughout the Americas and Western Europe. The NWSA and other women's suffrage organizations in the United States were only the *first* feminist associations. England's first equal rights movement began in 1851, a mere three years after the formation of the NWSA. In Brazil, Paula Manso de Noronha began publication of Brazil's first feminist journal in 1852, and in the mid-1850s Mexico's Liberal Party began calling for more female education. U.S. seminaries for girls had started to open in the second decade of the nineteenth century, and by the middle of the century women's colleges had begun to open, and some U.S. colleges were persuaded to open lectures and then degree programs to women. By the 1880s, it is estimated that some 80,000 women were studying in U.S. colleges—and many of these students were visitors from abroad.[11] All these American institutions admitted foreigners, and the mere existence of such colleges made it easier for women outside the United States to lobby for better women's education. Consequently, the United States, which offered the most positions for women's students, became the foremost international destination for women's education. Many alumnae returned to their home countries to agitate on behalf of women—for educational and professional opportunity, better medical care, or suffrage.

On both sides of the Atlantic, women entered the public realm in ever-increasing numbers. They became teachers. They started and ran charities and organizations for civic improvement. They fought for and achieved entrance into the universities of Europe, and a few became doctors and lawyers. Florence Nightingale (1820–1910), a British citizen, professionalized nursing and brought tens of thousands of women into the profession with her. Jane Addams (1860–1935), an American, invented the profession of social work and created not only an enduring institutional response to social ills but also another responsible profession that would be dominated by women for the next century and a half. Women went on missionary expeditions all over the world, where they founded and supported not only churches and hospitals but grammar schools, normal[12] schools, and eventually even women's and coeducational colleges. Women poured huge quantities of resources into education and into the intellectual infrastructure of their countries, with the result that by the end of the nineteenth century, middle-class and elite women all over Europe and North America were able to attend college. Literacy levels among women rose steadily throughout the period—most conspicuously in Western Europe and North America, but also throughout the Caribbean and Latin America.

Equal rights advocates were highly visible to the general public, and they were frequently censured strongly for their activities. Newspapers described them as mannish, ugly, shrill, and hysterical and suggested that their political activities were a way of compensating for their unattractiveness and inability to attract men. They were accused of wanting to destroy the traditional family, of being unnatural women, and of being either uninterested in men or, alternately, of wanting to be sexually promiscuous. In fact, suffrage and women's rights activists were just as likely to be married as other U.S. women. Despite these assaults on equal rights feminists' respectability, opponents of women's rights never quite succeeded in forcing the U.S. movement to back away from declaring women's rights to sexual autonomy—which they were better able to do in Britain. Cady Stanton, Mott, and Anthony were all young when they became activists and continued in politics until old age. Because they themselves all championed abolition, the rhetoric of the equal rights movement retained the language and concerns of abolitionists about women slaves. The sexual vulnerability of enslaved women was a traditional and continuing concern among abolitionists. Thus, women's rights advocates routinely referred to marriage and property laws as perpetuating a kind of slavery and, although they did not focus on assisting women labor activists, they opposed prostitution and the sexual harassment of female employees with the same anti-slavery rhetoric. Moreover, in the United States, equal rights feminists had support in this from less-visible advocates. Suffragists and equal rights feminists were only the most radical and most visible women acting to change women's position in society. Progressive women's organizations of many kinds that were not explicitly feminist in mission in fact advocated and supported suffrage and equal rights feminism as forms of social change that would strengthen the positions of wives and mothers in the home. For every suffragist and equal rights feminist in the newspaper, there were 5 to 20 of these "domestic feminists" paying dues to organizations that quietly supported women's rights.[13]

Even though the equal rights movement was the most high-profile feminist movement in the United States, most self-described progressive-minded women joined temperance movements, especially the Women's Christian Temperance Union (founded in 1873), rather than suffrage organizations. Temperance activists believed that alcoholism and alcohol consumption were two of the greatest social ills of the era. They led easily to poverty, wife battering, desertion, and prostitution (which temperance advocates understood largely as a social choice made by impoverished, frequently abandoned, women). Temperance movements sought to close saloons and persuade individual men to take the pledge—that is, swear to give up alcohol—which their literature depicted as the surest road to family harmony and at least modest prosperity. Progressive women also recognized that their legal system kept women from earning or controlling enough money and property to rescue themselves and their children from alcoholic or abusive husbands. Although they never spent as much time on advocating women's rights as suffrage organizations did, temperance publications increasingly advocated women's suffrage, married women's property rights, and the necessity for single women (whether never married, widowed, or abandoned) to receive assistance in supporting themselves.

Unlike equal rights feminists in Europe, temperance advocates had active help from their religious institutions. The Quakers in 1760, the Methodists in 1780, and the Universalists in 1800 all took a stand against alcohol, and the revival movements of the Second Great Awakening often asked people to declare not only *for* Jesus but *against* spirits. Temperance women therefore had a respectable base from which to launch their attacks on alcoholism and all the social ills they saw accompanying and exacerbating it. By the 1880s, membership rolls showed that between 2 and 6 percent of the entire population of many states (counting men and children) were active supporters, or at least dues-paying members, of the Women's Christian Temperance Union (WCTU), the nation's largest temperance organization. And for all their apparent traditionalism and respectability, temperance members came increasingly to favor an agenda of women's rights activism. In 1894 Alice Stone Blackwell described her local WCTU in Boston as having "nearly 400 members, and *I don't know of one who is not a suffragist.*"[14]

The Anglo-American (U.S., Canadian, and British) feminist movements depended on two contradictory ideas—first, that women had a duty to the wider society stemming from their special role as potential mothers and guardians of virtue; and, second, that women and men were equal in rights and responsibilities and that therefore women should have the same rights in law as men. Thus, women's movements of the era could insist that women were the best natural teachers of children and should therefore enter the teaching profession, because they had a greater natural inclination for working with children. At the same time, they could argue that women had an intellectual and moral capacity as great as men's, and that therefore they should have equal access to property and political influence. Most women's organizations today, even very conservative ones, deploy one or both of these ideological strategies to support their causes.

The first argument had—and still has—widespread appeal across political parties and national boundaries. Because it appeals to traditional, sentimental notions of women's activities and grounds women's activism in non-threatening images of mothers and wives, it attracts less ferocious opposition than equal rights feminism. Activists around the world have found it an effective tool through which to claim new responsibilities and state supports. Women's organizations still muster it in favor of increasing girls' and women's opportunities and participation in statecraft and the paid economy. For example, in the period before the 2006 election of Chilean President Michelle Bachelet, a physician and single mother, both political parties expressed a longing for female leadership, which they thought of as being more honest, trustworthy, and self-sacrificing than male leadership.

The second argument is broader and bolder. Since Seneca Falls, international feminism has always had its core of militants acting on behalf of liberating girls and women, not as mothers but simply as people deserving of as much consideration, economic power, civic protection, freedom, education, and political access as men. This position has been just as important for international women's movements as the more conservative one, but its champions have been perceived as much more overtly threatening to the status quo than the champions of better services for mothers. Although smaller in number, these more radical feminists have typically set the long-term agenda of women's movements.

ANTI-CLERICALISM AND ANTI-CATHOLICISM

The anti-clericalism (that is, cynicism toward and distrust of religious institutions) of the eighteenth century remained a reality of nineteenth-century political and philosophical thought. Especially in Catholic countries, Liberals and Socialists shared the opinion that the established church functioned mainly to preserve old privileges and stand in the way of beneficial change. When they came to power, their governments sometimes attacked the institutional church, seizing church properties and closing convents and monasteries. In Protestant countries, Socialists remained mostly anti-clerical, whereas Liberals settled for being anti-Catholic and criticizing the smaller and less-established sects of Protestants—especially the ones attractive to working-class people—as intellectually moribund.[15]

American and British feminism shared this anti-Catholic bent. To a very great extent, nineteenth-century middle-class women activists organized within Protestant churches or in the context of religious activities. Women's rights activists—those directly seeking suffrage, laws improving women's legal rights, and/or access to higher education—would form much smaller, separate organizations, but although they organized outside the churches, their organizations remained heavily Protestant in membership until quite late in the nineteenth century, and the writings and speeches of women's rights and temperance advocates showed it. Catholics were imagined as blindly obedient to the hierarchy of their church; as unpatriotic because they were presumed to put loyalty to the pope above loyalty to the state; and ignorant. Women from Catholic countries and Catholic women in general were imagined to be kept in ignorance, educated only for the most narrow of religious purposes, and much more oppressed than Protestant women and women from Protestant countries. It was true that Protestant areas put a greater value on women's education (and education in general) than Catholic ones, and that at least in the United States and in the dissenting sects of Britain, they encouraged lay people to be very active in the development of community life. Protestant women's writings on religion were tolerated and sometimes praised, if they championed a conservative view of feminine propriety. And as we have seen, Protestant churches worked hand-in-hand with Progressive women activists. But Protestantism itself was not normally supportive of feminism, and Protestant education could be just as rigid and restrictive as Catholic education was accused of being.

Yet nineteenth-century Catholic sisters generally behaved much like other Progressive women, engaging in activities very similar to their domestic feminist counterparts in temperance movements. Despite— perhaps in part because of—the persecutions of the era, convents and new orders sprang up throughout the Christian world, and the numbers of feminine religious waxed. They educated large numbers of girls and women as well as men; they entered professional fields; they founded and ran hundreds of institutions for social housekeeping, like orphanages and hospitals; and they undertook mission work. Convents sometimes clashed with their local hierarchy, seeking ways to stay independent of diocesan authority, and many of them provided extensive instruction and scope for self-improvement for their members. Anti-Catholic sentiment therefore kept organized feminists from working with the many Catholic women, especially nuns, who should have been their natural allies.

MOVEMENTS IN BRAZIL AND MEXICO

In Latin America the first pro-woman activism began in the 1840s with calls for the better education of girls, which was the central goal of Latin American feminism for most of the nineteenth and early twentieth centuries. This region produced no individual, influential female political leader like Catherine the Great of Russia or Empress Haruko in Japan (see "Russian Activists" and "The First Japanese Feminists" below). Nor was there a strong tradition of lay female organizations engaged in charitable work or political activism that could be the core of a domestic feminist movement. Convents were centers of learning, charity, and education, but—unlike some of the Native American missions organized by male clergy—they were not sites of overt political activity, nor did they mobilize women for collective action. Indeed, Latin American women lagged far behind their sisters in North America and Western Europe in education and activism. Instead, public suggestions that women required better educations first came from Liberal men, who claimed they wanted to establish secondary schools for women to make them better mothers and wives.[16]

By the 1850s, some middle-class and well-educated women began to argue in favor of better education and the "emancipation" (as Brazilian activists called it) of women, a call that would eventually be heard throughout Latin America. The first Brazilian periodical published by women, for women, was explicitly feminist. *O Jornal das Senhoras* was founded in 1852 by Joana Paula Manso de Noronha,[17] who declared it was time for women to speak for themselves and for each other. So unconventional was the idea of Brazilian women writing for a public audience that almost all the writers insisted on publishing anonymously during the journal's four years of existence. *O Jornal das Senhoras* was widely imitated from the 1860s on by other explicitly feminist periodicals like *O Bello Sexo*, *O Sexo Feminino*, and *Jornal das Damas*, which were quite popular among women in the regions where they were published. *O Sexo Feminino*, for instance, had 800 subscribers in a metropolitan area where there were probably no more than 1,500 literate women. At the same time, the Sisters of Charity of St. Vincent de Paul immigrated into Brazil and began opening private schools that educated some poor and middle-class women. Educated Brazilian women began to demand entry into the most prestigious male-dominated professions as soon as they heard about women in the United States and Europe doing so—at first traveling to the United States to attend college and enter medical school, then persuading the Brazilian government to permit women to enter colleges. In Brazil this ended up being less controversial than in the United States: Many free Brazilians saw the entry of a few middle-class women into the professions as evidence of their country's modernity, rather than of women's declining femininity. The first Brazilians campaigning for education couched their desire in terms of their longing to build a noble, heroic, daring, and modern future for Brazil. Instead of arguing for their needs as future mothers, these women modeled themselves on the virgin warrior Joan of Arc, a familiar and persuasive image for the Brazilian public. With the abolition of slavery in 1888 and overthrow of the monarchy in 1889, it became possible for Brazilian women to dream of the franchise, and the first demand for it was made in 1891. In 1932 under the leadership of Bertha Luz, Brazilian suffragists won their cause for those women who could pass the literacy qualification, at least until the elected government was replaced by a dictatorship in 1937.

In Mexico the Liberal Party came to power in 1855, promising to create secular secondary schools for girls. We know at least some women wanted these schools badly, because in 1856 a delegation of women delivered a petition demanding one for their city. The Liberal government not only failed to deliver on their promise (the first government-sponsored girls' school was not founded until 1867), but they also closed all convents and monasteries in Mexico—shoving a dagger into the heart of the educational system that did exist—even as they declared teaching a suitable profession for unmarried *secular* women. The first Mexican feminist organization (*Siempreviva,* a society that also published a feminist newsletter and a literary society) fought back against this neglect, founding its own girls' school, led by Rita Cetina Gutièrrez, in 1870. Gutièrrez later ran the first state-run normal school[18]—which was founded in 1886, 31 years after the Liberals came to power—in 1902 in Yucatan, thus personally overseeing the education of almost every teacher in Yucatan for a generation.

Yucatan, which already had a long history of popular dissent and revolt, became the wellspring of feminism in late nineteenth- and twentieth-century Mexico, with feminism itself being largely a movement of educated women, especially teachers. Collectively Mexican feminists fought for some of the things their U.S. counterparts had sought: restoration of married women's property rights (taken away in the 1884 Civil Code), protections for low-wage workers, and vocational education for all women, so that none would have to resort to prostitution. It was not until well into the twentieth century that Mexican women feminists sought suffrage, however, because prior to the Mexican Revolution (1910–1920), the machinations of the previous government and political parties had convinced most women that politics was too dirty and corrupt for a good woman to engage in—a sentiment still widely held in Latin America.

RUSSIAN ACTIVISTS

Aside from convents, the first secondary schools in Russia for girls had been founded by a ruler, Catherine the Great. In 1764 she began sponsoring dozens (later hundreds) of institutes created to educate the daughters of Russia's elites. Following in their trail were dozens of boarding schools, run largely by foreigners, providing slightly less elite, but still wealthy families the opportunity to educate their daughters in the manner of aristocracy. Thus throughout Russia an extensive network of girls' secondary schools was educating perhaps 5 to 10 percent of women, while convents educated a smaller but also significant number.[19]

The education offered at such places was not very thorough and of course did not extend to very many women. Moreover, it was intended mostly to turn aristocratic girls into suitably ornamental and pleasant wives, focusing heavily on topics such as exhibiting good manners, recognizing and choosing fashionable clothing, obeying authority, pleasing a husband, and making decorative textiles. Women who grew up to write of their experiences at such boarding schools and institutes often remembered them as harshly authoritarian, anti-intellectual, boring hothouses that prepared them for nothing more real or important than sewing and embroidery.

These institutes and boarding schools also taught women to read and write in Russian and French, to do at least basic arithmetic, to understand the essentials of their religion, to dance, and to play musical instruments. Clearly, this is not an education intended to prepare a woman for employment, self-sufficiency, or even for effective parenting. But it *is* an education that, however unintentionally, could not help but prepare adult women not only to long for self-expression but also give them the vocabulary to do it. The schools also housed girls in isolated and exclusively female company for years at a time, which has certain consequences probably unforeseen by their founders. Although educated nineteenth-century women throughout Europe often complained of the stifling atmosphere of boarding schools, they learned important things about girls and women while they were there.[20] Nineteenth-century rhetoric about women's special nature as nurturers of the next generation, as naturally gentle, kind, self-effacing, and obedient flowed from the pens of men, of women educated by tutors and, later, of women educated in coeducational institutions. Anyone who spent years as a pupil or teacher in an all-girls' school knew this was claptrap, no matter what nonsense about feminine purity they had believed on entering the school.

Because they were educated to dance, play music, and read French, middle-class and elite Russian women of the nineteenth century got most of their opinions about the way the world should work from novels, especially French novels, and the ones they most often chose to read were, unsurprisingly, about the plight and struggle of educated women. George Sand—the French baroness who had taken a male pen name, lived with famous musician Frederic Chopin, and dressed in male clothes—authored some of the favorite novels of Russian women. Eighteenth- and nineteenth-century moralists throughout Europe decried the influence of the novel on girls' and women's intellectual formation, declaring that they gave women inappropriate expectations about their lives and made them silly and immoral—all of which doubtless increased their appeal, especially among the young. The dangerous novels Russian women chose to read were those penned by women and men who dreamed of a new ethic of love, romance, and personal fulfillment, where women chose the men they wanted even after marriage; where a lover had to be faithful or lose his love; and where, increasingly, women devoted all their impulses for self-sacrifice not to husbands, children, or lovers, but toward a social cause. Novels proposed that the tyranny of the family, especially of the father, had to be overthrown if justice was to prevail, and women had to become equal partners with men.

Russian radical women were at least as likely to be socialists or anarchists as they were to be feminists. Overthrowing tyranny was as much a woman's as a man's goal, and the Russian anarchists and radicals resorted to both civil disobedience and terrorism to disrupt what they saw as a morally bankrupt system. The first Russian terrorists to be executed included women radicals, and their example of heroism, extremism, and self-sacrifice became a model for future activists. For Russian women radicals, giving their all to a cause and becoming the person they were meant to be was an explicitly political goal. To be fully oneself was not necessarily to be a wife and mother. Radical women—even some atheists—modeled their lives on the spectacular self-sacrifice and dedication celebrated in Russian Orthodox saints. The radical reinvention of the self called for in religious practice became a model for political growth. The conviction that women should determine their own sexual destiny and that they have an *obligation* to become the best possible version of themselves was new to Western political thought, and may be Eastern European feminism's most significant contribution.

Certainly not every educated Russian accepted these goals—many actively opposed the ideas in such novels and wrote scathing criticisms of them—but they had all heard of them. The result was that by the 1860s in Russia, debates about women's education were held in a completely different framework than in Latin America, Japan, England, or the United States at this time. The question was not whether women should be educated—all thought they should—but how the existing educational system should be expanded and reformed to include women. Should women be allowed to enter universities as well as primary educational institutions? If so, on what basis? Depending on the whim of the current minister of education, by the 1870s varying options had been tried. First women were permitted to attend lectures; then some were permitted to register as students; then eventually women's academies were created; then the government made those classes open to men—but so many women attended them that men avoided them.

As in other countries that have opened up higher education for women, Russia found that there were far more women eager to obtain an education than there were places available for them. Russian women were most interested in medicine and the sciences, and when the government began creating technical schools for subjects such as engineering and architecture, they flocked there—or at least showed up in much larger numbers than the government had anticipated. Especially early on, women from upper-class backgrounds suffered what must have seemed terrible deprivation to be able to attend university. They lived four to a room, on funds barely sufficient to feed and clothe them. Jews were limited by law to 3 percent of the total student population and moreover were forbidden to leave the Pale (the area designated by the government as Russia's Jewish territory). But they came from a cultural tradition that set enormous value on literacy and education, and many wanted higher education badly. They always made up a larger percentage of students than their percentage in the population, and a much larger percentage than their quota. So desperate were they to study that Jewish women often registered with the police as prostitutes (who had different quotas for entry) and wore the yellow star regulations insisted all registered prostitutes display.

Russian activists may have mostly come from the aristocratic and middle classes, but the ideological climate of the nineteenth and early twentieth centuries forced them to choose between activism on behalf of labor and the peasantry or on behalf of women. In the Russian Empire, of Eastern and Central Europe, formal feminist activism was dominated by middle-class issues, whereas labor activism was dominated by the issues most important to male industrial workers. The biggest successes of nineteenth-century Russian feminism were, first, that it gained women entry into education and professional employment; second, that it convinced most people to treat women's emotional and sexual freedom and their potential for development as human beings as a political issue. The first of these achievements Russian activists shared with successful feminist movements around the world; the second was a singular contribution.

THE FIRST JAPANESE FEMINISTS

Feminism was not a purely Western phenomenon in the nineteenth century. Japan has a long history of both state-led and grass-roots feminist activism dating from the 1870s. Many state initiatives were started by a woman—the Empress Haruko (1868–1912). Her efforts occurred at the same time as the earliest grass-roots activism. As we have seen before, the

Meiji state made industrialization and modernization a high priority, and part of setting that priority was rethinking the roles of men and women in Japan. What kind of new workers and new citizens would be needed to make Japan successful in the future? It was clear there would have to be change, but what kind and to what extent? Because of the great reverence the Japanese hold for the imperial family, the life choices and public demeanor of the emperor and empress were highly influential—and the imperial family knew it. Empress Haruko took on the responsibility of redefining Japanese womanhood through her own life choices, modeling a lifestyle in which she enjoyed new freedoms, took on wider social responsibilities, and (like previous empresses) participated in the production of Japanese high culture. Contemporary accounts of her are almost universally complimentary.[21]

Although Haruko's immediate successor lived a much more enclosed life (because her son was unwell and her husband was unstable), later empresses emulated much of her behavior. Unlike her predecessors, Haruko involved herself in the public life of the court and interacted directly with visiting dignitaries, quietly insisting on at least a social equality with her husband similar to that of Western women at the time. The emperor and empress had decided as a matter of policy that they wanted to encourage Western dress among Japanese elites, believing that changing the way people dress changes the way they act. Haruko wore corsets, wide skirts draped over multiple layers of undergarments (including hoops earlier in her life and bustles later), gloves, and tight high-heeled shoes. She also banned the blackened teeth and heavy white makeup of prior custom. Obviously, the empress had no more freedom of movement in these clothes than in traditional Japanese styles. Nevertheless, the restrictive fashions symbolized new freedoms to Japanese women.

The empress used Western dress as the outward marker of the ways she acted like an elite Western woman, as hostess, social arbiter, and philanthropist. Haruko and her husband greeted visitors together instead of him greeting them alone. She spoke directly to courtiers and foreigners and wrote foreign leaders in her own name. She appeared in public once to say goodbye to her husband when he left the country, and she once traveled with him in his carriage instead of in a separate carriage behind him. Like Hannah More and like Anglo-American domestic feminists, she visited schools and hospitals instead of just sending them money and supported the foundation of the Japanese branch of the Red Cross. Like a traditional empress, she supported the arts, writing poetry and supporting poetry contests, and she kept a court etiquette in which polite people whispered and—although she spoke with visitors—no man outside her family was to touch her.

Empress Haruko was dedicated to women's education. She founded and supported the Peeresses School for Girls, the first government-sponsored women's secondary school. This Western-style school educated daughters of elite families, and it faced considerable opposition from the rest of the state. Officials and male educators did not like seeing material and financial resources being "wasted" on girls when they could be spent on boys. On one occasion the empress had to step in to save the school from having their new building seized, as the Peers School for Boys (also run by the imperial household) tried to appropriate for themselves a brand-new edifice supporters of the Peeresses School had just built. Haruko's intervention, along with the protests of the girls and the resignations of all the faculty, managed to keep the building for the girls. In 1871, she also sponsored five girls (the oldest were 15 and the youngest, 8) sent to study in the United States. The two oldest became ill and had to return, but the other three remained and finished their schooling. Two went to college and graduated from Vassar.[22]

The empress seems to have been determined to create a wider sphere of activities and responsibilities for women and was a lifelong supporter of women's education, but the Meiji government in general was ambivalent about supporting women's education and opposed women's equality. Despite the risk that education might make Japanese women less docile and obedient, the Meiji government decided universal literacy was a necessity for modernization and put forth an enormous effort to achieve it. Official figures reported that whereas in 1875 only 18.6 percent of girls and 50.5 percent of boys were enrolled in school, by 1930, 99.5 percent of both girls and boys were enrolled. (These figures may be misleading: Other sources indicate that peasant children were unlikely to attend school more than a year or two.) Certainly, it was important to the Japanese government that girls be educated—but in the right sort of things. Although the original goal in the early 1870s had been to give boys and girls the same education in Western-style schools (hence the project that had sent five girls to the United States), by the 1880s the idea was to give girls and boys educations the government considered appropriate to their sex.

The most successful champions of women's education were actually male reformers. Except for Ueki Emori (1857–1892), the most radical of the educational philosophers, these men did not believe that women were or should be equal to men. Rather, they wanted to reform marriage law and prepare women to be good wives and mothers. Even so, the changes they wanted to see in Japanese society were radical for their time. Nearly all of them wanted to end concubinage and make marriages between men and women more equal—they did not believe it was right for a wife's role to be described solely in terms of her duty to her husband, as it had come to be during the Tokugawa, and they disapproved of polygyny and concubinage. The best-known and most influential of these men was Fukuzawa Yukichi (1835–1901), a professional educator and reformer. Fukuzawa found the whole concept of polygyny scandalous, especially the idea that a woman should have to accept her husband's child by another woman into the household. He went so far as to declare that if men could have concubines, women ought to be able to have them, too! He also seems to have thought that girls should have an education equal to and similar to that of boys and was instrumental in helping organize the 1871 delegation of five girls to America.

Yet Fukuzawa's view that women needed an education equal to men was not shared by most other reformers. They felt women needed an education so they could converse on a more equal level with their husbands and contribute directly to their husband's educations—exactly the arguments early feminist reformers in England and the Americas had deployed for the last two decades. There was no interest in educating women so that they would be better able to express themselves, participate in public life, or choose careers of their own. The government did not, however, consider taxing women less because they were receiving less education than their brothers; rather, women's taxes and lesser access to education would subsidize male education. Of course, the education of Japanese boys and men was also discussed solely in terms of potential benefits for the state; no one (at least on paper) was really interested in promoting the intellectual or creative growth of the Japanese people simply for the benefit of the recipients of that education.

The official reason for privileging boys' and men's educations over girls' and women's was cost. Because universal education is expensive, the Meiji government decided that it could only afford to educate boys past elementary school level. Boys' education, in their view, was of direct benefit to the state because men participated in the wage labor economy and women, according to government policy makers, did not—or at least should not. We already know that this imagined view of the world was deeply flawed, as women not only did most of the work of the household economy but also made up the majority of industrial workers in Japan. By the late Meiji, men made up only about 48 percent of all factory workers and less than 20 percent of workers in textiles—at that time Japan's most successful and important modern industry. But such inconvenient facts had no impact on government decision making, which was based on the lives the middle- and upper-class men involved imagined most women to lead—lives like those of their mothers, sisters, wives, and daughters. This lack of imagination is a consistent problem with governments' and nations' attempts to implement reforms on behalf of women: The men in power—and sometimes the women working with them—rarely know much about the lives of women outside their own social class. So, in Japan, secondary schools and colleges would therefore be for boys and men only, and it would be the work of men that would lead Japan into the modern age. When he founded a major Japanese university, even Fukuzawa himself, despite his published opinions, was forced to limit its enrollment to men.

To be fair to the government, the Japanese people were hardly clamoring for girls' education. Girls might be insulted on the way to school, and newspaper editorials fulminated against the terrible things girls might learn there. Many feared that girls would become too much like the Japanese conception of Western women, too individualistic and rebellious. Of course, there was some justification for this fear. People with extensive educations often did and do question authority, insist on having their opinions heard, and refuse to let other people make major life choices for them. Western educators must have understood this perfectly well, even if they did not say so in public very often.

Therefore the secondary schools and universities founded for women were the work of women themselves, usually in concert with American and European educators. This pattern would be repeated in most of Africa and Asia. If the Japanese government was uninterested in higher education for women, a number of parents nevertheless *did* want such an education for their daughters. These people sent their daughters to schools that had been set up by Christian missionaries (many of whom were domestic feminists in practice, even if they did not self-identify as such). About half the women who wanted to attend schools of higher education or acquire professional skills, such as nursing, left the country to study, and they did not always choose to return. But a number of women who had received a Western-style advanced education built Japanese schools of higher learning. Tsudo Umeko, one of the original five girls sent to America, had attended Vassar and Bryn Mawr. She founded a women's college and used her international contacts to connect a web of women who provided the financial and intellectual support the institution needed. Dr. Yayoi Yoshioka founded Tokyo Women's Medical University "with the purpose of improving the social position of women," as it appears in her own words on the university's Web site,[23] and Hani Motoko (1873–1957) not only created a progressive girls' school but also a magazine. Motoko's memoirs make it clear that getting an education on a par with boys' was difficult for a Japanese girl and probably impossible for most. It was only because she was especially interested in learning and was her grandfather's only heir that Motoko got access to education after primary school. There was no public secondary school for her to attend, but because she was the only heir, her family spent the money to have her taught in a

private school in Tokyo, where she found her education, which emphasized memorization rather than comprehension, too dull to hold her previously keen interest in study:

> Study of English was very popular at the time, and a number of teachers
> taught reading and translation classes usually consisting of a handful of
> girls and a score of boys, among whom I was one of the youngest. While
> translating Parley's *History of the World* with the class, I memorized the
> meaning of every word in it. If my teachers had emphasized a broad
> comprehension approach rather than the verbatim translation method,
> my study might have proved more useful in my later years. My English
> study, as well as feverish pursuit of academic knowledge, ended with this
> period of my life.[24]

A number of grass-roots feminist activists also jumped into the fray
beginning in the 1870s. Kita Kusunose (1836–1920), a widow and head of
household, wrote a letter demanding that women heads of household—
who paid the same taxes as men—should have the right to vote and to
make contracts on their own behalf, just as men heads of households did.
Her letter was debated and publicized all over Japan and began a discourse
of women's rights. Kishida Toshiko, a courtier in the service of Empress
Haruko, began to make public speeches on the subject of women's rights.
She championed equal education for girls, supported the right of women
to divorce, opposed concubinage, and criticized the traditional Confucian
"Three Obediences" prescribed for women: to father (as a child), husband
(when married), and sons (when widowed). Fukuda Hideko joined her,
and together they and other women started a formal feminist movement.
Japanese activists joined political parties, started lecture societies, and
sponsored social gatherings where women could discuss their concerns.
Unfortunately, the Meiji state was hostile to feminist activism. Toshiko
and other women were arrested several times, and in 1889 the government wrote a new constitution that specifically forbade women's suffrage.
New regulations in 1890 made it illegal for women to join political parties,
go to political meetings, or start political organizations of their own.

The heavy hand of the government thus ended the earliest wave of
the women's movement in Japan, just as it began to attract widespread
attention. It would be another 20 years before feminists were able to work
in public again. Even though the oppressive reforms of 1889 and 1890
were still in place, by 1910 women found they could get a public hearing
by writing about their concerns in women's magazines. Hiratsuka Riacho
(1886–1971) started the most radical of these publications, *Seito,* or *Blue-
stocking* (named after an intellectual movement started by women in
eighteenth-century Britain). She persuaded one of the most well-known
and influential poets in Japan, Yosano Akiko, to publish in it, along with a
number of other women who criticized the government. Fukuda Hideko,

who had been forced out of her feminist activism in 1890, returned to politics and to writing. These authors wrote about birth control, sex, and the ways Japan's contemporary economic and political system oppressed women. The government did not appreciate the feedback. The post office would sometimes refuse to send the magazine, and the government banned several issues. Ito Noe (1895–1925), one of the strongest government critics, was arrested and murdered in prison by a police officer. At the start of World War I (1914), the government banned the magazine entirely. But it was too late to ban feminism: The activists had gained too much experience. Hiratsuo Riacho went on to form The New Women's Society, the Women's League, and a women's suffrage party in the 1920s, and the women who joined her there would form the core of Japan's later, more successful feminist party.

Japanese feminism was much weaker than its sisters in Europe and the Americas, not least because the government fought against independent political activity. Feminist goals included reforms in marriage law, availability of family planning for women, and a good education for every girl and woman. They did not succeed in recruiting large numbers of laborers or peasants, who had very limited energy for political activity, but they did raise awareness of women's rights as a political issue.

CONCLUSION

Industrialization, imperialism, and the ideologies developed in response to them form the backdrop of women's public activism during the long nineteenth century. More girls and women than ever before attended school, if only for a short while, and this raised their expectations. An international conversation about modernization and progress developed around women's importance as mothers, wives, and citizens. Women like Mary Wollstonecraft, Hannah More, Fukuda Hideko, and Rita Cetina Gutièrrez sought to shape that conversation, with some success. Industrial workers also tried to negotiate the terms of their labor. Leadership in the male-dominated labor movement wanted to return women to a home they had never really occupied in the first place. Women activists succeeded more often when they demanded concessions to their femininity than when they demanded better wages.

Suffrage movements around much of the Western world culminated in many countries granting women's suffrage by the end of the 1920s. Domestic feminists and equal rights feminists had succeeded in persuading most governments and political parties to consider women important citizens whose voices should be heard—or at least, whose votes and activist energies should be courted. In victory, Western feminist movements themselves would be less interested in international cooperation during the late 1920s and 1930s, coping as they found themselves educating new female electorates and dealing with activists who turned to other social movements.

Women activists outside the West devoted most of their energies toward supporting movements for national sovereignty, trusting nationalist parties to enact major reforms for women when they gained independence. Unfortunately, Chapter 5 will show that the next three decades would see most states pulling back from commitments to women's emancipation, instead devoting more resources to warfare, developing a modern male citizenry, and expanding industrial capitalism in ways that systematically favored men over women and citizens over colonized subjects.

STUDY QUESTIONS

1. How did industrialization change the division of labor within families? If you were a man working in the early textile or mining industries, how would you feel about and respond to these changes? If you were a woman?

2. What kinds of work did women do for wages in industrialization? How was women's industrial work in Russia different from their industrial work in Japan and England?

3. Why did nineteenth-century governments want to educate girls and boys? Consider at least two different countries.

4. Based on what your own country teaches children and what you hear government officials say about school, what is or was the purpose of your own education? Do you agree with the goals you think your government has?

5. Women's movements have often found it difficult to work together across class differences. What might be some reasons for this? Do women of different social classes and income levels face barriers to working together that are not shared by men? How would you make it easier for women from widely different backgrounds to work together?

BIBLIOGRAPHY

*indicates contains whole primary sources or secondary works containing substantial extracts.

WESTERN EUROPE

Blom, Ida, Karen Hagemann, and Catherine Hall. *Gendered Nations: Nationalism and Gender Order in the Nineteenth Century.* Oxford: Berg, 2000.
*Bronte, Charlotte. *Villette.* London: J. M. Dent, 1993.

Caine, Barbara. *English Feminism, 1780–1980*. Oxford: Oxford University Press, 1997.

Forster, Margaret. *Significant Sisters: The Grassroots of Active Feminism, 1839–1939*. London: Sucker and Warburg, 1984.

Levine, Philippa. *Feminist Lives in Victorian England: Private Lives, Public Commitment*. Oxford, UK: Blackwell, 1990.

Morgan, Sue, ed. *Religion and Feminism in Britain, 1750–1900*. New York: Palgrave Macmillan, 2002.

Moses, Claire Goldberg. *French Feminism in the Nineteenth Century*. Albany: State University of New York Press, 1984.

Offen, Karen M. *European Feminisms, 1750–1950: A Political History*. Stanford, CA: Stanford University Press, 2000.

*Sand, George. *Indiana*. New York: Signet Classic, 1993.

Sharpe, Pamela, ed. *Women's Work: The English Experience, 1650–1914*. London: Arnold, 1998.

*Wollstonecraft, Mary. *The Works of Mary Wollstonecraft*. Edited by Jane Todd and Marilyn Butler. New York: New York University Press, 1989.

RUSSIA

Farnsworth, Beatrice, and Lynne Viola, eds. *Russian Peasant Women*. New York: Oxford University Press, 1992.

Glickman, Rose. *Russian Factory Women: Workplace and Society, 1880–1914*. Berkeley: University of California Press, 1984.

*Khvoshchinskaia, Nadezhda. *The Boarding School Girl*. Translated by Karen Rosneck. Evanston, IL: Northwestern University Press, 2000.

*Nikitenko, Aleksandr. *Up From Serfdom: My Childhood and Youth in Russia 1804–1824*. New Haven, CT: Yale University Press, 2001.

*Purlevskii, Savva Dmitrievich. *A Life under Russian Serfdom, 1800–1868*. Translated and edited by Boris Gorshkov. Budapest: Central European University Press, 2005.

Stites, Richard. *The Women's Liberation Movement in Russia: Feminism, Nihilism, and Bolshevism 1860–1930*. Rev. ed. Princeton, NJ: Princeton University Press, 1991.

*Verbitskaia, Anastasia. *Keys to Happiness: A Novel*. Translated and edited by Helena Goscilo and Beth Holmgren. Bloomington: Indiana University Press, 1999.

UNITED STATES

Aleman, Ana M., and Kristen A. Renn, eds. *Women in Higher Education: An Encyclopedia*. Santa Barbara, CA: ABC-CLIO, 2002.

*Beecher, Catherine. *The American Woman's Home, or Principles of Domestic Science*. New Brunswick, NJ: Rutgers University Press, 2002. First published 1861.

Cogan, Frances B. *All-American Girl: The Ideal of Real Womanhood in Mid-Nineteenth Century-America*. Athens: University of Georgia Press, 1989.

Jones, Martha S. *All Bound up Together: The Woman Question in African American Public Culture 1830–1900*. Chapel Hill: University of North Carolina Press, 2007.

Keller, Rene. "An American 'Escaped Nun' on Tour in England: Edith O'Gorman's Critique of Convent Life." *Feminist Theology* 14, no. 2 (2006): 205–220.

Kerber, Linda K. *Women of the Republic: Intellect and Ideology in Revolutionary America*. New York: W.W. Norton: 1980.

*Langley, Winston, and Vivian C. Fox. *Women's Rights in the United States: A Documentary Reader*. Westport, CT: Greenwood Press, 1994.

*Monk, Maria. *Awful Disclosures of Maria Monk*. New York: Arno Press, 1977. An anti-Catholic hoax first printed in 1836 and frequently reprinted since.

*O'Gorman, Edith. *Trials and Persecutions of Miss Edith O'Gorman, Otherwise Sister Teresa de Chantal of St. Joseph's Convent, Hudson City, New Jersey*. Hartford, CT: Connecticut Publishing Company, 1871.

*Robinson, Harriet. *Loom and Spindle, or Life among the Mill Girls.* Kailua, HI: Press Pacifica, 1976.

*Sklar, Kathryn Kish. *Women's Rights Emerges within the Anti-Slavery Movement: A Brief History with Documents.* Boston: Bedford/St. Martin's, 2000.

*Stanton, Elizabeth Cady. *Eighty Years and More: Reminiscences, 1815–1897.* Amherst, NY: Humanities, 2002.

Zollinger, Janet. *Two Paths to Women's Equality: Temperance, Suffrage, and the Origins of Modern Feminism.* New York: Twayne Publishers, 1995.

LATIN AMERICA

Hahner, June E., ed. *Emancipating the Female Sex: The Struggle for Women's Rights in Brazil, 1850–1940.* Durham, NC: Duke University Press, 1990.

Hahner, June E., ed. *Women Through Women's Eyes: Latin America in Nineteenth Century Travel Accounts.* Wilmington, DE: S. R. Books, 1998.

Lavrin, Asunción. *Women, Feminism, and Social Change in Argentina, Chile, and Uruguay, 1890–1940.* Lincoln: University of Nebraska Press, 1995.

Macías, Anna. *Against All Odds: The Feminist Movement in Mexico to 1940.* Westport, CT: Greenwood Press, 1982.

Maza Valenzuela, Erika. *Liberals, Radicals, and Women's Citizenship in Chile, 1872–1930.* Notre Dame, IN: The Helen Kellogg Institute for International Studies, 1997.

JAPAN

*Aoki, Michiko Y., and Margaret B. Dardess. *As the Japanese See It.* Honolulu: University of Hawaii Press, 1981.

Bernstein, Gail. *Isami's House: Three Centuries of a Japanese Family.* Berkeley: University of California Press, 2005.

Bingham, Marjorie Wall, and Susan Gross Hill. *Women in Japan from Ancient Times to the Present.* St. Louis Park, MN: Glenhurst Publications, 1987.

*Hane, Mikiso, ed. *Reflections on the Way to the Gallows.* Berkeley: University of California Press, 1998.

Keene, Donald. *Emperor of Japan: Meiji and His World, 1852–1912.* New York: Columbia University Press, 2002.

Kodansha Encyclopedia of Japan. 10 vols. Tokyo: Kodansha, 1993-.

Partner, Simon. *Toshié: A Story of Village Life in Twentieth-Century Japan.* Berkeley: University of California Press, 2004.

*Shidzue, Kato. *Facing Two Ways: The Story of My Life.* Stanford, CA: Stanford University Press, 1984.

Sievers, Sharon L. *Flowers in Salt: The Beginnings of Feminist Consciousness in Modern Japan.* Stanford, CA: Stanford University Press, 1983.

*Yukichi, Fukusawa. *Autobiography of Yukichi Fukuzawa.* New York: Columbia University Press, 1980.

AUDIO-VISUAL RESOURCES

Mill Times. With David Macauley. PBS Video, 2002.

Not for Ourselves Alone: The Story of Elizabeth Cady Stanton and Susan B. Anthony. PBS Home Video, 1998.

CHAPTER FIVE

IMPERIALISM AND ACTIVISM, 1830–1930

Probably the most important world historical development during this period was the rapid expansion and extension of colonialism. Women's roles as colonizers and as colonized tend to be underestimated in world history narratives, as is the importance of gender ideology to the political activities of their menfolk. This chapter provides a brief overview of how and why imperialism expanded in the nineteenth century and then discusses the most common experiences of colonized women and of colonizing white women. It examines four particular cases of Western imperialism and the roles and responses of women in those cases. In British Egypt and India, we consider the responses of elite Indian and Egyptian women to Westernized education and the ideology of domesticity; in Zimbabwe and Puerto Rico we will consider the responses and activities of Zimbabwean and Puerto Rican working-class women to industrialization. Finally, we will consider a case of Islamic imperialism in West Africa, the Sokoto Caliphate, where we will encounter a political program that considered gender ideology and women's education a critical part of social transformation. The agenda of the Sokoto Caliphate was in some ways very similar to that of other colonizing powers during that era—yet because the leaders of the caliphate came from a strong family tradition of female religious scholarship, they stimulated substantial change in family life in ways that colonized women apparently came to embrace. Today the descendants of the people ruled by the caliphate remember the leaders not as conquerors, but as reformers.

During the nineteenth century, certain technological changes made it much more feasible for European governments to expand their activities in regions where they had not previously been able to do much more than coastal trading. Steam power permitted large ships to travel upriver easily, deep into the Congo, Niger, Yangzi, and Huang Ho River valleys. For the first time, Western governments could bring mobile artillery into the heartlands of China, India, Japan, Borneo, and Africa. At the same time, the discovery that malaria could be prevented by drinking water mixed with quinine[1] made it possible for Westerners to travel inland in the equatorial latitudes without contracting the dreaded disease. Railroads transported raw materials from the interior to the coastline, troops from the coastline to the interior, and native laborers from rural areas to the rapidly expanding mines, plantations, lumberyards, factories, and cities that needed workers. Engineering, technical innovation, science, and industrial manufacturing were thus critical to Western military dominance and political expansion.

Westerners embarked on a second wave of colonial expansion during this period. Figure 5.1 shows the resulting extent to which people were able to migrate across the globe. Although the official triggers were different in each case, the British, French, Dutch, Germans, Belgians, and Italians all seized extensive landed territories in Asia and Africa and ruled them directly. The Russian government solidified its rule over the territories in Siberia and Central Asia that they had colonized in the previous centuries, expanded its influence in Afghanistan and Iran, and sent settlers into Alaska and down the Pacific Coast of North America into California. In the rest of North America, the British and the newly emerged United States governments marched to the Pacific, and fledgling Central and South American governments struggled to enforce their will on jungle and mountain interiors. In the British, Dutch, Portuguese, and French possessions of southern and Southeast Asia the local, independent governments that had focused on trade were replaced by governments managed much more directly from the home country of the colonizers. In 1875, the British purchased control of the Suez Canal (built in 1858–1859) through Egypt. The United States supported a Panamanian insurrection in Colombia (1903), backed the new government with military force, and helped build the Panama Canal (1906–1914). To the colonizers, military control of strategic internal geography became as important as the control of overseas trade routes. In contrast to the successful bids for independence in the United States, Haiti, and the mainland Spanish Americas, the rest of the Caribbean colonies remained under European (and, later, U.S.) control—a continuity made easier by the development of the steam engine and the eventual laying down of the trans-Atlantic telegraph cable. Historians refer to this era of new conquests and increasingly direct control over previously colonized areas resulting from the availability of new technologies as the age of imperialism, as distinguished from the earlier era of colonialism.[2]

Meanwhile, the spread of the Industrial Revolution transformed the material and economic bases for wealth the world over, pulling local economies deep into an international market and introducing new methods of production that changed divisions of labor along lines of class, sex, race,

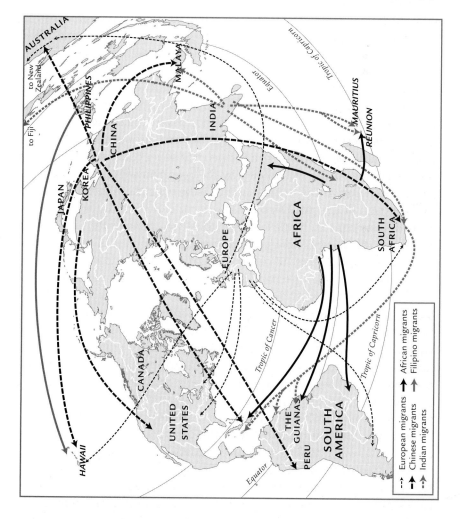

Figure 5.1 Migration Routes

Imperialism and migration during the nineteenth and early twentieth centuries. This map shows both free and unfree migration.

Legend:
- European migrants
- Chinese migrants
- Indian migrants
- African migrants
- Filipino migrants

age, and geography. Growing industries required ever-increasing supplies of raw materials from distant lands and ever-increasing numbers of workers to supply the raw materials and turn them into finished goods. The earliest mechanized labor appeared in textile production with the invention of the spinning jenny (see Chapter Four). With the invention of the cotton gin (to de-seed cotton bolls), cotton became the cash crop of the southern United States, the Nile River, and India. This embedded early industrial production deep in the economy of Atlantic slavery and converted many Egyptian peasants from subsistence farmers to exporters of raw material—cotton. Whole geographic regions thus specialized in particular kinds of industrial fabrication or production of raw materials. Divisions of labor within societies had to change to meet these new market demands, especially as the colonizing powers achieved the strength to insist. In Tanzania (then Tanganyika), for example, German governors forced local men to migrate to grow cotton, leaving the women to try farming alone—even during the weeks of the growing season that required someone to watch the fields 24 hours a day.

The notion that there was a separate white racial identity reached its peak during this period, helping to provide psychological justification for seizing new territories and for forcing Western governments, economic divisions, and class divisions on the peoples being colonized. The earlier understanding of race was refined by the development of a political idea called Social Darwinism, which claimed to be scientific in that it borrowed the language of Charles Darwin's theory of evolution. Darwin's theory states that species of living beings evolve, or change, over time. Each individual member of a species that reproduces (successful reproduction being proof of what Darwin called "fitness") passes on its inherited characteristics to its offspring. Changes in the environment (climate, surrounding predator species, disease, and so on) can make certain characteristics more successful than others. Over time, many changes accumulate, and species change significantly: Some populations of a species evolve into separate species, and some populations and species die out. This process is neither good nor bad in evolutionary theory, because the theory itself makes no claim that there is a goal, endpoint, or purpose, of evolutionary change. Determining the purpose and meaning of life is not the normal domain of science. Many nineteenth- and early twentieth-century people, however, interpreted fitness as an indication of a species' worthiness. For Social Darwinists, fitness meant not just that a group was able to survive, but that they were morally superior and *ought* to survive. Social Darwinism tried to apply the theory of evolution to each nation or society as if it were a separate species in competition with other societies, much as individuals and populations within a species compete. In its rawest form, this philosophy justified domination and conquest as necessary elements in human progress and improvement. Social Darwinism declared that some societies were more evolutionarily fit than others; that it was most desirable for the most fit to survive; and that powerful, wealthy, conquering countries (and individuals) were obviously the most evolutionarily fit. Conquest was therefore always morally justified, and conquered peoples could only benefit from having their laws, institutions, and family structures changed to resemble those of the conquerors. Women's role in this ideology was to create fit children, but not to step out of what most Social Darwinists thought of as their proper biological place.

Many people, even in colonized countries, accepted some of the assumptions of Social Darwinism. For instance, the notion that change is usually good, and that continual progress is therefore possible and desirable, was shared by almost anyone with a Western intellectual background. Eugenics, a social/scientific movement of the early twentieth century, sought to apply evolutionary theory to individual human reproduction, leading to government policies that called for the sterilization of people declared unfit—usually the mentally ill, convicted criminals, prostitutes, and other powerless people. Members of minority groups were the most likely to be sterilized.

Because of imperialism, industrialization, and ideologies of racial superiority, colonial subjects encountered the most popular goals of nineteenth-century reformers—universal suffrage and public education; industrial efficiency; public transportation systems; and household management techniques that improved diet, cleanliness, and public health—in a context of brutal subjugation. Deciding which Western ideas were worth borrowing and modifying took decades. Change was clearly inevitable, but how much change, and in what areas of life? Women's roles in societies were among the most hotly contested points in these debates. On the one hand, the drive for self-determination, equality under the law, and self-rule went naturally with the international movements for women's rights. Domestic feminism, which promised to empower women to be the best possible wives and mothers, had a widespread appeal. On the other hand, women's roles in the family and their physical appearance had great symbolic importance. Would educating and empowering women make better representatives of their own peoples, or would it turn them into pale imitations of Western women? If they received greater legal protection and financial freedom, would they use them to serve their husbands and raise strong children, or would they just dishonor their families by choosing disobedience or sexual license?

Women played critical roles in imperialism as colonizers, subjects, workers, and activists. Colonized women across the world shared some experiences, whereas colonizing women shared others. Therefore, the first part of this chapter discusses colonized women and colonizing women separately. On the other hand, cultural context matters—as we saw in Chapter Three's discussion of the disparate effects of entering into the world fur trade upon Iroquois and Ojibway women. Another, larger, portion of this chapter therefore explores the roles and responses of women in particular colonized territories. Finally, Westerners were not alone in establishing new empires in the nineteenth century. As the Muslim Mediterranean industrialized and experimented with modernization, Muslim reformers in the Arabian Peninsula, the Sudan, and Sokoto Caliphate (in the northwest of modern Nigeria; see Figure 3.2, page 89) sought to build new societies based on rejecting what they considered pagan superstitions and watered-down Islam in favor of what they considered a more rational version of Islam. The last section of the chapter describes the importance of one of these new societies, the Sokoto Caliphate, for women, and explores their roles in adapting, expanding, and maintaining that culture.[3]

COLONIZED WOMEN'S EXPERIENCES AND RESPONSES TO IMPERIALISM

It is nearly impossible to avoid the word "native" when discussing imperialism, but we must do so with caution. It has different meanings for different populations, implying "authentic" to some and "backward" to others. When describing social practices, the visual and performing arts, and material culture, people often use the word "native" as a synonym for "unchanged since colonization." This can create the impression that native cultures never change, and that innovation, adaptation, and borrowing are undesirable artificial hybrids of native culture and a superficial overlay of the colonizers' culture. For purposes of this discussion, therefore, "native" refers to the cultures and populations of the pre-conquest period, as well as to the people and society considered indigenous by the colonizers and the colonized.

The word is inescapable in discussions of imperialism, because colonizers built their entire legal and social structures on the belief that they could draw a clear line between themselves and the native peoples they ruled. They were mistaken, of course, since every colonial region had not only numerous mixed-race inhabitants but also many immigrants and temporary residents from other regions. Immigrants and regular visitors were not perceived as part of the native culture and population. The descendants of colonizers and native people (usually native women) might or might not be part native culture. In South Africa, such descendants formed their own cultural sub-group within society; in Dutch

Indonesia, they identified as primarily Dutch; in British India, they straddled the line between both cultures.

The idea of native culture was particularly important during this period, because debates about what was and was not authentically native formed the background of most nationalist independence movements as well as of many imperialist legal systems. As we saw in Chapter Four, culture—as expressed through language, law, and religion—was becoming one of the most important criteria in defining natural boundaries of nation-states and national identity. This was the core principle behind Nationalist independence movements (see the discussion of Herder in the section on "Nationalism" in Chapter Four). Imperialist governments tried to serve the goals of their mother country while working through local elites, whose interpretations of native culture became the written law of the land and the basis upon which land annexations, taxation, and corveé labor (any tax collected in labor instead of cash or goods) were justified.

Colonized women typically found themselves, their behavior, their rights, and their responsibilities at the heart of struggles over the definition of native culture. Just as nineteenth-century Europeans and Americans argued for women's education in order to create better mothers, so male imperial elites (both colonizer and colonized) took women's actions seriously. For imperialists, the fact that the women they colonized in Africa, India, Central Asia, and the Americas did not live according to the expectations the colonizers held of their own (middle-class) women was an indication of the backwardness of native culture. In the modern, progressive world of the late nineteenth century, European and American colonizers thought that women should live as housewives and mothers, making a beautiful domestic retreat for their husbands and acting as the pure moral center of their nuclear families. The fact that native women did not live this way was evidence, in imperialist eyes, that native men failed to live up to their responsibilities as heads of households and therefore could not be expected to run their countries without Western assistance.

Native peoples' opinions about women's roles in society often fell along a spectrum. At one end, groups usually called "reformers" wanted women to become more modern and progressive, by which they meant that they wanted girls and women to be educated and able to raise educated children. The most reform-minded people would be converts to the imperialist religion; in most of the territories conquered during the nineteenth century, this meant Protestant or Catholic Christianity. Christian missionaries and their converts did not understand Christianity as simply a change of heart. To become Christian meant to adopt a Christian (that is, Western) lifestyle; not just to become a monotheist and a monogamist, but to wear Christian clothes, organize the household in a Christian manner,

and deport oneself in public the way other Christians did. It may seem odd
to equate adopting a religion with adopting an entire way of living, but it
makes a certain amount of sense—it takes considerable effort to practice a
minority religion, and adopting the visible, outward habits of other Christians must have made it easier to identify with the worldwide Christian
community and to maintain religious identity. Christian converts were the
native individuals most likely to push for reform and modernization and
the most likely to favor women's education and empowerment. This was
the group least ambivalent or hostile toward adopting what their fellow
citizens saw as foreign values.

Other reformers were less eager to adopt the colonizers' values, at
least inside their homes. Among those who did not adopt the colonizers'
religion, many nevertheless wanted to increase the level of women's education. For such people it was the educated woman's task to preserve and
pass on traditional customs. This opinion was most strongly held among
native elites, whose male members were likely to have to make their living by working for institutions (like banks, lawyers' offices, government
offices) that required them to behave during their work lives as if they
were thoroughly Westernized. The female members of their families, who
interacted much less with the colonizers, would be able to provide cultural continuity and, with their new educations, enlightened companionship and comfort to their men. Frequently these men also championed
a more patriarchal ideology than had previously been common; they
wanted husbands and wives to form closer partnerships and to resist the
authority of family elders.

Farther along the spectrum were native peoples for whom keeping
women's roles unchanged symbolized successful resistance to cultural
contamination. These people, usually considered traditionalists, were
really arguing for *less* change than reformers. They might be members
of elites or at least of the middle class (to the extent that a middle class
existed), and they were often in more direct ideological conflict with the
imperial government than the previous group.

Some native leaders tweaked their interpretations of tradition to gain
power. In attempts to stay independent of colonial control, they would
manipulate their traditional authority (usually over women and younger
men) to the greatest possible extent, often exaggerating it when consulting with their new rulers. They put their arguments to their followers
and to colonial powers in terms of tradition and perhaps believed they
were maintaining tradition. Yet these elite, favored informants of colonial
administrators tended to spin the information they provided about native
culture to stress the importance of traditional leaders at the expense of traditional consultative bodies and traditions of individual, especially female,

freedoms. If a traditional leader could pacify male followers angry over a new tax by increasing their authority over their wives' or daughters' inheritances, there were always some willing to do so. Women belonged to all of these groups: Some were converts, some came from families of reformers, and some from families of traditionalists.

Imperialism often brought about profound changes in family life and gender relations within it. A major reason for this was economic. One of the forces driving nineteenth-century imperialism was the need for raw materials to feed the burgeoning industrial centers of Europe and North America—governments wanted colonies to provide imports that could then be sold at home, abroad, and back to the colonies themselves. This meant imperial governments often insisted on revising the indigenous economic system in order to redirect male labor toward plantation agriculture, mining, road- and railroad-building, processing of raw materials, or other productive targets of the colonizing power. Frequently this meant gathering male laborers from regions miles away—in the case of rubber and sugar plantations, sometimes from thousands of miles away—and housing them in labor camps. Working-class men might have to leave their families for weeks, months, or even years at a time. Many tasks that men had done for the family in the past now fell to women and children, and many children grew up without the chance to know their fathers and uncles the way previous generations had.

During this era, colonized women were usually less interested in women's rights than in national independence. Activists—who, like their sisters in the industrialized nations, mostly came from elite or middle-class families—supported their brothers in forming nationalist political parties or military resistance movements. That is not to say that women did no work on their own or their daughters' behalf, but the activist women's goal was usually to make them more fit as mothers and wives.

COMMON GOALS AND EXPERIENCES OF COLONIZING WOMEN

A distinguishing feature of imperialism was the extensive participation of Western women in the expansion of empire. Western women did not carry arms or run colonial offices, but they were critical components in the importation of Western ways of practicing education, medicine, charity, cleanliness, and domestic life. Some were activists trying to improve the lives of the natives or of the colonial population. Some were adventurers seeking contact with landscapes and peoples they considered untamed and exotic. Some were professional women seeking opportunities less available to them at home, and some were homemakers, accompanying husbands or brothers and trying to create a familiar niche in foreign lands they found uncomfortable and among people whose personal habits they found baffling or annoying.

Some of the most influential Westerners never traveled to any of the colonies. Authors of popular household manuals like Catherine Beecher (the sister of abolitionist Harriet Beecher Stowe) and Mrs. Beeton had an international audience. Western women who did travel to the colonies were determined to bring as much of home with them as possible, and they sought to recreate middle-class domestic life abroad. Western-style middle-class households required one or two servants to assist in the heavy work and cooking. The women required Western-style buildings and servants trained to cook, clean house, serve food, launder, garden, dress, and speak like European servants—and they found that it was very difficult to persuade their own servants to travel to the colonies. Thus, they had to use native servants. Housewives relied on household manuals to assist them in teaching native servants how to run a "modern" (in this context, Western) home. In doing so they considered themselves to be at the heart of the imperial project. From the moment of rising to clean the teeth with a toothbrush to bedding down in a raised bed with mattress, pillows, and sheets, colonizer women set the standard of daily living native peoples either rebelled against or sought to emulate.

A handful of suffrage activists traveled to numerous countries around the world, but they were most influential among Western women and in countries that were independent, because colonized women felt national independence should have a higher priority than women's rights or female suffrage. The more long-lasting early collaboration emerged as professional women imported an ideology of domesticity and the domestic feminism that piggybacked in with it. The most visible transmitters of the ideology of domesticity were the mission schools that accompanied every imperialist government. Unlike the religious institutions of the first wave of colonialism, those in the imperialist period recruited women missionaries in substantial numbers. The nineteenth-century notion that men and women naturally had separate spheres of influence (the public world and the home, respectively) led missionaries from most denominations to prefer male educators for boys and female ones for girls. This led to the importation of women educators. The emergence of nursing as a recognized (and almost entirely feminine) profession in the late nineteenth century meant that bringing Western medicine to the colonies required importing women nurses. Among Protestant organizations, it was common for married couples to run a mission (whether medical or educational or both) together. Among Catholic organizations, sisters and nuns worked under the supervision of male doctors and priests. In urban areas, schools might employ a number of single women educators. Initially, all these women were Westerners (though not all were white; African-Americans sent missions to Africa), but over time they acquired native colleagues who embraced many of their ideas. Many of these women had themselves been educated in mission schools; some at North American or European universities.

Some women traveled to the colonies in search of opportunity. Professional women hoped to find it easier to get employment in the colonies than in the homeland. If they could not support themselves, they nevertheless found the supply of eligible men rather larger—and competition less fierce—than at home. White women never emigrated to the colonies in numbers equal to men, so they were always greatly outnumbered by white men. Furthermore, their standard of living in the colony, as members of the ruling class, would be much higher than at home. If they could learn to find pleasure in the unfamiliar atmosphere and climate of the colony—and many could not—white women could live very pleasantly in the colonies. White women in the colonies had more servants and larger homes than their counterparts in the homeland.

On the other hand, colonial life was not all a bed of roses. For colonizing men, colonizing women represented the heart of their ethnic identity. Protecting the women, who had the responsibility of building a little piece of the home country in an alien land, was a high priority. Because they shared racist assumptions that native men were sexually aggressive and intrigued by white women, colonizers thought native men were a constant threat to white women's sexual purity. Most colonizing women shared this fear of native men and accepted laws restricting their contact with natives. However, because most of their servants were native men and women, this made household management quite difficult. Just as colonizers expected the natives to toe the color line, colonial societies expected its members to pay constant attention to relative rank and status. Colonial societies were famously hierarchical and rigid. Married women's social status was tied directly to their husbands' status, and their behavior reflected directly on their husbands. Social life was much more formal than at home, and—because colonial society was so much smaller—a woman's circle of acquaintances and opportunities for entertainment and public service were much more limited. Colonizing women were, in fact, rather isolated. It is probably accurate to say that most found their position challenging at best, and that some found it frightening at worst.

ACTIVISM IN AN IMPERIALIST ENVIRONMENT: FOUR RESPONSES

EGYPTIAN FIRST-WAVE FEMINISM, 1840S TO 1950S

Egypt is the home of one of the oldest and most continuous feminist movements in the world, a movement that was originally homegrown. Muhammad Ali (1789–1849), the leader whose decades-long struggle against Ottoman control brought Egypt de facto independence, took a strong interest in education, including girls' education. His first move was to centralize midwifery and gynecological training, creating a state school for midwives. His government found it was too controversial to attempt widespread girls' public education during his administration, but he arranged for the royal wives and concubines to study with Western tutors, setting a standard that he could hope would be followed by other elite and would-be elite families. A short time later, the first schools for girls and women were built. At first only Jewish and Christian girls attended these mission schools, but the power of royal example led elite Muslim families to aspire to educate their daughters in the Western mode, too. It became customary by the end of the nineteenth century for elite families to pay for the education of their daughters. As was also the case in Japan and China, several prominent male intellectuals (with government approval and in some cases support) championed the cause of women's education, saying that a strong, modern Egypt required a modern, educated woman. At that time, Muslim intellectuals and theologians saw no conflict between Islam and what they would have called progress for women. In fact, the most influential theologians of the era thought women—and indeed, all Muslims—needed a thorough education.[4]

Huda Sharawi (1879–1947) not only led the first formal feminist organization in Egypt but also campaigned tirelessly on behalf of Egyptian independence. By the time she was a young adult, Egypt had lost its hard-won freedom from the Ottomans and had fallen under British control. Educated in her father's household in that first wave of girls who received an education in imitation of elites, Sharawi credited part of her love of learning to her father and his willingness to discuss intellectual matters with his children. Her earliest role models were women—a learned local woman named Khadija al-Maghribiyya inspired her with the knowledge that women could actually compose and debate classical Arabic literature and poetry on par with men. Later, her friendship with Eugénie Le Brun, the wife of Egyptian politician and independence activist Husain Rushdi Pasha, was instrumental in teaching her how to get along with other adult women and introducing her to new European ideas, such as the concept of learned societies and charitable organizations run entirely by women. Madame Rushdi ran a salon that became a gathering place for women of intellectual and artistic interests. In other words, Sharawi learned from Madame Rushdi the less overtly radical forms of elite women's activism that Empress Haruko had introduced in Japan a generation earlier.

All of Sharawi's organizational work was at first done in company with other very elite women like herself: She instituted and organized a series of lectures by and for women, and she encouraged and organized Egyptian women to found charitable organizations and run them on their own rather than simply joining organizations run by colonizing women. Her brief experience as a refugee fleeing Europe as World War I began (she had been visiting the region with her children) showed her for the first time that many women had to work for a living and that she herself was completely unprepared and uneducated to do anything of the sort. This revelation made her realize that elite women needed to learn from working women—but it would be a mistake to think of Sharawi as a major bridge-builder between Egyptian social classes. She was, however, a tireless activist on behalf of Egyptian independence, organizing the women's arm of the Wafd—the Egyptian Independence party, which was banned by the British.

After traveling to an international feminist conference in Rome in 1923, Sharawi returned home on fire with enthusiasm. As she disembarked in Cairo, she removed her face veil and threw it in the sea—an example followed by most upper-class Egyptian women within a few years. She founded the Egyptian Feminist Union (EFU) in 1924 and at first worked as much as she could with international feminist groups. But Europeans dominated international organizations like the Women's Suffrage Association, and the largely middle-class white population that made up the leadership of European movements was often unable to work effectively with women in colonized or recently independent countries. Under British rule, Egyptian activists had championed women's education in the cause of making Egypt modern, setting aside the issue of women's suffrage in favor of bettering women's education and acquiring national independence. During and after World War II, activists focused on pan-Arab nationalism and Palestinian independence as two of the issues most critical to Arab women. Here, Egyptian feminists (as their counterparts in India experienced in their campaigns for independence—see next section) found their Western feminist allies insufficiently interested in supporting Arab sovereignty and Palestinian independence and eventually turned to regional alliances.

INDIA, 1850–1950

> *. . . the responsibility for our own husband has been placed into the hands of each one*
> *of us women. The task that is our duty is to make him happy and to work strenuously*
> *to achieve his well being. Is it a small responsibility to add the weight of another life to*
> *our own little lives or an easy task to keep a constant watch on the peace and happiness*
> *of another person? Still, be it a hard task or an easy one, it is our essential duty.*
>
> NAGENDRABĀLĀ DĀSĪ, WOMAN'S DHARMA[5]

As in Egypt and Japan, in India the first activists to fight for women were elite men with Western educations. Most of them worked in British government offices. It was not so much that British education gave them an awareness of injustice, but that British traditions of public activism and journalism offered them new vehicles for public protest and organization. Particularly in Bengal—the territory where the British had been in power longest—men used the press and religious organizations to protest the evils they saw inflicted on the women in their own households. Most of their efforts were devoted to helping widows and educating their own wives. Hindu elites, in particular, believed that any man who married a widow would die soon after and therefore expected widows not only to remain single but to stay with their in-laws, subservient to all the other members of the family. Since elite Hindu girls were typically married before puberty—often to much older men—it was common for girls to be widowed well before they were 20. One activist saw this happen to numerous girls who had been polygynously married to the old man who had been his *guru* (religious leader) and was so disgusted and appalled that he began a life-long campaign to both raise the legal age of marriage for girls and convince his contemporaries that widows should be allowed to remarry. Other activists struggled to gain access to education for elite Indian women, a complex task given that both Muslim and Hindu girls acquired all the responsibilities that went with being mothers and wives during their early teens. They also lived enclosed, if possible, which made it harder to connect them with teachers. Reformers campaigned against *sati*, the practice of burning widows alive at their husband's funerals, and succeeded in making it illegal. Both the campaigns for a later age for marriage and against sati were very controversial among Hindus, and resistance eventually coalesced into a traditionalist Hindu political movement, the forerunner of contemporary Hindu fundamentalist politics. Early marriage ensured that a girl knew her husband's family well, that the women with whom she would spend her life would be the ones to teach her how to live as an adult, and that her husband would not be a stranger to her when she eventually became sexually active with him. No one knows whether sati was a common practice in any era of Indian history, but the women who did it were considered in much the same light as martyred saints in Catholic countries. The idea of the woman who would be so religiously devoted to her husband that she would die with him was deeply embedded in Indian popular culture, and many (including women) did not want to give it up.[6]

The results of these men's early efforts were not always beneficial for all Indian, or even all Hindu, women. Outside high-caste families, widows were much more likely to marry, and they had more rights to family property than their elite sisters. Thus, when Hindu activists persuaded the British government to create the Hindu Widow's Remarriage Act, which permitted widows to remarry under certain conditions and gave them limited rights within the family, only elite widows benefited. The average widow actually saw some of her opportunities reduced. Furthermore, the British used complaints about the oppression of Indian women as evidence that Indian men were too uncivilized to be allowed to govern their own country—they had to have the British there to create just laws for them and to protect women. Sati particularly horrified the British, and they often referred to it as the kind of barbaric practice it was the empire's responsibility to end. Nevertheless, activist men attempted a great deal for women with the resources they had, opening shelters and vocational schools for abused or impoverished widows, campaigning vigorously in favor of greater education for women, and attempting to improve their legal status and rights within the family. Probably unintentionally on the part of the photographer, Figure 5.2 illustrates some of the contradictory impact of the imperial regime. The woman in the train may well be traveling to a new destination at a faster pace than ever before possible. Yet the sign defining the legal occupants of the car reminds travelers that the government intended the social and gender hierarchies of India to remain firmly in place.

Although they could rarely resist their own families' choices of brides for themselves—only heads of household had enough power to marry a widow, for instance—men could educate or arrange for their wives' education. The biographies and autobiographies of early Indian women writers and activists are filled with stories of learning from or because of a husband's insistence and encouragement. One aspect of British domestic life in particular appealed to Indian men: Many cherished the idea of a companionate marriage and a romantic partnership with their wives. Creating such marriages could cause deep rifts in the family, particularly among the women. A wife's mother-in-law and her husband's aunts and grandmothers often felt threatened by the new kinds of close relationships modern husbands wanted with their wives, because the couple seemed to be split off from the rest of the household. One of the core values of Indian society was that the family as a whole should come before any individual, and if a husband and wife were too close they might make decisions that were only for their own good, and not for the family. Young Indian men who tried to become too close to their wives upset the family, and many of these men—who had to

FIGURE 5.2   NEW TRANSPORTATION, OLD RESTRICTIONS
Not all Indian women's journeys were spiritual—the introduction
of railroads made it possible for them to travel farther and faster
than ever before in India. This image was created by William
Henry Jackson for the World's Transportation Commission in 1895.
Here we see two Indian women traveling in a coach designated,
according to the sign in the image, for "Native Females" and as
"Third Class." Segregating the coaches made it possible for women
to travel without violating their own or their family's traditions
of modesty. Even as the railroads added to women's freedom of
movement, they reinforced gender and colonial hierarchies. Can
you think of any ways contemporary travelers are divided in ways
that reflect current hierarchies?

give up many of their traditions while they were working—already faced
rifts with their fathers and grandfathers over their apparent rejection of traditional values. Worse, a woman who worked too hard to become the new
kind of wife her husband wanted set what her female relatives considered
a bad precedent for the other women, and, in their opinion, set herself up
for a lifetime of being bossed around by a man who still had no idea what
her daily life was like. In her memoirs, Ramabai Ranade said her female
relatives had told her explicitly that she should consider the women in her
family more important than her husband. The women would be around all
the time, whereas her husband would be at home for relatively few hours:

> . . . even if the men folk like it, you should read just once in a while. Isn't
> this reading disrespectful to the elders of the house? What do the men
> know? We have to spend our whole life among the women of the family.
> The men are there for such a short while. They may ask once, twice, ten
> times. You can always stop listening. They will give it up after a while, in
> sheer disgust. Can we not manage it?[7]

The women of the household had to stick together if they were to resist male oppression, Ranade's relatives argued. Thus, many of the first women to acquire an education did so to please their husbands—with whom they spent little time alone—and in the teeth of constant opposition from the family members surrounding them. Ramabai Ranade, for instance, hid her studying from her family as much as possible.

For most, what seems to have made this kind of acceptance of household disharmony possible was the decision to sacrifice themselves not on the altar of their family but on the altar of marriage. For Hindu women, marriage was supposed to be the supreme sacrament. Their devotion to their husbands was supposed to be total, although in practice it was more common for them to be devoted to their whole family. Such devotion was not supposed to be dependent on his behavior toward them or his worthiness of it; the obedience, self-denial, and asceticism that monastic orders use for spiritual purification was available to Hindu women within their marriages. Women who chose to obey their husbands' desire that they be educated embraced their families' disapproval as a spiritual sacrifice necessary if they were to worship their husbands. Their education was a spiritual journey, and marriage was a mystical experience. A husband might be difficult or refuse to support his wife in front of his relatives when they criticized her for actions done in obedience to his wishes. Yet these stories appear in the women's narratives as spiritual challenges rather than complaints.

Companionate marriage offered wives both the opportunity for rebellion and for personal, spiritual growth on a scale rarely offered to Hindu women. The daughters and granddaughters of this generation of rebels would see themselves as powerful wives and mothers, imagining themselves as the inheritors of Lakshmi, the goddess whose self-sacrifice had made her the patron of and model for all wives. More than women activists elsewhere in the world, they would be ardent supporters of patriarchy within a nuclear family unit. Strengthening their husbands' authority freed them from obedience to older women and handed younger women households of their own to run. Unheard by most of the government and even outside middle- and upper-class households, husbands and wives were quietly revolutionizing family life by putting the nuclear unit of husband, wife, and children at the center of their concerns. By the end of the nineteenth century, middle-class and elite Hindu families expected that husbands and wives would form a companionate unit within the household and that the wife would be literate and well informed.

East Indian women did not create a separate feminist movement until the 1980s. Instead, most activist women campaigned for independence from British rule at the same time as they campaigned against particular laws that discriminated against women. Indians have practiced modern forms of populist, democratic activism since the early nineteenth century, when social reformers began using petitions to express their concerns to their British conquerors. Women's welfare and status were an important concern for activists, whether they were seeking Indian independence or Hindu (or Muslim) cultural revival. As in China and Japan, the first prominent pro-women activists focused on the education of girls and women—in the case of India, on the education and welfare of widows, especially virgin widows. Like the Chinese, high-caste Hindus expected widows never to remarry. But unlike the Qing dynasty, colonial India's legal and customary traditions provided little financial, emotional, or social support for widows. The earliest activists focused solely on widows' self-improvement and charity, eschewing political agitation. Pandita Ramabai (1858–1922) devoted her life to female education, founding schools in Bombay, Poona, and Khedgoan. She scandalized contemporaries by marrying beneath her caste and converting to Christianity. After a famine in 1890 she was able to provide homes, employment, and education for hundreds of women and their families. Her contemporary Swarnakumari Debi (1856–1932) started the Sakhi Samiti, a social welfare society designed to build networks among affluent women that would permit them to help widows and orphans by rescuing women from emergencies, educating them, and then paying the newly educated women to teach others.

Later activists were much more likely to combine First-Wave Feminism with ardent Nationalism, like Saral Debi Ghosal (1876–1946), whose organization Bharat Stree Mahamandal also educated women with the aim of sending them out as tutors. Ghosal also opened a martial arts academy and campaigned in Bengal to persuade men to take up swords, clubs, boxing, and wrestling in preparation for the certain armed struggle to come. By the second decade of the twentieth century, women activists were focusing on gaining independence. Bhikaji Cama's (1861–1936) cause was nationalist independence, and by 1908 she had begun to preach armed struggle against the British. The founder of the All India Women's Conference, Kamaladevi Chattopadhyaya (1903–1990), also led a major campaign of civil disobedience, joined the Congress Socialist Party, and in 1935 presided over its first all-India Conference. Women like these believed Indian independence would lead to improvement in women's condition and seamlessly combined their nationalist and feminist concerns. First-Wave activists desired reforms in family law that would forbid child marriage, end dowry, permit widow remarriage, and entitle widows and divorcees to some portion of the family wealth, and they requested these in meetings of the Congress Party (the most popular nationalist political movement), which had women's sections attached to local, regional, and national chapters. However, since the Congress Party had no power to implement these changes, women activists were willing to wait until independence to achieve change.

ZIMBABWE (SOUTHERN RHODESIA), 1900–1953[8]

If the activist movements of Egypt and India show us ways that colonized elite and middle-class men and women negotiated changes in gender ideology, Southern Rhodesia and Puerto Rico illustrate the impact of industrialization on colonized women. In Southern Rhodesia, as throughout imperial Africa, governments imposed radical economic reorganization. New laws required people who had lived for centuries in a barter economy to pay taxes in European cash. Such requirements forced Africans to enter a wage labor force paid and controlled by European settlers. Africans planted and harvested cotton and coffee for international markets, built roads and railroads, hacked gold and diamonds from mines, and worked as servants for white settlers. Colonial governments used their more advanced firearms to enforce the new economic and social order.[9]

Even though the new economy targeted male labor, controlling women was an integral piece of imperial policies. Most of the work for laborers in the new economies took place at centralized locations; men had to travel many miles to find paid work—so that to earn cash, they had to live far from home. This meant that the female members of their families had to do the work that provided subsistence for the family in the village. Tasks that had been split between men and women were suddenly left to women alone.

For imperialists, sexual and racial politics required that white women were to be kept rigidly apart from black men; black women were to become and remain more subordinate to black men. States granted local chiefs and kings more power over all black males, and all black men over the women in their families—strategies intended to pacify local leaders and men in general.

Administrators in Zimbabwe enacted policies much like those of other African colonies. While British women themselves were lobbying for the right to vote and entering professions as nurses, social workers, teachers, and secretaries, officials in Zimbabwe were explaining that there was no need to consider such advances for African women. African women, one of them wrote, "are many centuries behind [the men] in civilization, and absolutely unfit to be granted any measure of freedom for the present as their instincts are purely animal." At least one male missionary agreed that, "90 percent of the . . . women have immoral tendencies, are most irresponsible, readily give vent to their whims and fancies, and are void of all shame." One Jesuit missionary opposed letting African women teach because they were, according to him, "too ignorant, too volatile and feather-headed to allow them to be entrusted with such a charge."[10] Colonial officials saw Zimbabwean women as a stumbling block on the road to economic growth. In their ideal world, women would work quietly and chastely at home, obeying their husbands and fathers-in-law. Numerous new rules tried to prevent women from obtaining any measure of financial or physical independence. Laws against adultery targeted only women; colonial interpretations of customary law refused to acknowledge that women might have good reasons to leave a husband. If a husband took on a new wife without his first wife's permission; if his wife had never consented to the marriage; if he refused to support his wife financially; if he beat his wife regularly—none of these were good enough reasons for a wife to be granted separation or divorce. Certainly, women who left their husbands forfeited legal claim to their children.

If a woman did achieve a legal divorce, the new laws forced her family to return her bridewealth (*lobola*). In the past, most Zimbabwean men had sought the return of their wives, not their lobola. If a husband and wife had a dispute, she would leave for her family while both parties cooled off, and after a period of separation and negotiation she would usually return. Officials encouraged husbands whose wives had left to demand the return of lobola instead of the return of their wives. At the same time, the need for cash to pay taxes and the rise of the cash economy were causing a lobola inflation. Their daughters' marriages were one of the few times families could expect an infusion of wealth. Where lobola had once been a small symbolic exchange, it now became an opportunity for families to raise significant amounts of cash. Women were becoming cash commodities for both their families and their husbands, and when they fled their husbands, the men wanted—in fact, usually needed, if they were to marry again—their wife's lobola. The more expensive marriage became, the more abandoned husbands began to petition their brothers- and fathers-in-law for lobola instead of for help reconciling with their wives. The higher the sum they had received for their daughters and sisters, the more women's relatives tried to force women to return to their husbands, even in cases of serious abuse.

For some women, this meant their only recourse was to remove themselves from both their husbands and their own birth families. Cities and Christian missions were their chief refuges. Unlike European women, Zimbabweans could rarely find work as domestic servants—these positions were nearly all held by men. Instead, most of the separated wives we know about lived off the displaced men in the mines and factories. Using the new railway system to take them far from home as quickly as possible, they went away to live and work for themselves among strangers under assumed names. A small number of women lived solely by brewing beer, running boarding houses, or doing laundry. A much larger number seem to have taken on men in temporary, "cookpot" marriages. Few Southern African men knew how to prepare food and cook for themselves, and workers rarely had time to fetch and carry water and firewood even if they did know how to cook. These temporary arrangements do not seem to have involved bridewealth. Some women worked solely as prostitutes, but it seems likely that most of the women earning money or other forms of wealth in exchange for sex were also doing other work. Some other women fled to missions or convents, living there at night and working outside for wages. Gradually they could earn enough to pay back their lobola. By going a step further and taking vows as sisters, they could live a life of their own choice without interference from their families. In 1985, Veronica Chigomo explained, "Long back lots of [girls] came to be sisters because their parents wanted to marry them to old men."[11] Chigomo's sister, Mary, a nun, had worked as a nanny to pay back her lobola to her brother. Paying back lobola could take a woman years. Throughout sub-Saharan Africa, women who left their husbands or refused to marry the men of their families' choice felt responsible for returning bridewealth. Buchi Emecheta's historical novel *The Slave Girl*, set in colonial Nigeria, details the impact of this custom on one woman and her family.

Initially both the government and African patriarchs wanted Zimbabwean women to remain home in their villages. But gradually, over the course of the 1920s, many families began to need women to bring in some kind of cash income. Doing this required women have some mobility. Many village women brought food, wood, and small items to markets a few miles away from home. Others traveled long distances and remitted money and gifts home. Not all the women who worked in cities and around mining camps were there without the knowledge, permission, or even persuasion of their families. At the turn of the century and before 1920, fathers, brothers, and husbands complained to authorities that their wives had run away, gone off to distant villages or taken the train far from home. As the economy became more dependent on cash, men's most common complaints about women changed; now they were upset because their women had left home without remitting their earnings.

We might well ask how colonial officials justified the severe social disorder caused by forcing Southern Rhodesians to mine, farm, and process raw materials for export for low wages and under threat of arrest and physical correction. The ideological underpinning of colonialism—not just in British Africa but throughout the world—was the racism that had been forged under Atlantic slavery and reinforced with Social Darwinism.

Racism proclaimed that men and women with darker skin were naturally inferior to those with lighter skin. Social Darwinism said that all peoples would benefit from the proper education, even if some people were always going to be more fit to rule than others, and that the superior people had a duty to raise their inferiors to the highest level of development and civilization possible. For the French, this meant trying to make subject peoples think of themselves as French; for the British, this meant imposing legal and bureaucratic systems that were similar to their own. For all colonial powers, it meant attempting to modernize the economies of their colonies by bringing in railroads, hospitals, schools, and large corporate employers who would impose Western working habits and economic practices on their workers.

As was true under Atlantic slavery, maintaining a clear line of demarcation between the races was crucial for those who wanted to retain the system. Under imperialism, white women retained the special status they held in Atlantic slave societies: As a symbol of the purity of the race, white women had to be sexually available only to white men. African men had to keep their distance from white women as much as possible, which could be very difficult given that more than 80 percent of domestic servants in Zimbabwe were men. Even though there were very few cases of Zimbabwean men attacking white women, and even fewer of Zimbabwean men sexually assaulting white women, settler men feared for the virtue of their women. Colonists frequently exhorted the government to provide better protection, and they organized neighborhood vigilante groups if they did not get satisfaction. On the other hand, white men could have sexual relations with black women without serious reprisal, even where the relationships were non-consensual. It was actually more likely that the domestic servants white men sent to procure unwilling black women would be condemned for pimping than that any European man would be condemned for rape. African men did complain to officials about the racial mixing of white men and black women, and for a while, white women settler organizations also tried to have the law punish white men for adultery with black women, but these demands never resulted in legislation.

Southern Rhodesian officials claimed to want to follow tradition and customary law as much as possible, and as we have seen, they wrote about African women as if they were children in need of guidance—much as they wrote about British women. Yet their interpretations of custom and tradition were really quite flexible; they were quite willing to believe that tradition was whatever interpretation of family law fit most comfortably with economic policy. They may have considered African women frivolous, childlike, and immature, but they in no way considered that an important reason to arrange an economic system that would permit women to remain in the company and under the supervision of their own husbands and brothers. Instead, the Southern Rhodesian economy deliberately separated men from their wives and children for months and years at a time, provided no assistance to women living apart from their husbands, and turned a blind eye to men who committed adultery or refused to assist in supporting their children or wives. Officials mouthed concern for African marriages, but in fact this concern expressed itself not by easing taxation or providing marriage counseling or by educating women for employment; instead, the state stepped up punishments for women who committed adultery or left home to find work without their husband's, brother's, or father's permission. They were not so much concerned that women would be tempted into adultery but worried that fear of their wives' adultery would cause male workers to want to return home. Southern Rhodesian officials' solution for this problem was to try to force *all* young able-bodied men to leave home for work, so that there would be no temptation left in the village. If the temptation or threat to African women came in the form of a white man, that was not a problem from the point of view of Southern Rhodesia's officials.

Thus, even though very few African women engaged in industrial labor, mining, or plantation agriculture, they were nevertheless very important to the processes that inserted Southern Rhodesia into the international industrial economy. Lobola inflation helped increase the supply of men looking for work in order to earn cash for a brideprice. Colonial leaders tried to placate able-bodied workers and older male elites by granting them greater control over their wives and daughters' sexuality. They forced women's families to return lobola and forced unhappy wives to either return to their husbands or lose custody of their children. Yet *other* women's presence as laundresses, brewers, cookpot wives, and part-time prostitutes was indispensable for the maintenance of any large male labor force, and the income that traveling women sent home made it easier for their families to pay taxes. Southern Rhodesia's colonial economy required both subservient and disobedient women to function.

PUERTO RICO, 1898–1936

> We cannot go on living as slaves within the terrain of oppression, because we have been tyrannized for many years, because we understand that the labor movement is moving forward in giant strides. We are already knowledgeable in the political, physical, intellectual, and economic areas; we can embrace innumerable doctrines in order to undertake our own defense . . . and we will continue to espouse these as we prepare for this suffrage campaign. . . . we understand that suffrage is not simply a matter of women's vote, but a matter of the highest principles of liberty for us all.
>
> — CARMEN PUENTES, "LA MUJER PUERTORRIQUEÑA PIDE EL SUFRAGIO"[12]

For most of the nineteenth century, Puerto Rico was a Spanish colony. After the Spanish-American War ended in 1898, the colony became an American Protectorate until 1952, when it was granted commonwealth status. As in Russia and Japan, Puerto Rico's significant industrialization occurred in the late nineteenth and early twentieth centuries. Also like Russia and Japan, Puerto Rico's industrial economy employed large numbers of women. Most of them worked not in textiles, however, but in cigar manufacturing. And unlike any of the other industrial workers we have studied so far, Puerto Rican women integrated themselves successfully into the labor movement and the Socialist Party, which campaigned vigorously for better wages and working conditions for women and for female suffrage. Labor activists also worked effectively with middle-class equal rights feminists, which was, as we have seen, unusual in First-Wave Feminism.[13]

Before American imperialism, women had of course been active in the Spanish colonial economy. After the abolition of slavery in 1872, women had continued to labor on coffee plantations and to work as laundresses and seamstresses. But with the advent of U.S. colonialism, Puerto Rico's economy was sent lurching rapidly into industrialization, and by 1930 Puerto Rican women had become office workers, garment workers, needle workers, teachers, nurses, salesgirls, and—by far the largest new sector for female wage labor—tobacco factory operators. From the 1920s onward, large numbers of Puerto Rican women also emigrated to the U.S. mainland, most looking for employment in the large cities of the Northeast. Many went into the needle trades and garment industry, where they competed directly with Jewish and African-American workers, generally getting lower-paid and less-secure positions.

When Puerto Rican women first entered the tobacco industry in large numbers, they performed gender-specific tasks. As the century ended, cigar making was still a skilled craft performed mostly by male artisans in small shops. A small number of tobacco manufacturers also employed a few hundred male and female workers, with the men making the finished cigars and the women preparing the leaves by stemming and classing them. After the American invasion, the American Tobacco Company (ABT) expanded operations to Puerto Rico and opened new and larger plants. Within three years, the company was the leading manufacturer in Puerto Rico, and by 1903 it controlled 42.7 percent of the entire export market, a share that would increase until 1926, when it controlled 56.3 percent of the export market. To increase the speed of production, manufacturers divided the process of cigar making into more and smaller steps, so that even the highest level of skilled workers needed shorter and shorter training periods. ABT and other tobacco producers assigned the new, low-skill tasks to women, whom they could pay less than men. In 1910 men made up nearly 70 percent of all tobacco industry employees, but 25 years later they made up less than 30 percent. In two generations, women went from having very few jobs in the tobacco industry to making up over 70 percent of the labor force.

At first, male tobacco workers tried to keep women out of the industry entirely, because their low wages were driving down the men's value as workers. But labor organizers and Socialists quickly saw the handwriting on the wall: Women were entering the industry to stay, and if unions did not respond, its membership's wages would plummet. Rather than fight a losing battle to keep women out of the industry, unions determined to bring women into their membership and fight tooth and nail for higher wages at the lowest end of industry. Local union organizer Prudencio Rivera Martinez, of the Cigar Makers International Union, articulated the position clearly at a 1913 assembly meeting:

> [S]ince it is no longer feasible to stop completely the access of women to the industry, easy and practicable resolutions should be adopted to organize them in their work centers, and to stop where possible the growth of women in the cigar industry in Puerto Rico. Women, organized with us, struggling with us and prepared with us are not fearsome, cannot be our enemy, on the contrary, have to be our allies.[14]

Even as Martinez was saying this, the Stemmers and Classers Unions, organized by and for women, was already in its second year of operation. Tobacco workers' organizations on the whole decided it was best to organize the women and work together, and this had significant consequences for Puerto Rican politics for decades to come. The decision of the unions to organize women tobacco operators meant that women workers had an organization that fought actively for the issues working women wanted, rather than ones male organizers thought they should want. Since early twentieth-century labor unions were overwhelmingly Socialist in politics, this also meant that Puerto Rican Socialists actively recruited female membership and spent serious political capital trying to get women the franchise. If in Mexico, Liberals and Socialists alike were afraid to give women suffrage because they feared the women would vote them out of office, in Puerto Rico the mass of politically active women were union members and at least nominal Socialists. Socialists and unions expected, quite correctly, that women would vote for their issues. This is not to say Socialists thought only of political success; they also believed women should have a voice in politics to fight for improvements in their lives.

Tobacco workers organized as feminists as well as workers. Women labor leaders were not just prominent in unions but also in the Popular Feminist Association of Women Workers of Puerto Rico, an organization that represented primarily female workers and heads of households. The Popular Feminist Association worked to protect women workers from exploitation, fighting to change laws on minimum wages and improve the protection of women and children as well as to ensure that women workers' voices were heard in legislative debates concerning them. These feminists accepted and argued within the ideal of female domesticity, just like most feminists elsewhere at this time. But they deployed that ideal differently. As mothers and heads of household they asked uncomfortable questions—how can we be good mothers if we are not paid enough to feed our children, afford decent housing, have access to health care and clean water? Like First-Wave feminists in the middle of the nineteenth century, they fought the feminist war on many fronts, not just formal legal equality and suffrage.

Unionists were not the only feminists in Puerto Rico, however. Middle-class and elite women also formed explicitly feminist organizations. However, by the early twentieth century these associations—like women's rights organizations in Europe, Mexico, Brazil, and North America—focused on achieving suffrage and political office first, and other reforms later. Real change would not come before women had the political clout the vote could give them. They couched their arguments in favor of women's suffrage in terms of modernity and progress. Their role as mothers gave them important insights different from men's, and their very presence in the legislature would have a civilizing and gentling influence on the men debating there. In fact, they were classic domestic feminists, claiming public roles as the natural outgrowth of their femininity and capacity for nurture, and they called their version of this movement "social feminism." Their name had nothing to do with Socialism, however; the bulk of Puerto Rico's social feminists in the Suffragist Social League (their primary organization) were political and economic Liberals, highly educated members of elite families. Like their U.S. counterparts in the aftermath of the Civil War, they eventually separated on an issue of class. Whereas U.S. suffragists were divided over whether to give freed slave men the franchise (some had said yes, and some could not bear the thought of black men having the vote before white women), equal rights feminists in Puerto Rico split over literacy requirements.

U.S. women achieved suffrage in 1919, but suffrage came 17 years later for most Puerto Rican women. Like other colonies in the Caribbean, Puerto Rico expanded suffrage much later than the homeland. The United States wanted universal suffrage for men and, rather less urgently, suffrage for women. Male universal suffrage was a relatively new concept in Puerto Rico, and there was a strong movement among Liberals to grant female suffrage only to literate women. Many politically active women were illiterate. Although the Liberals argued that these women were not well enough informed to vote, the real problem was that they were Socialists. The Liberal feminists within the Social Feminist League divided over this issue in 1924, with half the league's membership splitting off to form the Puerto Rican Association of Women Suffragists, a group advocating limited franchise. From this time forward, the Social Feminist League, which supported the universal franchise for all adults, supported the Popular Feminists and the tobacco workers unions in word, if not very often in deed. The Social League engaged in few common activities with the Popular Feminists. Instead, they lobbied U.S. mainland feminist organizations like the League of Women Voters to put pressure on Puerto Rico. They managed to persuade one U.S. senator to introduce a bill granting suffrage to all Puerto Rican women (it failed), and they petitioned President Calvin Coolidge to include a message about Puerto Rican women's suffrage in his State of the Union address. In 1928 the governor of Puerto Rico asked the legislature to grant women suffrage—but only the limited franchise, for educated women, which they received in April of 1929. After this the Social League's activities declined rapidly; although the league pledged to continue the fight for universal suffrage, they did not. Instead, the Popular Feminists and the Socialist Party struggled on for another seven years, campaigning vigorously for universal suffrage. Finally, in the 1936 elections, all Puerto Rican women could vote their beliefs.

The Puerto Rican case highlights a number of aspects of women's movements not only of this period but of many. First, it demonstrates the importance of unionization for working women's participation in grassroots politics. Where unions had not supported women workers or put them in charge of deciding their own issues, they largely failed to organize women in large numbers. Thus, they also failed to politicize working-class women, who would continue to see political rallies and debates as men's activities. In Puerto Rico, however, women unionized to fight for their own concerns, joined shoulder-to-shoulder with union and with Socialist men, and experienced considerable success. Puerto Rico also highlights the difficulty of bridging class differences within women's movements, particularly when women of different classes do not work together directly. The Social League was willing to tear itself in half over the principle of universal suffrage, but as it turned out, the membership did not have the stomach for the fight after they had their own vote. The ability of affluent women to look away from poor women's political and economic issues has often been an obstacle to organized women's movements. The division between Puerto Rican activists was only one of many over the decades. In Chapter Seven, we will see that Second-Wave feminists in the second half of the twentieth century would have more success in organizing across social and political boundaries, but even today it remains difficult for people to trust with and work with each other where their economic interests seem dissimilar.

THE SOKOTO CALIPHATE, 1808–1903

The experiences of women in the Sokoto Caliphate, a state mostly located in what is now northern Nigeria (see Figure 3.2, page 89) mirror those of women in Western colonial arenas in a surprising number of ways. Like most Western colonies in Africa and Central Asia, the caliphate was established by conquest. Like Western imperialists in the nineteenth and twentieth centuries, the conquerors saw themselves as bringing a superior way of life to a heathen people. Purifying Islamic practice, educating women to teach their children to be proper members of the new society, introducing orderly forms of farming and land tenure, and forcing laborers to work on plantations controlled by educated urban elites are all patterns similar to those cataloged earlier. The caliphate did not deliberately steer the agricultural system toward production for international industry, but it did encourage widespread changes in land use and created a cultural climate that strongly encouraged food production for sale.[15]

There are, of course, some important differences. The leaders of the caliphate were not outsiders, but part of a social group that had lived in the region for many decades. Although most of the early members of the caliphate were ethnic Fulani, their social organization was significantly different from that of the ethnic groups around them. Membership in the group was not determined by ethnic background, but by the member's willingness to accept and practice the caliphate's beliefs. It was not language, skin color, or class that made one a citizen of the caliphate, but adoption of the state's version of Islam.

The early Sokoto Caliphate was led by Shehu Usman dan Fodio and his son Muhammad Bello. When these two men died, it was Bello's youngest sister, Asma'u, whose spiritual gifts supported the state's legitimacy. The Shehu's family and followers were members of the Qadiriyya Sufi order. Sufism serves many of the functions of monasticism in popular Islam. Although Islam disapproves celibacy, the Prophet's own example at Medina had provided a model for spiritual retreat and the formation of a separate religious community. Many Muslims desire a life spent in contemplation and direct service to the divine. Such people generally participate in Sufi orders. At the heart of such an order is a community led by a teacher (sheikh) of great spiritual authority and learning. Sheikhs are leaders of religious communities, and in the Sudan, North Africa, Central Asia, and the Arabian Peninsula these communities are sometimes separate villages or tribes of people. In West Africa these were the people who had produced the great centers of learning and scholarship in Timbuktu and Kano. They were connected to the entire Muslim community, and their libraries typically included manuscripts from all over the Muslim world and all Muslim periods. The Shehu was leader of a Sufi town made up of his family and followers. His community's tradition eschewed luxury; emphasized the importance of charity, justice, and mercy; insisted on greater sex segregation than was the norm in the Western Sudan; and considered access to education indispensable for all Muslims.

The Shehu was particularly concerned with injustice toward women. He despised men who failed to provide financial support to their wives, who played favorites if they had multiple wives, or (worst of all) prevented their wives from getting a good education. Himself the son, grandson, and brother of highly educated women, he considered female scholarship normal. Like nineteenth-century domestic feminists in the West, the Shehu and his brother Muhammad Bello considered women's education necessary to the creation of a proper (in their case, Islamic) state. It was Muslim women who had to convince captured peoples to abandon practices like spirit possession; who would teach children Muslim values and enforce them within the household. It was often women who would mediate within the household. Thus, unlike almost any other government of the early nineteenth century, the Sokoto Caliphate not only implemented just a policy of educating women but also devoted significant resources to that education. They created a government department to oversee this effort and put their most learned sister, Asma'u, in charge of it. Nana Asma'u, as she has come to be known, would create a network of teachers and a system of women's education that survives in Hausa-speaking areas to this day.

It is helpful to think of the caliphate in general and Asma'u's work in particular as a Muslim missionary effort. The government's chief goal was to spread and protect its interpretation of Islam, and the influence of that missionary effort extended far beyond the political borders of the caliphate itself. The caliphate was spreading a way of life, and converting women to that way of life was as important as converting men. Like Christian missionaries of the same period, the caliphate sought conformity in dress and housing patterns and the gender division of labor.

The leaders of the Sokoto Caliphate envisioned their society as being made up of cities surrounded by a stable, harmonious agricultural countryside, with most of the population living in *ribats*, which were agricultural village communities. In the western Sudan, they were fortified. Ideally, the ribat was large enough to build a lively Sufi community around it, supply travelers, and provide its own food supply. In reality, this vision was imperfectly implemented and somewhat ecologically unsound. The caliphate often experienced hunger and, by the end of the nineteenth century, farming had expanded into regions that did not really have enough water or sufficiently developed soil to support the population. Hunger seems to have been a common experience.

Then and today in Hausaland—the region of Nigeria most closely associated with the caliphate—families lived in walled compounds, and women spent most of the day outdoors in the open air of their own family compound. Whether singing, reading aloud, bargaining, chatting, or arguing, women's voices were distinctly audible throughout the ribat. Women of the caliphate spent a lot of time gathered together with female friends, and their descendants still do. Married women sent their sons, daughters, and servants on errands throughout the ribat or the city and the surrounding countryside, gathering news, trading in foodstuffs and textiles, and inviting friends to visit. There was a steady stream of scholars and merchants throughout the western Sudan and, wherever the Muslim culture of the caliphate took hold, it was women who organized lodging, food, and water for the travelers. Nineteenth- and early twentieth-century travelers assessed the extent to which an area of this region was properly organized and harmonious largely by the degree to which they could find Hausa food and accommodations—in other words, by the strength of women's participation in the formal economy.

The Shehu was serious in his demands for married Muslim women to keep from public view and in his demands for their husbands to provide financial support and opportunity for extensive education. Like many of the most vocal domestic feminists of the West, he imagined a world where women were chaste and submissive wives; ardent and activist leaders in charitable work; wise and trustworthy mediators of family disputes; and well-educated students of religion. Women who organized to support orphans, widows, or education were encouraged. Women's socialization with each other was perfectly permissible and also encouraged—learned women could correspond with whomever they liked. Women could not work with male tutors face-to-face unless they were relatives, and they could not have the same kinds of intimate friendships with men that they had with other women. Yet the expectation was that women could get just as good an education from other women as from men. Asma'u's own prolific scholarship in three languages (Arabic, Hausa, and Fulani) was one of the primary models for women.

Asma'u was responsible for creating a widespread system of female education as well as government propaganda in the form of poetry and literature. She wrote scholarly works in Arabic and personal letters and elegies in her native language of Fulani, but she composed the bulk of her writing in Hausa. This was the language of the conquered people and refugees whom the caliphate settled in ribats throughout the region. Her chief task was to instruct and convert the women in these populations, most of whom would have resided in the households of families already loyal to the caliphate. Her most famous work, "The Quran," is a song/ poem of mnemonic aids to help the reader memorize the titles of all the *suras* (chapters) of the Quran and their main points. It is intended as a first introduction to the Quran, an organizational framework for any course of Quranic study from the most elementary to the most advanced, and as an aid to meditation. By reciting it—the names of the suras are in the original and appropriate Arabic—the speaker participates in and benefits from communion with the eternal Word. Thus, just memorizing provides a basic spiritual guide for beginners. Asma'u also wrote poems explaining how pagans could replace the medicinal benefits of traditional spirit possession (practiced by many pre-reform Muslims and in fact still practiced among some African Sufis) with acceptable Islamic practices of prayer and other medical treatment. Her most important educational achievement, however, was institutional. A century after the fall of the Sokoto Caliphate to the British, the network of teachers and pupils she created survives.

Asma'u created a flexible educational system that employed learned women to educate other women. Unmarried girls, post-menopausal married women, and widows would travel to Asma'u every year to report to her on their progress, hear her instructions and blessing, and receive the official insignia marking them as traveling educators, *yan-taru*. They would travel from ribat to ribat educating married women—mothers with children not yet grown—in their own or their friends' homes. Apparently, there was little enough crime in the caliphate that there were no concerns about the women's safety on these journeys. Popular songs and stories from the era depict adolescent girls wandering on adventures far from home and village in search of good husbands, spiritual growth, and luxury trade goods, so it would seem that traveling the country as a teacher would not have raised any eyebrows. Leaders of this Sufi movement are still highly educated. A yan-taru was normally literate in Arabic, Hausa, and Fulani, was thoroughly grounded in scriptures, hadith, and sharia, and maintained a library of several hundred manuscripts. Like Asma'u herself, the yan-taru was steeped in Muslim scholarship.

It is easier to know what the caliphate intended for women and the extent to which they succeeded than to know how much their conquered peoples appreciated it. The caliphs spent the entire period of the state's existence putting down one rebellion or other among local nobility— clearly the fighting men they conquered were not always pleased. As the caliphate took over more and more territory, it produced larger numbers of refugees and captured many more people. Some of the orphaned and widowed girls and women might be assimilated into families of members and put under the supervision of the women. It seems unlikely they found this a pleasant experience. Refugee and captured populations were frequently set to building ribats and settling them as laborers and slaves—not necessarily a lifestyle they would have chosen. The literature left behind and most of the archaeological evidence so far examined was written by the conquerors, and the Hausa today are proud of the caliphate's past. It may be that its glory is enhanced by comparison with the British conquerors of the early twentieth century and the frequently corrupt government of the post-independence era, or it may be that even the people conquered by the caliphate experienced it as a golden age. In any case, it is clear that by the last quarter of the nineteenth century, the Sokoto Caliphate had created a uniform Hausa-speaking Muslim culture not just in its own territories, but also in much of the surrounding area. The caliphate and Hausa-speaking regions in general (Hausaland) consisted of agricultural communities surrounding cities. These cities supported a network of Muslim travelers, both merchants and scholars, that connected the caliphate to the wider Muslim world, and it was the work of women that kept these travelers supplied.

The cultural reforms its leadership fought for continue to affect Muslims throughout the Hausa- and Fulani-speaking world, as do the economic relationships they created when their successful military campaigns brought tens of thousands of refugees into their society to work as slave labor in clearing and then farming fortified agricultural villages. These villages became the model for land use throughout not just the caliphate but also Hausaland. The Shehu's version of Islam became the Islam of the whole region, and Asma'u's scholarship and her authority became watchwords for the average Hausa speaker, whether male or female. Her official histories of the caliphate and the biographies she wrote and had broadcast throughout the region formed the narrative of Hausa ethnic identity. The version of femininity and household organization they championed became the model for most Hausa, even if only fairly affluent households could provide the kind of enclosure considered ideal for married women.

It is not clear why the colonialism of the caliphate seems to be so much more fondly remembered by the local populace than the colonialism of the English and other nineteenth-century imperial powers. After all, tens of thousands of people were displaced and put into a form of slavery in the decades of war accompanying its establishment. Perhaps it was due to the Shehu's preaching of equality among all Muslims;

perhaps it was due to the creation of ribats, although there is considerable evidence to suggest that the ribat system over-farmed the region and created frequent hunger. Perhaps it was because the European conquerors were seen as more foreign, and perhaps it was all three of these put together. In any case, the Sokoto Caliphate provides an intriguing example not only of imperialism that appeared to work for the people colonized, but also of successful government intervention to significantly change women's daily lives.

CONCLUSION

Imperialism affected women's lives in many different ways, and their responses to and participation in it were equally diverse. Colonizing women could act as representatives of the conquering ideology, as both white women and women members of the caliphate did. Some sought to work with and assist the women their government had conquered, and in doing so they tried to impose their own notions of appropriate femininity—as we saw in India and the caliphate. For their part, colonized women experienced colonialism in very different ways. Whether their conquerors sought to pull their region's economy into the wider industrial world made a big difference in their choices, and whether they themselves could find employment as industrial workers also made a difference, as we saw in Puerto Rico and Southern Rhodesia. The support of either men's organizations or outside women's organizations was indispensable. Most especially in colonized countries, male supporters or female colonizing supporters were necessary for women to stake their own claims as women while resisting colonial oppression. In Southern Rhodesia, women who fled from unhappy homes relied on Christian missions to support them, and their weakened position stemmed as much from the agreement of male colonizers and male elites that women should submit to their husbands and fathers as it did from colonization. White women's lack of interest in African women's status and their belief in African men's sexual aggression made it very difficult for black women to mobilize on their own behalf. In Puerto Rico women's quest for suffrage found that male unions' support for female union membership and the support of international feminist organizations were indispensable. In Egypt and India, male support for female education gave a small cadre of women the opportunity to make regional and international connections, and it was Nationalist men's willingness to permit women to form female political arms of their parties that taught women how to succeed in the political arena.

STUDY QUESTIONS

1. How did women's movements in colonized countries differ from those in independent ones? In what ways were they similar?

2. This chapter and Chapter Four provide several examples of movements started by men on behalf of women. Do you find any common characteristics in these efforts?

3. Compare and contrast the effects of early industrialization on Puerto Rican and Southern Rhodesian women. With which other country's industrialization experience do you think each is most similar?

4. In what ways were the goals of the Sokoto Caliphate similar to those of other colonial powers?

BIBLIOGRAPHY

*indicates contains whole primary sources or secondary works containing substantial extracts.

GENERAL

Benton, L. *Law and Colonial Cultures: Legal Regimes in World History: 1400–1900*. Cambridge: Cambridge University Press, 2002.

Blom, Ida, Karen Hagemann, and Catherine Hall. *Gendered Nations: Nationalism and Gender Order in the Nineteenth Century*. Oxford: Berg, 2000.

Chaudhuri, Napur, and Margaret Strobel, eds. *Western Women and Imperialism: Complicity and Resistance*. Bloomington: Indiana University Press, 1992.

Collins, Robert O., ed. *African History in Documents*. 3 vols. Princeton, NJ: Markus Wiener, 1990.

Headrick, Daniel. *The Tentacles of Progress: Technology Transfer in the Age of Imperialism, 1840–1940*. New York: Oxford University Press, 1988.

———. *The Tools of Empire: Technology and European Imperialism in the Nineteenth Century*. New York: Oxford University Press, 1981.

Pierson, Ruth Roach, and Nupur Chaudhuri, eds. With assistance of Beth McAuley. *Nation, Empire, Colony: Historicizing Gender and Race*. Bloomington: Indiana University Press, 1998.

Said, Edward. *Orientalism*. New York: Pantheon Books, 1978.

Spivak, Gayatri Chakravorty. "Can the Subaltern Speak?" In *The Post-Colonial Studies Reader*, edited by Ashcroft, Griffiths, and Tiffin. New York: Routledge, 1995.

Stoler, Ann Laura. *Carnal Knowledge and Imperial Power: Race and the Intimate in Colonial Rule*. Berkeley: University of California Press, 2002.

Strobel, Margaret. *Gender, Sex, and Empire*. Washington, DC: American Historical Association Essays on Global and Comparative History, 1993.

EGYPT

Badran, Margot. *Feminists, Islam, and Nation: Gender and the Making of Modern Egypt*. Princeton, NJ: Princeton University Press, 1995.

Baron, Beth. *The Women's Awakening in Egypt: Culture, Society, and the Press*. New Haven: Yale University Press, 1994.

Meriweather, Margaret L., and Judith E. Tucker, eds. *A Social History of Women and Gender in the Modern Middle East.* Boulder, CO: Westview Press, 1999.

*Nelson, Cynthia. *Doria Shafik, Egyptian Feminist: A Woman Apart.* Gainesville: University Press of Florida, 1996.

*Sharawi, Huda. *The Harem Years: The Memoirs of an Egyptian Feminist 1879–1924.* Translated by Margot Badran. New York: Feminist Press at CUNY, 1987.

INDIA

Forbes, Geraldine. *The New Cambridge History of India.* Vol. IV.2, *Women in Modern India.* Cambridge: Cambridge University Press, 1996.

Gooptu, Suparna. *Cornelia Sorabji: India's Pioneer Woman Lawyer.* Oxford: Oxford University Press, 2006.

Kumar, Radha. *The History of Doing: An Illustrated Account of Movements for Women's Rights and Feminism in India, 1800–1990.* London: Verso, 1993.

*Mazumdar, Shudha. *Memoirs of an Indian Woman.* Edited by Geraldine Forbes. Armonk, NY: M. E. Sharpe, 1989.

*Sahagal, Manmohini Zutshi. *An Indian Freedom Fighter Recalls Her Life.* Edited by Geraldine Forbes. Armonk, NY: M. E. Sharpe, 1994.

Walsh, Judith E. *Domesticity in Colonial India: What Women Learned When Men Gave them Advice.* Lanham, MD: Rowman and Littlefield, 2004.

PUERTO RICO

Capetillo, Luisa. *A Nation of Women: An Early Feminist Speaks Out.* Houston, TX: Arte Publico Press, 2004.

Ferrer, Valle. *Luisa Capetillo, Puerto Rican Feminist.* Translated by Gloria Waldman-Schwartz. New York: Peter Lang, 2006.

Rodríguez, Félix V. Matos, and Linda C. Delgado, eds. *Puerto Rican Women's History: New Perspectives.* Armonk, NY: M. E. Sharpe, 1998.

Shepherd, Verene. *Women in Caribbean History: The British Colonized Territories.* Oxford: Markus Wiener Press, 1999.

SOKOTO CALIPHATE AND WEST AFRICA

Bivins, Mary. *Telling Stories, Making Histories: Women, Words, and Islam in Nineteenth Century Hausaland and the Sokoto Caliphate.* Portsmouth, NH: Heinemann 2007.

Boyd, J. *The Caliph's Sister: Nana Asma'u (1793–1865) Teacher, Poet and Islamic Leader.* London: Frank Cass, 1989.

*Boyd, J., and B. Mack. *Collected Works of Nana Asma'u, Daughter of Usman dan Fodiyo (1793–1864).* East Lansing: Michigan State University Press, 1997.

Chuku, Gloria. *Igbo Women and Economic Transformation in Southeastern Nigeria 1900–1960.* New York: Routledge, 2005.

Coles, C., and B. Mack, eds. *Hausa Women in the Twentieth Century.* Madison: The University of Wisconsin Press, 1991.

Cromwell, Adelaide M. *An African Victorian Feminist: The Life and Times of Adelaide Smith Casely Hayford 1868–1960.* Washington, DC: Howard University Press, 1992.

*Emecheta, Buchi. *The Slave Girl.* New York: G. Braziller, 1977.

Hiskett, Mervyn. *The Sword of Truth: The Life of the Shehu Usman dan Fodio.* New York: Oxford University Press, 1973.

Mack, Barbara B., and Jean Boyd. *One Woman's Jihad: Nana Asma'u, Scholar and Scribe.* Bloomington: Indiana University Press, 2000.

ZIMBABWE/SOUTHERN RHODESIA

Barnes, Teresa. "The Fight for Control of African Women's Mobility in Colonial Zimbabwe, 1900–1939." *Signs: Journal of Women in Culture and Society* (Spring 1992): 586–608.

———. *"We Women Worked So Hard": Gender, Urbanization, and Social Production in Colonial Harare, Zimbabwe, 1930–1956.* Portsmouth, NH: Heinemann, 1999.

Barnes, Terri, and Everjoyce Win. *To Live a Better Life: An Oral History of Women in the City of Harare, 1930–1970.* Harare, Zimbabwe: Baobab Books, 1992.

Pape, John. "Black and White: The 'Perils of Sex' in Colonial Zimbabwe." *Journal of Southern African Studies* 16, no. 4 (1990): 700–720.

Schmidt, Elizabeth. "Patriarchy, Capitalism, and the Colonial State in Zimbabwe." *Signs: Journal of Women in Culture and Society* (Summer 1991): 732–756.

———. *Peasants, Traders, and Wives: Shona Women in the History of Zimbabwe, 1870–1939.* Portsmouth, NH: Heinemann, 1992.

◀ PART THREE ▶

THE TWENTIETH CENTURY

We have seen that during the long nineteenth century, states' power kept increasing while more and more people came to see themselves as having a personal stake in and a role to play in strengthening and improving states. The twentieth century accelerated this trend. It became possible for governments to mobilize entire national populations, and they did so.

Chapter Six, "Women under Totalitarianism" looks at the most notorious cases of this in Nazi Germany, the Soviet Union, and the People's Republic of China. These three states provide extreme examples of the worldwide tendencies of governments to police, manipulate, and attempt to improve even seemingly trivial details of daily life.

Women participated in revolutionary movements in all three of these countries. Each country tried to adapt women's roles as workers, mothers, and wives to suit a particular political vision. Like the Sokoto Caliphate in the nineteenth century, each country tried to use women leaders to indoctrinate their female populations and persuade them to provide active support to the regime. These nations' most infamous practices would be extreme forms of policies enacted in other countries, rather than complete innovations.

Chapter Seven, "Cold War, Neo-Colonialism, and Second-Wave Feminism, 1945–Present" brings us from the end of World War II to the present. Two world wars (1914–1919 and 1938–1945) had cemented states' ability to rally their citizens, but also weakened the European powers enough that they were unable to hold onto their overseas colonies. Over the next generation, almost all colonies achieved national independence. The Western European powers gave up their colonies, while two new superpowers, the Soviet Union and the United States, vied for superiority in a decades-long cold war. The Nationalist and independence movements of the twentieth century were accompanied by liberation activism in many countries. Chapter Seven goes on to describe women's roles in post-war regimes, some of the kinds of organizations women created, and the reasons they created them. More and more women joined or formed activist groups, and again they looked past achieving independence or victory over the enemy toward improving the societies and the worlds they lived in. A second wave of feminist activism made significant progress toward improving women's lives, and the widespread increase in public education, health care, and access to birth control gave hundreds of millions of women new choices and opportunities. The increasingly rapid pace of change, however, was disturbing and disorienting for many people. Individuals, ethnic groups, and whole countries struggled to find their balance in a world that seemed to change almost beyond recognition in the course of a generation or two.

The Conclusion of *Envisioning Women in World History* is an exploration of women's self-expression. Of course, women have spoken for themselves, made art, performed, and engaged in critical inquiry for as long as there have been women. But World History as a field has not yet engaged itself in detail with the human quest for the good, the true, and the beautiful, and I could see no way to incorporate that quest as part of the general narrative of this text. Yet one of my colleagues, after reviewing an early outline of this text, noted, "You've left yourself out." Where, she asked me, were the women scholars? And I decided that this text ought to have one space entirely devoted to the arts and sciences and their meaning for women. My own experience as an educator has taught me that students often overlook indications of women's agency in chapters that also discuss their oppression. Completing the text with an exploration of women's self-expression is my attempt to provide an antidote to the depression that can accompany the study of any oppressed group.

CHAPTER SIX

WOMEN UNDER TOTALITARIANISM

In Chapters Three and Four, we considered the period historians think of as the "long nineteenth century," an era of industrialization, imperialism, and the expansion of popular participation in politics. Industrialization would continue to expand in the twentieth century, creating a truly global economy by the end of the century. Formal colonial empires would gradually disappear in the second half of the century, but their legacy would remain in the form of economic interference in and dominance over many former colonies. Grass-roots political movements and massive popular revolts became staples of twentieth-century politics.

Women continued to be an important source of labor for low-paid, light industrial work. Countries all over the world looked to their women as symbols of national identity and achievement, and women themselves participated in and helped shape debates about their own and their nations' futures. Throughout the twentieth century, women participated in even the most dangerous grass-roots politics, their support often proving crucial to a movement's success. At the same time, early development policies and globalization often hurt women's economic standing more than they helped.

The technological advances of the nineteenth century accompanied increasing state power and centralization. New tools of information literacy and mass communication—such as libraries, museums, public schools, telegraphy, typewriter, radio, and motion pictures—emerged. New methods of international travel such as railroads and steamships made it possible to communicate ideas and transport goods farther and faster than ever before. In the twentieth century, governments achieved the ability to interact with citizens on a daily basis, and they seized this capability with gusto. World Wars I (1914–1919) and II (1939–1945) only increased the tendency of governments to centralize power, silence opposition, and mobilize their citizens by making daily activities revolve around patriotic service.

The three states examined in this chapter represent extreme cases of these tendencies as they were manifested in three of the most notorious twentieth-century states. Their governments used their power to police and limit citizen mobility, to spy on citizens, and to deport or kill thousands or even millions of people. Yet the powers they had were not unusual for twentieth-century states, and the shocking uses to which they put them were in fact extreme forms of practices engaged in by many other nations. If the Nazis of Germany were obsessed by racial purity, the Romanians of the 1930s were hostile to German speakers, Jews, and Hungarian speakers within their own borders. If the People's Republic of China forced most of its citizens into Communist re-education programs and political meetings, nations across the world introduced adult education classes, and political parties everywhere created neighborhood associations. If the Union of Soviet Socialist Republics (the Soviet Union, or USSR) closed down churches, told its Christian and Muslim citizens that religion was nothing but lies and superstition, and murdered or exiled political and religious dissenters, the Mexican Revolution of 1911 was sometimes violently anti-clerical, and government policies in Mexico had been trying to erase non-Christian religions for centuries. The differences between totalitarian states and "normal" bureaucracies had to do with where, how, upon whom, and by whose permission states employed coercion. All states have the power to exert great pressure on the majority of the population; but totalitarian states sought to micromanage the economic and social organization of their entire populations and ruthlessly rooted out not just active opposition, but also open expressions of dissatisfaction. Less overtly totalitarian bureaucratic states satisfied themselves with tweaking the edges of economic and social organization—mostly suppressing the work opportunities, health care, and freedoms of minority populations while using state education and modern communication systems to acculturate the majority of the population.

Radio, film, newspapers, magazines, and networks of publicly funded schools made it possible for governments and political parties to mobilize citizens on an unprecedented scale. The governments of industrialized and partly industrialized countries could pry into their citizens' lives, prod citizens into voluntarism, and demand active service. Nationalist ideology ruled the day. Colonial peoples learned in school, radio, and print that they were citizens of France, England, The Netherlands, or Portugal, and not just denizens of Senegal, India, Dutch Guiana, or Angola. Intellectuals the world over took up the problem of national identity with renewed vigor, trying to imagine the kind of citizen best suited to build and lead modern, twentieth-century nation-states. For some, the goal was to produce men who could be successful revolutionaries against colonial rule. For others, the goal was choosing the aspects of modernization most compatible with their own values, deciding which could be modified and which were essential to achieving autonomy, prosperity, economic stability, and cultural growth. Whereas in the nineteenth century, most serious thinkers had believed education was the most important tool of modernization, the success of anarchists and revolutionaries in Russia convinced many that the road to freedom led through militarism and unswerving devotion to the cause—whether the cause was Nationalism, Socialism, or Imperialism.

In theory, every society had unique agendas with respect to masculine and feminine behavior. On the surface, Adolph Hitler's dream that men become cheerful brutes and women mothers of healthy soldiers seems very different from Mao Zedong's vision of men and women as comrades working with equal zeal and competence toward a brighter tomorrow. In practice, totalitarian states shared a willingness to make deep alterations in the politics of the family; to shuttle women in and out of the paid labor force; and to demand changes in sexual practices, family planning, and childbirth.

The most infamous totalitarian governments of the first half of the century were Nazi Germany and the Soviet Union, which professed widely divergent ideologies as well as goals for women's participation in society. Both created official ministries intended to serve women or at least mold them into the kind of women the state wanted to see. Both states displaced the leadership of the women's movements and women's organizations already in place in their countries, installing women or even men as leaders based on criteria other than proven success in leadership; both failed in the end to produce the changes in family life and women's activities for which they had hoped.

In differing ways, each of these governments' use of women supporters and later attempts to control those supporters became models for later states. Reactionary governments in Chile, Argentina, and Brazil mobilized women supporters with rhetoric similar to that of the Nazis and then borrowed from the most successfully implemented Nazi family policies. For the rest of the twentieth century, the Soviet Union's official position that sexism is caused by social stratification—and so would disappear on its own in a truly Socialist society—became the default position of later Socialist and leftist governments as well as for leftist movements.

The later People's Republic of China (PRC) differed significantly from the USSR with respect to reforming gender relations. Although Chinese Communists disliked formal Feminism as much as other Socialists, they put real resources into improving women's lives over a much longer span of time than the USSR did. Women in the PRC gained more freedom within the family, greater control over their earnings, and (in cities) many more opportunities for respectable paid employment. Although the leadership of the PRC always supported the notion that sexism resulted solely from classism, in practice the People's Republic spent enormous energy on women's liberation and on transforming gender ideology.

WEIMAR REPUBLIC (1919–1933) AND NAZI GERMANY (1933–1945)

At the end of World War I (1914–1918), Germany was in terrible economic shape, and the peace treaty its leadership signed in Versailles only exacerbated the situation. The Germans built a government, the Weimar Republic, with a president, a chancellor, and a parliament that housed elected officials from many political parties. After several decades of active women's movements and suffrage movements, women finally received the vote. As in the United States and United Kingdom, the government's official reason for granting women suffrage was not decades of political activism but women's extraordinary service during wartime. German women voted in numbers almost equal to men. Even women who had campaigned against woman suffrage voted and in some cases ran for office, so that they could have a chance of returning the country to what they considered appropriate values. Conservative women's organizations throughout Germany encouraged their membership to vote in order to prevent Socialists and Marxists from coming to power, and their membership often voted as requested. Over time it became clear that women did not vote in exactly the same way as men. Catholic women in the Weimar Republic were more loyal to the Catholic Center Party than Catholic men were, for instance, and women in general supported Socialist parties less than men did. In fact, women's greater participation in religious organizations had long been a reason Liberal and Socialist parties (for instance, in France and Mexico) had opposed or been lukewarm toward woman suffrage: They presumed, correctly, that women would be less supportive of anti-clerical political programs than men.[1]

The women's organizations in Germany—even the explicitly feminist ones—were ideologically conservative compared with the other movements we have examined. The majority of Germans looked with nostalgia at an imagined but recent pre-industrial past in which families had lived together in harmony, with fathers as supportive, wise leaders battling the outside world and mothers as the warm and loving guardians of hearth and home. In the late nineteenth- and early twentieth-century German imagination, women were closer to nature and more spiritual than men. High culture—theater, opera, literature, art—was believed to be more important to women than to men, and women were thought to be naturally better at caring tasks such as social work. Nearly all women's organizations in Germany, whether feminist or anti-feminist, shared this assumption. Even most feminists held this romanticized view of women and campaigned not for women's equal rights but for the political and economic tools that would permit women to be good wives, mothers, and supporters of what they considered the feminine realm of public life. Sometimes this led them into political campaigns modern feminists would find scandalous. The Reich Association of Housewives, for example, lobbied for decades not only for mothering and housework to be recognized as a profession (a goal of many contemporary feminist and women's organizations), but also against the unionization of domestic servants. Official Socialist positions on and attitudes toward women were virtually indistinguishable from the positions of more conservative parties and included no concern for women as a class of people with collective concerns. When Socialism triumphed, the evils of patriarchy would vanish along with the evils of economic inequality—or so Socialist parties claimed. Meanwhile, women should just shut up about their own group's interests and toe the party line, as did women in the Conservative and Liberal parties. Throughout the Weimar period, political parties all told women virtually the same thing about their proper roles in society, presuming, apparently, that women had no common political interests separate from men's—even though they continued to vote differently from men.

The 1920s and early 1930s were exceptionally difficult for Germans, especially for German women. In 1923 the Weimar government decided to solve the problem of its war debts by printing more and more money, creating rapid inflation—20 percent a day in January 1923. Businesses paid employees daily, letting them take a break in the late mornings so they could spend their earnings on food before the afternoon's inflation made their paper money worthless. Savings were wiped out. Young women who had scrimped and saved for years to build a dowry found their preparations for marriage ruined. Some women took many lovers as compensation for being unable to marry. Poverty was so widespread and so acute prostitution became a major means for women to feed themselves and their families. No sooner had the economy begun to recover from the terrible inflation of 1923, giving a couple of years respite and stability, when the New York Stock Exchange crashed in October 1929, dragging the international economy—in particular, Germany's—with it. This second economic collapse caused the Weimar legislature to declare a state of emergency and leave day-to-day decisions in the hands of President von Hindenburg, who appointed an exceedingly conservative cabinet. As the economy worsened, people began to look for scapegoats. The two most popular choices were public morality and the Jews.

As usual when societies start chalking up their troubles to other people's morality, popular opinion pointed to women as the source of trouble. Their hair was too short, their makeup too thick, their jobs outside the home too important to them, their children improperly cared for, their womanliness hidden under a pseudo-masculine veneer. They were not getting married in timely fashion or having babies. Male unemployment was at 30 percent, and women's at 10 percent (although they earned only 60 percent of what men did), and this must be women's fault. What was wrong with Germany? Women's emancipation!

Only the Communists failed to blame women's rights for Germany's ills. Even the feminist Federation of German Women's Associations (BDF), the largest women's group in Germany, failed to support women workers and publicly stated that "working women ought to share fully the sacrifices and deprivations that are vested upon the entire population by the economic emergency. *The Federation does not intend to be a lobby for women's interests*" (emphasis added). The most the BDF would argue for was better benefits for homemakers: "The best way to solve the problem of the employed mother is to make it possible for her to quit her job and devote all her energies to motherhood," said BDF president Marie Baum.[2] Whether she meant to include single mothers in this statement is unclear. How quitting work would help employed women who had no children or whose children were adults is equally unclear.

Women were not the only ones scolded for the supposed decline in public decency, however. The scholars and artists of the period were also raked over the coals. If only they would make more wholesome art or have more life-affirming ideas, they would build the society up instead of tearing it down! Many people thought that way and said so in public forums. As terrible as the economy was for much of the Weimar era, this period was also one of the most intellectually brilliant in Germany history. In painting, sculpture, architecture, music, theology, theater, literature, science, even film—Germany led the world in the 1920s. Käthe Köllwitz, Carl Jung, Bertolt Brecht, Richard Strauss, Arnold Schönberg, Fritz Lang, Karl Barth, Albert Einstein, Max Planck, and many other pivotal figures in modern art and letters wrote and worked in the cities of Weimar Germany, especially in Berlin. Artists and scholars who had been disturbed and frightened by the dramatic changes of the post-war era produced work that was itself disturbing, or had disturbing implications, or that simply re-examined and questioned older ideas and ideals. New ideas, new theories, new ways of seeing the world proliferated in the most exhilarating way, and for some people the barrage of novelties felt dangerous.

If women, scholars, and artists were to be blamed for not doing their part to hold up public morality, Jews were to be blamed for almost everything else. Anti-Semitism has a very long history throughout Western and Central Europe, and Germany's tradition of it was alive and well during the 1920s. Anti-Semitic feelings ran strong under the surface of the German psyche, perhaps all the stronger because so many people never interacted with anyone they knew to be Jewish. Jews, who made up only about 1 percent of the German population, had been emancipated (made full citizens) in the various German states during the 1870s, and they had responded to their new freedoms and the new recognition of their membership in the community with exuberance. If Germany was the jewel of the West in the 1920s, Jews like Anni Albers (1899–1994, textiles), Albert Einstein (1879–1955, physics), Lotte Lenya (1898–1981, theatrical performance), Lenya's husband, Kurt Weill (1900–1950, composer), Erich Mendelsohn (1887–1953, architecture), Lise Meitner (1878–1968, mathematical physics), and Gertrud Kolmar (1894–1943, poetry) did far more than their share to make it so. They joined enthusiastically in producing the literary, artistic, and scientific renaissance that was the Weimar Republic.

Although one might think that this evidence of their value to society would decrease anti-Semitism, in fact anti-Semites could curse Judaism even for the blessings it brought the nation. Jewish intellectuals and artists could be criticized as producing weak, nervous, and effeminate art—echoing stereotypes of Jewish men—and as having a poisonous effect on the minds and culture of Germany—just as medieval and Renaissance Jewish communities had been accused of poisoning wells during plagues. Jews placed a high value on education (especially for men) and the arts, and throughout Europe were disproportionately represented among artists and intellectuals. This made it easy for those who disliked the innovations of early twentieth-century thinkers to call them Jewish and insist that even the innovative work of Christians was "tainted" (as opposed to "influenced," which they were) by Jews' ideas.

Middle-class Jewish women who lived through the 1920s in Germany thought they were thoroughly assimilated. Although in absolute numbers few Protestants and Catholics married Jews, the thousands of annual interfaith marriages in Germany made mixed-faith marriage quite common in the small Jewish community. Jewish women belonged to the same neighborhood, women's, and political associations as did their Protestant and Catholic neighbors and often exchanged baby-sitting responsibilities on each others' Sabbaths. Their husbands had jobs similar to those held by the husbands of Christian women, and Jews were prominent among the literati and artists of the era. They believed, because they only rarely heard anti-Semitic slurs, that anti-Semitic feeling was rare and that their Christian friends would stand up for them. But they were wrong.

When the Great Depression arrived with the New York Stock Market Crash of 1929, it exacerbated already severe economic problems, and a substantial minority of Germans looked for someone to blame. The Nazi Party came to prominence in this climate of economic failure, rapid intellectual and artistic change, and scapegoating. Although not the most popular party in Germany (it never won a majority of votes in any election), the National Socialist Party had a strong core of followers willing to do anything for power. Its leader, Adolph Hitler, traveled all over Germany making speeches and attracting followers, many of them women. In a country where even the feminists were telling women they ought to think less of their own concerns, Hitler's message that women should all concentrate on being worthy wives and mothers while their husbands and sons went out to work and defend the nation struck a nostalgic chord. Nazism seemed, for many Christian women, to promise them a separate sphere (the household) that they could control and where they would be respected. Nazi men wore brown shirts; marched in formation; assaulted Communists, Socialists, and Jews of all political standings; and went to jail to support Hitler. Nazi women fed the men, nursed their wounded, visited and took care of their wives and children while they were in jail, sewed their uniforms, gave them houseroom when they were on the road, and raised money to support the party. They came to rallies in large numbers, and they believed Hitler would give them a Germany full of manly men they could trust to care for them and their children properly. According to their memoirs, his very voice and presence elevated their hearts and minds and gave them the strength to treat outsiders like enemies at the same time that they acted as loving mothers and helpmates in the movement. Possibly his status as unmarried and thus symbolically available contributed to his attraction.

The Nazis won power because they had the largest number of votes in the pluralistic Weimar Assembly. Half the people who had voted for them—the party that specifically wanted to end the franchise for women—were women. They were then able to persuade President von Hindenberg to declare a state of emergency and put Hitler, the chancellor, in charge for the duration. That duration turned out, just as the Nazis had promised during campaigns, to be the rest of Hitler's life. During his campaigning, he was able to say everything his audience wanted to hear and to promise everything they wanted. But once in office, the Nazis did not choose to deliver on their apparent promises to women. Helping housewives and mothers was not on the top of the Nazi agenda. The chief goals of the party, as reiterated repeatedly in campaign speeches, government propaganda, and policy statements, were "racial purity" (at home and, if possible, abroad) and the creation of strong, racially pure soldiers for the expanding German state. It was nice if women could be useful as mothers and kind and gentle wives, but the bottom line was that the Nazi Party wanted women to breed men willing and able to "die laughing" for their country.

Although Hitler talked a great deal about the sacred importance of the mothers of the race, what he meant was that women and men were simply tools of the state. He was not interested in creating separate spheres for women, separate education for girls, separate responsibilities for married women, and incentives for good homemaking—although the Nazi government gave badges of honor to women who had five or more children and required members of the Hitler Youth (the Nazi version of Boys and Girls Scouts) to salute them. Most late nineteenth- and early twentieth-century governments focused on women as citizens and concentrated on educating them for certain kinds of (usually unpaid) productivity, but the Nazi state did not think of women (or men) as citizens with individual gifts to contribute to the whole. Whereas other governments wanted to make women into good citizens, wives, and mothers, the Nazis really only wanted German women to produce new Nazi children and enter the workforce when and where the party felt they were needed. Although the Nazi state relied heavily on women to enforce its policies of "racial hygiene" (the state's euphemism for murder and forced sterilization), the relentlessly anti-intellectual leadership never seems to have devoted much thought to that fact.

Creating racial purity was, of course, impossible. The more the Nazis pressed scientists to find firm biological bases for recognizing someone as Jewish, Gypsy (also called Rom), or Aryan (an early group of Germanic-speaking people with whom the Nazis identified), the more clear it became that race is mostly a social construct. Thus, the government fell back on defining people as Jewish if they had a certain number of Jewish ancestors and requiring people to produce genealogical charts that proved they were or were not Jewish.

The Nazis felt they were on firmer scientific ground with eugenics—the selective breeding of humans—which in their hands meant the involuntary sterilization or euthanasia of people with supposedly hereditary illnesses and weaknesses. People with birth defects, mental illnesses, developmental disabilities, and "deviant" sexual preferences were to be sterilized, while those with severe chronic illnesses were to be euthanized. In addition to being morally abhorrent, the choice of whom to sterilize had little to do with the heritability of a particular illness or even with whether it was an illness at all. Schizophrenia, for example, could be diagnosed in women on the basis of nothing more than poor housekeeping and in men on the basis of chronic unemployment. Just as the state felt comfortable rounding up and sterilizing the weaker members of the populace and trying to force Catholic hospitals to practice euthanasia, it was also willing to round up and murder its own citizens, all in the name of racial hygiene.

Many other governments of this era had adopted eugenics policies. In its most respectable form, eugenics advocated voluntary birth control, up to and including sterilization, for those too poor to support additional children and for people with severe and potentially hereditary illnesses. However, the admixture of Social Darwinism and racism with eugenics produced policies in many states that actively pressured poor people and ethnic minorities to be sterilized and that sometimes prescribed sterilization for the mentally ill. By actively advocating euthanasia and forced sterilization, the German government went much further than most, but it is important to remember that their policies were part of a more general repression of individual rights, rather than a totally isolated case. In fact, the Nazi obsession with racial hygiene was another form of the racism that provided the justification for race-based slavery and for late nineteenth-century imperialism. For the Nazi Party, fears of racial contamination were not directed at Africans or Asians, who made up virtually none of their state's population, but at Jews, Roma (Gypsies), and Slavs—groups of people virtually indistinguishable from anyone else in Northern Europe.

In seeking ways to separate themselves from their racial enemies and potential sources of impurity, Nazis at first forced Jews out of all areas of public life, then insisted they wear yellow stars when in public, then moved them into locked areas of cities, called ghettos. As it became clear that the government would not be able to deport every Jewish person from conquered territories, leaders sought a final solution. In autumn of 1941, the government set up three death camps; the machinery of state bureaucracy and industrial production would be turned to the problem of systematically murdering every Jew, Rom, Socialist, and dissident in Europe (see the very efficient form listing victims in Figure 6.1). By the end of the war, the Nazi government had succeeded in killing between 5.1 million and 6 million Jews (about half of all living Jewish people at the time) and about 220,000 Roma (about a quarter of the European Roma population).

Women's activities made it possible for the government to carry out these policies. Although it was mostly men who ran the concentration camps and worked as the police who carried people away in the middle of the night, it was women who lived in the neighborhoods. They

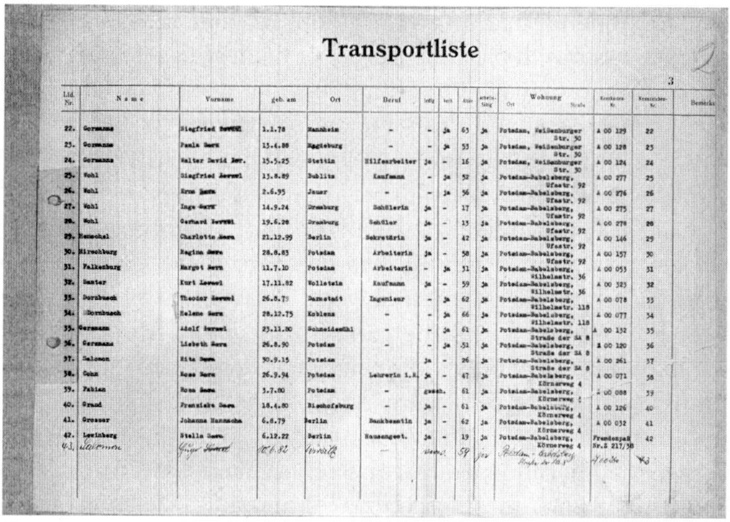

FIGURE 6.1   TRANSPORT LIST
List of German concentration camp inmates, 1946–1958.

were the ones who told their children not to play with Jewish children, who stopped inviting Jewish families to their homes, who asked Jewish women to leave women's organizations and sadly told their Jewish friends that it was too dangerous for them to keep associating together. It was women who refused to shop at Jewish-owned stores, and women who told storekeepers that if they kept serving Jews, Aryan women would stop shopping there. It was women who went door-to-door raising money and volunteers for Nazi charities and propaganda drives and who let it be known that they remembered the names of the families who had not made contributions. Women were the social workers who came to take Aryan children away from their Jewish relatives, the ones who came to school to pull Jewish children out of the classroom. They were the nurses and the nurses' aides in the hospitals charged with carrying out sterilization and euthanasia, and they were the ones who had to tell patients the lie that the operation they were about to undergo was necessary and leave out the fact that they would also be sterilized. Women reported to authorities when nice Aryan children had to live with a Jewish parent or grandparent and should be taken away for their own good. Women were the ones who noticed a family bringing in too much food to the house or noticed noises when buildings were supposedly empty and reported that Jews or dissidents were hidden there. Although many Germans may have disliked the Nazi Party and disagreed with the government, the fear of having their words and actions reported by women helped keep them in check.

Several women led large organizations of women Nazis during the era of the party's rise to prominence. All of them were effective and innovative leaders and managed to bring their followers along with them as well as raising money and votes for the party. Elsbeth Zander traveled all over Germany championing the wonders of motherhood and Adolph Hitler, publishing her own newspaper, creating rest homes for the SA (the *Sturmabteilung*, or paramilitary wing of the party), and recruiting women. In 1926 she was granted the right to call herself the leader of women Nazis, although that right would be taken away when the party came to power. She insisted on telling the party that it should honor motherhood more, and for her independent thinking she was cut out of the loop. Guida Diehl recruited thousands of women followers to the Fighting Women's League, which supported Hitler but was not an official Nazi organization (Diehl cherished her independence). She recruited conservative feminist members of the BDF and the national Protestant Women's Association and campaigned for segregated and sex-specific education. She wanted higher wages for married men (so their wives would not have to work) and state subsidies for the wives and adult daughters of men who could not support them, and she championed these causes vigorously. The Nazis welcomed her members and organizational skill, but her outspoken support for actually providing services to women was less welcome, and she too was edged out of influence after the party came to power. Other women leaders among the Nazis experienced similar fates; when Hitler came to power, he finally chose Gertrud Scholtz-Klink, a woman with no history of independent organization, to lead the women's department. Scholtz-Klink was an ardent Nazi, willing to accept and act on any order in exchange for absolute power over her subordinates. Scholtz-Klink successfully eliminated all her female rivals fairly early, and she did all that the party leadership expected. Even so, the party frequently made her task almost impossible.

Scholtz-Klink did her best to make Nazism attractive to average women, underplaying Nazi ideology and emphasizing women's roles as mothers. Hitler wanted Germany's real religion to be love of the Fatherland, the Führer, and the National Socialist Party, but Scholtz-Klink knew this held less appeal for most women than it did for her. Many Nazis treated National Socialism as their only religion, and perhaps as many as 10 percent of Christians were willing to treat loyalty to the party as more important than loyalty to their religion. But most of the religiously inclined people in Germany were not willing to worship the party, and women were then, as now, more active in the churches than men. Moreover, the only large, active, and successful women's organizations left after the Nazis destroyed the feminist groups were not focused on political activism, but on church work. Thus, the women with administrative and organizational experience were the ones least willing to choose the party over their church, which forced Scholtz-Klink to underplay ideology. Nevertheless, she was primarily a creature of the Nazi Party and was willing to demand of women almost anything the party asked for, no matter how ridiculous the demand or how little respect she herself received from the male leadership.

If women Nazis themselves were treated shabbily by the party, those caught opposing the government rarely survived. Most of those who lived did so because they went into exile. Some of these could not bear to stay away from their homeland and, when they returned, were likely to be arrested and killed. Käthe Niderkirchner, a Socialist from Brazil, left in 1933, but her longing to live in and save her country drove her back to Germany, where she was arrested, sent to a concentration camp, and executed in September of 1944. Lore Wolf, a lifelong Communist, traveled throughout Europe and in and out of Germany during the 12 years the Nazis were in power and was arrested 20 times, but either escaped or got herself released each time. As late as 1943, 200 non-Jewish wives of Jewish husbands staged a successful demonstration and secured the release of their recently arrested husbands. But the reason we know about the activities of most of the women involved in resistance movements was that they were caught and, according to German government records, died mysteriously or by suicide in prison without ever going to trial.

The ubiquitous Nazi propaganda machine and the party's cult of personality (itself an exaggeration of the Fascist cult of Mussolini in Italy) has been widely imitated, and other conservative regimes have copied Nazi methods of mobilizing supporters and population control. The Nazi claim that they could create social order by keeping social hierarchies intact and demanding obedience to state hierarchies still appeals to modern regimes in countries with wide gaps between rich and poor and a tiny middle class. In 1964, Brazil's women took to the streets in opposition to the government when the Brazilian Right called on them to march against the democratically elected government for "the Family, with God, for Liberty." Persuaded that Liberals and Socialists were going to take away what little autonomy they had as housewives, thousands of women demonstrated almost daily until the coup of April 1. They were hailed as heroines of the revolution—and, like their earlier German sisters, shunted aside in later policy decisions. The Nazi's instrumentalist attitude toward women—that they existed to serve the state, that they should be moved in and out of the marketplace at the will of the state, and that they should give birth to a state-recommended number of children—was widely shared by contemporary regimes and is still common in totalitarian and single-party states.[3]

Soviet Russia during the Revolution and under Stalin

Russian women lived very differently from German women at the start of World War I, and they had experienced very different histories of feminism, radicalism, and industrialization than the women of England, Japan, or Germany. Even as late as 1914, 86 percent of Russians were still peasants, and women made up a majority of these. Specifically women's organizations started late, and the numbers of women involved in either Feminism or radical Socialism were very low compared with the numbers in Western European countries. On the other hand, the goals of sexual liberation, women's equality, and supporting every person's full potential, so important to nineteenth-century radicals, remained important to Russian radical movements at the start of the twentieth century. Moreover, just as most radical men came from the educated classes of Russia, the radical and feminist women in Russia came for the most part from among the educated, and the few educational opportunities available for women accelerated their desires for self-improvement.[4]

Like many feminist organizations in the United States and Western Europe, organized feminists in Russia made a clear decision to focus on suffrage and vocational education, believing that these were the necessary bases for all future reform. Like their sisters elsewhere, although not as loudly as middle-class women's organizations in Germany, Russian feminists were particularly uninterested in improving the lot of women domestic workers. Access to cheap female labor was a necessary precondition for most middle-class women and their daughters to leave the home—no Russian woman in this era could expect her husband to take on half the housework or child care. Again, like feminists throughout the Americas, Russian feminists spent most of their political capital on education and the franchise. They got the improvements in education, but they did not get the franchise before the Revolution of 1917 (indeed, at a national level only Finns did, although many U.S. and New Zealand women voted in local and state elections before this) and so never had meaningful political access until after the breakup of the Soviet Union. And by then, the tide of public opinion was trying to force women out of any position of authority and all good-paying jobs.

Their emphasis on suffrage and education did not prevent Russian feminist organizations from addressing working women and peasants, and in fact they were much more successful at working with factory women than the Socialists were, at least before the 1917 Revolution. Women factory workers and peasants understood that the men in labor unions did not always share their interests—something Socialist organizers often refused to admit. Men wanted women to work fewer hours; but women wanted equal pay for equal work. Men wanted women to return to their homes and make way for men to take over their jobs; but women wanted the government to appoint female factory inspectors and on-the-job forewomen to protect them from sexual harassment and predation. Increasingly, though, early twentieth-century European feminists were half-hearted in their support of labor unions—not least because women Socialists, the activists who *did* care deeply about women's labor, had all been told repeatedly that feminists were anti-proletariat, bourgeois, and uninterested in creating a just world.

Most feminist organizations of the era worked on the assumption that they could not achieve widespread general improvement in women's lives without the franchise, because they did not trust men to serve women's interests. Therefore, efforts directed at providing immediate service to individual women were charitable, piecemeal, and articulated in ways that did not upset the status quo. Feminists opposed prostitution and spent decades lobbying for reforms in the ways governments treated prostitutes, but in the meantime spent a lot of energy persuading and helping individual women to leave the life and warning young women who came into the city about the dangers posed by predatory pimps and brothel keepers. Mainstream feminists set up refuges for women leaving dangerous husbands and in general tried to help women live in the world that existed rather than persuading them to throw themselves into a life devoted to overthrowing injustice. Socialists and Revolutionaries disapproved of such efforts, because they could not, in themselves, lead to revolutionary change and because they alleviated some of the tension that could have been channeled toward social unrest.

During most of the twentieth century, Socialist women opposed organized Feminism, which they saw as dominated by middle-class and elite women (true, but so was Socialist Feminism); uninterested in joining a revolution (true); and uninterested in helping poor, proletarian, and peasant women (manifestly untrue, as we have seen). Thus, the women who cared most about women's wage labor were the least likely to join feminist organizations. In this they were following the writings of August Bebel in *Women and Socialism* and Clara Zetkin, who ran the journal of the German Social Democratic Party's newspaper, *Die Gleichheit*. Zetkin hired numerous women correspondents and led the women's organizations within European Socialism. She was deeply committed to factory women and to class struggle, and she saw the feminist women's movements (which in Germany, as we have seen, were extraordinarily conservative) as classist.

Neither Clara Zetkin nor the Socialist Party would have any truck with a separate feminist movement, however, because she and party leadership believed the arrival of fully formed Communism could end sexism and racism, and that working to end them before that was a distraction from the roots of the problem. And nineteenth- and early twentieth-century Socialists had good reason to believe this fairy story; many of them personally experienced Socialist activities and organizations as egalitarian, at least on the local level. Women were welcome, responsible members of local Socialist movements, and Jewish women were just as welcome as Christian ones. This was, by the way, a nearly universal experience for Socialists in the 1920s and 1930s—many Americans of that era were drawn to Communism because they experienced in action a political movement that treated blacks, Jews, poor whites, and women of all ethnicities in basically the same way they treated middle-class whites. Radical Russian women were drawn to an organization that not only proclaimed the right and necessity of all people to reach their full potential as human beings but also actively denounced bigoted and sexist rhetoric, even if sexism and racism did not disappear from personal interactions.

It was not until Socialists got to the level of national and international organizations and began articulating women's interests that the rhetoric of women's equality was tested. The official position of Socialists throughout Europe, as articulated by Clara Zetkin on the party's behalf, was that in Socialism everyone was equal, and that what was required was a revolution on behalf of universal justice, not individual justice or justice for particular groups. The same justice and the same economic policies would universally benefit everyone. Socialist leaders were suspicious of even discussing the ways women's interests (or Jews' interests, or, in the United States, blacks' interests) might not be the same as everybody's. They feared acting on the basis of any categories other than class would lead to division. As the twentieth century wore on, the most common criticism of Feminism from the left was not that it was too middle class, too uninterested in the lives of everyday women, but that by treating women as a separate interest group, Feminism actually perpetuated sexism.

Women played a number of important roles in World War I and in the Russian Revolution. Like women in other countries, Russian women had begun serving as battlefield nurses during the mid-nineteenth century, and they continued that role in World War I. But they also served as soldiers in larger numbers than had ever been seen in modern warfare, and in more capacities than even their contemporaries in the Mexican Revolution did. Records were kept poorly, so historians have to guess at the total number who served, but most believe that between 50 and 70 thousand women served directly in the Russian armed forces during World War I, making up about 2 percent of military personnel. Even before the revolution, women joined the army as regulars. Anna Krasilnikova, for instance, entered the army disguised as a man, fought in 19 battles, and won the St. George's Cross, Fourth Class. Many women joined the army under their own name and were accepted, as the army had no formal policy against permitting women to sign up. Some became military drivers, and one Princess Shakhovskaya was assigned to active duty as a flier. A number of women's battalions were formed, the first under Mariya Bochkarëva, and some of them served in direct combat.

After the Russian Revolution of 1917, even more women joined. For the new government, women's participation in combat was most important for its propaganda value—if even women were willing to fight and die for their country, how could men refuse to do their duty for Russia by joining up? Nikolai Podvoiskii, the head of the Universal Military Training Institute, was the lone voice calling for women to be a regular part of the armed forces, or at least to ensure that all adult women under age 30 got sufficient military training to defend cities and villages in case of invasion. "The woman worker must know how to use a rifle, revolver, and machine gun, must know how to defend her city, her village, her children, herself from the attacks of the White Guard bands," he declared. But this was too much female equality even for the Bolsheviks, who ended up only actually *requiring* military training of some party members. Podvoiskii's desire to prepare women to defend themselves, their children, and their homes was seen as an assault on women's dignity rather than as an attempt to empower women. The heads of the Women's Department objected vociferously to the idea of making women receive combat training and said it would lead, inevitably, to women shedding blood in combat. Shedding blood was supposedly incompatible with women's natures, which Russian Socialists agreed were naturally nurturing and gentle. Podvoiskii had to settle for basic physical education for girls aged 16 to 18; voluntary participation in the institute's exercises teaching military administration, sanitation, communications, and provisioning; and voluntary opportunities for women to learn the use of rifles and machine guns through the Universal Training Administration.[5]

Until the 1960s, the official position of the Communist Party was that women and men were now equal. In fact, in 1930 the Soviet Union announced no more work needed to be done to achieve equality, as it was now in place. The state had passed legislation intended to make it easier for women to get out of difficult marriages, to get alimony from divorced husbands, and to get informal marriages (which were very common among ordinary people, who often could not afford the cost of a formal wedding) recognized. Unfortunately, these laws also made it easier for men to become bigamists and avoid paying alimony or child support, and so undercut the Communist Party's original goals. Proclaiming that everyone was equal now also permitted the government to create universal education for women, to put women into every profession in Russia (though not in large numbers in every one), and to place women into the lower and middle ranks of party administration and government.

However, multiple feminist movements in the second half of the twentieth century decided that two practical problems existed with the Communist Party's attitude toward "the woman question." First, simply announcing that men and women are now equal does not eliminate sexism, any more than simply announcing that race no longer matters eliminates racism. Sexist and racist feelings, ideas, and practices really only disappear when actively combated. Second, the simple idea that women are "equal" to men ended up being expressed in policy formulas that presumed women are also *the same as* men, and that they have the same (as opposed to similar) interests and backgrounds. Soviet policy therefore was not enough to put women into positions where they might have access to serious political power, or even a significant voice on the Central Committee. It put women in responsible jobs and meaningful work (though by no means all women; most of the really boring and physically taxing jobs in agriculture and industry were still performed by women). But it left them still solely responsible for child care and housework, while making it easier for men to divorce their wives and avoid responsibilities for either alimony or child care. The party could decide it was necessary to communicate specifically with women and recruit them as active party members, but it could not persuade local and regional leaders to take the mobilization seriously, to consider the absence of women's voices in their deliberations to be an important problem, or to support the mobilization of women with funds and personnel.

To a certain extent the Soviet Union had to adjust its policy of not treating any group separately in order to meet reality. Party activists and leaders were primarily well-educated people. Education, study, and activism had transformed their lives and given them purpose, and they wanted that kind of purpose to be shared by the rest of the Russian people. They knew that fully functioning citizens had to be active participants in building the new state; they had to be politically savvy; they had to have a broad view of the world; they had to be technically adept, literate, numerate—in short, they had to be many things the typical Russian, a peasant, was not. At least, the party—which was made up almost entirely of people who had never lived as peasants and so had very little idea how complicated farming can be or how difficult village politics could be—expected very little political savvy from peasants, and they *knew* few peasants were formally educated. Women had been active—indeed, critical participants in the revolution and the civil war; the party knew they could be a huge asset. But peasants already shared a vocabulary to discuss politics, a village political structure, and expectations of who should be their designated political agents—male heads of households. Indeed, many peasant men and industrial workers actively opposed women's participation in decision-making bodies. Peasant women, for their part, had no experience of political activity or debating, thinking, or acting on behalf of the group. When first asked to participate in political debates, women would say they were not familiar with such "men's activities." It quickly became clear that women in general were *not* going to be included in the revolution without direct state intervention and support specifically on their behalf.

Reluctantly, and with frequent complaints, a Women's Department, the *Zhenotdel*, was created within the party. At first it was led by Inessa Armand until her death from cholera in 1920, then for a few months by Alexandra Kollantai, who became too ill to serve effectively, and then by Anna Itkina as acting director. The leaders and organizers of Zhenotdel did heroic work on behalf of women throughout the Soviet Union and created an organizational structure that allowed for average women in villages, factories, and even the tents of Central Asia to communicate their concerns to the central offices of Zhenotdel. Sometimes when Armand or Kollantai brought women's specific concerns to the Central Committee, they got a hearing. However, often they were told that they were acting like feminists and trying to split women away from the party. Complaints that women's interests might not be identical with men's, or that cherished party policies and programs worked at women's expense for the benefit of men, were unwelcome. Any consideration of women *as a class* was inherently dangerous to party unity.

The party had great difficulty staffing Zhenotdel, especially after Kollantai—arguably the most well-known and respected woman in the Russian Socialist movement—left office. None of the other women leaders in the party were specifically interested in women's issues or in organizing women, and they refused transfer to the Zhenotdel. Likewise, at the local and regional levels of party activism, most women could see that working in the women's section was not going to get them any respect from the men in the party and saw such an assignment as a dead end. The most capable and most respected activists rarely wanted to work on women's issues, which they, like the men, saw as peripheral to the great task of Socialist liberation.

Moreover, local party leaders and members made working for Zhenotdel as difficult as possible and sometimes very dangerous. Zhenotdel organizers described male party leaders as patronizing at best, as refusing to give them office support, travel funds, or any other resources that would cost money, time, or labor. And this occurred in the easier areas to work; in many places, local men actively fought the education and organization of women. In Central Asia, some 800 women activists were murdered, with most of the perpetrators remaining uncaught.

Nevertheless, Zhenotdel continued until 1930 despite lack of funds and paid personnel. Like other nineteenth- and twentieth-century women's organizations, it relied heavily on volunteers and donations to support its work. The Women's Department succeeded in having villages appoint women representatives to the local and regional party apparatus. Many women joined its activities and learned the basics of party political doctrine as well as Socialist organization and political activity. In Central Asia they changed the lives of thousands of women—who joined or worked for or assisted the Women's Department, changed the way they dressed, and started demanding human rights they had never asked for before (the latter being the main reason the 800 Zhenotdel organizers were murdered). Russian radical women had always seen dress reform as a critical part of women's emancipation and, like the Egyptian Feminist Union, they saw the practice of veiling women's faces as the outward symbol and most powerful expression of women's domination. Muslim women throughout the Soviet Union removed their veils and demanded freedom, though in fact the government was not prepared to pay a high price for them to achieve it.

Here the party's own imperialist policies worked against women's emancipation. Freeing women became, in the minds of party leadership, a mark of modernization and Russification, and they tried to force women to unveil as a sign of their families' loyalty to the state. By making the Russification of Central Asian women a symbol of Muslim acquiescence to Russian rule, the government made the continuing oppression of women a matter of nationalist pride in these regions—women had to choose between being properly Uzbek or Azerbaijani and being "liberated." As violence escalated, the majority chose—at least in the early years—to side with their ethnicity. (This sort of pattern has repeated itself in all sorts of conflicts between ethnic minorities or colonized peoples under pressure to assimilate, for instance among Hindu Nationalists in the nineteenth century and American Indians over the last couple of centuries—although American Indians have more typically resisted the enforced enculturation of men.)

Despite all the difficulties, women who worked with the Women's Department had the new and empowering experience of contributing to an organization (the Zhenotdel, not the local party leadership) that took women's concerns, women's intellectual contributions, and women's political acumen seriously. Even though the Women's Department was not able to convince the government to socialize child care (or at least provide

some public child care), to curb drinking, or to focus on domestic violence, it changed minds. Zhenotdel did succeed in publicizing to women
the idea that they ought to be the equals of men and that they ought to be
equal contributors in shaping the ongoing Socialist revolution, rather than
waiting patiently for the revolution to finish its work and finally, incidentally, liberate women on a schedule determined by the party.

Stalin's rise to power in the party put an end to this Bolshevik experi-
ment in activism on behalf of women, which he and party leaders had
come increasingly to see as feminist. And, indeed, the agenda Zhenotdel
leaders brought to the leadership—child care, domestic violence, wom-
en's development as full human beings, women's participation in policy
making, women's conflicts with men—were classic feminist themes. But
the real problem with the women's department from Stalin's and the party's point of view was not that it was for women, but that it kept delivering the same unwelcome news—that party policies often hurt women
more than men and wasted women's potential contribution to society. In
Stalin's Russia there was not only no room for dissent, there was to be no
room for consultation. In the 1920s, party leadership was still open to suggestions for dealing with reality—for instance, the reality was that women
were often leaders of popular rebellion—and Zhenotdel had argued effectively that the women's department was probably the most effective tool
for bringing potential rebels into the fold. But Stalin, who was paranoid,
power hungry, and not only openly sexist but also misogynist, was uninterested in employing consultation or in permitting any separate organizations within the party. Throughout the 1930s until the German invasion
of 1941, activists of either gender who did not keep their heads down and
obey the party line were likely to be arrested and jailed, exiled, or killed.

Official Soviet ideology of the 1930s in fact embraced patriarchy, repu-
diating by implication earlier party belief that patriarchy was a by-product
of class relations and produced social injustice. Where Lenin had vigorously argued for communal kitchens and the creation of communal child
care for those who desired it, Stalin and the party leadership in the 1930s
valorized the nuclear family. For all the Stalin era's reputation in the West
for "de-feminizing" women, in fact the official press of the 1930s lauded
not women workers, but the wives of important men. Women who stayed
at home and did volunteer work, who were gentle, maternal, and supportive of their menfolk, were held up as the model of the new Soviet woman.
In part this new version of Soviet femininity was a sop to Soviet men; as
Stalin's government took away more and more autonomy from its citizens, it gave men more and more freedom and power in the household—a
familiar theme. Russian feminists call this the Little Deal, and it remained
intact through the end of Stalin's regime.

Thus at the same time the Nazis were proclaiming that their government would keep women protected in the home and save them from the radical, unfeminine lifestyle of Socialists, Socialists in the Soviet Union championed an ideology of femininity so traditional it could hardly be distinguished from that of their Western European neighbors. Moreover, the ideal of the womanly housewife had only ever been achievable by middle-class women. It was no more possible for the Soviet economy than for any other twentieth-century economy to take women out of the officially recognized workforce, especially not during the worldwide Depression. What the government really wanted was for women to continue to work in factories and on farms and everywhere else in the Soviet economy *while* they married, had children, and worked a second shift at home to cook, clean, and tend to their husbands and children. Regardless of official intent, women were for the most part to work in the jobs that had the least potential for advancement, the lowest pay and prestige, and the least job security, so that they could be pulled in and out of the paid labor force more or less whenever convenient. From an economic standpoint, Soviet socialism's treatment of women's work is hardly distinguishable from that of any other industrializing power, whether it was Japan, Egypt, the United States, or Nazi Germany.

On the other hand, the Soviet Union did provide universal education, so that women's literacy rates skyrocketed, and did recruit women into higher education. While the party might not want women to be too influential in politics, it did envision women as appropriate producers of culture and as engineers, technicians, and scientists, so that the Eastern Bloc intelligentsia was, by the end of the Soviet era, much more open to women than elsewhere in Europe and the Americas. Women held more teaching and editorial positions and were much more fully represented in medicine, math, science, and engineering—the fields that had most appealed to Russian women since the nineteenth century. The Soviet Union was not a regime that supported free inquiry—libraries and archives in the USSR and Soviet Bloc countries were famous among historians, for example, for purportedly losing manuscripts and documents that might have evidence contradicting official positions, as well as for pretending certain documents had never existed. Intellectuals in all fields were restricted in what they could say, and this hampered everyone's work in these fields. Nevertheless, the intellectual and scientific achievements of the USSR depended heavily on female members of the intelligentsia, who made up about half the participants in most fields.

The Soviet model of femininity forged during revolution, the 1920s, and the Stalin years became a model for radical Socialist movements and Socialist states throughout the second half of the twentieth century. In

Cuba, Mozambique, Zimbabwe, Egypt, and (to a lesser extent) Baathist Syria and Iraq, this model of woman as freedom fighter, wife, worker, and intellectual in service to her country would be repeated and elaborated, then discarded. Early revolutionary eras emphasized women's abilities as workers and freedom fighters, but as soon as the government achieved stability, old models of the woman as nurturer would emerge to justify continuing inequality. Other regimes, like Saudi Arabia, would imitate the Soviet Little Deal to keep their male population satisfied.

The other huge Socialist revolution of the twentieth century, which resulted in the creation of the People's Republic of China, would take a different approach. Perceiving the stagnancy of Stalinist Russia and its return, in many ways, to earlier ideologies, the younger Communist Party of China would seek to create a climate of ongoing revolution. Mao Zedong, the first party chairman, was—like Lenin—committed to improving women's lives and making them active participants in the revolutionary process. And unlike Lenin, he stayed in power long enough to implement many of the anti-patriarchal reforms Lenin and Kollantai had only been able to imagine.

THE PEOPLE'S REPUBLIC OF CHINA

Chinese women of the late nineteenth and early twentieth century lived under great oppression, both as women and as inhabitants of a semi-colonized country. Slavery remained common, and most slaves were women whose parents had sold them as small children in order to support the rest of the family—especially the boy children of the family. Patriarchy was as powerful as ever, but Western encroachment and Chinese interest in modernization had created some new possibilities for girls and women. Mission schools and universities had begun providing non-gentry women with educations they would never have been able to obtain before, and in the 1920s some women began to attend government universities. As in many other parts of the world, girls and women were more likely to be sent to mission schools than boys, because the unorthodox educations offered there were seen as less fit for boys who had ambitions in traditional arenas.[6]

The Qing dynasty had been in serious decline since the mid-nineteenth century as it fought internal rebellions and foreign intervention. Although China did not participate in World War I, the first half of the twentieth century continued this era of almost uninterrupted upheaval. From the Boxer Rebellion in 1900, the Japanese invasion of Manchuria in 1905, the last emperor's abdication in 1912, to the rise of the warlords, drought, Depression, civil war, and the later full-on Japanese invasion, China experienced almost constant warfare and frequent regime change. After the Nationalists (1937–1945) ended the era of warlordism, they attempted to reform China while fighting a war against the Japanese and a civil war against the Communists. Indeed, the Communists were doing the same thing. When, after Japan lost World War II, the Nationalists lost the civil war, they left the mainland in the hands of Mao Zedong and the Communist Party and fled to the island of Taiwan.

In many ways Mao fit the classic pattern of Chinese revolutionaries and founders of new dynasties. Like Ming Taize, founder of the Ming dynasty, he was the son of a peasant and led an army of disaffected peasants/bandits. His models were the revolutionaries of the classic Chinese epic *The Water Margin*, who had lived as bandits in the hills until they could swoop down and change the government. In public statements, he quoted as often from the classics of Confucian literature as from classic Communist writers such as Marx, Engels, and Lenin. He had been taught in the new school system before going to Beijing, where he found work as a librarian and read widely and without direction from anyone else. Coming across Communist writings, he joined the party, and it was through Communists that he got most of his adult education. Like other Communists of his era, he believed firmly in the importance of education for the masses of people everywhere, but it should be a *Communist* education—one intended to produce revolutionaries and party supporters, not little followers of Confucius.

In a society where obedience to parents, to employers, and to government officials was a moral duty and disobedience a kind of crime, and where even free women were servants to the men in their families, Communism and Socialism were a revelation. In particular, Mao took seriously the Communist claim that patriarchy was a cornerstone of oppression. Perhaps because in China the family dynamics were so visible, or perhaps because his own father had been abusive, Mao's opposition to the traditional Chinese family arrangements—especially those of the elite—was steadfast.

Although the Nationalists had made some attempts to improve women's lives and limit the power of husbands, they had not had a great deal of success. Campaigns against footbinding had experienced some successes,[7] and the practice had diminished very considerably, even in urban areas, by mid-century. In Mao's PRC, his legal reforms were widely publicized and enforced.

Footbinding was the most visible and trumpeted immediate success, although historian Dorothy Ko has found that the practice was already dying when Mao came to power. While in internal exile during the Nationalist era, Mao had campaigned against and forbidden footbinding;

in the PRC it was finally outlawed successfully throughout China. This was very good for young girls—for older women whose feet were already bound, it was problematic. A foot bound into the bowed arch of the late Qing period never healed to look or work like a normal foot. Xue Shaohui, the editor of *Chinese Girls' Progress,* had already pointed this out in an 1898 answer to a letter from one of her readers, saying, ". . . no magical pill can grow a new set of bones; a severed head cannot be reattached."[8] Moreover, unbinding hurt. Today one sees the lotus foot only on women who were children before the Communists came to power. The last factory devoted to making shoes for bound feet closed in 1999.

Anti-footbinding campaigns were not the only reforms the PRC made regarding women. Divorce was made easier for women; slavery, concubinage, and polygyny were abolished; the age of consent was raised; and it was forbidden to marry off women without their consent. Today, although it is still common for parents to arrange an adult child's marriage, it is done with consultation and consent of both prospective spouses. Moreover, the women's department of the People's Republic of China was not, like Zhenotdel, disbanded after a decade. The All China Women's Federation has received consistent funding and personnel since its inception, remaining a so-far permanent administrative body within the Communist Party. Although one of its main responsibilities is to disseminate party policies and propaganda among women and recruit them for party plans, to an extent the Women's Federation also serves women's interests *as women themselves* articulate those interests. It has had value as a central organizing tool for women and, no matter what official party project it is supposed to be working on at any particular time, in practice local offices have considerable autonomy and can work well with the other women's groups if they choose to do so. But neither did it espouse the kind of feminist radicalism that the early Zhenotdel leaders advocated.

BUILDING ON THE PRO-WOMAN ACTIVISM
OF NINETEENTH-CENTURY CHINA

In supporting what he thought of as women's equality, Mao drew on a Chinese tradition of feminism dating back to the late nineteenth century. China had had an active pro-women movement since 1895, when the first known anti-footbinding society wrote its charter. As is so often the case, men were the first vocal public advocates of making specific improvements to women's lives (as opposed to piously mouthing support for women's beautiful nature, motherhood, and widow chastity). Late nineteenth-century Chinese intellectuals, especially men with Western educations, began to argue against footbinding and in favor of women's education.

Footbinding (as we have discussed in Chapter Two) was a practice carried out by women in pursuit of good husbands for their daughters. Having tiny feet did not just make a woman more sexually attractive to the men of her era; it was also an outward sign of her family's determination that she would belong to the better class of people, that she would marry or at least be the concubine of a man who did not need his wife to work. Peasant women (always and still today the majority of all Chinese women) were notorious for having "big," or natural, feet. In the nineteenth century, footbinding was becoming very widespread—almost universal among the upper and middle classes—and very common even among the working classes in urban areas. At the same time, educated Chinese men encountered the idea that bound feet were unnatural and bad for women's health. Seeing footbinding through the eyes of Japanese, Southeast Asian, European, and American educators and business colleagues made some Chinese men think differently about the practice, and they began to oppose it. They chartered anti-footbinding societies to create a climate where families could afford to take the risk of not binding their daughters' feet. Members took oaths that they would neither marry their sons to women with bound feet, nor permit their daughters' feet to be bound (it was not possible for unmarried men to promise to choose a wife with natural feet, because Chinese parents still expected to choose their sons' brides). Societies published attacks on the practice of footbinding, wrote letters to newspapers opposing it, and campaigned to persuade people that it was cruel, bad for women's health, and bad for China—because by hurting girls and crippling women, it weakened the economy.

Like many other successful pro-woman movements, the members were mostly from fairly well-off, even elite families, and the problems of women they knew best were the problems of women from their own social classes. These men campaigned not just against footbinding but also against infanticide (which they knew was usually practiced against girls), concubinage, polygyny, and slavery—the injustices they were most often exposed to in their own households. Historically, a strong element of instrumentalism usually motivates elite support for women's issues. Governments and political parties want women to be more educated so they can be better mothers and citizens, for instance. Here, though, it seems clear that the primary motive of Chinese male feminists was moral outrage: They simply saw the treatment of women in their society as unjust.

These feminist men also argued in favor of educating women, especially the middle- and upper-class women they were most likely to marry. Obviously, this would have been good for the women themselves, but it also showed men's concern for their own welfare. By the early twentieth century, many educated Chinese men craved educated wives with whom they presumed they could have a companionable partnership of greater equality. Rather than desiring a gentle lotus blossom with tiny bound feet, excellent cooking skills, and practice in silent obedience, they wanted to marry a modern girl with an education and a modern outlook. They did not want for themselves the lives of authoritarian isolation they saw their fathers and grandfathers leading. Since far fewer women than men were educated and modern in outlook, and since relatively few parents desired a modern and freethinking daughter-in-law, many modern men ended up married to women completely unlike their own ideal. Of course, such misalliances happened to Chinese women, too, but they had fewer resources to turn their dissatisfaction into a recognized social ill.

The Communists went much farther than the pro-women activists of the Nationalist and earlier periods, however, and farther than the Soviet Union had managed under Lenin and Stalin. Mao perceived the overthrow of male dominance in the family as fundamental to the revolution, and the party itself expended considerable resources to present the nation with a vision of women as men's equals. During the 1950s, Lenin's dream of communal kitchens and communal child care emerged as a reality for Chinese women, though an unpleasant one. All housing and factories had been taken over by the state, and peasants made to farm collective units (1950–1953). During the Great Leap Forward (1958–1960), the party tried to industrialize China overnight, removing millions of farmers from the land and forcing them into factory work. Everyone was encouraged to sacrifice to build the new economy. Urban and factory workers were to devote every possible effort to production, and the workers remaining on collective farms were to try to double and triple their yield per acre. Communal kitchens were supposed to make it possible for families to avoid the time and expense of cooking and thus extend working hours. Children went not only into state educational and propaganda programs but also into work groups to assist the Great Leap. Unfortunately, the new factories were poorly designed and inefficient. China did not have enough engineers and technicians to keep them running, since purges the year before had executed or dismissed from office large numbers of engineers and scientists as "rightists" (antirevolutionary conservatives). China's agricultural economy—heavily dependent on intensive manual labor—had barely been productive enough to feed the population before the Great Leap. With millions of workers taken out of the agricultural economy, China was unable to feed itself. Millions died of hunger and related diseases—perhaps as many as 30 million. The Great Leap Forward was thus a terrible failure, but it was also one of the Communist Party's most important experiments in breaking down patriarchy.

The failure had been largely Mao Zedong's work, and his stature within the party plummeted as it became clear what a colossal disaster the Great Leap was. But Mao was a cagey politician, and he found a way to shore up his support within the party and the population in general by creating a new revolutionary movement within China. The movement began—without his official help but with his wife's support—in a series of student protests in his favor and blossomed quickly into the Cultural Revolution. One extraordinary feature of this movement was the way hundreds of thousands of women joined the Red Guards (the activists of the Cultural Revolution). They dressed and wore their hair like men, acted out rage by using foul language and violence like men, and in general acted in complete opposition to traditional stereotypes of women.

In part this must have been because of government propaganda. In addition to creating co-education programs and a women's department, the People's Republic tried to foster a climate of women's equality with men by mass-producing posters of athletic, muscular women and repeating slogans about women's equality. The USSR also tried to implement women's equality by making posters about it but had always chosen to show the typical Russian worker as male. Women in USSR propaganda were depicted as helpers of the male heroes of the people. Chinese propaganda, on the other hand, made an effort to image women workers as equal to, and the same as, men workers. The Red Guards explicitly tried to follow this policy, and Chinese fashions for decades dressed women and men in the same clothes—a policy the USSR rejected early. The Red Guards sought to overthrow all hierarchies and were more than willing to commit violence against any authority figure to do it. They eventually turned on some of their own leadership. They badly hurt China's cultural and intellectual legacy by destroying old arts and crafts, forcing intellectuals and artists to do nothing but repeat Red Guard cant, and beating up, imprisoning, and "re-educating" those whose existing works the Red Guards found unacceptable. When the movement ended, the women assumed more traditional manners, but they retained a relatively unisex habit of dress and a sense of themselves as important political actors with responsibilities toward the state. Victims of Red Guard's forcible re-education could be of any age, sex, or background, and could include former heroines and heroes of the revolution. Ding Ling (1904–1984), a radical author and an ardent early supporter of the May Fourth Movement and the Communist Party had been imprisoned by Nationalists for three years before their departure. During the Cultural Revolution she was arrested, beaten, humiliated, and put in solitary confinement. She was in prison until 1975.

Like other Socialist regimes, then, the Peoples' Republic of China increased women's education and paid-labor participation rates. They implemented reforms of family law that were meant to give women greater freedom of choice, and in the PRC, the new laws succeeded in doing so. They brought hundreds of thousands of women into scholarly and professional careers and low-level management positions. On the other hand, the government restricted the movements of rural women and put them to the hard manual labor of farming. The government also limited freedom of thought and religious expression (nuns and clergy needed official permission to exist), and, like other early Socialist parties, its leadership envisioned equality in terms of having women act like men. In practice, "equality" meant having some women do the same jobs as men, having all women do a second shift of housework after the Great Leap Forward failed, and putting token numbers of women into positions of authority.

Like the USSR, the PRC made enormous changes in women's access to education, public sector employment, and government service. Where before women who had worked outside the home had been scorned, now they were valorized. Newspapers, speeches, and posters all told women who worked to support themselves and their families that they were helping to make China great. Even though the PRC's schools were not always of high quality (especially at first and in rural areas), childhood education quickly became nearly universal. As in the USSR, female literacy skyrocketed. Women could join almost any industry, and they did. The contrast with pre-revolutionary China is undeniable; women who lived through the era experienced the arrival of Communism as a liberation and described it decades later as having brought equality with men. Even though few Chinese women are present in senior leadership positions in government and industries, the ordinary Chinese woman did feel that she was as important to China's development and to the government as her brother.

CONCLUSION

The three states described here were part of a worldwide tendency toward much greater state centralization and control over daily life. Their interests in controlling the ideology of the home; in indoctrinating children and citizens with state propaganda; and in directing as much social, political, and economic capital toward utilitarian ends were not unique. What makes them different from most other states was the relatively small range of debate about the direction of change and the states' willingness to sacrifice the lives of large numbers of their citizens to ends other than self-defense. Particularly with respect to state relationships with female citizens, their methods have often been imitated. Many governments and political parties—especially totalitarian ones—have followed the examples of Nazi Germany, the USSR, and the People's Republic of China in creating women's departments. The creators of these departments intend to mobilize women on behalf of government and party projects. They are all a little patronizing in the ways they address women, and their founders tend to imagine that all the women in their country are like the women in their own families and share the same concerns. Nevertheless, the existence of these women's departments in countries like Argentina, Chile, Uzbekistan, Brazil, Malaysia, Kenya, and Indonesia does give women a forum within which their concerns get brought to the attention of national and party leadership. They also create government slots that paid personnel—many of them women—to work with and organize women, in the process not only gaining leadership skills but also learning how to package women's issues in ways the authorities find palatable. Less positively, they also channel and limit women's participation, often forcing them to work only through the women's department or division, which is almost never empowered to make policy decisions on its own and never has a decisive voice in any decision-making body.

STUDY QUESTIONS

1. In what ways were the gender ideologies of the three major powers discussed here different? What assumptions about women did they share?

2. To what extent and in what ways did these governments require women's participation to succeed in their goals? To what extent did they acknowledge women's participation?

3. To what extent did each government attempt to serve women's needs?

4. Although this chapter focuses on the impact and role of women in totalitarian states, almost all women have strong relationships with at least some men. What do you think life in these countries was like for these women's brothers, husbands, sons, and friends? How would you have felt about these governments' policies concerning women and family life?

BIBLIOGRAPHY

*indicates contains whole primary sources or secondary works containing substantial extracts.

CHINA

Ebrey, Patricia Buckley. *The Cambridge Illustrated History of China.* New York: Cambridge University Press, 1996.

*Ebrey, Patricia Buckley, ed. *Chinese Civilization: A Sourcebook.* New York: Free Press, 1993.

*Edison, Victoria. *Cultural Revolution: Posters and Memorabilia.* Atglen, PA: Schiffer Publishing, 2005.

*Honig, Emily. *Personal Voices: Chinese Women in the 1980's.* Stanford, CA: Stanford University Press, 1988.

Ko, Dorothy. *Cinderella's Sisters: A Revisionist History of Footbinding.* Berkeley: University of California Press, 2005.

Schoenhals, Michael, ed. *China's Cultural Revolution 1966–1969: Not a Dinner Party.* Armonk, NY: M. E. Sharpe, 1996.

GERMANY

Allen, Anne Taylor. *Feminism and Motherhood in Germany.* New Brunswick, NJ: Rutgers University Press, 1991.

Ankum, Katharina von, ed. *Women in the Metropolis: Gender and Modernity in Weimar Culture. Weimar and Now:* 11. Berkeley, CA: University of California Press, 1997.

Bachrach, Susan, project director, and Dieter Kunz, ed. *Deadly Medicine: Creating the Master Race.* Washington, D.C., United States Holocaust Museum, University of North Carolina Press, 2004.

Bridenthal, Renate, Atina Grossman, and Marion Kaplan, eds. *When Biology Became Destiny: Women in Weimar and Nazi Germany.* New York: Monthly Review Press, 1984.

Gay, Ruth. *The Jews of Germany: A Historical Portrait.* New Haven, CT: Yale University Press, 1992.

*Goebbels, Joseph. *Michael.* New York: Amok Press, 1987.

Henig, Ruth. *The Weimar Republic.* London: Routledge, 2002.

Koonz, Claudia. *Mothers in the Fatherland: Women, the Family, and Nazi Politics.* New York: St. Martin's Press, 1987.

*Owings, Alison. *Frauen: German Women Recall the Third Reich.* Reprint. New Brunswick, NJ: Rutgers, 1995.

Stephenson, Jill. *Women in Nazi Germany.* New York: Longman, 2001.

Stibbe, Matthew. *Women in the Third Reich.* London: Arnold Publishers, 2003.

Usborne, Cornelie. *The Politics of the Body in Weimar Germany: Women's Reproductive Rights and Duties.* Ann Arbor: University of Michigan Press.

THE SOVIET UNION

Clements, Barbara Evans. *Bolshevik Women.* Cambridge: Cambridge University Press, 1997.

Engel, Barbara Alpern. *Women in Russia, 1700–2000.* Cambridge: Cambridge University Press, 2004.

*Engel, Barbara Alpern, et al., eds. *A Revolution of Their Own: Voices of Women in Soviet History.* Westview, CT: Greenwood Press, 1997.

*Engels, Friedrich. "The Origin of the Family, Private Property, and the State." In *The Marx-Engels Reader.* 2nd ed. Edited by Robert Tucker, 734–759. New York: W.W. Norton, 1978.

*Lenin, V. I. *Women and Society.* New York: International Publishers, 1938.

Stites, Richard. *The Women's Liberation Movement in Russia: Feminism, Nihilism, and Bolshevism 1860–1930.* Princeton, NJ: Princeton University Press, 1991.

Wood, Elizabeth. *The Baba and the Comrade: Gender and Politics in Revolutionary Russia.* Bloomington: Indiana University Press, 1997.

BRAZIL

Alvarez, Sonea E. *Engendering Democracy in Brazil: Women's Movements in Transition Politics.* Princeton, NJ: Princeton University Press, 1990.
Caipora Women's Group. *Women in Brazil.* London: Latin American Bureau, 1993.
*Patai, Daphne, ed. *Brazilian Women Speak: Contemporary Life Stories.* New Brunswick, NJ: Rutgers University Press, 1988,

AUDIO-VISUAL MATERIALS

Chinese Women: The Great Step Forward. 2 pts. Princeton, NJ: Films for the Humanities and Sciences, 2001–2002.
It's Right to Rebel. Directed by Julia Spark. Films for the Humanities, 1984.
To Live. Directed by Zhimou Yang. Los Angeles: Hallmark Home Entertainment, 1995.
Triumph of the Will (Triumph des Willens: das dokument vom Reichsparteitag 1934). Directed by Leni Riefenstahl. New York: Crown Video, 1984.
United States Holocaust Memorial Museum. http://www.ushmm.org/ (accessed February 15, 2007).
Women and the Holocaust. Center for Holocaust and Genocide Studies. http://www.chgs .umn.edu/Visual_Artistic_Resources/Women_of_Ravensbruck/Women_and_the_ Holocaust/women_and_the_holocaust.html (accessed February 15, 2007).
*"Women and Marxism." *Marxist Internet Archive.* Sally Ryan, webmaster. http://www .marxists.org/subject/women/index.htm (accessed February 13, 2007).

CHAPTER SEVEN

COLD WAR, NEO-COLONIALISM, AND SECOND-WAVE FEMINISM, 1945–PRESENT

The second half of the twentieth century saw the end of formal colonialism throughout the world. Colonized regions in Asia and Africa won their independence through war and political protest. The people living in colonies of the Caribbean and Polynesia either became recognized citizens of the nation that had colonized them (Puerto Rico, Hawaii, and American Samoa are examples) or else their countries became independent, but with a special connection to the colonizing country. In many cases, formerly colonized peoples retained a right to immigrate to the homeland of the old empire, and the homeland continued to be actively involved in the economic and industrial development of the old colonies. Migration increased—not only were expatriates returning to the former colonizing countries, but immigrants from all over the colonial empires also flowed into Europe in unprecedented numbers.

As former colonies declared or won independence, civil and human rights movements accelerated across the world. In India, untouchables (people of such low caste that their touch could ritually contaminate higher-caste people) campaigned for equal access to public spaces, government services, and employment. Blacks in the Caribbean and North America campaigned more vigorously for legal equality, and Native American and Aboriginal groups sought to strengthen recognition of treaty rights and reinvigorate their languages and traditions. Youth movements gained new prominence. Women's rights movements, which had been largely invisible during the Second World War and national independence campaigns, began to reappear, as women discovered that neither the end of the world wars nor the creation of new states would necessarily improve women's legal status or material welfare. This was the second wave of modern Feminism, called during its early years the Women's Liberation Movement.

THE COLD WAR

All this political activity occurred in the context of the Cold War, a decades-long political struggle between the Soviet Union (USSR) and the United States, fought by proxy in client nations. Winning World War II and enforcing the peace afterward had made the United States and the Soviet Union into "superpowers"—countries with so much military strength and so many dependent territories that no other nations could compete with them. The leadership of the two superpowers assessed political and cultural change at home and throughout the world in terms of their potential consequences for the Cold War. Despite having been allies during World War II, both countries' leadership saw the other as not only rivals but also as major security threats. Until the end of the Cold War in the early 1990s, leaders of other countries and activists throughout the world had to keep this rivalry in mind in all their planning. Countries that were not part of the Warsaw Pact or NATO were called the Third World, and eventually the Third World countries that did not align themselves with either superpower created an alliance of their own non-aligned states[1] (see Figure 7.1).

The old split between Socialist women activists and those working in equal rights movements therefore continued to be important—women's organizations in countries with strong Socialist governments or strong Socialist parties (and therefore USSR–aligned) tended to be Socialists rather than feminists, while those in U.S.–aligned countries tended toward equal-rights Feminism. Yet, as Socialists discovered that their political parties continued to ignore women's issues, and as equal-rights feminists discovered that helping working-class women required more than formal legal equality, Socialists began writing and talking about Socialist Feminism, and mainstream women's liberation activists began to write and talk more about the ways social class and race divided women.

World War II left the two superpowers in a position to rebuild or permit the rebuilding of those economies and political systems on the victors' terms. Obviously, the superpowers' direct impact on women differed.

THE SOVIET UNION

The Soviet Union remodeled the Eastern European countries along the lines of Stalinist Russia in an alliance of countries under Soviet leadership called the Warsaw Pact. The Communist Party created local branches to run each country and developed the infrastructure and industries of each member country to build a Socialist economy that

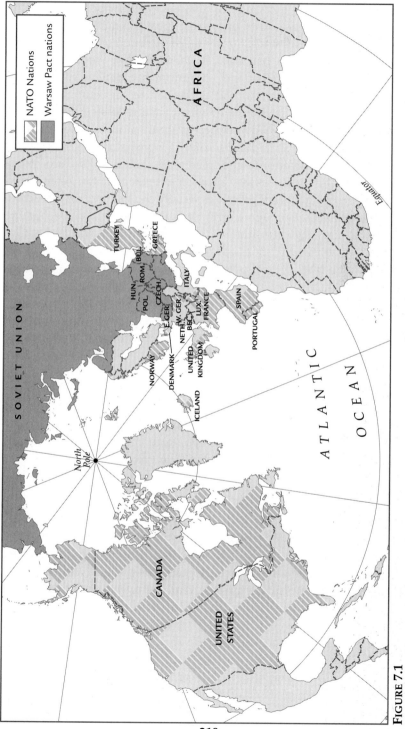

FIGURE 7.1

NATO and Warsaw Pact Nations, ca. 1955.

would feed the USSR's growing heavy industry. Other post-war policies included attempts to get rid of or at least greatly diminish the strength of religion and religious institutions—called superstitions in Communist philosophy—just as they had tried to do in Russia, the Ukraine, and Muslim Central Asia. The tendency to limit most women's employment to manual labor, light industry, and unmechanized agriculture that had already emerged in Soviet Russia now extended to Eastern and Central Europe. The Communists had less success shutting down religious activity, but it became difficult and dangerous for nuns, monks, and priests to live and work there. Some orders adopted plain clothes and separate housing to survive. The USSR was also opposed to sexual freedom (considered immorality, from their standpoint), especially women's sexual freedom, and wanted to encourage higher birth rates. Even as birth control became more reliable and easy to use, the Soviet Union made it harder and harder for citizens to access. Abortion was legal, cheap, and common; but condoms and, later, birth control pills were hard to find. The idea seems to have been that abortion would punish women for their supposed sexual transgressions, and condoms and birth control pills would just encourage promiscuity. On a more positive note, the Socialist goal of universal education and faith in women's relative intellectual equality meant that girls and women were extended primary, secondary, and post-secondary education on par with men.

Currently, the average literacy rate for women in former Soviet and allied countries is 99.8 percent, and women are as likely to attend secondary and post-secondary schools as men.[2] Contemporary Eastern European and Central Asian women are, therefore, much better-educated and able to support themselves on their own than their great-grandmothers.

THE WEST

In Western Europe (outside Spain and Portugal), Japan, and the Philippines, the United States operated differently—undertaking to rebuild the devastation from the ground up, changing schoolbooks, instituting and facilitating the creation of democratic governments, and rebuilding the industrial and transportation infrastructure destroyed in World War II. Although Japan, West Germany, and some Western European returned to, remained, or became democratic states, Spain, Portugal, and the Philippines either remained (in the case of Spain) or fell under the leadership of dictators. The United States and its allies created the North Atlantic Treaty Organization (NATO) for mutual defense, and (like the members of the Warsaw Pact), NATO countries tended to stick together in matters of international relations. Universal child education was a high priority for the United States and its allies, and the current rates for female literacy and secondary school enrollment is also very high in all these countries, with Japan now having succeeded in enrolling 100 percent of girls of the appropriate age in secondary school. On the other hand, although the United States had instituted some Socialist ideas, such as workers' compensation and social security, the major political parties' ideologies were still quite traditional when it came to women's issues. Post-war legislators envisioned U.S. and European women as wives and mothers and considered it their role to educate girls for those roles. Formerly popular images of women as scientists (Marie Curie), adventurers (Amelia Earhart), and capable industrial workers (Rosie the Riveter) that had been popular in earlier decades gave way to images of women as mothers and pretty ornaments. Girls and the children of the working class did not necessarily need to take the most prestigious classes, especially in the sciences, in school, and there was much more focus on the higher education of men than of women. U.S. and Western European laws still treated wives as subordinate to husbands for economic purposes, and in the middle of the century female employment was largely considered a negative thing. The nineteenth-century ideal of a nuclear family headed by a father who worked for wages and a mother who stayed home remained alive and well, and women were actively discouraged from staying in the workforce. Whenever multinational corporations and industries went abroad, they brought these attitudes about women and family life with them.

EXPORTING ATTITUDES

U.S. and Soviet attitudes toward women's work, family role, sexuality, and education filtered out to client states. Although neither country limited its support to foreign governments that shared its ideology, where they did support insurgent movements, they supported ones whose ideologies were compatible with, and often more radical than, their own. The United States was thus more likely to support very conservative regimes that expected women to live in ways the leadership considered traditional. The Soviets were more likely to support radical Socialists who put significant numbers of women into military action, preached atheism, and insisted that since men and women in the movement were already equal, there was no need to work on any lingering sexist attitudes within the revolution. These contradictions played themselves out most violently and visibly in Latin America. In 1980s Nicaragua, Socialist women guerilla fighters were still complaining that the men they fought alongside expected women to do all the cooking and cleaning in the camp, and a few years later conservative Chilean women activists were disappointed when the government they had put in office ignored the political goals of middle-class mothers.

POST-COLONIAL GENDER IDEOLOGY

Everywhere, late twentieth-century states debated issues of identity in terms of masculinity and femininity. During the late imperial period feminists, anti-feminists, and colonial regimes had justified imperialism partly by claiming that the men in colonized regimes were unable to care for their women properly, were undisciplined, and in general were bad to women in a way Western regimes were not. Both Communist theory and European notions of progress held as an article of faith that truly developed nations treated women equally with men. Of course, as we have seen, "equal" in these cases never meant that women were to have access equal with men to political authority or economic resources, although women in both societies had some access to both. Rather, in the Soviet Union it meant that women should work in the public sphere for pay, choose a husband, be allowed to serve in some middle management positions, and have roughly the same access as men to education—but also to do most of the housework, the heavy manual labor of agriculture, and light industrial jobs. In the United States it meant that girls should have a public education somewhat different from boys, nearly all women should marry, and a small handful should have careers—which they ought to give up when they marry. To a lesser extent in both societies, it meant that women and men should appear at and host parties, enter many public spaces as social equals with men, and that women should have considerable freedom to choose their husbands and lovers. Both societies permitted but frowned on women having lovers to whom they were not married—of course, the double standard treated male promiscuity as acceptable and even attractive—but permitted it. Both societies ignored as much as possible the large populations of women who worked grueling hours for low wages. Modernizing states had to decide whether they believed women's emancipation (as it was put during the period) was necessary to their country's transformation or merely a frill.

As we saw in Chapter Six, new totalitarian states went to great lengths to support or at least enforce the kinds of masculinity and femininity they thought most appropriate to their leaders' vision of the new regime. Newly independent regimes across the globe had similar concerns. Becoming a nation-state requires considerable work on national identity; political and cultural leaders had to decide what was distinctive, valuable, and necessary to make them not only stand out from other countries but also hold the loyalty of their populations. Some embraced modernization as an obvious good—this is especially true of countries in East Asia, such as China, Japan, and Malaysia. Some were suspicious of modernization projects, especially those supplied by the United States or USSR, fearing they might be Trojan horses disguising cultural and economic imperialism. For formerly colonized countries, the debate about how to modernize for self-defense and economic growth grew heated. Was modernization a repeatable process? Could it be achieved in the context of their own countries—most of which had entered the industrial economy not as manufacturers but as producers of raw materials for factories overseas? Was modernization the same as Westernization, and could it be achieved without losing their own traditions and culture? And if so, how? It did not help that the leaders of the United States and the USSR thought everyplace should modernize, and that their own respective values should predominate in decisions about how to do it.

Both late nineteenth-century countries and twentieth-century emerging nations saw the woman question as central to modernization. Even where governments did little to implement equality between men and women, they often included it in their constitutions and paid attention to women's activities. Like many other countries, for example, Indonesia and Malaysia started women's divisions of their governments to address what they thought of as women's issues: mothering, family health and hygiene, and children's education. Individual successful women, especially in new and highly visible fields like flight attendants and newscasters, were presented as emblems of each nation's up-to-date modernity. Cuba, which had its own Communist Revolution (1956–1959), relied on a Soviet model of male and female equality, announcing that everyone was equal and putting women into the same sectors of the paid economy as Soviet women.

For many emerging nations, women's emancipation was a mark of progress, a sign that they were part of the modern world. Governments saw girls' education and women's paid employment as obvious goods (although Indonesia and Malaysia, like many other countries, imagined employed women as single) and as natural extensions of their own values. Other countries, like Iran, went further trying to enforce modernization. The Shah of Iran, Reza Pahlavi (1924–1941) sought to modernize his country through, among other things, dress reform and education. At the same time he maintained a despotic and tyrannical regime, and he banned both independent women's organizations and women's journals. His son Muhammad Reza Shah (1941–1979) continued these policies and allied himself very closely with the United States (in part as a counter to the USSR, which was right on the Iranian border). The Pahlavis' support for some women's rights actually hurt the popularity of women's rights in Iran, not only because many Iranians despised the Shahs, but also because of the way Muhammad Reza implemented reforms of women's dress and education.

It is certainly possible to liberate Muslim women without angering the masses of people. In nearby Turkey, Mustafa Kemal Ataturk had been able to institute Western-style dress for men and women without much protest, emancipate women within the family, outlaw polygamy, and eventually grant all adults (including women) the right to vote in the parliamentary democracy. But for Ataturk, women's rights were part and parcel of gaining political freedom for everyone, whereas for Iranians, the Pahlavis' policies associated dress reform and women's work outside the home with injustice and foreign domination. Iranian citizens believed the shahs were more interested in maintaining control than in liberating anyone.

During the 1950s and 1960s, most countries paid at least lip service to the idea that a strong nation needed to invest in its women and children. Universal public education was a goal of nearly every nation, because a well-educated populace was considered the nation's most important resource. Even if all patriotic mothers were to do was raise good children—especially boy soldiers—that task should be done with the best modern methods, including at least basic training in family health care and hygiene. Few states were successful at implementing schools to serve every child, but they almost all tried. In most countries parents were more willing to send boys than girls to school and usually were willing to send them for longer. Girls were often needed to help take care of siblings, perform chores, and sometimes to take part in the family business. They were often married off younger than their brothers, and their education was often considered to be wasted on them, because they would not need it. Nevertheless, despite such all-too-familiar attitudes toward female education, female literacy rose dramatically across the world in the second half of the twentieth century. Though the modern world has not always succeeded in improving women's material conditions, it has become the norm for girls in nearly every part of the world to receive at least some formal education.

The visions new nation-states and emerging political parties have of the citizens of their society almost always include some ideas about appropriate sexuality and gender norms and focus more on women's bodies and women's sexual choices than on men's. So, for instance, in a story that would be familiar to the earliest groups of feminists, attempts to combat prostitution usually wind up as attempts not to close down the market for sexual services but to limit women's freedom of movement and association, regardless of whether they are engaged in prostitution.

RESULTS OF INDUSTRIALIZATION

Industrialization in its early stages eliminates jobs faster than it creates them, disrupts family structures, and pollutes the environment. It also requires an educated workforce accustomed to working at a pace regulated by machines; highly trained technicians and engineers to support, service, and design equipment; and a metalworking and mining infrastructure able to supply raw materials and power. All these things took nearly a century to evolve in Great Britain, the first industrial nation, and they have not evolved much faster in the Third World. The biggest successes have been in Latin America, where serious industrialization efforts had begun in the late nineteenth century.

Industrial development in the Third World has had the same kinds of disruptive side effects on women's work and family lives as it did elsewhere, earlier. Most women in the industrial sector work in textiles, canning, and other industries involving repetitive manual labor and limited education. Such low-paid industrial labor depends very heavily on women's work, with industries often employing almost exclusively women at the bottom rung of employment and offering them virtually no protections or benefits. Officially expressed desires to protect women from exploitation usually come to nothing. When the Dutch colonial government in Indonesia debated labor protection for women during the 1920s and 1930s, for instance, they protected the industries that most relied on women's work: tea, coffee, fireworks, batik (a kind of textile printing) workshops, and other industries that relied on female labor.

In such industries today, the situation is often still similar. Although a few women work as supervisors, nearly all the highly paid, skilled laborers and managers are men. Bosses presume that women's work is a temporary diversion from their long-term career path as stay-at-home mothers and wives and that they are earning money to supplement a male's income, not to support themselves or their families on their own. During the late 1980s in West Java, for instance, one tea picking plantation made nearly 7 percent of male employees supervisors, but only .15 percent of women (two women worked as supervisors). Indeed, the company's official policy was to deny married women employment (since their husbands were supposed to support them and since that would deny jobs to single men) and to deny benefits such as medical care, nursery facilities, funeral expenses for close relatives, and kindergarten care—for which male employees were eligible—to the 1,300 women it did employ. When the state of Indonesia passed a law stipulating equal rights for employees, the company responded by denying women the time they had previously been given for leave during menstruation, by cutting leave for pregnancies in half for a woman's second child, and by denying leaves entirely for further children.

GLOBALIZATION, FAMILY PLANNING, AND INTERNATIONAL DEVELOPMENT

One of the most distinctive characteristics of the twentieth century has been the increasing interconnectedness of not just economies but also of political, intellectual, and artistic movements throughout the world. As mass media such as magazines, radio, television, and film became available in very remote locations, more and more people began to be able to participate in an international, even a global, cultural and intellectual life. Corporations and non-governmental organizations created branch offices in multiple countries and marketed their products or offered their services in an even larger number of places. Political and religious organizations were able to connect with like-minded people in far-flung regions.

When World War II ended, governments around the world recognized a need for an international forum, think-tank, and part-time referee. The United Nations was chartered to replace the old League of Nations to give voice to international opinion and create an international organization to consider regional and global issues. Each nation could vote equally in the General Assembly, whose resolutions are only recommendations. Only the Security Council has the power to make binding resolutions. It had and has five permanent members, the victors in World War II: the United States, the Soviet Union, France, the United States, and China (at first Taiwan, later the People's Republic). At first 5 and later 10 other members were elected to represent world regions.

The UN had an immediate impact on the shape of national and international economic policies, refining international law; defining human rights; and identifying the problems women, children, and the poor faced worldwide. It has also been a gathering place for pooling ideas and resources to develop widely applicable policies. Even though the superpowers often held themselves aloof from the international treaties sponsored by the UN, these treaties have provided opportunities for international efforts.

The UN has played an especially important role in creating publicity for issues of women's rights. Despite the harsh reality of women's oppression in much of the world, on paper, delegates to the UN and the governments they represent have articulated a shared vision that accords women consideration. The United Nations' 1948 declaration of human rights insisted that strong mothers were the necessary backbone of a just and prosperous society. On paper, most states agreed. Some wanted their women to follow models of development similar to Western women. Turkey, for example, continued pursuing a version of modernization where women's equal participation in the political and economic realm was considered an obvious good, and women there today have access to education, finance, religious freedom, and political office as great as or greater than women anywhere else. Other countries insisted that the Western model of womanhood was inappropriate for their women and proclaimed the special virtues of their own female citizens. These special virtues were often very similar to those trumpeted by domestic feminists in the previous century—women's superior and innate gift for self-sacrifice, nurturing, and modesty were described in unimaginative and repetitive ways by the new male leaders of revolutions across the globe. The actual policies of such states can be surprising, however. For example, despite state rhetoric insisting on women's special character and their instinctive behavioral differences from men, Uruguay, Peru, Argentina, and Chile increased the educational and business opportunities available to middle-class women to the point that most college students in these countries are women. Of course, these successes were not always translated into gains for ordinary women, and they did not always succeed forever. Women's absolute literacy rates and girls' rates of attendance in school have declined substantially in recent years in Peru, for example.

Family planning was a critical piece of the economic puzzle for underdeveloped, non-aligned, and Third World states. These states saw rapid population increases during the twentieth century. Western states had seen most of their rapid population increase in the nineteenth century, when vaccination, prenatal care, and infant care had dramatically improved. In the Third World also, better access to prenatal care, better medical care for infants, better health care for young mothers and, in many parts of the world, better health care and nutrition for adults led to rising life expectancies at all age levels and lower rates of maternal death during labor. As in other countries earlier, it was not so much that women were having more babies (though, as women lived longer, sometimes they did) as it was that the babies they *did* have were more likely to live. Their parents themselves lived longer. These are, of course, wonderful developments in and of themselves and mirrored those in the Americas and Western Europe during the previous century. But they also meant that there were more people who would need more of the planet's unequally distributed resources. Governments across the world, but especially the governments of the most powerful countries that controlled the most resources, saw this as a potentially disastrous problem. How would the billions of people be fed, clothed, and housed? Where would the resources come from? Would people in rich countries be willing to use less? Could they be made to? Could there be a way to make more? Many countries implemented family planning policies designed to lower the number of births per adult, with China notoriously implementing a one-child policy forbidding most married couples to have more than one child (unless they were twins).

The one-child policy was successful in bringing down the birth rate in China, but at a high cost. Today, infanticide and roadside abandonment are illegal, but girl babies are frequently left at state orphanages (almost exclusively filled with girls), where they often die from neglect. Since the development of amniocentesis, which facilitates sex testing of fetuses, Chinese women abort female fetuses far more often than male ones. China has had a slightly skewed sex ratio for as long as we have had demographic studies, because female infanticide has been practiced for centuries and because girl children were always more likely than boys to be sold into slavery when slavery was still legal. But today the sex ratio among all Chinese has reached 106 men to 100 women (exactly the reverse of the ratio in most other countries). Most of the variance dates from the enforcement of the one-child policy in the early 1980s and is to be found among the youngest Chinese; there are 110 Chinese boys and men aged 19 and younger for every 100 women.[3] The sex ratio of Chinese men to women in the age groups from 20 to 60 are much closer to parity, with men being a slightly larger part of the demographic until age 60, after which women rapidly outnumber men—as they do in most societies—with good health care for the aged. This sex ratio hurts every young man's chance to have even the one child permitted by law. It will be interesting to see how the increasing scarcity of adult women affects Chinese social life over the next few decades. Already the government has made noises suggesting it may relent on some aspects of the one-child policy.

Across the world, previous family planning policies practiced in other countries had encouraged women to have *more* rather than *fewer* children (as in Nazi Germany and Fascist Italy) and had been ineffective. It turns out to be just as difficult to persuade families to limit the number of children they have as it is to persuade them to have additional children. Current programs that simply distribute birth control and hold classes about it have largely failed, especially if the targeted population sees the goal of the program as simply being to limit births. Even if families want to control the number and spacing of the children they have, they rarely trust their government, United Nations–sponsored agencies, or non-governmental organizations to serve their personal interests. People often perceive these birth control agencies as tools of governments and international corporations that simply want to lower the number of inconvenient or undesirable people in a country. Today, even when women want family planning help and are willing to accept it from agencies, it is often their sex partner who decides when, whether, and in what manner a couple will use birth control or have heterosexual intercourse. Couples may not be able to get birth control, even when both partners are willing to use it. In cultures that conflate honor with women's modesty, and women's modesty with keeping the women separate from unrelated men, it has often been hard for women to travel to health care workers to get information about family planning. Clinics may be too far away. The women themselves or their families may not trust the staff to deal appropriately with strange women. Even if they can reach clinics, women may find that preventive birth control is often unavailable or too expensive—in some parts of the world, a packet of condoms can cost the equivalent of half a day's wages, which has been a huge problem for AIDS prevention programs among prostitutes. Fertility awareness methods (like the rhythm method) of birth control can be effective, but take time and coaching from an experienced practitioner or medical professional and often require women to have intercourse only in the days of the month they are least interested in sexual activity if they want to limit births. Abortion is often very hard to obtain, especially because the United States, which funds a significant percentage of international family planning initiatives, intermittently insists on a gag rule preventing medical workers in family planning organizations from even discussing abortion if their clinic receives any U.S. funding. Around the world, especially in Africa, this has resulted in clinics that provide generalized family planning and basic health care having to close or greatly reduce their services. Three of these clinics in Kenya, for instance, were the only providers of basic health care in the urban areas they had served.

On the other hand, where the legal age of consent to sex and marriage is higher, women marry and have their first children later. First-Wave feminists around the world had advocated both encouraging grade school and higher education for girls and raising the age of consent. India, for instance, had permitted marriages to girls aged as young as 9 (though the age of consent was 10). Feminists had argued that such very young girls are unable to be good wives and mothers and will perform both tasks better if they have some education. In emerging post-colonial nations, progress toward legal protections for girls' sexuality had slowed, even halted, by the end of World War II. In the highly nationalist era of the world wars and early post-independence, governments were less interested in promoting girls' well-being than in having mothers give birth to new sons for the nation and in creating a new understanding of the state.

DEVELOPMENT POLICIES

Two kinds of economic policies have transformed most of the non-aligned or Third World countries. The first of these was the focus on development policies that began in the 1950s. Economic theories of the time explained that some countries were poor because they were underdeveloped. Having no modern industrial infrastructure, no modern educational systems, no modern bureaucracies, and little experience of diplomacy, underdeveloped countries needed to transform their economies—a goal shared by the United Nations, the superpowers, and most of the governments of emerging independent nations. "Development" and "modernization" meant the creation of an industrial base; an infrastructure of paved roads, railways, and airports; universal public education; high-quality health care, especially for infants and children; and clean water supplies. Most economists and public policy offices thought the best way to foster development was through industrialization—that is, through installation of industrial factories and mechanized agriculture.[4]

The focus on mechanization occurred partly because policy advisors saw these as necessary preconditions for the creation of wealth. But it was also because they wanted to rescue people from the backbreaking manual labor involved in traditional farming without tractors, cultivators, harvesters, and irrigation canals driven by electricity and wind. These useful tools require extensive use of fertilizers, pesticides, and petroleum products. But they also enormously magnify the productivity of each individual farmer or laborer.

This concept of development devastated food production in many parts of the world, especially those places where women did most of the farming—which still includes most of Africa and India. Whether nations hired Western industrial and agricultural experts or sent their own citizens to colleges and factories to learn the latest methods, all the experts came back with a vision of agricultural and industrial production firmly American, Western European, or Soviet in its assumptions.

The same deadly combination of expectations that had decimated American Indian systems of production and women's status in communities during the seventeenth and eighteenth centuries repeated its work across much of Africa, India, and Southeast Asia. Factory workers, farmers, and entrepreneurs were imagined as men; women were imagined as homemakers and consumers of goods. Thus, when factories were built or designed, even where they employed large numbers of women, the *real* workers—the ones with important jobs and opportunities for promotion—were always presumed to be men. Unions focused on men (in Peru in the 1960s and 1970s, for example, only male factory workers, their wives, and their widows could become union members, even though almost all the workers in the canning industry were women). Land tenure issues were dealt with even less appropriately. Prior to development schemes, in many countries land was owned by a lineage or a village instead of by individuals. Many new governments created systems of formal landholding in which only individuals owned land, and then chose an individual to speak for the lineage or village—inevitably, the rules for selecting the individual landholder from among the rest of the family made the landholders men, not women. Extension classes educating farmers in the latest agricultural methods were aimed at men. Loans and assistance for improving land went to men, the presumed farmers of the land. Plans to finance new companies and loans for new businesses went to men, who were presumed to be the ones to start them.

Unfortunately for agricultural development schemes focusing on men, in a very large part of the world the people who did the actual farming of land were women. In some villages of Africa and India *all* the men are absent, leaving their wives, mothers, and sisters solely responsible for the family land and for the day-to-day support and feeding of their children. In Africa, where nearly all industrial workers are men and where those men often work hundreds of miles from the land that supports their family, such agricultural policies devastated women farmers, who in fact do almost all the subsistence farming. Early development policies also harmed the families of women farmers, especially in Africa and India. When farmers cannot get credit—whether because development schemes are not lending to women or because governments do not recognize a woman farmer as having legal claim to the land she works—they cannot invest in fertilizers, seeds, improvements to the land, or new equipment. Thus, the productivity of women's farming declined. Yet their families often relied on women's produce as their sole source of food and income while the men in the family were away working in factories, mines, or cities. Therefore, the new methods succeeded mostly in separating women from control of their own land. Modern, mechanized agriculture and land ownership became an increasingly industrialized affair, with crops grown primarily for export or regional sale, not local consumption. Meanwhile, agricultural land ownership was increasingly centralized in the hands of men who did not work the land themselves.

Because of these problems, a good deal of economic development policy in the last 20 years has focused on improving women's access to capital and material resources. Micro-lending has been among the most successful of these. In micro-lending, a bank loans very small sums (often well under $100) to an entrepreneur, usually a woman, for low interest, thus permitting her to start up or expand a small business. The women often are connected to support groups of other entrepreneurs. Micro-lending has been very successful in the sense that very few women default on their loans, and many are able to continue and expand their small businesses.

It was in the 1960s and 1970s that economic development policies began to emphasize the importance of limiting the number of children born to each family while decreasing the mortality rates among pregnant women, infants, and small children. The emphasis was to be on each family raising fewer children and giving those few children a higher material standard of living. After attempts to provide decent clinical care for pregnant women, mothers, and small children, the next most effective way to achieve this is to increase the average age of first marriage for women. Women who have children in their late teens or early twenties are much less likely to have health complications than those who marry earlier, and their babies are more likely to be healthy. Women who marry later also have fewer children (or at least, fewer pregnancies). A girl who marries at 14 is likely to have five or six more pregnancies than a woman who marries at 21, even if neither uses any birth control. The younger woman is also likely to be less well-prepared to act as a mother, because the older one has attained intellectual and physical adulthood—her brain has finished developing—and the younger one has not. Societies that practice child marriage recognize this by having the couple live in the household of one set of parents and putting the bride under the authority of her mother or mother-in-law.

The one thing most likely to persuade girls and their families to marry late is education; girls who have the opportunity for high school or college educations are much more likely to take the opportunity and then to marry. They thus will marry at a later age and will also be better equipped for the responsibilities they will take on.

In Mexico City in 1975, the United Nations held its first state-sponsored international conference on women. The UN Decade for Women was announced, and among the many issues addressed by the conference were family planning, birth control, women's education, and women's human rights. For the first time, the UN articulated the position that there was a clear connection between women's education, age at first marriage, the number of children they had, and the health of those children. Women who did not marry and have children until their late teens or twenties had healthier children, and there was a direct correlation between the number of years a girl or woman spent in school, her children's health, and the material welfare of her family. Also for the first time, the UN tied the connection between economic development and women's health, education, and welfare explicitly to demographic and economic statistics. Many states that did not care much about women's emancipation *did* care about economic development and family planning and so took notice.

Less popular were the further findings and declarations of the congress, which included statements that domestic violence, rape, incest, prostitution, and various forms of genital mutilation are a violation of women's human rights. Previously, international law had treated these kinds of harms to girls and women as individual crimes committed against individuals. Human rights violations are *state* crimes against individuals. At Mexico City, the UN declared tolerating systematic violence against women to be just as much a violation of women's human rights as actively suppressing freedom of speech or religion. In most of the world, women were and are afraid to report crimes like rape, incest, domestic violence, or forced prostitution, because local police not only failed to protect them but punished women for reporting the crime. To this day, some states forcibly return escaping prostitutes to brothels where they have been enslaved and some prosecute rape victims for having had sex outside marriage. In fact, some states, like Serbia in the Bosnian War, use rape in warfare and others, like India and Guatemala in the 1980s and 1990s, have used it in attempts to put down dissident movements.

The Mexico City pronouncements made the neglect of women's complaints of abuse, the use of rape in warfare, and the use of rape to punish dissidents into recognized human rights violations. The UN also declared that it is a human rights violation to restrict women's freedom of movement and citizenship opportunities (for example, by forcing a married woman to get her husband's permission to travel or by attaching a woman's nationality to her husband's, so that if he changes his citizenship she loses hers).

These declarations of women's human rights were not universally popular, and many states have refused to honor them. Even where regimes have made sincere attempts to address issues like domestic violence, it has not always been easy, or even possible, to change the culture of local police forces. U.S. police officers, for instance, have the highest rate of domestic violence within their own marriages of any profession in the country; it has proven very difficult to make such officers treat as a serious offense behavior in which they themselves or their partner officers (on whom they rely for protection in very dangerous situations) engage on a regular basis.

SECOND-WAVE FEMINISMS: 1970S TO THE PRESENT

When women lived in colonized countries, they supported nationalist movements in huge numbers, often making up the majority of demonstrators. When independence was won, women were praised and credited with helping create the new state, but few new states put women's interests high on their list of priorities for domestic and international policy. Instead, the special qualities of what the new governments and political parties thought they saw in the values of traditional womanliness would be praised, and women would be encouraged to support the new state by enacting the roles tradition assigned them. Depending on how economically secure the new states were, they might or might not devote resources to assisting women to perform these supposedly traditional roles more effectively. This neglect of women's issues has led women in many countries to begin a second wave of feminist activism. Here, a few examples from different continents and decades will stand for the whole. India's movement, because it is well-documented but relatively unknown outside the country's borders, will receive particular attention.

SECOND-WAVE FEMINISM IN DEMOCRACIES

THE UNITED STATES.   "Second-Wave Feminism" is the phrase historians use to describe a period of intense feminist activism in North America and Europe from the late 1960s through the early 1980s. It began as an outgrowth of women's participation in student protests in the 1960s and in civil rights movements across the Atlantic. In the 1960s, women like Simone de Beauvoir (author of *The Second Sex*), Betty Friedan (author of *The Feminine Mystique*), and Gloria Steinem (journalist and activist) discovered—just as their predecessors in the Abolitionist movement had discovered—that their male colleagues expected them to act as subordinates. And, just like their predecessors, whose history few of them had had an opportunity to study in any depth,[5] many women activists decided that the only way to go forward on a path of their own choice was to create a separate women's movement. Black women and their compatriots in the American civil rights movement had learned that the first step toward political power was to free the mind, and so early Second-Wave Feminism focused on what it called consciousness-raising. Women met in small groups to discuss the ways they had felt sexism in their lives, so that they could see how instances that might have seemed isolated to them were in fact shared by many women. For example, being denied the chance to open a bank account because a bank had a policy against opening separate accounts for married women, would be a common experience they could identify as part of a pattern of discrimination and repression. Like their predecessors in First-Wave Feminism, Second-Wave feminists challenged everything they saw—political organizations, educational institutions, medical institutions, clothing styles, legal codes, restrictions on women's employment, and even the language used to describe occupations. Their efforts were met with derision and with the usual accusations that feminists hated men, wanted to destroy the family, or were just bitter because they were too ugly to attract a man's attention.[6]

Second-Wave Feminism in the United States focused on several issues that had been important to First-Wave feminists: education, children's rights, reproductive health, birth control, dress reform, and fair employment practices. Activists also pressured colleges and universities in North America and Europe to form women's studies departments or programs, creating new intellectual centers for feminist activism (much to the dismay of anti-feminists) in male-dominated educational institutions. Second-Wave feminists campaigned to have women's achievements put into textbooks and curricula, to create research positions in women's studies, and, on an even more practical level, to get girls equal access to education in male-dominated fields and women equal access to colleges and graduate schools. They campaigned for laws requiring fathers to support their children even after divorce and for access to birth control, prenatal care, and abortion for women—not just in their own countries but around the world. They fought to gain access to professions and crafts largely closed to women before and to enact legislation making it illegal to force a woman to accept sexual exploitation as part of her job. Dress reform, remembered in popular consciousness as bra-burning, was a major piece of feminist consciousness-raising. Feminists did more than question the reasons for wearing bras, however. They asked why the clothes women wore for work cost so much more than men's and why women were charged more for such services as dry cleaning and haircuts than men. Activists were more divided over sex work than their predecessors, although it was still a major area of feminist concern. Some saw sex work as so exploitative it had to be opposed in all its forms, whereas others campaigned for laws to protect prostitutes, and still others tried to change the sex industry by, for example, creating pornography controlled by women and directed toward a female audience.

Second-Wave feminists brought international attention to the problems caused by violence against women and by poor environmental practices. They created new educational programs and centers to support women. Environmental activists had their first major successes in the 1970s, largely due to the heroic campaigns of individual women. Others campaigned successfully for girls and young women in public schools and colleges to have the same opportunity and access to sports as boys and young men, with spectacular results. U.S. girls are now 10 times more likely to participate in athletics than they were in 1972, when the passage of Title IX made it a requirement for public schools, colleges, and universities to provide girls and women access equal to that of boys and men to athletics and athletic scholarships.

INDIA.   The first re-emergence of an active women's movement was in 1972, with the organization of the tribal non-caste people of Maharashtra into the movement called Shramik Sangathana. These Shahada tribal people sought, like many indigenous peoples around the world, to retain control over their lands, which were owned in common but frequently appropriated by the government or high-caste landlords. Women were the most vehement protesters, persuading men to join the movement, leading demonstrations, and taking the hardest lines in negotiations with landlords. As activists grew more experienced, they began to see additional, gender related, problems to solve. They realized that their husbands were spending their wages on alcohol as soon as they were paid. The women themselves had been pushed out of the wage labor market, which hired men, gave the land to the men, and left the women to work the land alone and without pay. Like the activists in the Women's Christian Temperance Union in the nineteenth century, Shramik Sanganatha began to agitate against alcohol production and consumption, going into liquor dens and destroying the liquor pots just as radicals from the WCTU had gone into taverns and destroyed bottles and kegs. Shahada's movement spread throughout Maharashtra, and its members began also to protest the uncontrolled rise of consumer prices. Housewives in groups of 10 to 20 thousand began to hold protests at offices of ministers and industrialists, beating metal plates with rolling pins, and handing over bangles to symbolize that *real* men (Indian men do not normally wear bangles) would not gouge consumers. By 1975 Maharashtra had become a center of self-consciously feminist agitation, with the Shahada movement protesting the continuing existence of dowry. Although it was then and is now illegal to charge a woman's family dowry for her husband, it remains common for the bride's in-laws to demand presents from her natal family. Sometimes wives are murdered because their families do not provide enough dowry. Agitation against dowry escalated throughout the 1980s, as feminists drew attention to the frequency of dowry murders and to the lax handling of such cases by the police.[7]

In the late 1970s and 1980s, feminists also began to experience some success in drawing attention to the issue of rape, which in India is frequently used by landlords, police, and the army as a tactic to undermine movements of political protest (in violation of the UN's new human rights standards concerning violence against women). According to activists, sometimes police come in large numbers to a village and systematically beat and/or rape every woman there, as they are accused of having done in the village of Belidha in December of 1978. More often, however, individual women are taken into custody and assaulted in order to punish them or their husbands for political activity. Enormous national attention came to focus on the problem, and activists used it to organize demonstrations against and teach-ins about violence against women generally, as well as to start mobilizing national attention to the fact that acquaintance rape is also a serious problem in India.

The protests of the late 1970s and the nationwide protest of 1980 persuaded the government to take limited action. Custodial rape of prisoners became a recognized crime, but in general laws against rape were not well enforced. Feminists therefore began creating women's centers that offered health care, counseling, and legal assistance. These differed from earlier women's centers in that they tried to treat women's problems holistically, not focusing on just one or two problems in each center but trying to deal with a woman's life in context. They were also explicitly feminist in orientation, ideology, and practice, which was new for women's organizations. Previous Indian feminists, steeped in Socialist theory, had often felt it was wrong to separate feminist work from more general work for social justice, but by the 1980s Indian feminists felt that they had to have separate institutions and movements focused on women only. The centers tried to act on an ethic of sisterhood and friendship, to treat the women who came to them as equal partners, and to celebrate women's joys as well as their sorrows. They not only counseled women in marital distress and sponsored public debates and conversations, but also created forums for music, dance, singing, and painting. Using these traditional and nonverbal forms of expression helped Indian women work with each other across class, caste, and cultural boundaries, but it took considerable time and effort to discover ways to combine feminist political theories and calls for action with artistic expression. Feminist ideas began to spread throughout the whole of Indian society (although the word "feminism" was often treated with hostility). All the major English-language newspapers pay at least one woman to report on feminist issues, and in 1980 the first women's studies center, the Centre for Women's Development Studies, opened its doors. These developments mark significant progress in making Feminism and women's issues part of mainstream cultural awareness, if not necessarily part of mainstream cultural values.

As in the Atlantic countries, eco-feminism became a driving force in Indian women's activism in the last quarter of the century. As the world has become increasingly industrialized and as industries have spread manufacturing facilities not just around countries but around the world, it has often been women who noticed the ways poor neighborhoods and poor countries have disproportionately borne the environmental costs of industrial production. In India it was rural village women who first began protesting logging. The Indian government has long recognized the erosion of forests as a major environmental problem, because the disappearance of forests not only dries out the land but makes it harder and harder for women, who typically gather all the firewood for cooking and all the family water, to do their work. By 1993 some rural Indian women were walking 8 kilometers a day to gather firewood, water, and fodder for their family.

The first women to begin organized protests were trying to save a handful of walnut trees in and next to their own village from destruction and to prevent developers from running tractors and rows of donkeys through their irrigation. Many rural Indians live on and farm land that belongs to absentee landlords, who may sell rights to developers without consulting or even informing the village. In this particular village—as in many African ones—nearly all the men worked as migrant laborers, while some 500 women lived in the home village and did all the farming. At first they only attempted to save the eight walnut trees, but later they defended the forest beside their town by the simple method of surrounding trees and clinging to them—called "chipko," or clinging. The women organized everyone in the village to develop and implement a conservation plan that would both protect trees and increase the fuel supply. The women were so successful in saving trees that activists all over the state and over India have imitated their methods. Women farmers have also gathered successfully to oppose mining companies that used paths through their land to bring in large shipments and then dirtied the water. By narrowing and even blocking paths through their villages, women have successfully forced local industry to bargain with them, and this tactic, first initiated in one small village, has been adopted by environmental activists throughout India. Women have made up the vast majority of environmental protesters in India, even and especially with respect to the protests of the infamous incident in Bhopal in 1984. The Union Carbide plant had accidentally released over 20 tons of methyl isocyanate into the atmosphere, killing several thousand and injuring as many as half a million more. Only through the persistent clamor of campaigns dominated by women (at first men made up 40 percent of protesters, but by the time they achieved their first victory, women made up 90 percent of all protesters) have victims of the scandalous accident finally gotten government action and some relief.

It would be incorrect to say that Second-Wave feminists have utterly transformed Indian society. Yet their efforts have made substantial inroads in the public consciousness. Women's issues are now widely recognized as important in India, so that even centrist and right-wing political parties now seek to articulate ways in which they serve women's interests and to mobilize women on those issues.

ZAMBIA, ZIMBABWE, AND MALAWI SINCE INDEPENDENCE. In the Central African countries of Zambia, Zimbabwe, and Malawi, women joined male-dominated trade unions and political parties, supporting strikes and rallies on the road to independence. During the 11 years from 1953–1964 that the (now) three countries were joined as one, women activists worked for all the Nationalist political campaigns that succeeded in turning Zambia and Malawi into independent nations. Since then, a few women have been permitted to join the national elites, work in universities, become business leaders, and work in government ministries. Both have become multiparty democracies—Zambia in 1991 and Malawi in 1993—with regimes that tolerate a degree of free expression and assembly. But government policies have done little to improve women's lives; what resources have been available to allocate toward alleviating poverty have been placed in male hands, helping solidify the economic and political supremacy of men over women in these two countries. Since Zambian and Malawian independence, women in these two countries have had more success gaining opportunities for education and waged work, but are still likely to be poor and to work without pay on farms owned by male family members. Banks rarely give credit to women, companies are largely uninterested in investing in job training for women, and land (the vast majority of which is controlled by men, who quite often work for wages far from the family farms they own) is even harder for women to purchase than for men. The women who do work for wages (10 percent of all workers) typically work in the lowest-skill industries. Zimbabwe's liberation struggle ended in 1980, and women there received more rewards for their participation in the war. Prime Minister Robert Mugabe's government gave women new legal rights and provided women with better access to education and jobs. However, these policy changes have been limited, and they meet with active resistance from Zimbabwean men. Moreover, Mugabe's regime has become increasingly repressive over the years, so that freedom of expression, the press, and assembly no longer exist. Mugabe's stated program to take land from white settlers and return it to the people has actually taken land from the rich and given it to his cronies, exacerbating the economic problems it was supposed to help solve and certainly not helping the average Zimbabwean farming woman. Popular protests have met with intense reprisal, and it becomes more and more clear that democratic reform is not part of Mugabe's agenda.[8]

SECOND-WAVE FEMINISM IN HISTORICALLY UNDEMOCRATIC COUNTRIES

Today, except for Saudi Arabia, everywhere men have the right to vote, women do, too. In Kuwait, almost the last holdout against women's suffrage, women voted for the first time June 30, 2006. But much of the world's population lives in places where no one has a vote or where single-party systems make elections perfunctory. In these countries, advocates for women's rights have had to frame their campaigns differently than women who live under long-standing democratic regimes. Whereas sexual and reproductive freedom, access to prestigious positions and good education, and increased political participation were major concerns of Second-Wave Feminism in the West, other feminists were more interested in obtaining day care, improving labor conditions and union participation, and opposing repressive or economically failing regimes.[9]

Some past Latin American governments (today Latin America is almost entirely made up of democratic regimes) and political parties sought to mobilize women for their agendas. Feminists in South America have pointed to the ways gender ideology frequently justifies oppressive states and question whether *any* state can avoid trying to champion particular images of masculinity and femininity to shore up its authority. Conservatives may claim that they intend to protect women's interests (as wives and mothers) but rarely follow that by making better education, health care, and security available to women. Socialist and social democratic governments have promised greater participation but have often failed to include women in positions of power or to take up women's issues. Feminists in Brazil, Argentina, Uruguay, Chile, Peru, and the Arab world have asked themselves whether states are more likely to work toward gender equity or to use patriarchy to shore up their rule. Oppressive states often use images of the patriarchal household, of the proud wife and mother and the strong providing father, as images to proclaim that all is well with the state and as goals for men and women to desire in place of political autonomy. Whereas feminists in long-standing democracies often take it for granted that changing laws and state policies will help women, activists in countries with a history of repressive regimes are painfully aware of the gap between having a law passed and seeing it enforced. Even where women's efforts have toppled old authoritarian regimes (as, again, in Brazil and Iran), they do not necessarily trust that straightforward political campaigning is the best way to achieve gender equity.

From 1971 to 1973, Chilean women were pivotal in the movement opposing Salvador Allende's socialist government. In the March of the Empty Pots in 1971, middle- and upper-class women protested in large groups for the first time. Shortages of basic foods and supplies led to violence in the streets. By 1973 these conservative women were begging the military to intervene in the government, sending the wives of military leaders to be their spokeswomen. In 1973, the military staged a coup, ousting and killing Allende. The new government immediately detained, punished, and killed women who had been former leftist activists, not only raping them but applying electric currents to the mouths, nipples, and vaginas of prisoners.

Leftist and reformist political parties regimes could also succumb to the desire to use gender ideology to shore up their legitimacy. Although Brazil had strong opposition movements throughout the 1970s and 1980s, and although the majority of urban activists in those movements were women, the institutions through which women worked were hostile to feminism. Socialist parties and some elements in the Roman Catholic Church were very active in supporting social justice for the poor *in general* but considered feminist concerns trivial and middle class—even when it was very poor urban women bringing them up.

Tens of thousands of Iranian women marched in support of the Revolution of 1979, which promised to provide a protective, just, and traditional Islamic framework for women. Almost the first reforms the regime made were to change family law to lift restrictions on polygyny, make it easier for men to get a unilateral divorce, make it harder for women to get a divorce, and curtail women's custody rights. Currently, Iranian women need permission from their male guardian to travel even within the country. On the other hand, Iranian women can vote, run for political office, own businesses, and enter most professions—and girls all go to school.

Many Third World activists have seen that it is one thing for a government to *say* it supports women and another thing for a government to provide that support. Governments and political parties can, however, use the assertion that everyone is now equal as an excuse to treat women's activism as, at best, a bourgeois distraction and, at worst, a danger to the state. Blindness to the issues that would drive feminist activists from the late 1960s forward was typical of leftist parties worldwide—not just in China and the Soviet Union as we saw earlier but also, for example, in Brazil, Cuba, and Nicaragua under the Sandinistas.

Even governments that sincerely desired to improve women's lives did not necessarily empower women to choose their own priorities. Maoist Chinese reforms reflected the concerns of Chinese feminist men in the 1920s and 1930s, not the concerns of women in the second half of the century. The leadership of the Communist Party was then, as now, made up almost entirely of men, and their reforms were dependent on what reformist men had thought women needed. Conspicuously absent from the agenda of the Chinese government and other Socialist movements of the mid-twentieth century were such staples of worldwide Second-Wave Feminism as domestic and sexual violence, the double shift of housework and paid employment, glass ceilings in the workplace, environmentalism, access to child care, and sexual freedom beyond the right to refuse marriage to a particular man. In fact, the Chinese government expected and very nearly required all adults to be entered into hetero-sexual monogamous marriage and, like its Qing dynasty predecessor, strongly discouraged adults from remaining single and punished homo-sexual relationships.

When the Cultural Revolution was over, the actual status of Chinese women had changed little, and the state showed no interest in consider-ing women's issues in and of themselves. The All China Women's Federa-tion (Fulian) was and is the official voice of feminism in China, but it is an arm of the government, and part of its function was and is to shield the Chinese government from any unauthorized women's opinions or com-mentary. In China, the government represses all independent ideological activity, whether it be political, cultural, or religious. Thus, overtly femi-nist organizations are not permitted to exist, and one recourse Chinese women who disagree with the government's agenda for women have is to refuse to be identified with Fulian and state-sponsored pseudo-feminism. Some Chinese women activists refuse to refer to themselves as feminists (because in their country "feminists" work for the government and sup-press women's activism). Instead, they may emphasize having a "female position" or "female consciousness." Lesbian activists do not call them-selves anything in public, because homosexuality is officially deemed deviant, and organizing homosexuals is a crime.

Many states strive to keep a supply of women constantly available as a cheap, intermittent labor force. The economies they plan require large numbers of people (whom they prefer to be young women or married women working seasonally, whose wages are considered relatively unim-portant compared with men's) to work as cheap labor in low-skill indus-tries. Their small but dependable salaries function as a buffer for their families in times of economic trouble, and the industries themselves can hire and fire the women without feeling concerned that they are firing someone who supports a family. The Malaysian government actually says this explicitly in pamphlets extolling the modern Malay wife and mother and describing the necessity for a supply of educated part-time women workers. Peruvian women work in canneries not only without benefits but without knowing from day to day whether they are meant to be at work. Employers tell women they are needed the day of their shift, may require double shifts without notice, and may require workers to wait four or five hours (without pay) for a shift to start or not start. Grape packers in Chile (a woman's job in that economy) worked 12- to 16-hour shifts in the 1980s and 1990s, which put a huge strain on their marriages, because their husbands were working the earlier shift that picked the grapes. There was little money or opportunity for homemaking or child care, and the men were not accustomed to doing it. But an economic downturn in this period meant that many families were losing their farms, making it necessary for women to work to pay for the necessities they had once grown themselves. Although having paid work made many of these women feel independent and helped some of them negotiate marriages that were more egalitarian, their jobs just as often contributed to breaking up marriages.

FUNDAMENTALISMS. As Second-Wave Feminism began to experience success, a backlash against Feminism has appeared in areas where it has organized women and gained access to education, better-paying jobs, and some political power. Over the last 25 years, opponents of Feminism have experienced unusual success in rolling back hard-won gains for women's freedoms. Instead of opposing women's education, political access, and workforce participation, they opposed "Feminism" and "Westernization" and defended traditional families (that is, patriarchy) in the name of religion and of women's true nature. Since gaining national attention in the mid-1980s, Indian feminists have been accused of being too Westernized, too middle-class, and too far removed from the concerns of ordinary, real Indian women. Likewise, since the Iranian Revolution of 1979 and with the rise of Islamic fundamentalism in the Arab world—partly in response to the situation in Palestine and partly as an attempt to combat the spread of Western cultural decadence—Islamism has become a convenient symbol of Muslim success in maintaining cultural and religious identity, just as it had been in Soviet Central Asia during the 1920s and 1930s. Feminists such as the Indonesian women shown in Figure 7.2 are described as anti-Islam, anti-family, and anti-freedom; as dupes of the West; as overeducated in Western values and therefore not true representatives of Arab or Muslim women (even though the speakers who make these accusations are often themselves middle-class men with some Western education). Many women activists, especially in the Arab world, refuse to self-identify as feminists, even when they are engaged in activities that not only Westerners but also members of the old Egyptian Feminist Union would have considered radically feminist. There is a strong social stigma, and in some places a risk of damaging reprisal (including beatings or arrests) for speaking out in favor of anything explicitly feminist or against Islam in any way.[10]

In some places, this reaction came in the form of shutting women out of public accomplishment, as in China, post-revolutionary Iran, and the various newly independent republics of the Soviet Union and Russia. In Latin America, it takes the form of blocking women's groups from participation in mainstream political organizations and preventing women's divisions within the organization itself from having a say in policy development.

FIGURE 7.2   INDONESIAN FEMINISTS PROTEST

On May 11, 2006, a performance group of four Indonesian feminists protested an anti-pornography bill, wearing chains to symbolize the bill's oppression of women. The bill was sponsored by very conservative Muslim groups. Women's groups feared the bill would lead to long jail sentences for such offenses as kissing in public, wearing the traditional dress of Indonesian minorities such as the Balinese and Papuans, or even baring legs or shoulders. The fervent opposition of women's groups caused this bill to be considerably watered down. As of this writing, it had not yet passed. What image of Indonesian women do these Muslim protesters seem to want to project and to whom? Does it affect your analysis to know that other feminist protesters carried signs in English that said, "Diversity, Freedom, Equality" or "My Body. My Rights" and directed onlookers to their organizational Web site?

Religious fundamentalisms have been important to the lives of many women across the world. Fundamentalist movements began in the mid-nineteenth century as pious members of various faith traditions searched for ways to reconcile their beliefs with the changes wrought by increasing modernization and popular activism. Today, fundamentalist Muslim, Jewish, Christian, and Hindu movements all have radical social and political activists as well as widespread infrastructures of traveling speakers, practitioners, communications networks, places of worship, and approved political candidates or parties. Fundamentalists of all faiths share a number of characteristics. These include a marked emphasis on particular interpretations of sacred texts, denunciation of co-religionists who do not share those particular interpretations, a desire to force state institutions to support their particular beliefs, and the idea that tolerance of religious pluralism actually oppresses fundamentalists by preventing them from imposing their beliefs on others. Fundamentalists claim for themselves the sole right to define

religious orthodoxy and traditional practice and typically claim that orthodox practice and interpretation of sacred scriptures requires women to be
subordinate to men. It is often further claimed that tradition forbids permitting women to act in any significant way as leaders in the establishment
or interpretation of orthodox practice and interpretation. Female scholarship and leadership in these areas and any female activities that could con-
ceivably be interpreted as feminist are perceived as affronts to the divine,
thus neatly preventing women from having a systematic opportunity to
participate in building definitions of appropriate feminine behavior.

Fundamentalisms are deeply concerned with regulating women's
behavior; defining women in terms of marriage and motherhood; placing
great emphasis on modesty and chastity; and pushing states to enact policies discouraging female employment, making divorce harder (at least for
women), and giving men more authority over their families—especially
over women and minor children. Fundamentalists are not typically concerned with parental authority over adult males or wives' rights in marriage and in fact may insist that laws that actively oppress women and
girls are absolute requirements of religious faith. Thus, traditions permitting parents to force 12-year-old girls into marriages with much older men
are inviolable parts of tradition, even if laws permitting slavery are out
of date. Polygyny and the right of men to divorce wives at will are central to the very nature of Muslim marriage; but Muslim women's rights
to inheritance and independent property can legitimately be modified or
ignored in countries where this is claimed to be traditional. Furthermore,
regardless of whether fundamentalists consider women to have a greater
or lesser sex drive than men, they consider it women's responsibility to
prevent what they define as illicit sex. It is women's responsibility to dress
modestly, to act in such a way as not to arouse men's lust, and to resist
sexual advances. Women are the ones blamed for sexual activity outside
permitted parameters, even where the blame is not placed directly on an
individual. For example, most U.S. research on teenage girls' sexual activity and unwed pregnancies indicates that girls are 2 to 3 1/2 times more
likely to behave promiscuously or to become pregnant if they have been
subject to incest or other sexual abuse.[11] Yet in the public preaching of U.S.
fundamentalism, depictions of young unmarried mothers presume they
got pregnant simply because of their own poor choices. The prevalence
of sexual and other forms of domestic violence is downplayed, while the
individual responsibility of women is discussed in detail. Fundamentalist charitable groups spend considerable social capital trying to persuade
young mothers or soon-to-be mothers to marry the fathers of their children and very little discussing the large percentage of these young women
(and young fathers-to-be) whose introduction to sex came through rape.

Indeed, in some countries rape victims are considered criminals and fair game for rape by police and other government officials.

Despite the hostility fundamentalist religious organizations express toward women's sexuality, they attract large numbers of female members. Fundamentalist organizations are typically very good at grass-roots organization and creating supportive communities—small groups proliferate so members can make friends, join support groups to sympathize with and help address their problems, and even find mates. On an ideological level, fundamentalist women often perceive that secular governments have failed to serve women's interests or, indeed, to deliver justice for society in general, and believe that a government based on religious principles would do better. They do not just believe that their religious organizations' views are accurate, but that those views, put into action, will necessarily improve society. They may be disaffected from secular organizations, but they are often very active in grass-roots religious organizations and political organizations that support views they agree with.

Fundamentalisms appeal to women for many of the same reasons they appeal to men, but also for some sex-specific ones. Women may be raised in a fundamentalist family and thus never question their religious faiths (though many of the feminists most hostile to organized religion or to the major world religions were themselves raised in fundamentalist households or schooled in fundamentalist institutions). Very often, however, older girls and adult women choose fundamentalist sects on their own. In a rapidly changing world, fundamentalism promises security, eternal truths, and enduring traditions to hang a life on. In daily practice, fundamentalist organizations' emphasis on chastity for both men and women can make women feel protected from sexual predation. Fundamentalist women are often in rebellion against media-generated images of women. Just as First- and Second-Wave feminists campaigned for dress reform, seeking comfortable and practical clothing, fundamentalist women feel liberated when they reject the constant demands of keeping up with mainstream fashion. Their organizations' interpretations of modest dress make women members feel valued for their personalities, ideas, and contributions rather than for their appearance. This is of course a two-edged sword: When strict interpretations of modest dress are forced on all women, conservative women will feel that their willing sacrifice of fashion and frivolous dress no longer has any special value.

The emphasis most fundamentalist religions put on men's responsibilities as patriarchs and on strengthening the family unit appeals to many women. They believe they are less likely to be abandoned, cheated on, or divorced by a fundamentalist man, and that such a man will also be a better father for their children. Like early feminists, they use their religion's definitions of women's proper roles and appropriate sexuality to insist on policies that reflect the most ennobling vision of women's roles their religion affords and, despite pious male and female pronouncements that women should not teach or act as leaders, fundamentalism in fact produces many female leaders. So long as their teachings include significant emphasis on the importance of female subordination, use titles that do not infringe on those reserved for men, promote some key fundamentalist doctrines, and do not take away resources from boys or men, female fundamentalist leaders usually find that male leadership will tolerate and even support some of their activities.

Women who live in states with fundamentalist regimes (for example Saudi Arabia, Iran, or Pakistan) may find that the only way for them to have any freedom or influence is to join Islamist movements. For example, the only Iranian women who have felt safe speaking in favor of secular law or Feminism have been expatriates. To voice such sentiments inside Iran is to risk heavy reprisal. By acquiescing to fundamentalist demands regarding modesty and sexuality, they can enjoy greater freedom of movement, access to employment, and some freedom to articulate and express their own ideas. Islamist women have achieved the creation of at least three women's theological colleges, have brought more women into mosques, have created respected positions for some learned women, and have successfully argued against some official statements and policies that harmed women. Yet these benefits are for the most part available only to urban, educated Islamist women. Rural, poor, and marginally educated women more typically find that the imposition of new, stricter fundamentalist norms just takes away some of the few freedoms they have.

POST-MAO CHINA AND POST-SOVIET RUSSIA.   Both China and the former Soviet Union suffered from misogynist and anti-feminist backlash during the last quarter of the twentieth century. From 1978, Mao's successor, Deng Xiaoping (d. 1997), embarked on an ambitious program of economic liberalization. Peasants were allowed to save surpluses for sale; urban dwellers were allowed to open businesses; of late, even large socialized industries have been permitted to split into smaller units and enter part of their assets into the international market. Chinese heavy and light manufacturing have boomed and, even though the gap between rich and poor has grown, the per capita income of Chinese has grown, and the gross domestic product has more than quadrupled. Although on average Chinese are wealthier, the introduction of capitalism has created large disparities in wealth and given rise to new opportunities for employment discrimination against women, minorities, and the elderly. Women have paid a higher price for the new economy than men. In fact, women have lost ground in employment and leadership positions and, although the Chinese government claims that female entrepreneurship is as frequent as male entrepreneurship, women make up only one-fifth of Chinese entrepreneurs and start businesses primarily in the service sector. Female-run businesses are the main source of responsible positions for business-women, because they (unlike male-run businesses) are more likely to hire women than men.[12]

Economic liberalization has allowed employers to choose whom to hire and whom to fire. Since most Chinese industries were already run by men, men had the best contacts and the best credit to open businesses. As the private sector expanded, it turned out that most of these men had no interest in hiring or promoting women to management or in hiring older women for anything at all. Young and pretty women were desirable for front of the house retail and service tasks and for secretarial appointments, but that was about the extent of female opportunity in the new business. Moreover, as formerly state-run industries were privatized, the few women who had already been in (mostly low-level) management would be let go. Even the government stopped championing women's economic equality. Instead the new female symbol of China's economic success was the housewife whose husband made enough to support the whole family.

Economic liberalization and *Perestroika* (Soviet Premier Mikhail Gorbachev's policy of openness) changed the Soviet economy in similar ways during the 1980s, until the actual demise of the Soviet Union after 1989. After that, women's position worsened rapidly. The macho posturing of official Soviet self-images and the Little Deal allowing men to expect their wives to work full-time and still serve men and home had created a society where many men neither knew nor cared what contributions women made, and who saw women mainly as potential or inadequate sex toys and domestic servants. There were no longer quotas for women's participation in the *Duma* (the parliament), and so women almost disappeared from political office at the very time that those offices started to have political clout. There were no laws against sex discrimination or sexual harassment in employment. Women lucky enough to have jobs often found themselves expected to have sex with their employers as a regular part of their jobs. Older women, even those with management experience, were fired and ended up with few options outside domestic labor. Young women frequently turned to prostitution and pornography, deciding that if having any job required them to prostitute themselves, they might as well make decent money at it. One result of this was that feminist activism was reborn in the former Soviet Union as it had not been since the closing of the Zhenotdel under Stalin.

CONCLUSION

The twentieth century has brought huge changes in women's material welfare. The end of colonialism brought neither the material wealth nor the improvement in women's legal standing for which they might have hoped. Early development schemes actually hurt the economic positions of many women and their families, and family planning programs rarely focused on what women themselves might want but on the goals of governments run mainly by men. The rapid increase in world population has, in fact, meant diminishing access to food, clean water, and health care for women in parts of the world, and much greater access for others. Thus, the century has widened the divisions between women.

In fact, the century has been revolutionary for women. Their opportunities for education, for political participation, and for sexual choice have expanded in most of the world. The idea that women have rights both as human beings and as women has become mainstream in most of the world, as have the goals of universal female education and access to reproductive health care. The rapid pace of change made many people uneasy, and changes in gender roles, especially female gender roles, have often been the most disturbing to people. Whereas on the one hand the twentieth century has been pivotal in creating new options for women, the very presence of those new options has prompted considerable opposition to improving women's political standing. This opposition does not come entirely from men, either; as we have discussed, fundamentalism and other conservative movements enjoy widespread female participation. Yet even these women are not interested in creating a world where they have no power in the public realm. Rather, in many ways, the writings of conservative and fundamentalist women echo the goals of First-Wave domestic feminists. To what would probably be the delight of First-Wave feminists like Mott, Wollstonecraft, and Anthony, the desires of the many of the more conservative governments and religious movements in the world today share with these early feminists an agenda that was considered shocking and radical in the first half of the nineteenth century: to provide women with a thorough and progressive education; to improve the health of women and their families; and to include women in policy making.

STUDY QUESTIONS

1. What are some issues Second-Wave feminists had in common with First-Wave feminists? What new concerns did they have?

2. How did early development policies affect men and women differently? What steps have been taken to fix some of the damage done?

3. In what ways do the labor practices of the early Industrial Revolution still seem to be in place?

4. To what extent is the presence of religious movements and organizations in your own life or that of your female friends and relatives restrictive? To what extent is their presence liberating?

BIBLIOGRAPHY

*indicates contains whole primary sources or secondary works containing substantial extracts.

COLD WAR

Clements, Barbara Evans. *Bolshevik Women*. Cambridge: Cambridge University Press, 1997.
*Engel, Barbara Alpern, et al., eds. *A Revolution of Their Own: Voices of Women in Soviet History*. Westport, CT: Greenwood Press, 1997.
Engel, Barbara Alpern. *Women in Russia, 1700–2000*. Cambridge: Cambridge University Press, 2004.
Wood, Elizabeth. *The Baba and the Comrade: Gender and Politics in Revolutionary Russia*. Bloomington: Indiana University Press, 1997.

DEVELOPMENT POLICIES AND INTERNATIONAL FAMILY PLANNING

Chuku, Gloria. *Igbo Women and Economic Transformation in Southeastern Nigeria 1900–1960*. New York: Routledge, 2005.
Goebel, Allison. *Gender and Land Reform: The Zimbabwe Experience*. Montreal: McGill-Queens University Press, 2005.
Heyat, Farideh. *Azeri Women in Transition: Women in Soviet and Post-Soviet Azerbaijan*. London: Routledge Curzon, 2002.
*Honig, Emily, and Gail Hershatter, ed. and trans. *Personal Voices: Chinese Women in the 1980s*. Stanford, CA: Stanford University Press, 1988.
*Hooks, Margaret. *Guatemalan Women Speak*. Washington, DC: Ecumenical Program on Central America and the Caribbean, 1993.
*Lo, Jeannie. *Office Ladies, Factory Women: Life and Work in a Japanese Company*. Armonk, NY: M. E. Sharpe, 1990.
Locher-Scholten, E., and Anke Niehof, eds. *Indonesian Women in Focus: Past and Present Notions*. Dordrecht, Holland: Foris Publications, 1987.
Made, Patricia, and Nomasomi Mpofu. *Women in Zimbabwe: A Profile of Women in Zimbabwe*. Harare, Zimbabwe: Zimbabwe Women's Resource Centre and the Southern Africa Research and Documentation Centre, 2005.
*Menchú, Rigoberta. *I, Rigoberta Menchú*. New York: Oxford University Press, 1997.
Meriweather, Margaret L., and Judith E. Tucker, eds. *A Social History of Women and Gender in the Modern Middle East*. Boulder, CO: Westview Press, 1999.
Myula, Peter, and Paul Kakhangwa. *Women in Malawi: A Profile of Women in Malawi*. Zomba, Malawi: University of Malawi Center for Social Research, 1997.
Ng, Cecilia, et al. *Positioning Women in Malaysia: Class and Gender in an Industrializing State*. New York: St. Martin's Press, 1999.
Partner, Simon. *Toshié: A Story of Village Life in Twentieth Century Japan*. Berkeley: University of California Press, 2004.
White, Seodi Venekai-Rudo, et al. *Women in Malawi: A Profile of Women in Malawi*. Limbe, Malawi: Women and Law in Southern Africa, Research and Education Trust, 2005. This

work takes the Myula and Kakhangwa study (cited above) forward from 1997. Available as hard copy and on the World Wide Web at http://databases.sardc.net/books/malawi2005/index.php (accessed March 2, 2008).

The World's Women, 2005: Progress in Statistics. New York: United Nations, 2005.

SECOND-WAVE FEMINISMS AND RELIGIOUS ACTIVISM

Alvarez, Sonia E. *Engendering Democracy in Brazil: Women's Movements in Transition Politics.* Princeton, NJ: Princeton University Press, 1991.

*Andreas, Carol. *When Women Rebel: The Rise of Popular Feminism in Peru.* Westport, CT: Lawrence Hill, 1985.

Brasher, Brenda, ed. *Encyclopedia of Fundamentalism.* New York: Routledge, 2001.

Brasher, Brenda. *Godly Women: Fundamentalism and Female Power.* New Brunswick, NJ: Rutgers University Press, 1998.

Brownell, Susan, and Jeffrey Wasserstrom, eds. *Chinese Femininities/Chinese Masculinities: A Reader.* Berkeley, Los Angeles: University of California Press, 2002.

Chaudhuri, Matrayee, ed. *Feminism in India.* New York: Palgrave Macmillan, 2005.

Croll, Elisabeth. *Feminism and Socialism in China.* New York: Schocken Books, 1980.

Downs, Laura Lee. *Writing Gender History.* New York: Oxford University Press, 2004.

Fernea, Elizabeth Warnock. *In Search of Islamic Feminism: One Woman's Global Journey.* New York: Anchor Books/Doubleday, 1998.

Forbes, Geraldine Hancock. *Women in Modern India.* Cambridge: Cambridge University Press, 1996.

Kumar, Radha. *The History of Doing: An Illustrated Account of Movements for Women's Rights and Feminism in India 1800–1990.* New Delhi: Kali for Women, 1990.

Kurbanova, Mohira R. "The Role of Traditional Gender Ideologies in the Empowerment of Women in Post-Soviet Uzbekistan." MA thesis, Ohio University, 2005.

Martin, Christina K., Gail Hershatter, Lisa Rofel, and Tyrene White, eds. *Engendering China: Women, Culture, and the State.* Cambridge, MA: Harvard University Press, 1994.

Marty, Martin E., and R. Scott Applebee, eds. *Fundamentalism and Society: Reclaiming the Sciences, the Family, and Education.* 3 vols. Chicago: University of Chicago Press, 1993.

Noonan, Norma Corigliano, and Carol Nechemias, eds. *Encyclopedia of Russian Women's Movements.* Westport, CT: Greenwood Press, 2001.

Ping-Chun Hsiung, et al., eds. *Chinese Women Organizing: Cadres, Feminists, Muslims, Queers.* Oxford: Berg, 2001.

Reed, Betsy. *Nothing Sacred: Women Respond to Fundamentalism and Terror.* New York: Thunder's Mouth Press/Nation Books, 2002.

Whelan, Imelda. *Modern Feminist Thought: From the "Second Wave" to "Post Feminism."* New York: New York University Press, 1995.

Winn, Peter. *Americas: The Changing Face of Latin America and the Caribbean.* New York: Pantheon Books, 1992.

AUDIO-VISUAL SOURCES

Jamison, Gayla, director. *Forging Peace in Guatemala.* VHS. Princeton, NJ: Films for the Humanities, 1997.

Sarmiento, Carmen, director. *Women of Latin America.* 10 videos. VHS. Princeton, NJ: Films for the Humanities, 1997.

JOURNALS

Journal of Women's History. Bloomington: Indiana University Press, 1997–Present.

Ms. Arlington, VA: Liberty Media for Women, 1971–Present.

Signs: Journal of Women in Culture and Society. Chicago: University of Chicago Press, 1975.

CONCLUSION

THE POLITICS OF CREATION AND THE SEARCH FOR TRUTH AND BEAUTY

It was when my mother-in-law told me I did not have to follow nobody's ideas that I learnt myself to follow my head. . . . And that's what I did, and I do it yet, and it's a good way, too.

— ARLONZIA PETTWAY, B. 1925, ON DEVELOPING HER OWN STYLE OF QUILTING[1]

No history of women should ignore the extent to which women strive to express themselves and to understand the world. A survey of women's creative and scholarly accomplishments through the last 500 years would fill a library of books. But it seemed best—after six chapters largely devoted to women's struggles for freedom, security, child care, political influence, justice, and mere survival—to remind ourselves that the human spirit is not simply the victim of outside forces. Nor do women live by bread, rice, and family alone. They also need intellectual, spiritual, and creative outlets to grow as whole persons. Yes, misogynist efforts and anti-feminist backlash seek to take away women's gains in political, economic, sexual, and reproductive freedom. Yet more girls and women have greater access to education and training in all areas of life than ever before, resulting in a worldwide proliferation of artistic and scholarly works in all media and genres. If it is true, as a popular slogan of Second-Wave Feminism claimed, that "the personal is political," the personal decisions of so many women to work as scholars, artists, and artisans have a political dimension.

SOME POLITICAL IMPLICATIONS OF DOMESTIC CRAFTS

The most domestic and traditional of women's activities can have powerful political meaning. Industrialization and development notwithstanding, some women still fabricate many of the objects they and their families wear and consume. Whether they are very wealthy or living in dire poverty, most women are engaged in some kind of artistic or craft production, from preparing special foodstuffs and crafting ceremonial objects to fabricating basic necessities such as clothing, furnishings, or houses. Women use crafts like sewing, weaving, basketry, cooking, and pottery not just to fulfill their own and their families' basic needs but also to maintain cultural identity, to make political statements, and to express themselves.

Using traditional methods of craft production is one way women choose to pass on their heritage to their children and to remind themselves and others what it means to be a member of a particular community. Such a purpose for craft production has been especially important for indigenous peoples and members of minority groups, whose craft and cooking practices can help community values and lifeways survive under external threats and pressure (for example, the Hopi women in Figure C.1 are using traditional grinding stones to prepare their meal). Rigoberta Menchú, a Guatemalan labor activist, explains that when she was growing up, the women of her community made tortillas in the traditional way every day:

> It's not the custom among our people to use a mill to grind the maize to make dough. We use a grinding stone; that is, an ancient stone passed down from our ancestors. We don't use ovens, either. We only use wood fires to cook our *tortillas.* First we get up at three in the morning and start grinding and washing the *nixtamal,* turning it into dough by using

FIGURE C.1   HOPI WOMEN PREPARING MEAL
Four Hopi women grinding meal in 1906 in much the same way that Rigoberta Menchú describes Maya women grinding corn. Is there any kind of laborious food preparation that your family continues to do in order to maintain tradition or nurture bonds among family members?

the grinding stone. We all have different chores in the morning. Some
of us wash the *nixtamal,* others make the fire to heat water for the coffee
or whatever . . . there were four women working in the house. Each . . .
had her job to do. . . . Whoever gets up first, lights the fire. She makes the
fire, gets the wood hot and prepares everything for making *tortillas.* She
heats the water. The one who gets up next washes the *nixtamal* outside,
and the third one up washes the grinding stone, gets the water ready and
prepares everything needed for grinding the maize. . . . When the fire
is made and the *nixtamal* washed, everyone starts grinding. One person
grinds the maize, another grinds it a second time with a stone to make it
finer, and another makes it into little balls for the *tortilla.* When that's all
ready, we all start making *tortillas.*[2]

Corn, she explains, is the basis of Maya indigenous culture, and the methods used to cultivate, process, and cook maize shape the community in
ways that it would be very difficult to reproduce by other means. Likewise,
when a Navajo seeks to weave by traditional methods, she is also seeking
to maintain or return to her roots and, like Rigoberta Menchú, involving
her community in the process. Traditional Navajo blanket weaving requires
a particular lifestyle. Ideally, the wool would come from a woman's own
sheep, which her husband, brothers, or sons herd, and which she and they
follow, moving from summer to winter grounds. She should clean, comb,
and dye the wool herself from fibers available locally and use a particular
kind of loom and—because the fabric is made by hand and all by her and
her daughters—here and there the fabric will contain stray hairs of their
own woven into the whole. The pattern should look "right" when the blanket is draped over the body a certain way and may well be designed with
a particular person in mind. Thus, a Navajo blanket made by traditional
methods is more than a decorative object—it stands for a commitment to
living traditionally. When Ashkenazi Jewish women around the world
make bread and prepare their households for the Sabbath, they are doing
something similar—creating a Jewish space that not only their grandmothers and great-grandmothers but also Jewish women on the other side of
the world would recognize. In Mali, in the ancient city of Jenne, women
who marry into families of blacksmiths from outside ethnic groups often
take up pottery making, not just to make money, but because women from
blacksmith's families have traditionally worked in that craft. Going through
an apprenticeship in pottery helps a woman integrate into her new family,
who often press her to take it up. Most readers can probably recall ways
that special foods, gift textiles (in this author's own circle, usually quilts),
seasonal household ornaments, or the choice of particular gardening methods or plants connect them to their own family heritage.

Women also make crafts with explicit political messages. In the 1960s
and 1970s the women of Gee's Bend, Alabama, made "freedom quilts"

in support of the civil rights movement. Pacific Islanders have been particularly attentive to the ways tradition becomes part of modern cultural identity and national self-awareness. For instance, Maori women and men in New Zealand and Samoan migrants in the United States and New Zealand wear tattoos in part as a way of connecting to and carrying on their traditions. And in Papua New Guinea the *bilum,* or net bag—a women's craft that has spread throughout the country in the last few decades—has become one of the most important and widely recognized symbols of traditional culture and of Papuan womanhood. Each region produces its own kinds of net bags, ranging from the purely functional to the ceremonial and highly decorated.

Even though simply making craft items of a particular sort may have a broad cultural meaning, when a woman makes a particular object it is usually for a specific person, occasion, or purpose, and the actual design will often be chosen for purely aesthetic reasons. Arlonzia Pettway, quoted at the start of this chapter, is typical of the other quilters in her small town, most of whom say that although they may have gotten inspiration from formal patterns, in general they designed quilts to please themselves, in variations of patterns they saw their mothers make. The quilts themselves served an important function—they had no central heat and no fireplace in the bedrooms, so every bed needed four to six quilts. The quilts, being made mostly from the remains of old work clothes and rags, were not very sturdy, so most women needed to make several a year for their families. But each individual one was made to please the eye as much as possible using the often faded and stained materials available. Their meanings could be very specific and personal. After her husband died, one widow and her daughter made a quilt from all of her husband's work clothes so that she could wrap herself in it and be surrounded by him. Some years, coming together to make quilts and sing was the only recreation the women had.

Like the women of Gee's Bend, Chilean activists turned a folk art—in their case, the *arpillera,* appliqué images of rural life and landscapes sewn on burlap to make tapestries—into political protest. Working in the basements of Catholic churches with donated supplies, Chilean women in the mid-1970s and 1980s used the arpillera to document the kidnappings and disappearances of their relatives. The churches displayed and sold the tapestries to support the women and their families (who were often deeply impoverished), at once supporting the protest movement and providing the women an outlet to express their grief and pain.

Crafts, which have only recently begun to receive serious scholarly attention as art forms, can resonate through several dimensions of women's lives and have both covert and overt political meaning. They can commemorate events and people in the life of a woman and her family, helping them keep their family or their ethnic traditions alive. They can act as an anchor for tradition while a world of unnecessary change tries to sweep families along. They can unite women for common purposes, function as a form of political advertisement, and pay for social and political movements.

"MEN'S" ARTS AND SCIENCES

As feminist ideas have become current throughout the world and as governments have sought to modernize over the last 200 years, many girls and women have had access to education in arenas that were once open only to men. Educational levels that had previously been attained only by Buddhist and Christian nuns, members of leading Sufi Muslim families, and the daughters of the most privileged classes became available to more and more women. Even though illiteracy remains much higher among women than men, women now participate in most of the forms of learning and self-expression that until recently were controlled by men and forbidden to women. Their work is a testament to the fact that women can contribute to the process of discovery as well as men.

One of the most important results of this for world and women's history has been the proliferation of women's own ideas about themselves and the world around them. We have also seen that, even where women have the same training as men, the same professional goals and ideals, their professional choices may be shaped by their experiences and their obligations as women. For example, despite the fact that many regimes in the Arab world are generally repressive of independent political organization, Arabs revere the spoken and written word too much for their governments to censor most forms of written expression. As more and more Arab women have become educated, they have begun to write about their own lives and concerns in novels, short stories, and poems, many of which have been translated and published internationally. Some of what they have had to say has been shocking to the Arab public, especially to men and to governments. Arab women like Hanan al Shaykh (*Women of Sand and Myrrh; The Story of Zahra*) have written about their own and other women's sexuality, about polygyny, and about education. Egyptian feminist and physician Nawal el Saadawi's novels, essays, and speeches (for which she has spent years in jail) focus on women's oppressions and desires.

In Africa, Nigerian-born writer Buchi Emecheta (b. 1944) has written an autobiography and two semi-autobiographical novels and has also made it a personal quest to tell the history of Nigerian women's lives since the nineteenth century in a series of historical novels, of which *The Joys of Motherhood* (1979) is the most famous. Bessie Head (1937–1986) of Botswana criticized the racism of Bantu Africans toward Bushmen in her novel of tragic romance, *Maru*, one of the first post-colonial works to consider black Africans as appropriate protagonists of romance.

Similar stories can be found in the fine and performing arts. Education in these areas is typically harder to come by than literacy, and access to venues for exhibition and performance is harder to get. Even in countries where more women than men study the fine and performing arts, the most influential theaters and festivals, the funds required to stage performances, the heads of film studios, the major museums and galleries that exhibit art works, and the professional intellectuals (professors, curators, and reviewers) who act as gatekeepers for the arts are still mostly men. Thus it is rare for the content of performances involving large numbers of performers to have been determined by a woman writer, choreographer, or director; for films to be produced, directed, and written by women; and for major exhibitions of artwork to focus on individual women artists or on trends in women's artistic production. Nevertheless, many individual women have been very successful as performers, writers, directors, and (in particular) as choreographers and heads of dance companies. Umm Khulthum (1898–1975) was the most influential singer in the Arab world—her music is still played daily on radio stations throughout the region. She was the first major star of recorded Arab music, and her body of work, which is highly revered and influential among contemporary singers, symbolized for many the best of Egyptian national culture. Yvonne Rainer's dance manifesto saying "no" to most of the ideas about dance current in the 1950s and early 1960s became the centerpiece of modern dance theory, challenging and revising ideas about and the performance of classical dance throughout the Atlantic World. Twyla Tharp has probably been the world's most influential modern dance choreographer since the late 1970s. Amalia Hernandez founded and has directed the extremely influential Ballet Folklórico de México for 40 years. In India, Chandra Lakha, Malliki Sarabhai, and Mrinalini Sarabhai have created influential dance companies and used dance to promote feminist and environmentalist causes. Their Darpana Academy of the Performing Arts teaches thousands of students and collaborates on hundreds of projects throughout India.

The work of these artists, performers, and writers is not simply beautiful or entertaining, although much of it is both these things. The meanings of their work are not limited to the works themselves or to their audiences' interpretation of the works. A career spent creating art, music, literature, dance, or theater is only rarely one that pays huge financial rewards—the women who are successful rarely pursue their art for the money, but for the intangible rewards of self-expression and interacting with an audience or readers or for the pleasure of helping others express themselves. Like the radical Russian activists of the nineteenth century, these women are attempting to become the best version of themselves, to attain the highest goals for the sake of striving. To spend a lifetime engaged in creative accomplishment other than or in addition to motherhood is to engage in a radical form of self-definition.

SCHOLARSHIP

First- and Second-Wave feminists in Europe and the Americas focused enormous attention on gaining access to education for girls and women. Consequently, for the last 20 years women in these regions have actually been more likely than men to finish elementary and secondary education and to attend universities. This has not resulted in women's wages in general reaching parity with men's or with Western women having equal access to high-status jobs in universities. However, it has meant that many more women than ever before have become university instructors and professional researchers and that they have persuaded colleges and universities to create programs in Women's Studies and Gender Studies.

Women's Studies and Gender Studies programs are often highly contested in the institutions that house them and, even at very large and wealthy universities, typically have only a handful of faculty, small budgets, and limited space. Nevertheless, these small programs have made it respectable—or at least permissible—for instructors and researchers to study and teach about any aspect of women's lives and/or the implications of gender for almost any subject. They have acted as central meeting points for people researching women and for feminist activists, sponsored conferences, published academic journals, and created a visible market for texts, films, and recordings by and about women. It is because of the proliferation of these departments and the scholarship produced in cooperation with women's studies that it was possible to write this textbook, which could not have been written in 1980, 1990, or even in 2000. Even today, most people researching women's studies concentrate on Europe and North America, because most of the jobs available in the field are at North American and Western European institutions seeking scholars researching and teaching about those regions. The bulk of all women's studies research on women has, therefore, focused on Western women. Nevertheless, as this book indicates, research on Third World women has grown rapidly since the 1980s. Women's Studies departments, albeit small, have appeared in India, China, Japan, and other countries across the world.

Because women's studies programs have been so important in making this book possible, I have begun the discussion of late twentieth-century women's scholarship with such departments. However, the vast majority of women scholars over the last half-century have not chosen to specialize in women's studies. Rather, the late twentieth century has seen mostly middle-class women from all over the world enter and succeed in all the scholarly fields of science, engineering, the humanities, and business. Every scholar has her own reasons for entering and staying in a particular field, but a handful of reasons come up repeatedly.

Curiosity motivates many researchers. The words of Priscilla Auchincloss, a specialist in high energy physics, are not atypical. Physics, she explains, " . . . sparked in me an intense fascination with logical, analytical problem-solving. . . . I often return to an image of gazing upon 'truth,' simple, unadorned, gleaming, and beautiful. . . . "[3] In an era when many women can have access to advanced education and some can have access to extensive research facilities, many women want learning for its own sake. First-Wave feminists often said this explicitly, saying or writing that they felt deprived of the education they wanted because they were female. Huda Sharawi, for example, wanted to learn Arabic grammar, but Said Agha, the eunuch who guarded the women's quarters of her family, refused to allow her tutor to teach her, because "The young lady has no need of grammar as she will not become a judge!" "I became depressed," Sharawi wrote, "and began to neglect my studies, hating being a girl because it kept me from the education I sought." Some women just love learning in a particular field—medicine, entomology, literature, primatology, theology—for its own sake and make that field a lifelong study simply because they can. As Sharawi said, "I have a natural love for poetry and bought every book I came across. My passion increased all the more because of the itinerant poet, Sayyida Khadija al-Maghribiyya, who often visited our house, where she stayed several days at a time . . . composing verse."[4] As the previous chapters have shown, most human cultures have discouraged intellectual development in women, especially defining particular kinds of scholarship as off-limits.

Most nineteenth- and early twentieth-century feminists, as well as governments that championed women's educations, championed women's education because it would make women better citizens, mothers, wives, or workers. Second-Wave Feminism, however, not only in the West but in India, the Middle East, and Japan, has borrowed from Russian radicalism and dares to pay explicit attention to women's own desires—not just women's desires for autonomy, economic justice, sexual and reproductive freedom, and civil rights, but also women's longing to better themselves. Second-Wave Feminism coincided with an era in which governments and corporations all over the world began to consider it important to fund what is called "basic research," that is, research done just out of curiosity, because the scholars doing the research think it might be important *someday.* The idea is that the best new innovations and ideas happen serendipitously, often as unexpected by-products of experiments or research projects. There is also a renewed tendency to fund research tangentially related to problems governments and corporations think it would be good to solve, again on the assumption that we never know exactly where unexpected new ideas and solutions may come from. Because of this openness to basic research and the focus of Second-Wave Feminism on women's own desires, people throughout the world now accept as natural the radical new idea that it may be all right for women to study things and to engage in scholarship *just because they want to and have a talent for it.* In the past, women scholars and artists could get educations only if their fathers or guardians were willing and could only work as scholars in the fields of their choice if they were extraordinarily lucky (nuns needed less luck, but have always been a very small portion of the population). Now, although family support is often critical in starting a career, women can find state and private support for later scholarship. It is often harder for women to gain that support than it is for men, but it is possible, and hundreds of thousands of women the world over have taken advantage of it.

If it is true that scholars undertake their studies in part because curiosity and natural talent drive them to it, it is also true that curiosity is rarely the only thing motivating scholars. Nobel Laureate Gertrude Belle Elion became a scientist because her grandfather's death from cancer made her want to contribute to cures and treatments for it. She went into chemistry rather than medicine because it was almost impossible for a woman to get a medical degree when she was a girl. She worked in industry (for Burroughs Wellcome) rather than in academia because it was the only place she could find a position of independent responsibility. "I could do as much as I wanted to," she said of her mentor there, " . . . there was never any barrier to my jumping into a field in which I had no formal training."[5] Women and men scholars are both often motivated by a desire to serve the community or to serve a particular population. Because societies have different expectations for women's service than for men's, women scholars often choose differing forms of community service. The particular projects a woman undertakes and the questions she asks come from her own sense of what matters. It has turned out that the priorities of women scholars, like those of women voters, are not always the same as those of men scholars—and that some men scholars have changed their own priorities after considering the results of the new questions women ask. National Academy of Science member Sarah B. Hrdy's work on langur monkeys demonstrated for the first time that male langurs killed only the infants of females with whom they had not had intercourse. Her work transformed the study of the ways primate females select mates.

In every country, some professions and forms of scholarship attract women in larger numbers than others. It is not clear yet whether this is because more women are predisposed toward these fields than others or because women are discouraged more from some fields than others—most scholars studying such trends suspect the latter. Certainly in the United States, women were still being actively discouraged from fields such as engineering, mathematics, biology, and physics as late as the 1980s. Encouraged and discouraged professions vary considerably from one country to another—as we have seen, the former Soviet Union strongly encouraged women to work in mathematics, medicine, and engineering, for instance, whereas most educational and research institutions in the United States discouraged women from entering those fields until recently. Turkey, for example, has produced almost as many women as men engineers since the mid-twentieth century and currently has the largest proportion of women scientists among developed countries.[6]

Much of the most radical thinking and doing has been the work of women engaged in one of the oldest projects of feminism: re-envisioning, rereading, and re-evaluating religious traditions from a woman's perspective. More women today than ever before have access to not only a secular but also a thorough religious education, and they have taken advantage of it. Muslim intellectuals in much of the world have learned to use the rhetoric of Islamism, the Quran, and traditional scholarship to articulate a theology that accords women equality with men, dignity, and respect. On a very practical level, the Women's Centre for Legal Aid and Counseling (WCLAC) in Palestine has published and disseminated numerous brochures explaining to women the rights they do have under current family laws. North African scholar Leila Ahmed has researched the early history of the transmission of Islamic texts. Her conclusion has been that the misogyny apparent in many contemporary Muslim countries and religious practices results from men misreading the Quran, deliberately choosing interpretations of it and of the *hadith* (traditions of the Prophet Muhammad) that benefit men over women, and preventing women from having a voice in interpretation. Her ideas have become common among activist Muslim women.[7] Zaynab Al-Ghazali has described women's obligations under Islam in language as similar to that used by nineteenth-century feminists describing women's obligations to the family. According to Al-Ghazali, women's primary concern should be their religion, their marriages, and their children—but these concerns often force women to activism or work in the world outside their homes. Perceived by many conservative Arab Muslims as a hero, martyr, and saint because of the way she transcended terrible experiences as a political prisoner, Al-Ghazali envisions a world where women are actively engaged in all areas of politics, serving in any post up to (but not including) the head of state.[8] Catholic theologian Mary Daly has challenged the entire edifice of Christian theology, while Rosemary Radford Ruether has devoted a career to building a feminist Christian theology, and Phyllis Trible to understanding the women of the Hebrew scriptures.[9] In short, theologians and philosophers around the world have been challenging and revising interpretations developed over many centuries without regard to the feminine perspective. The degree to which established religious institutions have taken women's interpretations to heart varies widely, of course, but it is surely significant that only two generations of sustained critique have caused some institutions to make major changes and all of them to respond (sometimes with great heat) to the criticism.

In Closing

This conclusion does not suggest that only contemporary women have sought to express themselves, to seek wisdom, and to explore the nature of the universe and our place in it. Rather, it reminds readers that just because much of women's history has been determined by other people's decisions—husbands, mothers, fathers, in-laws, governments, and religious institutions—it does not mean that women's lives are entirely circumscribed by the society they live in. Contemporary women as a whole enjoy more freedom of self-expression and inquiry than women a century ago. Yet each chapter of this text contains examples of how women's own concerns and choices have contributed to shaping not just their own lives, but the culture around them. It is my desire to end this text by reminding my readers that we all have some power to act for ourselves, to make decisions to better the world around us, and to become better representatives of humanity. Terrible things have happened and sometimes continue to happen to women and to oppressed peoples everywhere. Yet at the same time, countless women living in difficult circumstances choose to continue every day; they choose life, growth, wisdom, and beauty; and they choose these things not just for themselves but also for their families and their communities. And this is what I hope readers will remember most; that it is important not only to honor women's struggles and sufferings, but also their courage and their contributions.

STUDY QUESTIONS

1. Are there any kinds of crafts or foods the women in your own family make as part of maintaining tradition? What are they? If there are no such traditions in your family, why do you think that is?

2. If you had an extra 10 hours a week to spend in voluntary or other kinds of activist service, what would you choose to do?

3. How do you make room to search for truth, beauty, and meaning in your own life?

4. Talk with the women in your own family. How many of them have engaged in voluntary or activist work?

BIBLIOGRAPHY

It would be impossible to list all the important works done by women in the last half of the twentieth century; this bibliography provides a very limited introduction.

*indicates contains whole primary sources or secondary works containing substantial extracts.

FEMINISTS

Barlow, Tani E. *The Question of Women in Chinese Feminism.* Durham, NC: Duke University Press, 2004.
*Beauvoir, Simone de. *The Second Sex.* New York: Modern Library, 1968.
*Buckley, Sandra, ed. *Broken Silences: Voices of Japanese Feminism.* Berkeley: University of California Press, 1997.
*Daly, Mary. *Beyond God the Father: Toward a Philosophy of Women's Liberation.* Boston: Beacon Press, 1973.
*———. *Gyn/Ecology: The Metaethics of Radical Feminism.* Boston: Beacon Press, 1978.
*Friedan, Betty. *The Feminine Mystique.* New York: Dell, 1963.
Karam, Azza M. *Women, Islamisms, and the State: Contemporary Feminisms in Egypt.* New York: St. Martin's Press, 1998.
*Oliver, Kelly, ed. *The French Feminism Reader.* Lanham, MD: Rowman and Littlefield, 2000.
*Soskice, Janet Martin, and Diana Lipton, eds. *Feminism and Theology.* New York: Feminist Press, 2003.

VISUAL ARTISTS

Agosin, Marjorie. *Tapestries of Hope; Threads of Love: The Arpillera Movement in Chile, 1974–1994.* Albuquerque: University of New Mexico Press, 1996.
Arnett, William, et al. *The Quilts of Gee's Bend.* Atlanta, GA: Tinwood Books, 2002.
Arnett, Matt, and Vanessa Vadim. *The Quilts of Gee's Bend.* VHS. Atlanta, GA: Tinwood Media, 2002.
Freeman, Linda, prod. *African Art, Women, History: The Luba People of Central Africa.* VHS. Chappaqua, NY: L&S Video, 1998.
Karanja, Peter, ed. *African Art and Women Artists.* VHS. Films for the Humanities. Princeton, NJ: Author, 1992.

LaViolette, Adria. "Women Craft Specialists in Jenne: The Manipulation of Mande Social Categories." In *Status and Identity in West Africa: Nyamakaw of Mande*. Edited by David C. Conrad and Barbara E. Frank. Bloomington: University of Indiana Press, 1995.

Nashashibi, Salwa Mikdadi, ed. and curator. *Forces of Change: Artists of the Arab World*. Washington, DC: The National Museum for Women in the Arts, 1994.

PERFORMING ARTISTS

Goldman, Michael, dir. *Umm Khulthum: A Voice Like Egypt*. VHS. Seattle, WA: Arab Film Distribution, 1996.

Jha, Prakash. *Parampara: Indian Classical Dance Forms*. VHS. Dubai, UAE: Vista India, n.d.

Kroll, Nathan, prod. *Martha Graham in Performance*. VHS. West Long Branch, NJ: Kultur International Films, n.d. Originally released by Rembrandt Films in 1957, 1960, 1959.

Lewett, Linda, dir. *Woven by the Grandmothers: 19th Century Navajo Textiles*. VHS. Washington, DC: WETA, 1998.

Mack, Barbara B. *Muslim Women Sing: Hausa Popular Song*. Includes CD. Bloomington: Indiana University Press, 2004.

SCIENTISTS

Ambrose, Susan, et al., eds. *Journeys of Women in Science and Engineering: No Universal Constants*. Philadelphia, PA: Temple University Press, 1997.

McGrayne, Sharon Bertsch. *Nobel Prize Women in Science: Their Lives, Struggles, and Momentous Discoveries*. Secaucus, NJ: Carol Publishing Group.

Shearer, Bejamin, and Barbara S. Shearer. *Notable Women in the Life Sciences: A Biographical Dictionary*. Westport, CT: Greenwood Press, 1996.

———. *Notable Women in the Physical Sciences: A Biographical Dictionary*. Westport: CT: Greenwood Press, 1997.

WRITERS

*Daymond, M. J., et al. *The Women Writing Africa Project*. 3 vols. New York: The Feminist Press of the City University of New York, 2003–2007.

*Dooling, Amy D., and Christina Torgeson. *Writing Women in Modern China: An Anthology from the Early Twentieth Century*. New York: Columbia University Press, 1998.

*Emecheta, Buchi. *The Joys of Motherhood*. Oxford: Heinemann International, 1988 (copyright 1979).

*Head, Bessie. *Maru*. London: Heinemann Educational, 1972.

*Leonard, Kathy S., trans. and ed. *Cruel Fictions, Cruel Realities: Short Stories by Latin American Women Writers*. Pittsburgh, PA: Latin American Literary Review Press, 1997.

*Shaykh, Hanan al. *The Story of Zahra*. New York: Anchor Books, 1994.

*———. *Women of Sand and Myrhh*. Translated by Catherine Cobham. New York: Anchor Books, 1992.

*Tharn, Susie, and K. Lolita, eds. *Women Writing in India: 600 B.C. to the Present*. New York: Feminist Press of the City University of New York: 1990.

NOTES

INTRODUCTION

1. Lerner's most well-known work is *The Creation of Patriarchy.*
2. "Compulsory Heterosexuality and Lesbian Existence," *Signs* 5, no. 4 (Summer 1980): 631–660.

CHAPTER ONE

1. Examples and statistics in this section are from Lee and Daly, eds., *The Cambridge Encyclopedia of Hunter-Gatherers;* and Frances Dahlberg, ed., *Woman the Gatherer.* Both provide excellent starting points for students researching women's roles in foraging societies. For more detail on Native Americans and Africans, see Atmore and Atmore, *Medieval Africa,* and the Bibliography at the end of Chapter Three.
2. Lee and Daly, *Encyclopedia of Hunter-Gatherers.*
3. Ibid.
4. Ibid.
5. See Atmore and Atmore, *Medieval Africa,* and the Bibliography at the end of Chapter Three.
6. Stanley R. Witkowski and William T. Divale, "Kin Groups, Residency, and Descent," 673–680, in *Encyclopedia of Cultural Anthropology,* ed. Levinson and Ember (New York: Henry Holt, 1996), 673–674.
7. The most readable introductions are in Bingham and Gross, *Women in Africa of the Sub-Sahara;* and Page, *Encyclopedia of African History and Culture.* Part 3 of Henry Louis Gates, Jr. *Wonders of the African World* focuses on Timbuktu.
8. See Ibn Batuta, *The Travels of Ibn Batuta, AD 1325–AD 1354.* Edited and translated from the Arabic text by C. Defrémery and B. R. Sanguinetti. London: Hakluyt Society, 1994.
9. See Cass, *Dangerous Women,* and Widmer et al., *Writing Women,* for an overview of the Ming period and women writers during it. See Ebrey, *Cambridge Illustrated History of China* (cited in Chapter Two) for an overview of Chinese government and social structure.
10. Ropp, "Ambiguous Images," in Widmer and Kang I-Sun, *Writing Women,* 22, 33.
11. Thomas Brady, Heiko Oberman, and James Tracy eds., *Handbook of European History 1400–1600* (Grand Rapids, MI: W.B. Eerdmans, 1996) provides a good overview of scholarship on most of the general history of Europe during this period. For women's history, the best overviews are Wiesner, *Women and Gender,* and Hufton, *The Prospect Before Her.*
12. See A. S. Kline, *Petrarch: The Canzoniere.* http://www.tonykline.co.uk/PITBR/Italian/Petrarchhome.htm.
13. Chava Weissler, "The Traditional Piety of Ashkenazic Women."

14. McVay, "Celibacy," in *Greenwood Encyclopedia of Love, Courtship, and Sexuality Through History,* vol. 3 (Westport, CT: Greenwood Press, 2008).

15. Students who wish to follow up on this subject may find that Tanya Bayard's 1992 translation of a medieval housekeeping manual provides fascinating details about gardening in fourteenth-century France.

16. Wiesner, *Women and Gender,* and Hufton, *The Prospect before Her.*

17. Christine de Pisan, *Ditié de Jehanne d'Arc,* ed. and trans. Angus Kennedy and Kenneth Varry (Oxford: Society for the Study of Medieval Languages and Literature, 1977), 41–42.

18. Miller, *The Art of Mesoamerica,* provides an introduction to Meso-American art, inscriptions, and interpretive challenges. Leon-Portilla, *Fifteen Poets,* discusses the fifteenth-century context of Aztec and Nahuatl-language literature. Two excellent overviews of Aztec social life and customs that vary greatly in tone and approach are Carrasco and Scott, *Daily Life of the Aztec People,* and Clendinnen, *Aztecs: An Interpretation.* I also owe a debt of gratitude to Dr. Jasmin Cyril, the art historian who provided my initial introduction to the art and social history of pre-Columbian Central America.

19. Leo-Portilla, *Fifteen Poets.*

20. Ibid., 182–185.

CHAPTER TWO

1. For general information about Chinese history, social life, and customs see Ebrey, *The Cambridge Illustrated History of China,* and Ebrey, *Chinese Civilization: A Sourcebook.* Spence, *The Death of Woman Wang,* provides an excellent introduction to seventeenth-century rural life; Ko, *Teachers,* is excellent on women's lives. Widmer and Kang I-Sun Chang, *Writing Women* (cited in the Bibliography of Chapter One) discusses women writers.

2. Ebrey, ibid.

3. Cao Xueqin, *Dream of the Red Mansions.*

4. On women in Buddhism, see Falk and Gross, eds., *Unspoken Worlds;* Findley, ed., *Women's Buddhism;* and Ruch, ed., *Engendering Faith.* For women's history in the Tokugawa period, see Bernstein, ed., *Recreating Japanese Women,* and Bingham and Gross, *Women in Japan.*

5. Ivan Morris's translation of Sei Shonagon's *The Pillow Book* (New York: Columbia University Press, 1991) is readable and readily available. Although Arthur Waley's translation of Shikibu's *The Tale of Genji* is probably the most engaging, it is out of print. Readers may also enjoy Edward Seidensticker's unabridged translation (New York: Knopf, 1978). Seidensticker's abridged translation can be difficult to follow because it leaves out so many early chapters.

6. For general information about early Ottoman history, see Imber, *The Ottoman Empire, 1300–1650.* For women's history, see Peirce, *The Imperial Harem,* and Zilfi, ed., *Women in the Ottoman Empire.* Zilfi is particularly strong on legal history. For minority history, see Levy, *The Jews of the Ottoman Empire,* and Greene, *Minorities.*

7. Wiesner, *Women and Gender,* devotes a chapter to witchcraft and witch hunting. Levack's *Witch-Hunt in Early Modern Europe* is the standard overview, and his *Witchcraft Sourcebook* provides excerpts from numerous medieval and early modern sources.

8. Wiesner, ibid.; Levack, ibid.

9. Wiesner, ibid.

10. In Otten, *English Women's Voices.*

11. Rapley, *The Dévotes,* discusses the early history of the Ursulines and the Vincentians.

12. Monson, *Disembodied Voices,* Chapters 8 and 9.

CHAPTER THREE

1. See Diaz, *The Conquest of New Spain,* and Leon-Portilla, *The Broken Spears,* for Spanish and Aztec perspectives at the time of the conquest. For a general history of the conquest and biographies of Cortés and his translator, La Malinche, see Meyer and Breezely, *Oxford History of Mexico.* Michael Woods' *Conquistadors* (filmed on location) provides overviews of each of the major Spanish conquests.

2. Crosby's *The Columbian Exchange* is still the standard introduction. His *Ecological Imperialism* and *Germs, Seeds, and Animals* are also instructive for this and Chapters Four and Five. Magner's *History of Medicine,* Chapters 6 and 7, describes European and Native American medical history during the early modern period. Part Six, "The Columbian Exchange," of *Columbus and the Age of Discovery* is a solid visual introduction.

3. Magner, ibid., and Crosby, ibid.

4. Ibid.

5. See Lavrin, ed., *Latin American Women;* Socolow, *Women of Colonial Latin America;* Navarro and Korrol, *Women in Latin America and the Caribbean;* and Veira, *Women in the Crucible of Conquest,* for colonial women's history. For Peru in particular, see Van Deusen, *The Sacred and the Worldly,* and the introduction to her translation of Ursala de Jesús' *The Souls of Purgatory.*

6. Hence the lack of specificity as to precisely where their territory began and ended.

7. On Ojibwa women's history and culture, see Anderson, *Chain Her by One Foot;* Devens, *Countering Colonization;* and Landes, *The Ojibwa Woman.* Mary Jo Tippeconnic's chapter on the Ojibwa and Iroquois in Vivante, ed., *Women's Roles in Ancient Civilizations,* is a good starting point. Lawn and Salvucci, eds., *Women in New France,* provides the observations of Catholic male (Jesuit) missionaries in North America.

8. The original Five Nations confederation that constituted the Iroquois included Seneca, Oneida, Onondaga, Cayuga, and Mohawk. The Tuscarora were adopted in the eighteenth century.

9. On Iroquois women, see Graymon, *The Iroquois;* Mann, *Iroquoisan Women;* Navarro and Korrol, *Women in Latin America and the Caribbean;* Lawn and Salvucci, *Women in New France;* Spittal, *Iroquois Women;* and the Tippeconnic article in Vivante, *Women's Roles.* See also the Web site of the Shako:wi Cultural Center of the Oneida Nation for information on Iroquois history and culture, http://oneidanation.net. For general information about the Iroquois and others, see Sturtevant, ed., *Handbook of North American Indians.*

10. The seminal work on the demography of the slave trade is Curtin, *The Atlantic Slave Trade.* For maps, see Walvin, *Atlas of Slavery.* On the history of enslaved women, see Bush, *Slave Women in Caribbean Society;* Shepherd, *Women in Caribbean History;* and Shepherd and Beckles, *Caribbean Slavery in the Atlantic World.* For the history of black women in North America, including Canada, see Hine, King, and Reed, eds., *We Specialize in the Wholly Impossible.* For the impact of slavery on gender ideology in the Americas, see Hine et al., *We Specialize,* and White, *Ar'n't I a Woman?* For stories by former slaves, see the works of Ursala de Jesús, *The Souls of Purgatory;* Mary Prince, *The History of Mary Prince;* and Harriet Jacobs, *Incidents in the Life of a Slave Girl.*

11. Quoted in Shepherd and Beckles, *Caribbean Slavery*, 847. But see also Mary Prince's autobiography, which is available online and free to the public through the series *Documenting the American South.*

12. Prince, *History*, 4.

13. On the slave trade in Africa and its political and social impact, see Bonlanle, ed., *Nigerian Women;* Curtin, *The Atlantic Slave Trade;* Ogunyemi, *Queen Amina of Zazzau;* and Walvin, *Atlas of Slavery.* On Amina and Nzingha, see Ogunyemi, *Queen Amina;* Mvuyekure, *West African Kingdoms;* and volumes 4 and 5 of UNESCO's *General History of Africa* (cited in Chapter One). McKissick, *Nzingha,* provides the only substantial English-language narrative of Nzingha's life, but her book is historical fiction.

14. On gender and slavery, see White, *Ar'n't I a Woman?* For daily life in the southern colonies of North America, see Spruill, *Women's Life and Work.* For white women in the Caribbean, see Shepherd, *Women in Caribbean History.* For white women in Mexico and Latin America, see Socolow, *Women of Colonial Latin America;* Van Deusen, *The Sacred and the Worldly;* and Veira, *Women in the Crucible of Conquest.* For a case study of the ways gender, race, and class ideology intertwined, see Stolcke, *Marriage, Class and Colour.*

15. Although they might earn more than servants and laundresses, white women sex workers who accepted clients across racial lines could be seen by other whites as a source of contamination and were therefore more likely to be abused than other white prostitutes.

16. On women missionaries, see Pencak and Richter, *Friends and Enemies in Penn's Woods,* and McNamara, *Sisters in Arms,* cited in the Introduction to this book. Mann's *Iroquoisan Women* describes Iroquois perceptions and experiences of missionaries in detail, and Perdue's *Cherokee Women* frequently touches on Christianity and missionaries among the Cherokee.

17. McNamara, ibid.

CHAPTER FOUR

1. For the Industrial Revolution in Britain and its impact on women, see articles 4–6 in Sharpe, ed., *Women's Work.* Bronte's *Shirley* (London: Penguin Classics; first published 1849) recounts early industrial unrest in northern England from the point of view of a fictional industrialist and his family and friends.

2. Statistics from Sharpe, ibid.

3. Nikitenko's memoirs (*Up from Serfdom*) are available in English, as are those of Savva Dmitrievich Purlevskii (Gorshkov and Purlevskii, *A Life under Serfdom*). For peasant women's lives, see Farnsworth and Viola, eds., *Russian Peasant Women.* For the later industrial period, see Glickman, *Russian Factory Women.*

4. For Japanese political history, see Keene's biography of the Meiji emperor, the *Cambridge Illustrated History of Japan,* and "Meiji" in the *Kodansha Encyclopedia of Japan.* For industrial workers, see Sievers, *Flowers in Salt;* the articles by Lebra and Maloney in Bernstein, ed., *Recreating Japanese Women* (Berkeley and Los Angeles: UC Press, 1991); and Bingham and Hill, *Women in Japan.* For a micro-history of daily life, see Bernstein, *Isami's House.*

5. Sievers, ibid.

6. For twentieth-century farming, see Bernstein, *Isami's House* and Partner, *Toshié.*

7. On women and early socialism, see Stites, *The Women's Liberation Movement in Russia;* Offen, *European Feminisms;* Caine, *English Feminism;* Moses, *French Feminism;* and Sharpe, *Women's Work.* On Nationalism and feminism, see Blom et al., *Gendered Nations;*

and Offen, *European Feminisms*. On Liberalism, see works by Hahner, *Emancipating the Female Sex;* Caine, *English Feminism;* Macías, *Against All Odds;* and Blom et al., *Gendered Nations*.

8. Wallace's poem by this title is his most famous work and continues to be reproduced repeatedly on Web sites honoring Mother's Day, tradition, and women's activism within the family.

9. There is an extensive scholarly literature on U.S. and British activism. For the origins of U.S. women's activism, see Kerber, *Women of the Republic*. On equal rights feminism, see Langley and Fox, *Women's Rights;* Sklar, *Women's Rights Emerges;* Stanton, *Eighty Years;* and Giele, *Two Paths*. On temperance, domestic feminism, and domestic feminism's gradual adoption of the goals of equal rights feminism, see Giele, ibid., and Cogan, *All-American Girl*. For "the woman question" among African Americans, see Jones, *All Bound Up Together*. For British feminism, see Caine, *English Feminism;* Forster, *Significant Sisters;* Levine, *Feminist Lives;* and Morgan, *Religion and Feminism*. Wollstonecraft's *Maria* and *Vindication of the Rights of Women* (both collected in her *Works*) formed the intellectual bases for both equal rights and domestic feminism, though women activists were more inclined to mention her in private letters than in public statements.

10. Kerber's *Women of the Republic* argues that women's participation in the American Revolution was based on a sense of themselves as Republican Mothers.

11. In fact, from the time of its first opening in 1833, Oberlin College (then Oberlin Collegiate Institute) admitted students without regard to race or sex. The first three women to graduate from the institute did so in 1841. The institute was chartered by the state of Ohio in 1850, the first state-recognized college in the world to admit women to degree-granting programs. See also Lisa Wolf-Wendel's article, "Women's Colleges," in Aleman and Renn, *Women and Higher Education*.

12. Teacher education schools.

13. Giele, *Two Paths*, Chapter 3 and especially Figures 3.1–3.4, maps WCTU organizations and compares their membership with suffrage organizations.

14. Quoted in Giele, ibid., 93.

15. On anti-clericalism in Mexican politics and the Mexican Revolution of 1911, see Macías, *Against All Odds*. Charlotte Bronte's *Villette,* most of which is set in a private girls' boarding school in Belgium (likely modeled at least in part on the one where Bronte herself had taught), is particularly scathing in its description of what the author considered the superstition, active repression, and stultifying effect of Catholic society. Elizabeth Cady Stanton's entries in the fascinating all-female Bible commentary, *The Woman's Bible* (first published 1895–1898), can be pungently anti-Semitic and anti-Catholic. The nineteenth century generated a wide array of anti-Catholic writing, particularly narratives claiming to be "true accounts" of young girls who had narrowly escaped the terrible oppression and (at least implied) sexual violations supposedly common in convents. Some, like O'Gorman's (in Keller, "An American 'Escaped Nun'"), were really written by ex-nuns. Others, including Maria Monk's debunked *Awful Disclosures,* were written by Protestant men. Lyman Beecher, the father of two of nineteenth-century America's most prominent women writers, Catherine Beecher and Harriet Beecher Stowe, delivered the sermon that incited a mob to burn down an Ursuline convent in Charleston, Massachusetts. Catherine, at least, shared his contempt for Catholics. For Catholic sisters' domestic feminism, see McNamara, *Sisters in Arms* (cited in Introduction).

16. On Brazilian feminism, see Hahner, *Emancipating the Female Sex*. For Mexico, see Macías, *Against All Odds*. Lavrin, *Women, Feminism, and Social Change* and Maza, *Liberals, Radicals, and Women's Citizenship* provide context for Chile, Uruguay, and Argentina. For women observers' thoughts about nineteenth-century Latin American women, see Hahner, ed., *Women Through Women's Eyes*.

17. See Hahner, *Emancipating the Female Sex,* 26–29.

18. A normal school is a teacher education school.

19. On the history of Russian girls' and women's education (including a brief discussion of Jewish women), see Stites, *The Women's Liberation Movement in Russia.* For a fictional account of girls' schooling that illustrates the ideas many other women expressed about their educations, see Khvoshchinskaia, *The Boarding School Girl.* Verbitskaia's novel *The Keys to Happiness* was influential among middle-class women, attesting to widely shared doubts and ideals.

20. Stites, ibid., 4–6.

21. Besides Bernstein, there are few English-language histories of nineteenth-century Japanese women. On the history of Japanese feminism and of movements for Japanese women's education, Bingham and Hill's 1987 *Women in Japan* remains essential. Memoirs of women activists include Shidzue, *Facing Two Ways,* and Hane, *Reflections.* For the thoughts of one of the most important male reformers of education, see Yukichi, *Autobiography.* Bernstein traces the impact of Meiji reforms on an individual family in *Isami's House.* For a description of peasant life in the first half of the twentieth century, see Partner, *Toshié.*

22. Bingham and Hill, ibid., provided data for girls' schooling and industrial statistics in this section.

23. "Yoshioka, "Faith and Compassion," http://www.twmu.ac.jp/U/english/e01_founder.html (March 13, 2008).

24. See "Memoirs of a Successful Woman" in Aoki and Dardess, *As the Japanese See It.*

CHAPTER FIVE

1. Currently marketed (with added sweetener) as tonic water.

2. For general histories of the importance of technology to imperialism, see Headrick's works. For a general history of women and gender in imperialism, see Strobel, *Gender, Sex, and Empire.* Stoler's *Carnal Knowledge and Imperial Power* analyzes and critiques the historiography of women in imperialism. The two collections co-edited by Napur Chaudhuri (*Western Women and Imperialism* with Strobel, and *Nation, Empire, Colony* with Pierson) provide multiple viewpoints on the interconnection of race and sex in imperialism. For Tanzania, see the "Records of Maji Maji" collected by C. K. Gwassa and John Iliffe and quoted in Collins, *African History in Documents,* vol. 2, 124–141 (first published as *Records of the Maji Maji Rising,* Historical Association of Tanzania, Paper 4, 3–30, Nairobi: East African Publishing House, 1967). For colonial legal regimes, see Benton, *Law and Colonial Cultures.*

3. Here I owe thanks to Dr. Mary Bivins, who first guided me through the extensive literature on West African women and then called my attention to the role of educated women in spreading the values of reforming Islam among the Hausa people. For the social and economic impact of the caliphate and for British imperialism on Hausa women, see her *Telling Stories, Making Histories.*

4. On feminism in Egypt, see Sharawi's memoirs, *The Harem Years,* and Badran's introduction to them. See also Badran, *Feminists, Islam, and Nation;* Baron, *Women's Awakening in Egypt;* Nelson, *Doria Shafik, Egyptian Feminist;* and Meriweather and Tucker, eds., *Social History of Women and Gender.*

5. Quoted in Walsh, *Domesticity in Colonial India,* 150.

6. The English-language literature on modern Indian women's history is very large; the bibliography in this chapter provides only a bare introduction. On the ideology of domesticity in India, see Walsh, *Domesticity in Colonial India.* On the history of feminism, see Kumar, *The History of Doing,* and Forbes, *Women in Modern India.* For a biography and memoirs of individual Indian women activists from different points on the nineteenth-century political spectrum, see Gooptu, *Cornelia Sorabji;* Mazumdar,

Memoirs of an Indian Woman; and Sahagal, *An Indian Freedom Fighter.* For an extensive bibliography of Indian women's history in general, see Forbes, *Women in Modern India.* For classic analyses of the ways Western colonial and post-colonial gender stereotypes supported imperialist attitudes of cultural superiority, see Said's *Orientalism* and Spivak's "Can the Sub-Altern Speak?"

7. Quoted in Walsh, ibid., 79.

8. I owe a particular debt to Dr. Raphael Njoku, who provided specific editorial and bibliographic advice.

9. Barnes and Win, *To Live a Better Life,* and Pape, "Black and White" are the classic introductions to women's history in colonial Zimbabwe.

10. All quoted in Schmidt, "Patriarchy, Capitalism, and the Colonial State," 736–737. For colonial and imperialist legal regimes in general, see Benton, *Law and Colonial Cultures.* For an overview and critique of male-centered historical views of relationships between colonized men and women, see Stoler, *Carnal Knowledge.*

11. Schmidt, ibid., 749.

12. *Union Obrera,* February 7, 1920, 3; quoted by Maria de Fátima Barceló-Miller, "Halfhearted Solidarity: Women Workers and the Women's Suffrage Movement in Puerto Rico During the 1920s," in Rodriguez and Delgado, *Puerto Rican Women's History,* 133.

13. The literature on Puerto Rican women's history, whether in English or Spanish, has recently grown, although there is more on Puerto Rican women in the mainland United States than in Puerto Rico. The best place to start, and the source of the quotes and statistical information in this section, is Rodriguez and Delgado, eds., *Puerto Rican Women's History: New Perspectives.* For a Puerto Rican feminist's own perspective, see Capetillo, *A Nation of Women.* For Capetillo's biography, see Ferrer, *Luisa Capetillo.* For a wider perspective on women in the Caribbean, see Shepherd, *Women in Caribbean History.*

14. Quoted in Juan José Baldrich, "The Decomposition of the Cigar-Making Craft in Puerto Rico, 1899–1934," in Rodriguez and Delgado, ibid., 105–106.

15. For a history of popular feminine gender ideology during and after the caliphate, women's economic contributions, and an overview of scholarship on the caliphate, see Bivins, *Telling Stories, Making Histories.* For the Caliph's attitudes toward women and Nana Asma'u's institutional contributions, see Boyd, *The Caliph's Sister,* and Mack and Boyd, *One Woman's Jihad.* For the writings of Nana Asma'u, see Boyd and Mack, eds., *Collected Works of Nana Asma'u.* For the ongoing importance of the caliphate among contemporary Hausa women, see Boyd, *The Caliph's Sister,* and Coles and Mack, eds., *Hausa Women in the Twentieth Century.* There is an extensive English-language literature on the Sokoto Caliphate; the bibliographies in Bivins, *Telling Stories,* and Mack and Boyd, *One Woman's Jihad,* provide excellent starting points. Mervyn Hiskett's *Sword of Truth* is the standard biography of Usman dan Fodio. Barbara Cooper, *Marriage in Maradi: Gender and Culture in a Hausa Society* (Portsmouth, NH: Heinemann, 1997), can provide a good a comparison of the impact of British colonialism in Zimbabwe with its impact on women in the former caliphate.

CHAPTER SIX

1. The bibliography in this chapter scarcely scratches the surface of the immense English-language literature on women, gender, and the body in Weimar and Nazi Germany. For an introduction to the Weimar political history, see Henig, *The Weimar Republic.* For an introduction to women's history in the period, see Usborne, *The Politics of the Body.* Bridenthal et al., *When Biology Became Destiny,* is the classic overview of both periods. Allen, *Feminism and Motherhood,* introduces the history of German feminist movements; Koonz, *Mothers in the Fatherland,* is indispensable for the history of Nazi women's

activism; and Stibbe, *Women in the Third Reich,* sums up the "state of the question" on women in Nazi Germany. For the international connections among European socialists, see Stites, *Women's Liberation Movement in Russia.* Bachrach and Kunz's *Deadly Medicine* provides an overview of the National Socialist sponsored medical "science." For basic information about the Holocaust, including an encyclopedia of terms, maps, and statistics, see the United States Holocaust Memorial Museum Web site, www.ushmm.org.

2. Quoted in Koonz, ibid., 102.

3. On twentieth-century Brazilian women's history, see Alvarez, *Engendering Democracy in Brazil;* Patai, ed., *Brazilian Women Speak;* and the Caipora Women's Group, *Women in Brazil.*

4. For an overview of Russian women's history, see Engel, *Women in Russia.* Stites, *Women's Liberation Movement in Russia,* remains the classic discussion of radical women's activism up to 1930. For women in the ruling party, see Clements, *Bolshevik Women.* For the relationships between rural women and the party, see Wood, *The Baba and the Comrade.* The chapter bibliography lists sources for major works of Lenin and Engels concerning women. For the writings of women Socialists, including Alexandra Kollantai and Clara Zetkin, see "Women and Marxism" in the *Marxist Internet Archive.* Engel et al., *A Revolution of Their Own,* provides autobiographical histories of women's participation in and feelings about the revolution and the Communist Party.

5. Quoted in Wood, 53.

6. Ebrey, *Cambridge Illustrated History of China,* is the best general overview of Chinese history. Numerous documents from twentieth-century China are translated in Ebrey, ed. *Chinese Civilization.* The film *Chinese Women: The Great Step Forward,* although painting rather too rosy a view of women's role in the PRC, documents women's lives from the late Qing to the late twentieth century and interviews numerous women.

7. Ebrey, *Chinese Civilization,* provides several examples of pre-Nationalist and Nationalist documents concerning attempts to improve women's status.

8. Quoted in Ko, *Cinderella's Sisters,* 40.

CHAPTER SEVEN

1. For an overview of the Cold War in the United States and USSR see John Lewis Gaddis, *The Cold War: A New History* (New York: Penguin, 2006) and Lawrence Freedman, *The Cold War: A Military History* (London: Cassell and Co., 2001). For the rest of the world, see Odd Arne Westad, *The Global Cold War: Third World Interventions and the Making of Our Times.* (Cambridge, England: Cambridge University Press, 2007).

2. See *The World's Women* for most of the statistical data on women cited in this chapter.

3. *Financial Times World Desk Reference,* 5th ed. (London: Dorling Kindersley, 2005), 188.

4. For early development policies and their gendered impact, see Chuku, *Igbo Women.* For gendered labor practices and state policy initiatives and their impact during the twentieth century, see Lo, *Office Ladies;* Ng, *Positioning Women in Malaysia;* and Locher-Scholten and Niehof, eds., *Indonesian Women in Focus.* For examples of contemporary policies on women and development, see Made and Mpofu, *Women in Zimbabwe;* Myula and Kakhangwa, *Women in Malawi;* and White et al., *Women in Malawi.*

5. For instance, a search of the Ohiolink combined catalog of all academic libraries of Ohio located only five studies of Susan B. Anthony, two of Elizabeth Cady Stanton, three of Mary Wollstonecraft, and two of Lucretia Mott published between 1940 and 1970. All three biographies of Wollstonecraft were written by men. Between 1971 and 2007, over 35 documentaries, critical editions, and book-length studies appeared on Anthony alone.

6. On varieties of Second-Wave Feminism in North America, see Downs, *Writing Gender History,* and Whelan, *Modern Feminist Thought.*

7. Both Forbes, *Women in Modern India,* and Kumar, *The History of Doing,* provide solid introductions to Second-Wave Feminism in India. For more recent developments, see Chaudhuri, ed., *Feminism in India.*

8. For Malawi, see Myula and Kakhangwa (1997) and White et al. (2005) reports, *Women in Malawi.* For Zimbabwe, see Made and Mpofu, *Women in Zimbabwe.* For a detailed history of land reform, see Goebel, *Gender and Land Reform.*

9. For Brazil, see Alvarez, *Engendering Democracy in Brazil,* and for Peru, see Andreas, *When Women Rebel.* Winn, *Americas: The Changing Face,* summarizes women's roles in several social movements in Latin America and the Caribbean. For interviews with and activism of specific Latin American women, see the videos of Jamison, *Forging Peace;* Sarmiento, *Women of Latin America;* the interview in Hooks, *Guatemalan Women Speak;* and Menchú's autobiography, *I, Rigoberta Menchú.* For strategies of activists in China, see Ping-Chun Hsiung et al., eds., *Chinese Women Organizing.*

10. On Muslim women activists in general, see Fernea, *In Search of Islamic Feminism.* On women's responses to fundamentalism, see Reed, ed., *Nothing Sacred.* On fundamentalism in general, see Brasher, ed., *Encyclopedia of Fundamentalism,* and Marty and Applebee, eds., *Fundamentalism and Society.* For a detailed examination of the role of American women in Christian fundamentalism, see Brasher, *Godly Women.*

11. The statistics for U.S. boys who experience sexual abuse are even more alarming. For instance, according to a survey of Minnesotans, men who self-reported as having been sexually abused as boys were *6 to 10 times more likely* to be involved in a teen pregnancy than their peers reported experiencing no sexual abuse. See Elizabeth M. Saewyc, Lara Leanne Magee, and Sandra E. Pettingell, "Teenage Pregnancy and Associated Risk Behaviors among Sexually Abused Adolescents," *Perspectives on Sexual and Reproductive Health,* 36, no. 3 (May–June, 2004): 98–105.

12. On the social condition of late twentieth-century Chinese women, see Honig and Hershatter, *Personal Voices;* Martin et al., *Engendering China;* and Ping-Chun Hsiung et al., *Chinese Women Organizing.* On post-Soviet women, see Engel, *A Revolution of Their Own.* On women in post-Soviet Central Asia, see Kurbanova, "The Role of Traditional Gender Ideologies," and Heyat, *Azeri Women in Transition.*

CONCLUSION

1. Quoted in the exhibition *The Quilts of Gee's Bend,* Cleveland Museum of Art, June 27–Sept. 12, 2004. Organized by the Museum of Fine Arts, Houston, and the Tinwood Alliance, Atlanta.

2. Menchú, Rigoberta. *I, Rigoberta Menchú.* New York: Verso, 1983, 43–45.

3. Quoted in Ambrose, "Priscilla Auchincloss," in *Journeys of Women.*

4. Huda Sharawi, *Harem Years: The Memoirs of an Egyptian Feminist 1879–1924,* translated by Margot Badran. New York: The Feminist Press, 1987, 40–41.

5. Quoted in Ambrose, "Gertrude Belle Elion," in *Journeys of Women.*

6. Dr. Muserref Wiggins, personal communication, March 3, 2008; Patricia Kahn, "Turkey: A Prominent Role on a Stage Set by History," *Science,* vol. 263 (March 1994), 1487–1488.

7. See Ahmed, "Early Islam and the Position of Women," in Nikki Keddie and Beth Baron, eds. *Women in Middle Eastern History: Shifting Boundaries of Sex and Gender* (New Haven: Yale University Press, 1991).

8. Karam, *Women, Islamisms, and the State,* is a good starting point for Islamist women theologians.

9. Soskice and Lipton's edited anthology *Feminism and Theology* is a good introduction to Christian feminist perspectives.

◖ INDEX ◗

145